# Saint Albon and Saint Amphibalus

Garland Medieval Texts

*Number 11*

# Garland Medieval Texts

## A.S.G. Edwards
### General Editor

# Saint Albon and Saint Amphibalus
*by John Lydgate*

edited by

## George F. Reinecke

GARLAND PUBLISHING, INC.
NEW YORK & LONDON
1985

Library of Congress Cataloging in Publication Data

Lydgate, John 1370?–1451?
Saint Albon and Saint Amphibalus.

(Garland medieval texts ; no. 11)
Bibliography: p.
Includes index.
1. Alban, Saint, d. 304?—Poetry.  I. Reinecke,
George F.  II. Title.  III. Series.
PR2034.S24  1985    821'.2    83-48229
ISBN 0-8240-9436-0 (alk. paper)

Printed on acid-free, 250-year-life paper
Manufactured in the United States of America

# CONTENTS

The legend of Saint Alban, written by ... John Lidgate at the request of Mr John Whethamstede, Abbot of St Albans. In the year 1439.

O that Clio my dulnesse to redresse
With alle hir sustren dwellyng at Elicon
What myght availe to write the parfitnesse
Of this holy martir slayn ful yore agon
for cristis feith, the blessid man Alban
called of right thorugh eny Region
protomartir of Britis Albion

That aqueynted is ampis of Maro
nor with metris of Lucan nor Virgile
nor sugred dites of Tullius Cithero
Nor of Omerus to folwe the fresshe stile
semed to clymb on so hygh a stile
or for to folwe the steppis Auncient
of Fraunceis Petrak, the poete laureat

The golden trumpet of the hous of fame
With ful swyfte wengis of the pegasee
hath blowe ful fer the knyghtly mannys name
born in Verolamye a famous gret cite
baptised in Rome, the cronicle who list se
and as I fynde, this yong lusty man
took first the ordre of chevalrie

Whos liff to write, of liff I am bareyn
tho that affectioun curiously to telle
dredyng my labour shuld be in veyn
that never drank of pegasens welle
but for the goodnesse, so hihly doth excelle
I stond in hope, his influence shal shyne
my tremblyng penne bi grace to enlumyne

F. 96 r. of the British Library's MS. Landsdowne 699. Reproduced by permission of the British Library.

# PREFACE

Gratefully I acknowledge the help of many people in the production of this edition. First of all, I must thank Professor Bartlett Jere Whiting, who first set me to work on Lydgate's *Saint Albon*. The late Fred N. Robinson and Francis P. Magoun, Jr., also of Harvard, gave me much advice when my work was in its early stages. Professor Francis Wormald of London located the Talbot Book of Hours for me. Dr. K. J. Höltgen of Bonn and officials of the University Library there arranged for the microfilming of an important unpublished dissertation. Professor N. R. Ker twice gave me useful advice concerning the description of manuscripts. Professor W. H. Bond of the Houghton Library at Harvard frequently advised me on palaeography when I was transcribing the manuscripts, and Professor David Hart of the University of Arkansas supplied knowledgeable information on fifteenth-century armor.

Special thanks are due to the professional staffs of Widener and Houghton Libraries for their frequent assistance, especially in the filming of manuscripts in various British, Irish and American libraries. The authorities of the British Library, the Bodleian Library, the Fitzwilliam Museum, the Henry Huntington Library, the Library of Congress, the Library of Trinity College, Dublin, the Lincoln Cathedral Chapter Library, and the Library of Trinity College, Oxford, and the Library of the Inner Temple willingly allowed the photocopying of their manuscripts. Dr. G. J. Eberle, until recently Director of the Long Library at the University of New Orleans, and his staff have assisted me in many ways.

Prof. R. W. Burchfield at Oxford gave me much practical advice on the apparatus. Later, Prof. A. S. G. Edwards of the University of Victoria, general editor of this series, read the text and made dozens of practical and bibliographical suggestions.

Among the numbers of typists who have worked at one phase or another of this study, I must single out Rosemary Hoag, Jean Porte,

Mary Clark and especially Sally Cole Mooney, who produced the camera-ready copy for this edition.

I have dealt with several members of the staff of Garland Publishing, all of whom I must thank for their friendly information and courtesy.

A grant from the Southern Fellowships Fund some years ago helped me to start the research for this edition; a sabbatical and secretarial assistance from the University of New Orleans furthered its completion. I gratefully acknowledge this help.

Last, I must thank my wife, Marie Elina Duvic Reinecke, who transcribed, read copy, and otherwise sustained my life while I worked on *St. Albon*. To her I dedicate this book as a token of abiding love.

G. F. R.
*University of New Orleans*

John Lydgate completed <u>St</u>. <u>Albon</u> <u>and</u> <u>St</u>. <u>Amphibalus</u>[1]
in 1439, when he was about sixty-nine. Except for the <u>Life</u>
<u>of</u> <u>Our</u> <u>Lady</u>, it is the longest and most ambitious of his
saints' legends. It is also his last. This double saints'
life, chiefly in rime royal, is in three books. The first
treats of the early lives of Albon and the clerk Amphibalus;
the second, of Alban's conversion by Amphibalus and his subsequent martyrdom; the last, of the deaths of Amphibalus and
his other converts.[2] John Whethamstede, Abbot of St. Albans,
commissioned the poem. A friend of Duke Humphrey and patron
of early humanists and of education as well as an administra-
tor and encyclopedist, Whethamstede was doubtless prompted to
commission <u>St</u>. <u>Albon</u> by his knowledge of Lydgate's <u>St</u>. <u>Edmund</u>
<u>and</u> <u>St</u>. <u>Fremund</u>, done not long before for his own monastery
of Bury St. Edmunds. Whethamstede's commission and its date
are attested to not only by the colophons of four manuscripts,
but also by surviving records of the abbey.[3]

In writing <u>St</u>. <u>Albon</u> <u>and</u> <u>St</u>. <u>Amphibalus</u>, Lydgate relied
heavily on his sources. Although these are almost entirely
nonhistorical, Lydgate doubtless believed in them. Thus his
pious conscientiousness reinforced his customary close depen-
dence on sources, and he strayed but little from his data as
far as names, places and events are concerned. On the other
hand, he freely heightened and adorned his material with
rhetorical and figurative passages, as the very length of the
poem would suggest.

It may have been the classical interests of his patron[4]
or a late development of the poet's own taste that accounts
for the markedly epic details and scope of <u>St</u>. <u>Albon</u>. Far
more than the earlier <u>St</u>. <u>Edmund</u>, which alone among Lydgate's
saints' lives approaches it in length, <u>St</u>. <u>Albon</u> contains
mythological and historical allusion, descriptions of cere-
monies, and nature passages in an elevated traditional style.[5]
The invocation, the long set speeches, and the choice of
princely and military metaphor to characterize the central

figure are all evidence of Lydgate's wish to make of this
poem more than an ordinary saint's legend.  The notion that
length adds dignity no doubt partly explains Lydgate's word-
iness, though it may be due merely to the prolixity of age,
which probably accounts for such other features as the rep-
etitions and the development of tangential ideas (e.g. III,
745 ff.) which also characterize the work.

Although certain literary historians, taking their cue
from the colophon (p. 198 in this edition), have discussed
St. Albon as though it were a translation in the modern sense,
these are mistaken; the poem is in fact a fairly close versification of the known prose sources (probably, as we shall
see, at one remove), interlarded with a variety of additional matter, part original with Lydgate, but chiefly derived.
Most of this additional matter is added to give solemnity,
rhetorical emphasis, and such moral instruction as would make
it of help to the knight or gentleman of the fifteenth century.

The harsh judgment of the nineteenth and twentieth centuries on St. Albon[6], though perhaps deserved, may be attributed in some measure to the poem's inaccessibility.  It was
not available in print in medieval form until 1974.[7]  When
the monks of St. Albans had it printed in 1534, they modernized it and modified it substantially.[8]  Much later, in 1882,
when Carl Horstmann undertook to edit the poem, though aware
of the existence of three early manuscripts, he incomprehen-
sibly chose to edit the 1534 edition, though a priori it
seemed the least likely choice, whether textually or linguistically.  Collation rapidly reinforces this a priori judgment.[9]
The present editor's unpublished doctoral thesis (Harvard,
1960) and J. E. van der Westhuizen's edition (Leiden, 1974)
are the only editions from the 15th century manuscripts before
the present one.

*THE MANUSCRIPTS*

Of fifteenth century manuscripts there are four in reasonably complete form, another about four-fifths complete,
and a fragment of thirty-five lines.  All the above have
been collated, as has the 1534 edition.  The editor has based
his text on MS. Lansdowne 699 in the British Library.  The
manuscripts are as follows:[10]

      Lansdowne 699, referred to below as La;
      Lincoln Cathedral Library 129, referred to as Li;

Inner Temple Library Petyt 511 (xi), referred to as In;
Trinity College, Oxford, 38 (kept in Bodleian), referred
   to as T;
Huntington Library HM 140 (formerly Phillipps 8229),
   referred to as H;
Fitzwilliam Museum, Cambridge 40-1950 (McLean MS. 40), a
   fragment in the Talbot Book of Hours), referred to as
   Tal.
The 1534 edition, existing in a unique copy at the
   British Library, having independent textual authority,
   has also been collated, and is referred to as Ed.

The National Library of Wales' MS N. L. W. 5135 is a nineteenth century transcript of Lansdowne 699, and has not been
consulted further than was necessary to establish this proven-
ance.

   Lansdowne 699 is a small volume of 176 leaves, measuring
7 and 3/8 inches by 5 and 1/2.[11] It is chiefly of paper, with
the outside and inmost sheets of each quire in parchment. The
paper is watermarked with a bull's head surmounted by a vertical rod, imposed on which is a "chi" or St. Andrew's cross
(e.g. ff. 97, 106, 107, 113, 122 etc.). C. E. Wright, then
Deputy Keeper of MSS. at the British Museum, estimated the
handwriting to be of about the year 1450, or little more than
a decade after the composition of the poem.[12] Like the similar Lincoln MS, it has many traits typical of mid-to-late
fifteenth century vernacular verse manuscripts. Yet it probably ought not to be classed as being in Malcolm Parkes'
"Bastard Anglicana" hand, because of the absence of many cursive traits. The individualizing aspect or duct (what our
grandparents meant when they spoke of someone's "hand") has
fewer cursive elements by far than Lincoln or the page Wright
attributes to William Ebesham in his English Vernacular Hands
(Lydgate and Burgh, "Secrees of the Old Philisoffres," British Library Additional 43491), a manuscript in a hand otherwise quite similar to both Lansdowne and Lincoln.[13] For
instance, Lansdowne usually does not recurve the "h" ascender
or descender; the "d" ascender does not loop. The first
stroke of minuscule "w" is quite tall and straight, as is the
descender in the tall "s" when it is used, for it commonly
does not appear initially. Absent are the "reverse e," the
"g" written open, then closed with a horizontal stroke above;
Lansdowne forms the "g" of two circles, one above the other,
like an arabic "8." The modern minuscule or "gallows" form
of "r" is general except after "o" where the "2" form is
fairly regular. It may be said that though not pretentious,

the Lansdowne hand shows a number of "formata" traits. The
paragraph signs alternately are blue and red. There is a red
stroke in the initial letter of each verse. The large ini-
tials are in blue with red decoration.

The closeness in size and lay-out of text in the two
halves of the manuscript (St. Albon occupies the latter half;
the first is made up of seventeen secular and religious
pieces by Lydgate, including "The Churl and the Bird," "Die-
tarium," "Guy of Warwick," "Machabre" and "St. Augustine."
The hand is much the same in both halves.) suggests some association between them from the beginning, though the varying
size of the quires in the first segment suggests that they
were not continuous. The Albon is in five quires of sixteen leaves. Nothing is known of the history of Lansdowne
699 until the 16th century, when it was owned in its entirety
by one David Martyn, who inscribed irrelevant marginalia
passim. From these, it seems that Martyn was from Rutland.
In 1615, William Browne, almost certainly Browne of Tavistock,
author of Britannia's Pastorals, was its owner.[14] In the next
century it was owned by Edward Umfreville, author of Lex
Coronatoria (1761). Acquired by the first Marquis of Lansdowne (1737-1805), it passed with the rest of his manuscripts
to the British Museum in 1807.[15]

Ff. 96-176 contain St. Albon in one hand in five quires
of eight (sixteen leaves), four stanzas to the page. Absent
from Lansdowne are some fifty lines apparently by Lydgate
which occur in other manuscripts (I, 383; II, 1801-1814; III,
953-959, 966-973, 1030-1043). It also lacks the prayer to
St. Alban, 195 lines long, which is found at the end of three
other manuscripts and, in much revised form, at the end of the
16th century edition. Perhaps the Lansdowne scribe did not
view the prayer as an integral part of the poem, since the
colophon is present as in the fuller manuscripts. Indeed the
prayer may have been a separate composition, and its presence
(fragmentary) by itself in the Talbot Book of Hours seems to
reinforce this possibility, as does the separate existence of
the earlier "Prayer to St. Edmund,"[16] which bears an otherwise analogous relationship to St. Edmund and St. Fremund.

Lincoln Cathedral 129 was apparently once a parchment
and paper manuscript, also in quires of eight (sixteen leaves).
It is of the mid-fifteenth century, and very likely from the
same shop as Lansdowne, if not from the same scribe. Through
most of the poem, Li corresponds, four stanzas by four stanzas
to the side, with the lay-out of La. There are eighty-nine

leaves extant, beginning at I, 113 of <u>Albon</u>.  The description
in the modern catalogue of Lincoln Cathedral Library[17] is
rather full but inexact as to collation.  Fourteen leaves of
text are missing (i.e. about 800 lines of verse).  They are
as follows:

> I, 1-112 (two leaves)
> I, 841-II, 24 (two leaves)
> II, 254-309 (one leaf)
> II, 534-589 (one leaf)
> II, 814-925 (two leaves)
> II, 1710-1835 (two leaves)
> III, 526-637 (two leaves)
> III, 1449-end (at least two leaves)

Most or all of the instances of two leaves lost except the
second folio ending at I, 112 were probably parchment, and
removed for some ignoble use.  They doubtless constituted
the outside leaves of each quire.  Thus what remains may
properly be called a paper manuscript.  The manuscript presumably began with <u>Albon</u>, which occupies all the quires, except for most of the last (vi); the remainder contains Lydgate's "Churl and Bird," "Miracle of St. Augustine," and
"Dance of Machabre," all of which are also found in the
first segment of La in the same order.

Though the hand is similar to La, it is more cursive,
having more recurved and looped ascenders and descenders (notably in "b" and "d.")  The "g" is closed above by a horizontal stroke, unlike La.  Unlike La, the "r" is sometimes initially of the "v" shape, and the "2" form appears not only
after "o" but after "p."  All in all, it follows Parkes'
criteria for Bastard Anglicana more than La.[18]

President MacCracken believed that this manuscript was
the richly illuminated volume that Abbot Whethamstede caused
to be made for the Abbey Church.[19]  But he was surely mistaken, for the manuscript is small, partly secular, and (what
remains of it) ornamented only by a few large capitals.  It
is not known how or when it was acquired by the Lincoln chapter.

The Inner Temple's Petyt MS 511 (xi), a composite volume
of 247 leaves, begins with <u>St. Albon</u> almost complete, and
includes the final prayer (II, 1850-1919, between ff. 40 and
41, lost).  It too is a fifteenth century manuscript of
parchment and paper; the scribe was one Panox (see text. note

to III, 1602) about whom nothing is known.  The quires are
chiefly in sixes.  It is illuminated in red and blue, rather
simply, with decorated capitals.  The initial letters of each
verse have red strokes.[20]  Much larger than La or Li, the
manuscript measures 11 and 3/8 by 8 inches.  St. Albon is followed by the Brute Chronicle of England, ending with the
early reign of Henry VI and written in a different hand.  This
volume may well have been owned by members of the Inner Temple
even in the days of Elizabeth, for Gerard Legh, who had close
ties with that society,[21] used Lydgate's poem in his  Accedens of Armory (see expl. note to I, 435-539).  It was left
to the Inner Temple by William Petyt, a former treasurer, in
1707, as part of a large bequest of manuscripts.  Of much the
same size as Huntington and Trinity manuscripts, In is written with five stanzas to the page.  The hand is broad-nibbed
and relatively small and compact.  Characteristically the
reverse form is used for "e," "r" has three forms:  the cap-
ital-like initial form, the "v" type internally, and the "2"
form after "o."  Ascenders and descenders are short, or stick
close to the line, being curved, recurved and looped.  An
exception is the initial and internal "s," which is long
and broad, as is the "f."  The minuscule "g" is closed with a
horizontal stroke.  Many nouns are underscored or capitalized.

     Trinity College Oxford 38, deposited at the present time
in the Bodleian, is a parchment and paper manuscript in
folio, measuring about 11 and 1/2 by 8 and 1/2 inches, well
written in one rather spiky hand.  The five quires are of
fourteen folios each, the two outer and two inner folios of
each quire being of parchment.  It contains only the St.
Albon, which is complete, including the final prayer, and
occupies 67 folios.  The manuscript is of the mid-to-late
fifteenth century.  The hand is a rather large cursive vernacular, marked by long ascenders and long, thick descenders.
The "d" ascender is recurved into a loop; most of the occurrences of "g" are marked by the open top closed by the horizontal stroke.  There are several forms of "e" including the
reverse "e" (most common) and the "theta" type as well as
the more usual forms.  The "2" form of "r" is used after "e"
and "o"; a small capital form appears initially; otherwise
the "gamma" or "gallows" form of "r" is used.  The "w" is
marked by a tall center vertical loop; the strokes of "w"
are tight and close so as to form an enclosed area.

     The watermark (bull's head, surmounted by St. Andrew's
cross, and ring with diamond) both appear on paper made in
Utrecht about 1462, which would agree well with the hand, but

since each appears on papers made in numerous other places at
various times in the century, this is no real evidence.[22]
Nothing is known of its early history until it was presented
to Trinity College in 1630 by its head, Dr. Ralph Kettel.

The manuscript was perfunctorily revised in the sixteenth
century by someone who collated it here and there with the
1534 edition.  It was perhaps the same person who expunged
the word "pope" wherever it appears, doubtless in keeping
with the law of Henry VIII.  Van der Westhuizen sees two correcting hands, the latter almost entirely limited to the last
three hundred lines of Book III.[23]  If he is right, both re-
visors were about much the same task at much the same time.
It is conceivable that these are not derived from Ed but intended for a rough draft of the 1534 edition.

Huntington HM 140 is a parchment and paper anthology,
well known because Chaucer's "Clerk's Tale" follows immediately on St. Albon, which occupies ff. 1-66r.   HM 140 measures about 11 and 1/2 by 8 inches, and, like In and T, disposes Lydgate's text five stanzas to the page.  The whole
text, including the final prayer, is present, but H has been
misbound, so that the fourth quire of sixteen leaves precedes the third, also of sixteen, so that lines II, 1157-III,
175 follow III, 176-1294.  St. Albon occupies four full
quires and shares the fifth with the "Clerk's Tale."  There
are five hands in the manuscript, but only three are present
in St. Albon; these are markedly different and easily distinguished.

The first hand goes from the beginning to III, 175, the
second to III, 1330, and the third from that point to the end.
Hand 1 is a cursive hand of mid-to-late fifteenth century,
characterized by heavy descending strokes, and frequent use of
the "2" form of "r" before "u."  It even appears in some
cases initially.  Many though not all "a's" are marked by a
looped tall stroke, starting as high as "l" or "d."  Three
downward strokes of diminishing size, slanting to the right
make up the minuscule "w," while "g" is sometimes circular
with a curved descender and sometimes open above, with the
horizontal stroke above.  Tall "s" is not used initially,
and reversed "e" occurs here and there.

Unlike hand 1, hand 2 is slanted like modern italics;
the lines waver and are not perfectly horizontal, so that
the page has an amateurish look.  The "2" form of "r" appears after "a," "e," and "o" as well as sometimes initially;

elsewhere the "v" form of "r," with and without descender
below the line is common.  There is no tall ascender in the
letter "a," which usually is oval and short.  Sometimes "d"
has a loop, but more commonly has a short straight diagonal
ascender.  Tall "s" appears initially.  The "g" has the
separate horizontal stroke above; "w" is much as in hand 1.

Hand 3 is more professional than hand 2.  Like hand 1,
it is a vertical and regular cursive, characterized by much
use of the "2" form of "r" after consonants and round vowels.
Unlike hand 1, it uses no tall ascenders in "a"; the "w"
made with three diminishing downward strokes is present,
along with another, in which the middle stroke is as high as
the first, or higher.  Some "d's" are looped, but an approx-
imately equal number of short, straight diagonal ascenders is
found; some ascending almost vertically.  A nearly closed
"g" is sometimes marked by the vertical stroke above.  Initial "s" is tall.  In all positions "e" is usually in the
modern "lower case" shape.  Initial "t" often has a tall
form.

Formerly MS 8299 of the Phillipps Collection and so
designated by Manly and Rickert in their full description,[24]
it passed to the Huntington Library in 1923.  This manuscript
contains paper with a watermark quite similar to the bull's
head number 14261 of Briquet bearing the date 1473.  All
three portions seem to have been copied (though with varying
degrees of attention and accuracy) from the same source manuscript.  The whole volume is known to have been in the hands
of William Marshall, a member of Princess Mary's household,
in 1527.  In the late eighteenth century, it belonged to
Richard Gough.  Many other ownerships may be inferred from
the names which appear here and there in the volume; for
these see Manly and Rickert.

The "Talbot Hours" is MS. 40-1950 in the Fitzwilliam
Museum at Cambridge.  It is fully described in the Yates
Thompson Catalogue as No. 83.[25]  It has no known history from
the fifteenth to the nineteenth century.  The catalogue associates it with the great Talbot of Henry VI's day.  It is
a narrow "holster" manuscript of parchment, 10 and 3/4 by 4
and 1/2 inches, such as might have been carried in a saddle-
bag.  On the recto of f. 135 of this devotional book the
title "Oracio ad prothomartyrem Albanum" is followed by five
stanzas corresponding to III, 1499-1526, though not in the
same stanzaic order.

A printed book, the black letter quarto The glorious
lyfe and passion of Seint Albon ... and also the lyfe and
passion of Saint Amphabel ..., exists in a unique copy in the
British Library.  Probably, it was printed by John Hertford
at St. Albans in 1534.  Certain aspects of the 1534 edition
as it differs from the original are further discussed in the
Appendix.  The 1534 editor (or perhaps the printer) revised
the spelling greatly to conform to sixteenth century usage,
and was free in adding or removing words and even phrases
here and there.  The editor was also responsible for one
major piece of revision and one major addition, which are
discussed in the Appendix.

The revisor-editor prepared his text chiefly from a hypothetical manuscript closely related to the Huntington and
Trinity manuscripts, which we will designate as $*Ed^2$; he took
readings rather often from another manuscript, quite superior,
and closely related to Lansdowne and Lincoln, less closely to
Inner Temple, and at farthest remove from Trinity and Huntington.  This putative source, called $*Ed^1$ is much used in
Book II, and nearly as much in Book III, though it never re-
places $*Ed^2$ as the editor's main source.  There are a handful
of correspondences between 1534 and the Inner Temple only,
but these are insufficient to prove contamination by yet another manuscript.  See the stemma below.

Although the Lansdowne lacks about 155 lines that occur
in other manuscripts and give every evidence of being genuine
(perhaps added, perhaps discarded), it has been chosen as the
text best suited to be the basis for a new edition.[26]  On the
grounds of clear sense, freedom from gross blunders, conform-
ity to meter, and accord with the extant sources it is superior to the others, though the closely allied but much more
fragmentary Li approaches it in quality.  Altogether, about
200 readings (chiefly of one or two words) have been adopted
from other manuscripts and italicized.  As large as this number may seem, it will be obvious from the textual notes that
on a basis of sense, metrics, and the sources, there would
have been many more emendations if In, T, or H had been so
used.  Lansdowne's faults are primarily those of omission.
Those lines and passages which it lacks have been supplied
from Li (when available) or from T.  They are labeled and ascribed by the textual notes.  All added passages are in italics except for the long final prayer, taken from T.

The apparent relationship of the manuscripts on the basis
of the text may be represented as follows, with asterisks

designating hypothetical manuscripts:

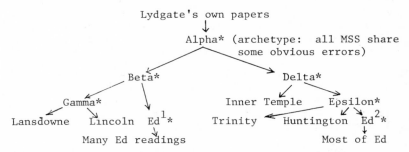

Lydgate's own papers

Alpha* (archetype:  all MSS share
some obvious errors)

Beta*                    Delta*

Gamma*            Inner Temple        Epsilon*

Lansdowne    Lincoln    Ed[1]*    Trinity ← Huntington    Ed[2]*

Many Ed readings                              Most of Ed

    The textual variants are remarkably numerous for a work extant in so few manuscripts.  La and Li are quite closely related, as is the "contaminating" MS, Ed[1].  The other three manuscripts, along with the principal source of the early print, and, so far as one may judge, of the Talbot fragment, form another family.  T, the first, is the product of a scribe with little sense of meter and a dislike for Lydgate's telegraphic and asyntactic style.  He continually "improved" his text.  Although H lacks most of the conscious improvements of T, it is full of gross blunders, and is by far the most corrupt of the manuscripts.  Ed[2]* must have been closely related to H, for it shares many bad readings with it (less frequently with T as well.)  Ed[1] shares some plausible readings with La, Li, and In, as against the other evidences.  More often, it agrees with La and Li only.  Tal is too brief to be placed in the stemma, but it consists of matter found only in the "delta" manuscripts.  It is worth noting that the two extant "gamma" manuscripts are very similar in hand, size, and lay-out, and also share some northerly grammatical forms, notably the northerly forms "ther, them" against "her, hem" in the "delta" manuscripts, though they are all pretty much of an age, and indeed, the "gamma" MSS are probably older.  The "delta" manuscripts which survive are close both in size (folio), and in the arrangement of five stanzas to the page, so that bibliographical and linguistic data tend to support the textual conclusions.

*The Legend of St. Alban*

    The historical existence of Albanus can be assumed from the fact that there has been a cult of the saint closely associated with a burial in Verulamium (today St. Albans, Herts.) since the early fifth century.  Hagiographers believe

that such circumstances as the early development of a cult
and the specific tomb are good indications that a historical
martyrdom is involved.[27]  The earliest written record of St.
Alban is found in the life of Bishop Germanus of Auxerre (St.
Germain l'Auxerrois) written by Constantius of Lyons about
480 A. D.; this is the same work which first records the
"Alleluia Victory."  It contains these data, synopsized by
Wilhelm Levison:

> Germanus and his colleague Lupus of
> Troyes had been sent to Britian in 429 to
> fight against the Pelagian heretics; having
> succeeded, they visited the tomb of St.
> Alban to offer thanks for their victory
> (c. 16 in <u>Monumenta</u> <u>Germanica</u>:  <u>Scriptores</u>
> <u>rerum</u> <u>Merovingicarum</u>, VII, 262):  "Com-
> pressa itaque perversitate damnabili eiusque
> auctoribus compositis, sacerdotes beatum
> Albanum martyrem, acturi Deo per ipsum gratias,
> petierunt."  The genuine text of the <u>Life</u>
> does not tell anything more of the martyr,
> who evidently could be presumed to be known
> to the reader....[28]

The first extant work devoted to the life of St. Alban is a
"passion" found in a manuscript of the eighth or ninth century preserved at Turin, and thought to represent a text
written in France, possibly at Autun, in the first half of
the sixth century.[29]  This prose work has been shown by
Meyer to be mainly non-historical, a composite from other
saints' lives, notably those of Irenaeus, Andochus, Benignus,
Thyrsis and Felix, and of Symphorianus of Autun.[30]  Levison,
however, believes the description of the place of martyrdom
to be accurate enough to reflect a genuine oral tradition
brought to the continent by Germanus.

The Turin passion tells of a nameless Christian cleric
who, fleeing the persecution of the Emperor Severus, is
given shelter by Albanus.  This latter, though still a pagan,
gives him a cloak and allows him to escape.  Albanus is ap-
prehended, brought before the emperor, and, confessing his
belief in Christ, is urged to abjure and worship the Roman
gods.  Albanus indignantly refuses, even when tempted with
the rewards of high office, gold, and a senator's daughter
in marriage.  Finally he is condemned to die by the sword.
When the large crowd which followed him out of the city is
prevented from passing a stream because of high water,

Albanus prays and the waters recede, whereupon his executioner
is converted. The other executioners then take him to the
top of the hill; there Albanus thirsts, prays, and causes a
spring to gush forth. Once Albanus is dead, the emperor
ceases his persecution. At a later time, Germanus visits
the wonder-working shrine, leaving there a collection of
relics of apostles and saints and taking away with him some
of the earth which had been watered with the British martyr's blood.[31]

The Turin Passion thus contains in essence all the matter of Lydgate's second and longest book. Meyer also stud-
ied two other early and related accounts. That of Autun,
extant in a manuscript of the ninth or tenth century, he
believes to be the source of Gildas, and therefore to have
existed before the year 600. This text is much abridged,
except for the account of the death and miracles. Another
manuscript of the ninth or tenth century is the Paris Passion, which corresponds closely to Turin and Autun in those
parts treating of the miracles and martyrdom, but differs
substantially in the earlier portion, adding details found
in neither of the others. Meyer's conclusions are supported
by P. Déléhaye:

> Reste à conclure que le point de départ
> est un des textes complets, celui de Turin,
> comme il n'est pas malaisé de le démontrer.
> Un second hagiographe, qui voulait mettre
> en lumière les miracles de S. Alban, a ex-
> trait de la passion l'abrégé, où tout le
> reste est condensé en quelques phrases.
> Survint un troisième qui s'aperçut du manque
> de proportion de la nouvelle pièce; il ré-
> tablit l'équilibre, en développant la première
> partie, et s'aida, pour l'interpoler, de ses
> souvenirs et de ses lectures. La resultante
> est le texte de Paris.[32]

It was this Paris version which Bede paraphrased in the
seventh chapter of his first book. The only essential part
of the Ecclesiastical History not found in the Paris text
is his attribution of the events to the time of Diocletian's
persecution. This Bede probably derived from Gildas' De
Excidio Britanniae, in which the author conjectures ("ut
conicimus") that the death of Alban occurred under that
emperor.[33] Somehow Bede (or his MS) transformed the conjecture into a fact. Certain modern authorities attribute

Alban's death to the Decian or Valerian persecutions of the
mid-third century, but nothing is known with certainty.[34]

The authority and general distribution of Bede's History
made his version of the legend of Alban so well known and
respected that for centuries there were no really independent
treatments;[35] indeed even Lydgate is at one or two removes
dependent upon Bede.

However, a daring departure was made by the monk William
of St. Albans during the abbacy of Simon (1167-1183). William produced a long and rhetorical account of his abbey's
patron which not only expands Bede's data but adds a great
deal of wholly new material concerning the deaths of "Amphibalus" and his many converts. It is only fair to admit that
William might have been a dupe, but it is more likely that he
was the originator of the clumsy fabrication. The work pur-
ports to be translated from the English of a convert from
paganism who lived at a time when most Anglo-Saxons were not
yet Christians. This convert would have based his work on
tradition and on certain inscriptions or sculptures then extant on the walls of Verulam:

> Cives quondam Verolamii, ob elationem
> cordis sui declarandam qualiter passus sit
> beatissimus Albanus in muris suae civitatis
> sculptum reliquerunt: quam scripturam (Trin.
> Dub. E. 1. 40, "sculpturam"), longo post
> tempore, in muris eorum, jam ruinosis...in-
> veni.[36]

Levison suggests that the hint for the fabrication came
from Geoffrey of Monmouth's Historia Regum.[37] Geoffrey it
was who first gave Alban's teacher the name Amphibalus.[38]
But this was not all that Geoffrey had to offer. His best-
seller of the twelfth century of course purported to be taken
from a "British" book in the possession of Walter, Archdeacon
of Oxford. Whatever the truth of this assertion, William
believed it. It would be ironic if one forgery, accepted as
genuine, were to have inspired another of much the same sort,
though admittedly lacking in the genius of the Historia.

William in his preface admits having taken the name
Amphibalus from Geoffrey, and incidentally thus testifies to
his knowledge of the Historia:

> Sciendum autem quod huic operi beati

        clerici nomen adjecerim:  quod non in
        libro quem transferro, sed in historia,
        quam Gaufridus Arturus de Britannico in
        Latinum se vertisse testatur, inveni.[39]

Though the hint may have come from Geoffrey, the <u>purpose</u> of the fraud was probably, as Levison suggests, the stimulation of pilgrimages to pay for the expensive ornaments just added to St. Alban's shrine by Abbot Simon.[40]  In 1177, certain supposed visions of a citizen of the town led to the finding of the relics of "Amphibalus" at Redbourn, four miles northwest of St. Albans.[41]  News of the finding, we are told, reached the brethren of the abbey dramatically during their common meal, just as one of them was reading aloud from William's book.  Not long thereafter, Amphibalus joined Alban in the abbey church.  We must agree with Levison's suggestion that these two occurrences, the "translation" of the old English book and the finding of the "relics of St. Amphibalus" came so close together as to suggest that they were both part of one plan, having as its aim the increase of pilgrimages.[42]

An interesting parallel exists in the finding of the supposed tombs of Arthur and Guenevere at Glastonbury Abbey in 1191.[43]  Schofield and others attributed this fraud to Henry II's desire to discomfit the Welsh by ending the legend of Arthur's return and to further the independence of the English church by increasing the prestige of Glastonbury and its connections with Joseph of Arimathea.[44]  More recently, R. S. Loomis, though less convinced of an attempt at fraud than his predecessors, referred to Giraldus Cambrensis' <u>De Principis Instructione</u>, which states that King Henry learned of the burial place from a "historico cantore Britone."  Here too one feels the pervasive influence of Geoffrey and his "source."

The <u>Gesta</u> <u>Abbatum</u> <u>Sancti</u> <u>Albani</u> of Matthew Paris tells of a semingly distinct discovery.  As some demolition work was being done in the old city of Verulam in the tenth century, says Matthew, the workers found in a niche a book chest containing a number of books in "idioma antiquorum Britonum."[45]  These could not be read until a learned old priest, Unwona by name, proved able to translate them.  Most, being pagan religious books, were immediately consigned to the fire.  One ornate volume however proved to be a history of St. Alban, "quam ecclesia diebus hodiernis recitat legenda, cui perhibet egregius doctor Beda testimonium, in nullis discrepando."  This history was translated immediately into

Latin, and the original manuscript thereupon crumbled into
dust.  The conservative eighteenth-century Bollandist editor
remarks that this was wonderful indeed, and would not un-
justly bring one to suspect a fictitious element.[46]  If
Matthew's account refers to a work other than William's Interpretatio, as obviously it would seem to do, no trace of
this work exists today.

The chief discrepancy between the "ancient author's
prologue" in William and the account in the Gesta relates
to the language in which the books were composed; otherwise
the accounts, though almost wholly different, are susceptible
of being harmonized.  If one attempts to do so, the following emerges.  A recent convert, British or Saxon, in the days
between the Anglo-Saxon invasion and the landing of Augustine,
wrote down in his own language the passion of St. Alban as
learned from oral tradition and from certain carvings on the
ruined walls of Verulamium.  Fearing for his life, he con-
cealed the volume, which was later found and turned into
Latin.  If we posit the translation of the "Unwona" version
into Old English, followed by the loss of the original Latin,
and the re-translation by William of the now lost Old English
version, the two accounts are not absolutely irreconcilable.

Yet, in spite of at least one modern voice raised tenta-
tively on the side of belief in suddenly crumbling codices,
we are almost certainly dealing with fiction in both cases.[47]
The puzzling element is the existence of two such differing
accounts in well-known writers of the same monastery, less
than a century apart.  Baring Gould suggests that Matthew
Paris rationalized the tale, having realized that William
"had not the wit to make his author write in British."[48]  Yet
William knew enough to refer to Geoffrey as a "historia de
Britannico" (see above).  From the forger's point of view, a
pretended original written by an eye-witness would have been
best, and William would no doubt have so written his account,
had it not been for the problem of credibility:  if William
knew no Celtic tongue how could he translate from British?
If the original were supposed to be in Latin, why not produce
it for all to read?  The only reasonably safe course was to
make the source an English old enough, and hence difficult
enough, to prevent questions.  In passing, one may note that
MS. E. 1. 40 of Trinity College, Dublin, once the property of
St. Albans Abbey and thought by some to be in the hand of
Matthew Paris, contains William's "translation" but omits
his preface which refers to the "liber Anglico sermone con-
scriptus."  This omission would tend to bear out the notion

that after William had completed his work, an oral tradition
developed in the monastery, based in part on honestly misin-
terpreted archaeological finds in the ruins of Verulam.
Matthew, a man of considerable historical sense, would then
have sought to rationalize this corpus of tradition on the
assumption that some of it was true, by suppressing William's
prologue with its incongruous detail.  However one touch
which tends to put Matthew's honesty in doubt is that the name
"Unwona" which he gives to the ninth-century translator was
already associated with St. Albans, as the name of a bishop
who had signed Offa's foundation charter a hundred years before, a cleric previously mentioned in Matthew's own works.[49]

*Direct Sources*

     Whatever its origin, the Interpretatio Guillelmi (to call
it by the name used in the Acta Sanctorum), whether as a separate work or as incorporated into a longer one, is the pri-
mary source of most of Lydgate's second and third books.
The explanatory notes to the present edition, which reproduce
most of William's text passage by passage as it corresponds
to Lydgate's, should make this abundantly clear.

     Emil Ühleman has suggested that there have existed both
an original Interpretatio and a revision reproduced in the
Acta.[50]  The Dublin manuscript, a microfilm print of which I
have examined, conforms very closely to the printed text in
the Acta, from which is derived the text given in the notes
to this present volume.  Ühleman's distinction seems a quib-
ble based on three brief and not too significant passages.
In any case, it is Ühleman's belief that Lydgate used the
revised form.[51]

     There are four other extant treatments of the St. Alban
legend which seemed to deserve examination as possible major
sources.  First we must consider the Latin verse of Ralph
of Dunstable, a fellow monk and contemporary of William's
at St. Albans.  The length and unpublished state of this
two-thousand-line poem have made a minute comparison impossible within the scope of this edition, but a cursory examination of microfilm prints of two of the manuscripts
(Cotton Julius D. III and Trinity College, Dublin E. 1. 40)
and close comparison of several passages with the corresponding ones in Lydgate have led me to agree with Ühleman that
the influence of Ralph on the later poet is unprovable and
insignificant.  Indeed, the only verbal parallels which

Ühleman can find between Ralph and Lydgate[52] one can match
more closely in earlier works of Lydgate himself.  Thus:

    Ralph:   Albani celebrem coelo terrisque triumphum
             Ruminat inculto carmine Clio rudis
                                         (ll. 1-2)

    Albon:   To calle Clio my dulnesse to redresse,
             With alle hir sustren dwellyng at Elicon
                                         (I, 1-2)

    Lydgate's
    Edmund &
    Fremund:  I dar not calle to Clio for sucour
              Nor to the musis that been in noumbre nine
                                         (I, 90-91)

and

    Ralph:   Non Maro sum, fateor, sed neque Codrus ego.
                                         (1. 4)

    Albon:   I nat acqueynted with musis of Maro
                                         (I, 8)

    Fall of
    Princes:  I nevir was acqueyntid with Virgile
                                         (IX, 3401)

Ralph's Latin contains an extremely long excursus into the
sacred history of the Jews which Lydgate would probably have
found irresistible had it been before him; Ralph gives an
incident of Alban's severed head speaking, which would have
especially appealed to Lydgate because the head of his own
abbey's patron, St. Edmund, allegedly did the same (Edmund
& Fremund, II, 904 ff.)  Ralph is rich in elaborate figures
of speech, carefully marked by name (Meth., Yronia, etc.) in
the margins of both copies examined, yet few or none of these
are utilized by Lydgate.  Hazlitt's opinion, given in his
edition of Warton's History of English Poetry, III, p. 66,
that Ralph is Lydgate's source is a reasonable conjecture if
one has no knowledge of William's version, but no one who has
compared all three could possibly believe that Ralph is the
closer to Lydgate.

    The second treatment to be considered is the thirteenth-
century Anglo-French poem, La Vie de Saint Auban, often

ascribed to Matthew Paris and found in only one manuscript,
Trinity College Dublin E. 1. 40, which also has William's
prose and Ralph's poem. The Auban, first edited by Robert
Atkinson in 1876 and more recently by Harden (Oxford, 1968),[53]
is written, like Lydgate's later work, in heroic style. Yet
the type is a much earlier one; both the verse form and diction suggest the chanson de geste. The extant portion, for
the beginning is lost, starts at Amphibalus' entry into Verulam and follows the matter of William's Interpretatio, though
not so closely as does Lydgate. It would be tempting to assume that the lost opening contains in germ the matter of
Lydgate's first book, the "enfances" of Alban and Amphibalus,
but the French poem refers to Amphibalus several times as a
"cleric from the East." This probably rules out the Welsh
origin and childhood friendship with Alban which characterize
the "enfances." Ühleman, who concludes that the Auban is
certainly not Lydgate's chief source for Books II and III,[54]
points out a number of minor correspondences which might suggest Lydgate's acquaintance with the French poem. Only one
of these is at all striking: the Auban at 1. 238 mentions
the vinegar and gall given to Christ during his passion.
With this we may compare Lydgate, II, 486. This detail,
though of course familiar to anyone who knows the gospels,
is not found in the Interpretatio. Of Ühleman's other points
of correspondence, the mention of the name Gabriel for the
angel of the Annunciation is such a commonplace as to be of
no consequence. The lines, "Il vent a Varlam, un liu emper-
ial,/Une cite nobile sanz gueres paringal" (Auban, 11. 10-11),
compared by Ühleman with "To Verolamye which of antiquyte/
Was in Briteyn a famous gret cite" (I, 874-5), involves
phraseology so usual in medieval verse as to make the similarity unimportant.

The name "Aracle" as applied to Alban's converted executioner first appears textually in the Auban, and then as
"Araclius" in Lydgate, but the name in its Latin form is
found in the marginal rubrics of the Interpretatio in the
Dublin MS, so that the French poem is not necessarily the
direct source. Ühleman says that Lydgate's poem, like the
Auban, has the betrayer of Alban first spy on him through a
window,[55] but in fact Lydgate mentions no window.

A similarity which Ühleman missed, but which seems more
telling than any of his, is that in both poems, though not in
William, Amphibalus weeps on being given Alban's cross (Aub.
11. 1201-04; Lyd. III, 110). The suggestion that Auban must
be a source because of the colophon to Lydgate's poem,

"translatid out of frenssh & latyn", Ühleman readily admits
to be extremely weak.[56]  We may conclude that although Lydgate probably had some knowledge of the Auban and that this
knowledge is reflected here and there in his work, the verbal
parallels are fewer, the situations less close than are those
of William to Lydgate's poem, and that therefore the Auban
is not a source of any consequence.

The third known treatment of the Alban legend is a brief
prose work in Latin, published for the first time by van der
Westhuizen[57], but long available in essence via the synoptic
rubrics printed by Thomas D. Hardy in his Descriptive Catalogue (I, pp. 18-19) and the fragment occurring in Ussher's
Britannicarum Ecclesiarum Antiquitates, in The Whole Works
of Most Rev. James Ussher (Dublin, 1864) V, pp. 197-98.  It
was Dr. Quistorp who first perceived that this Tractatus de
Nobilitate, Vita et Martyrio SS. Albani et Amphibali e Gallico in Latinum translatum as described by Hardy must be a
source or analogue of Lydgate's Alban.[58]  Although Dr.
Quistorp went no further than Hardy's Catalogue, the present
editor's close collation of MS. Bodley 585 with Lydgate has
shown her to be right.[59]  The Tractatus, or the unknown
French book from which it was translated, is pretty surely
the source, directly or at one remove, of much of Lydgate's
Book I, as the many verbal parallels cited in the explanatory
notes should make clear.

The innovation of the Tractatus is its narration of the
events of the youth of Alban and Amphibalus.[60]  It makes of
them both young aspirants to knighthood sent to Diocletian at
Rome in the train of Bassianus, son of Severus, king of
Britain.  In Rome, we are told, Alban distinguished himself
greatly in a tournament and was retained at court by Diocletian, whereas Amphibalus was converted to Christianity by
Pope Zephyrinus and took orders.  Years later, Diocletian,
having previously sent Alban back to become "princeps mil-
itiae" and seneschal of Britain, started persecuting the
Christians.  This caused them to disperse from Rome.  Amphibalus, returning to his native Wales, stopped at Verulamium,
where he encountered his old friend Alban.  In none of the
earlier accounts of the Alban legend is there any hint that
he had been acquainted with Amphibalus before the latter's
arrival as a fugitive.[61]

But it ought not to surprise us that between Henry II's
time, when William started the amplification of the Alban
legend, and Lydgate's day more than two hundred years later,

there should have emerged an "enfances" narrative, providing
the monks and pilgrims (especially the noble ones) with further, more impressive and more appealing information about
the birth and youthful exploits of the protomartyr.  Though
the first analogies which come to mind may be the infancy
narratives in Matthew, Luke and the apocryphal gospels, the
"enfances" genre in the France of the high middle ages was
more typical of chansons de geste and chivalric romances than
of religious narrative.  The author of Tractatus (or rather
of the French work it presumably translates) was very probably
attributing these youthful exploits to Alban and Amphibalus
for the first time.  But it seems likely that he found inspiration in an earlier account of two other saintly knights which
had long enjoyed widespread popularity in France and England.

The versions of the tale of Amis and Amiloun, sometimes
attached to the Charlemagne cycle and sometimes found separately as a double saints' legend,[62] bear a striking resemblance to the new matter of the Tractatus.  Obviously, the
names of the saintly knights resemble each other:  they al-
literate in "a" and the second is longer than the first.
This similarity might well have sufficed to bring the "Amis"
legend to mind when the author of Tractatus cast about for
saintly, knightly material to amplify the Alban story.

Amis (Amicus) and Amiloun (Amile, Amelius) were legendary knights who received their training at the same court
and later demonstrated an exaggerated spirit of friendship
and mutual sacrifice.  Like the British saints' even before
Tractatus their remains were eventually reunited long after
their burials.[63]  The Vita sanctorum Amici et Amelii dates
from the first half of the twelfth century; the pair of
knights appear in several chansons de geste of that century
and of the thirteenth.[64]  The legend concerns two noble
youths conceived simultaneously in separate regions of France.
Their eternal friendship being foretold, the parents bring
them to the pope to be baptised (cf. Albon, I, 332).  When
grown they separated (like Albon and Amphibalus), eventually
to meet again.  From their separation the tale bears no resemblance to the Tractatus until circumstances require the
surrender of Alban's garment to disguise the hunted Amphibalus, but William had already put this into the Interpretatio
(except for the princely British origins of Amphibalus.)
William's instance of self-sacrifice by one friend for another
may have been the point of connection with Amis for the
author of Tractatus:  given two saints who exchanged garments
to save the one who was being sought by enemies, two saints

who died separate holy deaths but were later rejoined in
death in St. Albans after the miraculous revelation of Amphibalus' resting place, and further given the wish to create
a fictional chivalric life for these saints, the analogy of
the Franco-Italian knights who lived and died for friendship
and were miraculously rejoined after death may well have provided the theme of Tractatus which Lydgate later utilized.
Previously Amphibalus was neither Briton nor of noble blood,
nor even previously known to Albanus.

This part of the Tractatus is set in fairly detailed
semi-history or pseudo-history drawn from Geoffrey of Monmouth (see explanatory notes to book I, passim). The Tractatus continues the legend with the events found in William,
though in greatly abridged form, then adds more matter from
Geoffrey concerning King Coel's avenging of the deaths of
the martyrs and also details of the church of St. Amphibalus
at Winchester.

Nothing much is known for certain of the origins of this
Tractatus, though one may speculate as to its inspiration.
The variant title found in the Bodley MS., Tractatus...de
quodam libro gallico excerptus & in latinum translatus, in-
dicates that the French original was probably not concerned
exclusively with St. Alban.  A search of the manuscript cata-
logues of the major French libraries has been fruitless.  The
only hint of attribution is found in a marginal note on f.
22r. of the Trinity College, Dublin, MS. of the Interpretatio, which reads "Erat namque dux & magister milicie totius
Britannie" and "Hoc de libro Johannis Mansel."  John Mansel,
one of Henry III's chief ministers, a cleric of military
leanings and of great wealth, had several known connections
with St. Albans Abbey (see DNB).  The marginal note corresponds closely to the Tractatus' "principem milicie totius
britanie" (f. 3 v.), but we cannot be certain as to the meaning of "de libro Johannis Mansel."  It might mean merely
that John Mansel passed through St. Albans and lent his book
to one of the monks; on the other hand it might imply his
authorship.

It would be tempting to connect the note with another
Mansel, Jean Mansel de Hesdin, a contemporary of Lydgate's
and author of the historical compendium, La Fleur des Histoires, which contains a great number of saints' lives, drawn
mostly from the Legenda Aurea.[65]  However, Prof. Joan Larsen
Klein, who generously investigated MS. Douce 333 at the Bodleian, has informed me that it contains no life of Alban;

M. J. Porcher of the Bibliothèque Nationale also has reported
negatively on his gratefully acknowledged examination of the
manuscripts in Paris.

The manuscript of the Tractatus examined in microfilm
for the present edition, Bodley 585, is in one fifteenth-
century hand, and also contains an extract from Vitae Duorum
Offarum dealing with the translation of Alban's relics and a
portion of the encyclopedic Granarium of Abbot John Whethamstede,[66] which is referred to in Lydgate's poem (I, 894).
This last fact suggests that the manuscript was copied at
St. Albans at a time roughly contemporaneous with Lydgate.

D. R. Howlett's suggestion based on Bale's attribution,
that Abbot Whethamstede wrote the Tractatus,[67] seems rather
improbable on three counts.  First, its contents are much
too naïve to have been acceptable to the encyclopedic abbot;
second, it seems most unlikely that scribes at his own abbey
would have referred to the longer French work from which
Tractatus was excerpted as "a certain book."  But if Whethamstede did not write the French, he is merely an excerpter
and translator, and his action in doing this work sheds little
light on Tractatus' origins.  Third, if we accept Galbraith's
dating of most of the contents of the Tractatus manuscript
(Cotton Claudius F iv)[68] as applicable to Tractatus, then
Whethamstede was not old enough to have written it.

Yet there is circumstantial evidence that neither the
Tractatus nor William as discrete works provided Lydgate's
immediate source.  We are led to this conclusion by the
existence of a fifteenth-century prose life of St. Alban in
English, occurring in at least seven manuscripts of the
English version of Legenda Aurea, known as the Gilte Legende.
It was this translation which Caxton seems to have abridged
and revised.  Pierce Butler's Legenda Aurea--Legende Doree--
Golden Legend is a discussion at length of the entire ques-
tion;[69] in our times Auvo Kurvinen, Manfred Görlach and
Richard Hamer have all discussed Gilte Legende at length.[70]
The manuscripts all contain varying numbers of English saints'
lives not in the Latin or French versions.  One of these is
an unusually long chapter on the life of St. Alban.  The
most impressive though not the oldest of these manuscripts is
Harleian 4775 of the British Library;[71] the other manuscripts
seem to vary from it only in individual words and phraseology.
The Gilte Legende "St. Alban" has two notable characteristics
relating to Lydgate.  First, it is a rather close translation
of the Tractatus and Interpretatio; second, like Lydgate's

Albon it follows the Tractatus for the episodes before Amphibalus' entry into Verulamium, then, again like Lydgate, turns
to William's work, reverting to Tractatus to insert the
"Maximian and Asclepeodotus" passage, which is an attempt to
harmonize the trial of Alban with the data as to his rank and
position previously given from Tractatus. The fact that it
is a close translation from known Latin sources proves that
the prose legend cannot have derived from Lydgate. Since the
splicing of the two sources in each work strongly suggests a
very close relationship, two possibilities would seem to
exist:  either Lydgate used the English prose as his immediate
principal source, or both derive from a common Latin original
now lost.

    The colophon of Lydgate's poem with its "translatid out
of frenssh & latyn" must now be reconsidered. Whatever else
this means, it is good evidence that the English prose was
not his chief source. Lydgate, unlike Chaucer, did not usually obfuscate his borrowings. The most likely interpretation
of the phrase from the colophon is that an anonymous monk of
St. Albans, probably at the beginning of the fifteenth century, crudely linked together the beginning and trial scene
of the Tractatus and the greater part of the Interpretatio,
making of them one volume (see Expl. Notes, II, 163; II,
1001,; II, 1220; II 1367). In his conflation he retained the
phrase occurring in the British Museum MS. of Tractatus, "e
Gallico in Latinum translatum." Conjecturally, then, Lydgate,
commissioned by the Abbey, would have been presented with
this hypothetical Latin version, the fullest of all extant
lives of the saint, and have assumed that the whole work was
a translation into Latin from the French. Hence the "translated out of frenssh & latyn" of the colophon. W. McLeod
is doubtless right in rejecting the supposition most recently
voiced by Howlett that the extant Seint Auban attributed to
Matthew Paris is the French work referred to.[72]

    Latinate constructions and Latin name-forms in Lydgate's
poem reinforce the statement of the colophon. Thus the
Interpretatio (p. 153 C) reads, "Tunc populus, in civitate
Iudice derelicto, proruit ad spectaculum." Lydgate (II,
1553) faithfully copies the absolute construction:

              Peeple cam doun his martirdam to see,
              The iuge allone lefte in the cite.

On the other hand, the Gilte Legende reads, "And all the
peple leving the iuge in the towne runne out to biholde this

merveille." (f. 100 v.).  Similarly, both the Tractatus and
Lydgate refer to Maximian as Herculeus, whereas Harleian 4775
calls him Hercule.  Amphibalus himself is "Amphiabel" or
"Amphabel" in the Harleian legend.  Lydgate usually has
"Asclepeodot" for the Latin "Asclepiodotus," vice Harleian's
"Askopedot" or "Asclepedot," and "Gallus" for the Latin
accusative "Gallum," as opposed to Harleian's peculiar reten-
tion of the accusative form.

That Lydgate does not chiefly derive from the Gilte Legende version is further shown by many correspondences with
the Latin, in which cases the Harleian differs from both.
The following, drawn from numerous examples, may suffice:

In book II, ll. 1626-27, Lydgate, referring to Araclius, speaks of "The same knyht astoned & a ferd/ Which
drouh Albon...."  This derives from William's "Miles ille
qui...trahebat" (p. 153 F).  Harleian 4775, on the other
hand, reads "one of the knyghtis that drowe Albon" (f. 101
r.), although only one is actually involved in the action.

Lydgate, like the Latin, includes among Albon's peti-
tions for the people during the great heat and drought which
accompany his passion, a request for a breeze:  "The smothe
wynd bi grace late enspire" (II, 1747); the translator of the
Harleian legend misreads the subjunctive "incipiat," and
sets down "Than anone the wynde bigan to blowe more freshly"
(f. 101 4.).  A little further on, Lydgate correctly refers
to the sun (II, 1786) in reference to William's "deo magno
Soli" (p. 154 C), whereas the Harleian MS reads "the gret
god Venus" (f. 101 r.).

Of the numerous passages omitted in the Harleian which
are present in both Lydgate and the Latin source, we may cite
Lydgate's close rendering of William's "ad scelus de scelere
transitum facientes" (p. 154 A) at II, 1708.  Though the
Harleian MS. has the preceding and following passages, it
omits the cited line entirely.

All the evidence above, however, fails to show that
Lydgate used the Latin sources as they now exist.  The collation of Lydgate with these Latin sources uncovers several
passages in which Lydgate and the Harleian agree with each
other but not with the Tractatus and Interpretatio; here we
call attention to three:  in matter coming substantially from
William's Interpretatio, which does not even mention Asclepiodotus, both English versions refer to the judge by that name,

thus identifying him with the king of Britain in the Tractatus.  See Lydgate, II, 1001 and Harleian f. 99a r.

At III, 167, Lydgate reads "commemoracioun."  The corresponding passage in the Harleian reads "mynde."  Yet the
Latin reads "commoratio" (dwelling), not "commemoratio."  At
III, 905 ff., Lydgate concurs with Harleian (f. 103 v.) in
having only one of the "tormentours" rush ahead of the crowd
to put an end to Amphibalus' life.  On the other hand, William is clearly plural: "pervenerunt ... declinarent ...
expoliaverunt" (p. 158 B).

There is thus good evidence for maintaining that there
once existed (and may still exist) a Latin conflation of the
Tractatus and Interpretatio (cf. the "Asclepiodotus" passage
just discussed).73  This lost Latin, with a few accidental
scribal changes from its originals, would be the main source
of both the English prose of the Golden Legend (e.g. Harl.
4775) and of Lydgate's poem.  From the usual fidelity of the
English prose to the known Latin sources we must conclude
that the Latin conflation was a mere patching together of
passages from the Tractatus and Interpretatio, differing from
them only in such chance errors as the rendering singular of
the disembowellers of Amphibalus and the reading of "commemoratio" for "commoratio."

McLeod independently reached in 1980 a conclusion which
was already expressed in the present editor's Harvard thesis
of 1960,74 that the interweaving of Tractatus and William's
Interpretatio in similar pattern by the Gilte Legende and
Lydgate's Albon brings one to the conclusion already expressed, that there was a common principal lost source in
Latin prose.75  But McLeod passes over the similarities between the Legende and Lydgate which are absent from the known
Latin sources as just pointed out.  He disposes of the possibility that Lydgate had by him and occasionally used the
very recent English prose as well as the hypothetical version,
saying merely that "the proximity of time makes this un-
likely.76  Because the attribution of the Gilte Legende to
"a synful wretche" is seen by at least one modern scholar as
derivative from the language of the nameless convert as
repeated in Lydgate, III, 1314 , it is not impossible that the
Gilte Legende was translated at St. Albans.77  If this be
true, then what could have been more likely than that Abbot
Whethamstede should make available to the poet the year-old
prose version, recapitulating the sequence of William's prose
and Ralph's versification many years before.  That Lydgate

should have used a Latin source while (like Chaucer in the
Clerk's Tale) occasionally referring to a vernacular version
is not unlikely.

Of minor sources, the Anglo-Norman _Auban_ has already
been discussed. There are indications that Lydgate used
Geoffrey of Monmouth's _Historia_ to reinforce his treatment
of Book I, e.g. the reference to Lucan in I, 120. For St.
Germanus' visit to Alban's tomb Bede's _Ecclesiastical His-_
_tory_, I, 18, is the direct or indirect source. The tale of
Offa's vision and discovery of Alban's relics is to be found
in _Vitae Duorum Offarum_ and in the _Chronica Majora_ of Matthew
Paris, but no direct source has been found for the oddity
which Lydgate shares with one later work, the Cologne volume
of 1502, _De incliti et gloriosi protomartyris Anglie Albani_
(see the Appendix). Both of these works make contemporaries
of Germanus and Offa, whereas in Matthew Paris the interval
between their lives is stated to the year.

_Versification, Stanzaic Punctuation and Language_

The reasonably satisfactory analysis of Lydgate's metrical system by J. Schick[78] was little challenged until 1938,
when C. S. Lewis' mildly revisionist study of the fifteenth-
century heroic appeared.[79] Since 1966 there has been renewed
interest in Lydgate's versification, largely because of attempts to apply Morris Halle and S. J. Keyser's analysis of
Chaucer's in "Chaucer and the Study of Prosody.[80] It is not
the intention of this editor to add his opinions to the rest
in any systematic way; however a few words specifically directed to the verse of _St. Albon_ are needed.

First, in _St. Albon_ the caesura, usually marked by a
virgule or slash in the manuscripts, is much more noticeable
than in the verse of Chaucer, though probably not much more
than in the earlier work of Lydgate. Second, if we apply
Schick's five main types to the poem, we find all present in
varying degrees, each with one or more variations, or in com-
bination with one of the other basic types, -- phenomena
recognized by Schick. Among the types, "A," the iambic five
stress line with caesura after the second stress, is the commonest; "B" with an extra weak foot gives the line a trochaic quality. However, in both "A" and "B" one variation
recurs with a surprising frequency; this is the inversion of
the first foot of the first or second hemistich so as to make
it trochaic. Schick paid little attention to the second

hemistich as compared with the first, except that type "B" presumes an initial stress, as does Lydgate's specialty, type "C," with stresses divided only by the caesura occurring at the end of the first and beginning of the second hemistich. A sampling based on all lines ending in "00" or "50" shows that about one third of the first hemistiches begin with a stressed syllable; by the same sampling, the first syllable after the Lansdowne virgule is stressed in 40% of the instances.

These two phenomena tend to make the verse movement very trochaic, -- more so than one might expect.

Schick, in treating the first half-line as of two stresses and four or five syllables, implies that the second half-line will have three stresses. Yet much of the time in St. Albon the middle stress of the three is so light (if it is there at all) that one may readily read the verse line as of four stressed syllables, two in each hemistich, so that the line resembles to a degree the historic English poetic line; occasional presence of alliteration adds to this impression.

In Chaucer, the flexibility of the rime royal stanza is often characterized by heavier punctuation, chiefly after the third or fourth line. There is perhaps less predictability about the stanzas of St. Albon. About one quarter of the stanzas do not require any major voice drop or punctuation heavier than the comma within the stanza. About one fifth need more punctuation at the end of line four, and an eighth or so at the end of line three. Together these make up about 34%. The greater part of the remainder have two pauses, the most common distribution being after lines two and four. Rarely, a single pause is seen at the end of line two, or after line five.

The Glossary and its length are indication enough that when he wrote St. Albon Lydgate had acquired or created a large vocabulary which he freely employed in composition. Lydgate shares with Chaucer a position at the zenith of Romance word acclimation. According to Reismüller,[81] working under a two-fold hardship, first, the over-dependence of the early volumes of OED on the much-published Lydgate, and second, the imperfections of the Horstmann edition of Albon, cites forty-three words as appearing in the poem which Lydgate used in English for the first time (though not necessarily here). Here is the list, chiefly abstracted from Reismüller, but omitting his errors:

abject

advert

aduertise

arable

aspection

aureat

azure (missed by Reismüller)

bezzle, besile

calion

chastiser

concern, II, 21 (missed by R.)

curas

denizen

depict

derision

detestable

disentrayled

duplicity

excel (earliest use?)

exemplify

fallible

feruence

fondresse

fringid

frument

headspring (missed, R.)

impotent (cf. Reismüller,
           "impotence")

lamentable

maligne

oblation

outrance

palestre

persuade

perturbance

podagre

prothomartyr

repertorie

rural

sanative

serpentine

signacle

splay

tarage

tugurrye

victorious

What is most striking about the list above, even if we
assume that it is only one-half or two-thirds properly attributed to Lydgate, is the frequency of words which are today in the vocabulary of every educated person; as against
calion, frument, outrance (modern re-introduction), palestre,
podagre, signacle, tarage and tugurrye, we have at least
twenty-nine rather usual modern terms, and a few more which
are easily recognizable, such as besile and splay (for dis-
play).  Thus the usual well-worn remarks of handbooks about
the difficulty and ornateness of Lydgate's language do not
much apply to St. Albon and St. Amphibalus.  We can hardly
complain of the difficulty or ineptness of such new words as
abject, arable, denizen, excel, fallible or persuade.  We
must rather be conscious of the debt which our language owes
John Lydgate.

Less commendable is the idiosyncratic and latinate treatment of the  English sentence, notably as regards omission of subject pronouns, use of absolute constructions and attempts to employ English nouns in introductory ablative constructions (these are further discussed on p. 210).  Also presenting difficulties are the frequent parenthetical expressions and the loose, run-on sentence structure.

The two most significant things that may be said of Lydgate's figurative language are that it is allusive to the classics of antiquity and to the scriptures and that it is applied quite consciously, cosmetically, like icing on a cake. Such figures are by no means spread thinly through the text, but are concentrated in passages which require heightened treatment, such as the conversion, trial and martyrdoms. Doubtless the passages which best illustrate these are the passage beginning II, 583 and the one at II, 835.  Book II has the greatest concentration of ornate language, and III, as though the first verve had ended and Lydgate was no longer much interested in his task, has far fewer examples of the purple patch.

## Remarks on the Treatment of the Text

All contractions in the Lansdowne Manuscript except those which represent a reduction in syllables, such as "t'" and "b'" have been silently expanded.  In some cases, when the proper expansion was in doubt and the text was clear without the ambiguous mark, that mark has been ignored as being probably a mere flourish.  The capitalization has been modernized and all underscoring omitted.  The virgules which are a common feature of La and Li, usually falling at the caesura, and constituting almost the only punctuation of these manuscripts, have been omitted.  Modern punctuation has been supplied. Lansdowne has numerous "e" flourishes and also a few internal, probably meaningless ornaments.  All of these have been omitted except when they extend over a preceding vowel, indicating "n" or "m."  Double "f" has been rendered by a capital letter where modern usage demands one, otherwise by a single minuscule initially and double minuscule medially or at the end.  Minuscule "h" has been transcribed a little hesitantly as "gh" when the letter has an elongated horizontal stroke.  The ampersand, very common in Lansdowne, has been rendered "and."

When the reading of a word or phrase in other manuscripts

has seemed to the editor either more grammatical or more in keeping with good sense and the sources than that of Lansdowne, it has been adopted.  Such readings have been examined in light of the stemma, but there has been no attempt to systematically apply the stemma to the text.  These readings not from Lansdowne have been italicized and introduced into the edited text.

The editor has tried to include in the textual notes all variant readings involving a difference in wording or morphological form, as well as a substantial sampling of spelling variants, which are of substantial interest, both metrically and linguistically.  Especially in the first three hundred lines, a great many of these have been recorded.  When form or meaning variation is the reason for citation in a note, even if the spellings vary, only one is ordinarily given, the spelling of the first manuscript referred to by initial immediately thereafter.

When it would not otherwise be clear which word in the line is referred to by a textual note, the text word has been repeated below and followed by a "close-bracket."  After this sign come the variant readings, each labeled with the abbreviation for the manuscript in which it occurs.  However, when no confusion is likely, the Lansdowne form is not repeated below; in such cases there is no bracket, and the variants immediately follow the line number.  See above, p. x, for the abbreviations used for the manuscripts.  References to folio numbers in the left margin of the text are to the modern numbering of Lansdowne, except when, Lansdowne being defective, another manuscript has been substituted for it, in which case the substituted MS. is similarly cited.

*NOTES*

1.  The form "Amphibalus" is used by the originator of the name, Geoffrey of Monmouth, and most modern writers.  Sometimes Lydgate used "Amphibal."  "Amphabel" is the form used in the Horstman edition, based on the first edition of 1534. Westhuizen in his recent edition prefers Lydgate's alternate form, while Derek Pearsall holds for "Amphabell."  "Amphable" and "Amphiable" are fifteenth and sixteenth century forms used outside the Lydgate tradition.

2.  The books are of markedly different length:  Book I has 930 lines, Book II has 2,087, and Book III (including the

detachable prayer of 105 lines), 1,602. Thus the whole poem
as edited consists of 4,619 lines.

3.    Internal and external evidence both serve to prove the
date and Lydgate's commission. Internally we have the allusions to the commission in the Epilogue to Book I, and in
the colophons appearing in four of the extant manuscripts.
Externally we have Cotton Nero D VII, f. 32 r., as published
by H. T. Riley, Registrum Abbatiae Joh. Whethamstede, Rolls
Series, xxviii, London, 1872, I, p. 462. which records that
Whethamstede appropriated "100 solidi" for the "translation,
writing and illumination." Dr. David Howlett of Corpus
Christi College, Oxford, has informed me by letter of data
concerning the ornate manuscript's early history which he
found in MS. Arundel 3 of the Library of the College of
Heralds, f. 41 r. and v. From MS Arundel 34, published by
Riley as Annales Monasterii Sancti Albani a Johanne Amundesham, Monacho, Rolls Series, xxviii, London, 1872, II, p. 256,
we learn that Lydgate himself, referred to as "cuidam monacho
de Burgo Sancti Edmundi," received three pounds, six shil-
lings, eight pence for the work; see H. N. MacCracken,
"Studies in the Life and Writings of John Lydgate," unpublished Harvard thesis, 1907, Appendix, p. 124.

4.    Roberto Weiss, Humanism in England, 2nd ed., Oxford:
Blackwell, 1957, pp. 30-38. See also "Whethamstede" in the
Dictionary of National Biography.

5.    Dr. Hildeburg Quistorp's unpublished dissertation, "Studien zu Lydgate's Heiligenlegenden," Bonn, 1951, takes up
this heightened style at length, p. 188. See also Walter
Schirmer's John Lydgate, ein Kulturbild, Tübingen: Tauchnitz, 1931, pp. 144-48 (pp. 150-55 in the English translation by Ann Keep, London: Methuen, 1961).

6.    Typical of the few critical notices is Gordon Gerould's
in Saints' Legends, Boston: Houghton Mifflin, 1916, pp. 263-
64. He terms the poem "even less successful" than St. Edmund. Though Sergio Rossi likes Edmund, he writes of St. Albon (Poesia cavalleresca e poesia religiosa inglese nel
Quattrocento, 2nd ed., Milan: Instituto Editoriale Cisalpino,
1960, p. 184: "valore intrinseco non ha...." Alain Renoir's
Poetry of John Lydgate, London: Routledge, 1967, ignores
St. Albon completely. Derek Pearsall in John Lydgate, Charlottesville, Va.: Univ. of Virginia Press, 1970, p. 284,
calls it pretentious, fatuous and repetitive. In Chaucer and
the Fifteenth Century, Oxford, Clarendon, 1948, H.S. Bennett
refers to it only once, as a prose work.

7.   J. E. van der Westhuizen edited The Life of Saint Alban
and Saint Amphibal, Leiden:  E. J. Brill, in 1974.  This edition is based on the editor's thesis of the University of
London, 1963.  Westhuizen was not aware of the present editor's thesis (Harvard, 1960).

8.   See Appendix, pp. 199 for data on added and suppressed
lines.

9.   S. Albon und Amphabel, ein Legendenepos in 3 Buchern von
Lydgate, nach der editio von S. Albans, 1534, in Festschrift
z. 50jahr. Bestehen der Konigstadtischen Realschule zu Berlin, 1882.  Horstmann always mistakenly describes MS. Trinity College, Oxford, 38 as the Cambridge MS. or MS. Trin.
Cambridge 39, though he cites it liberally.

10.   Carleton Brown and R. H. Robbins, Index of Middle English Verse, New York: Columbia Press for Index Society, 1943,
no. 3748.

11.   See H. L. D. Ward, Catalogue of Romances ... in the
British Museum, v. I, London, 1883, pp. 496-97.

12.   A personal communication to the present editor.

13.   See C. E. Wright, English Vernacular Hands from the
Twelfth to the Fifteenth Centuries, Oxford: Clarendon Press,
1960, plate 24, and A. I. Doyle, "The Work of a late Fifteenth Century English Scribe, William Ebesham," Bulletin of
the John Rylands Library, xxxix (1957), 298-325.  For Malcolm
Parkes' terminology, see English Cursive Book Hands, 1230-
1500, revised, London: Scolar Press, 1979.

F. N. Robinson, "On Two Manuscripts of Lydgate's "Guy of
Warwick," Harvard Studies & Notes in Philology and Literature,
v (1898), 188, notes that MS. Vossius 9 of Leyden contains
seventeen writings by Lydgate which are also in Lansdowne
699; they both also contain Chaucer's "Truth" and "Fortune."
Items 8-17 of Vossius appear in the same sequence as in Lansdowne.  J. A. van Dorsten in "The Leyden Lydgate Manuscript,"
Scriptorium xiv (1960) 320, concludes that both manuscripts
have a common source.  In the present editor's opinion, Lansdowne is somewhat the older.  Of course, Vossius does not
contain St. Albon. The Lincoln MS. is of the same anthology
type.  Van Dorsten's description of the principal hand in
Vossius (p. 321) mentions several features not typical of
Lansdowne.

14.   On f. 95 of Lansdowne are written the opening lines of

Britannia's Pastorals: Browne's poem, in turn (Book I, Song 4, 11, 315-21) has a passage which speaks of "Verolame, a stately nymph of yore / Whose waters are besmeared with Albon's blood."

15. Ward, v. I, p. 497.

16. See H. N. MacCracken, ed., Minor Poems of John Lydgate, v. I, E.E.T.S., E.S., cvii, 1911, p. 124.

17. R. M. Woolley, Catalogue of the Manuscripts of Lincoln Cathedral Chapter Library, London: Humphrey Milford, 1927, no. 124.

18. Cf. Parkes, pp. xiv-xxi.

19. MacCracken, "Studies," Appendix, p. 124.

20. J. Conway Davies, Catalogue of Manuscripts of the Honourable Society of the Inner Temple, London: Oxford University Press, 1972, pp. 222-23.

21. D. S. Bland, "Pegasus at the Inner Temple," Notes and Queries, ccxiv (1969), 16-18, and "Gerard Leigh and Stephen Hawes," Notes and Queries, ccxxiii (1977) 497 (with bibliographical notes).

22. Charles Briquet, Les Filigranes, Paris: A. Picard, 1907. no. 689 and no. 14, 236. The bull's head is the commonest of early watermarks. J. J. G. Alexander of the Bodleian generously offered much information about TCO 38 in a letter.

23. Van der Westhuizen, p. 8.

24. The Text of the Canterbury Tales, Chicago: University of Chicago Press, 1940, I, pp. 433-38. Herbert C. Schulz, former curator at the Huntington also provided information about HM 140.

25. A Descriptive Catalogue of the Second Series of Fifty MSS (Nos. 51-100) in the Collection of Henry Yates Thompson, Cambridge: University Press, 1902, pp. 218 ff.

26. Westhuizen reached the same conclusion independently.

27. Hippolyte Déléhaye, Les Passions des Martyrs et les Genres Littéraires, Bruxelles: Société Bollandiste, 1921, passim. A. W. Wade-Evans in his Welsh Christian Origins,

Oxford: Alden, 1934, pp. 16-18, rejects this evidence and
and favors martyrdom at Caerleon. Charles Thomas in the recent Christianity in Roman Britain to A.D. 500, Berkeley:
California Press, prefers the claims of Verulamium, pp. 48-50

28.  "St. Alban and St. Albans," Antiquity, xv (1941), 337.
This admirable essay deserves to be read in full.

29.  It was W. Meyer who first published and clarified the
relations of the three passions of Alban that precede Bede's
Ecclesiastical History (The Turin Passion, D.v. 3, Bibl. Nat.
Taurinensis, the Autun Passion and the Paris Passion) in
"Die Legende des h. Albanus in Texten vor Beda," Abhandlun-
gen der ... Kgl. Gesellschaft der Wissenschaften zu Göttingen, Phil.-Hist. Klasse, N. F. viii (1904), p. 1 ff.

30.  Hugh Williams, Christianity in Early Britain, Oxford:
Clarendon Press, 1912, p. 108, and Levison, pp. 346-47.

31.  Meyer prints the Turin, Autun, and Paris texts in their
entirety.

32.  Déléhaye, Passions, p. 407.

33.  Hugh Williams, ed., Cymmrodorion Record Series, iii,
London, 1901 (for 1899), p. 24.

34.  Levison, p. 350.

35.  Déléhaye, Passions, p. 407.

36.  "Interpretatio Guilelmi" in Acta Sanctorum apud socios
Bollandianos, "Die vigesima secunda Junii," v. 5, p. 149 c
(editio novissima) Paris: Palmé, 1867.

37.  Levison, p. 354.

38.  J. Loth in "S. Amphibalus," Revue Celtique, xi (1890),
349, put forth this suggestion as to how Geoffrey came to
mistake "amphibalus" for a name: "C'est en effet le nom sous
lequel on designait une sorte de chasuble.... On ne peut
cependant supposer, malgré l'aplomb dont Gaufrei a donné tant
de preuves, qu'il se soit livré a cette plaisanterie.... Il
devait ignorer le sens du mot amphibalus: a priori c'est à
une méprise de lecture qu'il a dû sa trouvaille. Il me pa-
rait aujourd'hui certain que le passage qui l'a si plaisam-
ment induit en erreur se trouve dans l'Epistola Gildae.
On lit, au debut à peu près de l'Epistola, dans l'imprecatio

contre le roi Constantin, qu'entre autres forfaits, Constantin aurait commis le suivant: 'In duarum matrum sinibus, ecclesiae carnalisque, sub sancti abbatis amphibalo, latera regiorum puerorum ... laceravit.' Gaufrei aura lu: 'sub sancto abbate Amphibalo'; la terminaison, dans le manuscrit qu'il avait sous les yeux, pouvait être en abrégé. La conjecture se change en certitude, si on se reporte au chapitre iv, livre xi de son _Histoire_: Et (Constantinus) praedictos filios Modredi cepit: et _alterum_ juvenem Guintoniae in ecclesiam sancti Amphibali fugientem ante altare trucidavit....'"

Later, J. S. P. Tatlock in "St. Amphibalus," _University of California Publications in English_, iv (1934), pp. 249-57, told of finding the "abbate" form previously hypothesized by Loth in certain MSS. of Gildas. He believed that the expression "sub sancte abbate Amphibalo" was used by Geoffrey to mean "in the very church dedicated to St. Amphibalus." This would explain the lapse of centuries between Alban and either of the two Constantines mentioned. The inspiration to give the name to Alban's unnamed confessor would then come by association: a saint whose name is "cloak" with one who exchanges cloaks. Tatlock finds such a leap well in keeping with the spirit of the _Historia_. The passage seems destined to be misunderstood. J. E. van der Westhuizen in his edition of Lydgate's poem takes "Guintoniae" as quoted above for the name of one of Modred's sons and translates, "The one Guintonia, a young man... (p. 34).

39. _Acta Sanctorum_, p. 149 c.

40. Levison, p. 354. See C. Jenkins, _The Monastic Chronicler and the Early School of St. Albans_, London: S.P.C.K., 1922, p. 33, and L. F. Rushbrook Williams, _History of the Abbey of St. Albans_, London: Longmans, 1917, pp. 77-78.

41. Matthew Paris, _Chronica Majora_, ed. H. R. Luard, Rolls Series 57, London, 1872, v. II, p. 301.

42. Levison, p. 356. R. M. Wilson, "Some Lost Saints' Lives in Old and Middle English," _Modern Language Review_, xxvi (1941), 161-63, agrees with Levison.

43. James Douglas Bruce, _The Evolution of Arthurian Romance_, 2nd ed., repr., Gloucester, Ma.: P. Smith, 1955,, pp. 77-78.

44. W. H. Schofield, _English Literature from the Norman Conquest to Chaucer_, New York: Macmillan, 1906, p. 246; R. S. Loomis, ed., _Arthurian Literature in the Middle Ages_, Oxford:

Clarendon, 1959, p. 67 and n.

45. H. T. Riley, ed., Rolls Series 28, London, 1869, p. 26-7.

46. Acta Sanctorum, June 22, p. 146.

47. Paul Grosjean, review of R. M. Wilson's Lost Literature of Medieval England in Analecta Bollandiana, lxxx (1952), 392.

48. S. Baring Gould and John Fisher, Lives of the British Saints, London: C. J. Clark, 1907, p. 155.

49. L. Williams, pp. 11, 241.

50. "Ueber die Anglonormanische Vie de St. Auban," Romanische Studien, iv (1880), 547-48.

51. Ibid., p. 556.

52. Ibid., p. 555.

53. Arthur Robert Harden, ed., La Vie de Seint Auban: An Anglo-Norman Poem of the Thirteenth Century. Anglo-Norman Text Society, xix, Oxford: Basil Blackwell, 1968.

54. Ühleman, p. 553.

55. Ibid., p. 554.

56. Ibid., p. 553; D. R. Howlett still believes on insufficient grounds that the "French" of the colophon refers to the Auban. See "A St. Albans Historical Miscellany of the Fifteenth Century," Transactions of the Cambridge Bibliographical Society, vi (1974), 199.

57. Van der Westhuizen, pp. 277-85. This transcription must be used with caution.

58. Quistorp, p. 177.

59. See Reinecke, Thesis, 1960, pp. xxxii ff.; Westhuizen reaches the same conclusion, p. 45.

60. Delehaye in his Passions points out the parallel development of "enfances" to supplement both chansons de geste and saints' lives during the later middle ages, p. 320.

61. Several works written after Lydgate's include the "en-

fances." C. Narbey in the Supplément aux Acta Sanctorum, Paris: Le Soudier, 1899-1919, gives Leland's rationalized account from Collectanea, no. 5105, v. iv, pp. 19 ff. and 25 ff. Percie Enderbie, Cambria Triumphans, London, 1661, pp. 159-65, also seems to derive from Lydgate. There are references in Gerard Legh's Accedens of Armory, London, 1562. The "Lyfe of Saynt Albone and of Saint Amphyabel" in the Caxton - De Worde Golden Legend of 1493 is adapted not from Lydgate but from the unpublished prose account found in the pre-Caxtonian Gilte Legende.

62.  See Joseph Bédier, Les Chansons Epiques, Paris, Champion, 1926-29, v. 2, pp. 178-90; MacEdward Leach, ed., Amis and Amiloun, E.E.T.S., O.S., cciii, esp. pp. ix-lxxxix; Kathryn Hume, "Structure and Perspective: Romance and Hagiographic Features in the Amicus and Amelius Story, " Journal of English and Germanic Philology, lxix, 89-107.

63.  Bédier, p. 179: "On vénérait à Mortara deux compagnons qui sont l'Oreste et le Pylade...des chansons de geste...A peu de distance de Mortara s'élève une antique église...de Saint Albin.... On conservait encore dans cette eglise au xviii$^e$ siècle la tradition que les corps de Saint Ami et de Saint Amile y avaient reposé...." One may note the suggestive church dedication and compare Lydgate, III, 845 for reference to Orestes. See also Bédier, pp. 181-82.

64.  Ibid., pp. 182-83.

65.  For more on Mansel de Hesdin see G. de Poerk, Introduction à la Fleur des Histoires de Jean Mansel, Ghent: Claeys-Verheughe, 1936.

66.  Falconer Madan and H.H.E. Craster, Summary Catalogue of Western Manuscripts in the Bodleian Library, II, Oxford: Clarendon, 1953, No. 2357. Mr. W.O. Hassall of the Bodleian generously provided further information. D. R. Howlett has shown this to be part of the same St. Albans manuscript as Cambridge D d, 6. 7.; see my footnote 56.

67.  Howlett, pp. 199-200.

68.  V. H. Galbraith, ed., St. Albans Chronicle, Oxford: Clarendon, 1937, p. xxxviii. W. McLeod, "Alban and Amphibal: Some Extant Lives and a Lost Life," Mediaeval Studies, xlii (1980), 417, also doubts Howlett's attribution.

69.  Butler, pp. 50-75. See also Sr. M. Jeremy's "Caxton and

the Synfulle Wretche," _Traditio_, iv (1946), 423-28.

70. A. Kurvinen, "Caxton's 'Golden Legend' and the Manuscripts of the _Gilte Legende_," _Neuphilologische Mitteilungen_, lx (1959), 353-85; M. Görlach, _The South English Legendary, Gilte Legende and Golden Legend_, Braunschweiger Anglistiche Arbeiten, 3, Braunschweig: Institut für Anglistik und Amerikanistik, 1972; Richard Hamer, _Three Lives from the Gilte Legende_ (with bibliography), Heidelberg: Winter, 1978.

71. A copy of this manuscript is available in the Library of Congress as MLA Rotograph 343.

72. McLeod, p. 418.

73. The most likely place for the occurrence of this Latin conflation is some manuscript of the Latin _Legenda Aurea_ in which the life of Alban has been inserted. Such a manuscript would account for the presence of Alban's life in all MSS of the English version. Accordingly, the present editor sent letters of inquiry to the librarians of fifteen manuscript collections in England, Ireland, and the United States known to possess copies of the _Legenda Aurea_ in an English hand. He gratefully acknowledges answers from Durham Cathedral, Cambridge University, Peterhouse and Pembroke College, Cambridge, the Bodleian, Balliol, Lincoln, Brasenose and Merton Colleges, Lambeth Palace, Trinity College, Dublin, and the H. M. Huntington Library, San Marino, California. MS. Laud Misc. 183 of the Bodleian and Pembroke 227 are the only ones to contain a life of Alban, and neither is the conflated life which was the object of search. The conflation must, at least for the present, remain hypothetical. Dr. Joan Larsen Klein generously examined Laud Misc. 183 for the present editor.

74. Reinecke, p. xlii.

75. McLeod, pp. 426-28.

76. _Ibid._, pp. 425-26.

77. Hamer, pp. 16-18.

78. J. Schick, ed., Lydgate's _Temple of Glas_, E.E.T.S., E.S., lx (1891).

79. C. S. Lewis, "The Fifteenth-Century Heroic Line," _Essays and Studies_, xxiv (1938), 28-42.

80. College English, xxviii (1966), 187-219. A brief conservative chapter is Walter Schirmer's in John Lydgate (trans. Ann Keep), pp. 70-77. See also Mahmoud Manzalaoui, "Lydgate and English Prosody," Cairo Studies in English (1960) 87-104; Dudley Hascall, "The Prosody of John Lydgate, " Language and Style, iii (1970), 122-146: Derek Pearsall, John Lydgate. pp. 58-62; Karen Lynn, "Chaucer's Decasyllabic Line: The Myth of the Hundred Year Hibernation," Chaucer Review, xiii (1978), 116-127.


81. Georg Reismüller, Romanische Lehnworter (Erstbelege) bei Lydgate, Münchener Beitrage, xlviii (1911). See also J. E. Mendenhall, Aureate Terms: A Study in the Literary Diction of the XVth Century, Lancaster, Pa. (1919), (passim), and Elfriede Tilgner, "Die Aureate Terms als Stilement bei Lydgate" (with bibliography), Germanische Studien, clxxxii (1936), 1-87.

*BIBLIOGRAPHY*

I. MSS. OF LYDGATE'S <u>ST</u>. <u>ALBON</u> <u>AND</u> <u>ST</u>. <u>AMPHIBALUS</u>

MS. HM 140, Henry Huntington Library, San Marino, California, formerly Phillipps 8299, ff. 1 r.-66 v.

MS. Petyt 511 (xi), Inner Temple Library, London, ff. 1 r.- 66 v.

MS. Lansdowne 699, British Library, London, ff. 96 r.-176 v.

MS. Lincoln Cathedral Chapter Library, Lincoln, ff. 1 r.-67 v.

MS. 38, Trinity College, Oxford, in the Bodleian Library, ff. 1 r.-67 r.

MS. McLean 40 (Talbot Book of Hours), Fitzwilliam Museum, Cambridge, f. 135 r.

MS. N. L. W. 5135 (Bourdillon), National Library of Wales (a 19th. c. copy of MS. Lansdowne 699), 160 pages.


II.  SOURCES AND ANALOGUES IN MANUSCRIPT

MS. Bodley 585, Bodleian Library, Oxford, containing <u>Tractatus</u> <u>de</u> <u>Vita</u>, <u>Nobilitate</u> <u>et</u> <u>Martyrio</u> SS. Albani et Amphibali, ff. 1 r.-17 v.

MS. Cotton Julius D III, British Library, containing Ralph of Dunstable's verse <u>Passio</u> <u>S</u>. <u>Albani</u>, ff. 125 r.-158 v.

MS. Cotton Claudius E IV, British Library, <u>Tractatus</u> <u>de</u> <u>Vita</u> ... <u>SS</u>. <u>Albani</u> <u>et</u> <u>Amphibali</u>, ff. 334 v/-336 r.

MS. Harleian 4775, British Library, "Lives of Seinte Alboun and Seinte Amphabel," <u>Gilte</u> <u>Legende</u>, ff. 97 r.-104 v.

MS. Trinity College, Dublin, E. L. 40, containing the Vie de
Seint Auban, Passio (or Interpretatio) of William of St.
Albans, and the Passio of Ralph of Dunstable, ff. 3 r.-5 r.


III.  EDITED VERSE OF LYDGATE REFERRED TO IN THIS EDITION


The Glorious Lyfe and Passion of Seint Albon ... and Seint
Amphabel.  St. Albans, 1534, (British Library shelf mark
C. 34. g. 17; S.T.C. no 256).

Horstmann, Carl, ed.  S. Albon u. Amphabel, Ein Legendenepos
in 3 Büchern von Lydgate, nach der editio von S. Albans,
1534, in Festschrift z. 50 jähr. Bestehen der Königstadt-
ischen Realschule zu Berlin, Berlin:  Winckelmann, 1882.
[Horstmann's edition is sometimes bound separately.]

Reinecke, George Francis.  "John Lydgate's Saint Alban and
Saint Amphibalus:  An Edition," a Thesis.  Cambridge,
Mass., Harvard University, 1960.

Westhuizen, J. E. van der, ed.  The Life of Saint Alban and
Saint Amphibal.  Leiden:  E. J. Brill, 1974.

                    * * * * *

Bergen, Henry, ed.  The Fall of Princes.  E.E.T.S., E.S. cxxi-
cxxiv, cxxvi.  London: Oxford University Press, 1924-35
(for 1918-20).

_____. The Troy Book.  E.E.T.S., E.S. xcvii,
ciii, cvi, cxvi.  London: Oxford University Press, 1906-
35 (for 1920).

Erdmann, Axel, ed.  The Siege of Thebes.  E.E.T.S., E.S.
cviii.  London:  K. Paul, Trench, Trübner, 1911.

Horstmann, Carl, ed.  "St. Edmund and St. Fremund" in Altenglische Legenden (neue Folge).  Heilbronn: Henninger, 1881.

MacCracken, Henry Noble, ed.  The Minor Poems, E.E.T.S., E.S.
cvii:  "The Religious Poems."  London:  Oxford University
Press, 1911 (for 1910);  E.E.T.S., O.S. cxcii:  "The
Secular Poems."  London:  Oxford University Press, 1934.
                                            ·
_____. The Serpent of Division.  New
Haven: Yale University Press, 1911.

Miller, James. "John Lydgate's Saint Edmund and Saint Fremund: an annotated edition," a Thesis. Cambridge, Mass.,
Harvard University, 1967.


IV. MANUSCRIPT LISTS, DESCRIPTIONS AND HANDS

Briquet, Charles M. Les Filigranes. Paris: A. Picard,
1907.

Brown, Carleton, and R. H. Robbins. Index to Middle English
Verse. New York: Columbia Press for Index Society, 1943.

Coxe, H. O. Catalogus Codicum MSS qui in Collegis Aulisque
Oxoniensibus hodie Adservantur, Oxford: Univ. Press, 1852.

Davies, J. Conway. Catalogue of Manuscripts of the Honorable
Society of the Inner Temple. London : Oxford University.
Press, 1972.

De Ricci, Seymour and W. J. Wilson. Census of Medieval and
Renaissance Manuscripts in the United States and Canada.
New York: H. W. Wilson, 1935-40.

Dorsten, Jan A. van. "The Leyden Lydgate Manuscript."
Scriptorium, xiv (1960), 315-25.

Doyle, A. I. "The Work of a late Fifteenth Century English
Scribe, William Ebesham." Bulletin of the John Rylands
Library, xxxix (1957), 298-325.

Madan, Falconer et al. Summary Catalogue of Western Manuscripts in the Bodleian Library. Oxford: Clarendon
Press, 1895-1953.

Manly, John M. and Edith Rickert. The Text of the Canterbury
Tales. Chicago: University of Chicago Press, 1940.

Parkes, Malcolm Beckwith. English Cursive Book Hands, 1230-
1500, revised. London: Scolar Press, 1979.

Robinson, Fred N. "On Two Manuscripts of Lydgate's 'Guy of
Warwick.'" Harvard Studies and Notes in Philology and
Literature, v (1898), 18.

Smith, T. Catalogus Librorum Manuscriptorum Bibliothecae
Cottonianae. Oxford: Sheldonian Theatre, 1696.

Ward, H. L. D.  Catalogue of Romances in the Department of
    Manuscripts in the British Museum.  London:  Trustees of
    the British Museum, 1883.

Woolley, Reginald M.  Catalogue of the Manuscripts of the
    Lincoln Cathedral Library.  London: Oxford University
    Press, 1927.

Wright, C. E.  English Vernacular Hands from the Twelfth to
    the Fifteenth Centuries.  Oxford:  Clarendon Press, 1960.


        V.  WORKS TOUCHING ON LYDGATE'S ST. ALBON


Bennett, H. S.  Chaucer and the Fifteenth Century, Oxford
    History of English Literature , ed.  F. P. Wilson and Bon-
    amy Dobrée, v. II, pt. 1.  Oxford:  Clarendon Press, 1947.

Edwards, Anthony Stockwell Garfield.  "A Lydgate Biblio-
    graphy, 1928-68."  Bulletin of Bibliography & Magazine
    Notes, xxvii, no. 1 (Jan.-Mar., 1970) 95-98.

Gerould, Gordon.  Saints' Legends.  Boston:  Houghton Miff-
    lin, 1916.

Holzknecht, Karl J.  Literary Patronage in the Middle Ages.
    Philadelphia: privately printed, 1923.

MacCracken, Henry Noble, "Studies in the Life and Writings of
    John Lydgate."  Doctoral Thesis, Harvard, 1907.

Pearsall, Derek.  John Lydgate.  Charlottesville, Va.:  Uni-
    versity of Virginia Press, 1970.

Quistorp, Hildeburg.  "Studien zu John Lydgates Heiligen-
    legenden."  Dissertation, Bonn, 1951.

Renoir, Alain and C. David Benson, "John Lydgate" in A Man-
    ual of the Writings in Middle English, ed. Albert E. Hart-
    ung, v. VI, pp. 1809-1920, 2071-2175.  New Haven:  Con-
    necticut Academy of Arts and Sciences, 1980.

Rossi, Sergio.  Poesia cavalleresca e poesia religiosa ing-
    lese nel Quattrocento, 2nd ed.  Milan:  Instituto Editor-
    iale Cisalpino, 1960.

Schirmer, Walter F.  Der Englische Frühhumanismus.  Leipzig:

Tauchnitz, 1931.

_____. John Lydgate, ein Kulturbild. Tübingen:
M. Niemeyer, 1952.

_____. John Lydgate: A Study in the Culture of
the XVth Century, trans. Ann E. Keep. London: Methuen,
1961.

Warton, Thomas. History of English Poetry, from the Twelfth
to the Close of the Sixteenth Century, ed. W. C. Hazlitt.
London: Reeves & Turner, 1871.


VI.  THE ALBAN LEGEND, ITS SOURCES AND ANALOGUES


Amundesham, Johannis. Annales Monasterii Sancti Albani a
Johanne Amundesham, monacho, ed. H. T. Riley. London:
Rolls Series, xxviii, 1871.

Baker, Eric. "The Cult of St. Alban at Cologne." Archaeological Journal, xciv (1937), 207-56.

Bédier, Joseph. Les Chansons Epiques. Paris: Champion,
1926-29.

Bruce, J. D. The Evolution of Arthurian Romance, 2nd ed.
Gloucester, Mass.: P. Smith, 1958.

Butler, Pierce. Legenda Aurea-Légende Dorée-Golden Legend.
Baltimore: John Murphy Co., 1899.

Caxton, William. The Legende named in Latyn Legenda Aurea.
Westminster: 1483, reproduced by Alfred Aspland, London,
1878.

Chevalier, Ulysse. Répertoire des sources historiques du
Moyen Age. Paris: A. Picard, 1905-07.

Déléhaye, Hippolyte. Les Légendes Hagiographiques, 3rd ed.
Brussels: Societas Bollandiani, 1927.

_____. Les Passions des martyrs et les genres
littéraires. Brussels: Societe Bollandiste, 1921.

_____. Review, Meyer's "Legende des h. Alban-
us." Analecta Bollandiana, xxiv (1905), 397-99.

Déléhaye, Hippolyte. "In Britannia dans le Martyrologe Hie--
    ronymien." Proceedings of the British Academy, xvii
    (1931) 300-315.

De Poerck, G.  Introduction à la Fleur des Histoires de Jean
    de Mansel.  Ghent:  Claeys Verheuge, 1936.

Enderbie, Percie.  Cambria Triumphans.  London:  Andrew
    Cooke, 1661 [Wing 728].

Galbraith, V. H., ed. St. Albans Chronicle.  Oxford:  Claren-
    don Press, 1937.

Geoffrey of Monmouth, Historia Regum Britanniae, ed. Acton
    Griscom.  London:  Longmans, 1929.

Gildas.  Gildae de excidio Britanniae, ed. Hugh Williams.
    Cymmrodorion Record Series, iii (1899).

Görlach, Manfred.  The South English Legendary, Gilte Legende
    and Golden Legend.  Braunschweiger Anglistiche Arbeiten
    iii, 1972.

Grosjean, Paul.  Review of R. M. Wilson's Lost Literature of
    Medieval England.  Analecta Bollandiana, lxx (1952) 389-
    99.

Hamer, Richard.  Three Lives from the Gilte Legende.  Heidel-
    berg:  Carl Winter, 1978.

Howlett, D. R.  "A St. Albans Historical Miscellany of the
    Fifteenth Century." Transactions of the Cambridge Biblio-
    graphical Society, vi (1974), 195-200.

Hume, Kathryn.  "Structure and Perspective:  Romance and
    Hagiographic Features in the Amicus and Amelius Story."
    Journal of English and Germanic Philology, lxix (1970),
    89-107.

Jenkins, Claude.  The Monastic Chronicler and the Early
    School of St. Albans.  London:  S.P.C.K. 1922.

Jeremy, Sister Mary.  "Caxton and the Synfulle Wretche."
    Traditio, iv (1946), 423-28.

John of Tynemouth.  Nova Legenda Angliae, ed. Carl Horstmann.
    Oxford:  Clarendon Press, 1901.

Kurvinen, Auvo. "Caxton's 'Golden Legend' and the Manu-
    scripts of the 'Gilte Legende.'" Neuphilologische Mit-
    teilungen, lx (1959), 353-75.

Leach, McEdward, ed. Amis and Amiloun. E.E.T.S., O.S.,
    cciii, London: Oxford University Press, 1937.

Legh, Gerard. The Accedens of Armory. London, 1562.

Leland, John. De Rebus Britannicis Collectanea. London:
    G. & J. Richardson, 1770.

Levison, W. "St. Alban and St. Albans." Antiquity, xv
    (1941) 337-59.

Loomis, Roger Sherman, ed. Arthurian Literature in the Mid-
    dle Ages. Oxford: Clarendon Press, 1959.

Loth, J. "S. Amphibalus," Revue Celtique, xi (1890), 349-50.

Matthew Paris, Chronica Majora, ed. Henry R. Luard. Rolls
    Series, lvii, London, 1876.

_____. Vie de Seint Auban, ed. Robert Atkinson.
    London: J. Murray, 1876.

_____. La Vie de Seint Auban: An Anglo-Norman Poem
    of the Thirteenth Century, ed. Arthur Robert Harden.
    Anglo-Norman Text Society, xix, Oxford: Basil Blackwell,
    1968.

McLeod, W. "Alban and Amphibal: Some Extant Lives and a
    Lost Life." Medieval Studies, xlii (1980), pp. 407-30.

Meyer, Wilhelm. "Die Legende des h. Albanus, des Protomar-
    tyr Angliae, in texten vor Beda." Abhandlungen der Kgl.
    Gesellschaft der Wissenschaften zu Göttingen, Philol.:
    Hist. Klasse, Neue Folge, viii (1904).

Narbey, C., Supplément aux Acta Sanctorum pour les vies des
    l'époque Mérovingienne. Paris: Le Soudier, 1912.

Riley, Henry T., ed. Registra quorundam abbatum monasterii
    S. Albani. Rolls 28, no. 6, London: Longmans, 1872-73.

Schofield, William Henry. English Literature from the Norman
    Conquest to Chaucer. New York: Macmillan, 1906.

Societas Bollandiana. Acta Sanctorum. (See William of St. Albans).

Stanton, Richard. A Menology of England and Wales. London: Burns & Oates, 1887.

Tatlock, J. S. P. "St. Amphibalus, " Essays on Criticism, 2nd ser., University of California Publications in English, iv, 249-57.

Thomas of Walsingham. Gesta Abbatum Monasterii Sancti Albani, ed. Henry Thomas Riley, Rolls Series 28, part 4. London: Longmans, 1869.

Thomas, Charles. Christianity in Roman Britain to A.D. 500. Berkeley: University of California Press, 1981.

Ühleman, Emil. "Ueber die Anglonormanische vie de St. Auban." Romanische Studien, iv (1880), 543-626.

Ussher, James. Britannicarum Ecclesiarum Antiquitates in The Whole Works of Most Rev. James Ussher. Dublin: Hodges & Smith, 1864.

Vaughan, Richard. Matthew Paris. Cambridge: University Press, 1958.

Wade-Evans, A. W. Welsh Christian Origins. Oxford: Alden, 1934.


## VII.   WORKS RELATING TO INDIVIDUAL PASSAGES


Baus, Karl et al. The Imperial Church from Constantine to the Early Middle Ages, trans. Anselm Biggs, in History of the Church, gen. eds. Hubert Jedin and John Dolan. New York: Seabury Press, 1980.

Bede, the Venerable. Historia Ecclesiastica, ed. Charles Plummer. Oxford: Clarendon Press, 1896.

Biblioteca Hagiographica Latina Antiquae et Mediae AEtatis, ed. Societas Bollandiani. Brussels, 1898-99.

Cary, George. The Medieval Alexander. Cambridge: University Press, 1957.

Cary, Maurice. History of Rome, 2nd ed., London: Macmillan, 1954.

Chaucer, Geoffrey. Works, 2nd ed., ed. F. N. Robinson. Boston: Houghton Mifflin, 1957.

Cook, S. A. et al. Cambridge Ancient History. Cambridge: University Press, 1923.

Coulton, G. G. "Knighthood," Encyclopedia Britannica, 11th ed. New York: Encyclopedia Britannica Company, 1910-11.

Ellard, Gerald. Christian Life and Worship. Milwaukee: Bruce, 1940.

Felix. Life of St. Guthlac, ed. B. Colgrave. Cambridge: University Press, 1956.

Friedman, J. B. Orpheus in the Middle Ages. Cambridge, Mass.: Harvard Press, 1970.

Hammond, Eleanor P. English Verse between Chaucer and Surrey. Durham, N.C.: Duke, 1927.

Keeler, Laura. Geoffrey of Monmouth and the Late Latin Chroniclers, 1300-1500. University of California Publications in English xvii, no. i (1946).

Lull, Ramon. The Book of the Ordre of Chyualry, trans. W. Caxton, ed. A.T.P. Byles, E.E.T.S., O.S. clxviii. London: Oxford University Press, 1926.

Magoun, Francis P., Jr. The Gests of King Alexander of Macedon. Cambridge, Mass.: Harvard Press, 1929.

_____. "The Theme of the Beasts of Battle in Anglo-Saxon Poetry." Neuphilologische Mitteilungen, lvi (1956), 81-90.

Matthew Paris. Vitae Duorum Offarum, in Opera Omnia, ed. William Wats. Paris: 1644.

Metham, John. Works, ed. Hardin Craig. E.E.T.S., O.S., cxxxii. London: K. Paul, Trench, Trübner, 1916.

Nicolas, Sir Nicolas Harris. History of the Orders of Knighthood of the British Empire. London: J. Hunter, 1842.

Norton-Smith, John. Review of van der Westhuizen's ed. of St.

Albon. _Medium Aevum_, xliv (1975), 325-26.

Offord, M., ed. _The Parlement of the Thre Ages_. E.E.T.S.,
O.S., ccxlvi. London: Oxford University Press, 1959.

Perrin, J. M. "Mercy, Works of," _New Catholic Encyclopedia_.
New York: McGraw-Hill, 1967.

Renoir, Alain. "Crist Ihesu's Beast of Battle: A Note on
Oral-Formulaic Theme Survival." _Neophilologus_, lxx (1976),
455-59.

Rickaby, J. "The Cardinal Virtues," _Catholic Encyclopedia_,
1st ed. New York: Encyclopedia Press, 1913-22.

Robertson, D. W. _Preface to Chaucer_. Princeton: University
Press, 1963.

Schroeder, Horst. _Der Topos der Nine Worthies in Literatur
und bildener Kunst_. Göttingen: Vanderhoeck, 1971.

Skeat, Walter W., ed. _The Alliterative Romance of Alexander
and Dindimus_. E.E.T.S., E.S., xxxi. London: Kegan Paul,
Trench, Trübner, 1878.

_____. _The Vision of William concerning Piers
the Plowman_. London: Oxford University Press, 1886.

Stanley, Thomas. _History of Philosophy_. London: W. Battersby, 1701.

Trevisa, John. _On the Properties of Things_, eds., M. C. Seymour et al. Oxford: Clarendon Press, 1975.

Warfield, B. B. _Studies in Tertullian and Augustine_. Westport, Conn.: Greenwood Press, 1930, reprint, 1970.

Weiss, Roberto. _Humanism in England during the Fifteenth Century_, 2nd ed. Oxford: Basil Blackwell, 1957.

Whitelock, Dorothy. _The Audience of Beowulf_. Oxford: Clarendon Press, 1951.

## VIII.  LYDGATE'S LANGUAGE AND VERSIFICATION

Hascall, Dudley. "The Prosody of John Lydgate." _Language and_

Style, iii (1970), 122-46.

Lewis, C. S. "The Fifteenth Century Heroic Line." Essays and
    Studies, xxiv (1938) 28-42.

Lynn, Karen. "Chaucer's Decasyllabic Line: The Myth of the
    Hundred Year Hibernation." Chaucer Review, xiii (1978),
    116-27.

Manzalaoui, Mahmoud. "Lydgate and English Prosody." Cairo
    Studies in English (1960), 87-104.

Mendenhall, John C. Aureate Terms: A Study in the Literary
    Diction of the Fifteenth Century. Lancaster, Pa.: Wickers-
    ham, 1919.

Pearsall, Derek. John Lydgate. Charlottesville, Va.: Univer-
    sity of Virginia Press, 1970. [Chapter 3, pp. 49-66]

Reismüller, Georg. Romanische Lehnworter (Erstbelege) bei
    Lydgate. Leipzig: Münchener Beitrage, xlviii, 1911.

Schirmer, Walter F. John Lydgate: A Study in the Culture of
    the XVth Century, trans. Ann E. Keep. London: Methuen,
    1961. [Chapter 9, pp. 70-77]

Tilgner, Elfriede. Die Aureate Terms als Stilement bei Lyd-
    gate. Berlin: Germanische Studien, clxxxii, 1936.

# SAINT ALBON AND SAINT AMPHIBALUS

## Book I

### Prologue

f. 96 r.      To calle Clio my dulnesse to redresse,
With alle hir sustren dwellyng at Elicon,
What myht availe to write the perfitnesse
Of the holy martir slayn ful yoor agon
For Cristis feith, the blissid man Albon,        5
Callid of riht thorugh euery regioun
Prothomartir of Brutis Albioun?

     --I nat acqueyntid with musis of Maro,
Nor with metris of Lucan nor Virgile,
Nor sugrid ditees of Tullius Chithero,        10
Nor of Omerus to folwe the fressh stile,
Crokid to clymb ouer so high a stile,
Or for to folwe the steppis aureat
Of Franceis Petrak, the poete laureat?

---

On f. 95 v. of MS  Lansdowne 699, the text which is here
substantially reproduced, there appears in a later
(Tudor?) hand, "Here followyth the [illegible] conquist
of the land by Julius Cesar and of the lyf of St Albon."
On f. 96 r. of La there is written in a late Italian
hand, "The legend of Saint Alban written by John Lidgate
at the request of Mr. John Whetehamsted Abbot of St
Albans. In the year 1439." The MS is not otherwise
titled; however, see the colophon.

1-112  Not in Li.
2    hir] her T; om. Ed        sustren] susters T In H; systers Ed
5    feith] sake H
6    thorugh] thorough T In; thurgh H
10   Nor sugrid] Nor with sugred T H     cithero T In H;
      Cicero Ed
11   folwe] folowe T; folow In H
13   for] om. H
14   Fraunces Petrark T In H

The golden trumpet of the Hous of Fame,          15
With ful swift weengis of the Pegasee,
Hath blowe ful fer the knyhtly mannys name.
Born in Verolamye, a famous gret cite,
Knyhtid in Rome (the Cronicle who list, see)
And, as I fynde, this yong lusty man          20
Took first the ordre of Dioclician.

Whos liff to write of liff I am bareyn
His high perfectioun ceriously to telle,
Dreedyng my labour shuld be in veyn
That neuyr drank of Pegaseus welle;          25
But, for his goodnesse so highly doth excelle,
I stond in hope his influence shal shyne,
My tremblyng penne bi grace to enlumyne.

f. 96 v.          In *tendre* age this goodly yong Albone,
Born as I seide in Brutis Albioun,          30
A lordis sone,-- more likly was ther none
To marcial prowesse bi disposicioun,--
Which, for his persone, as made is mencioun,
For condiciouns, and high birthe of bloode,
In gret fauour of all the lond he stoode;          35

And for that he in vertu did excelle,
Belouyd and cherisshid of euery maner man,
By Kyng Severus (myn auctour can wele telle)
Sent vnto Rome, to Dioclician,
With a yong prince callid Bassian,          40
Thei bothe tweyn, as the statute bonde,
To be made knyhtis of his owen honde.

---

16    wynges T In; wyngis H
18    gret] olde T In H Ed
19    Knyhtid] Knyghthode T In H Ed
21    first] furst In; furste H; fyrste Ed          the ordre]
        ordre H; order Ed          of] by T In H Ed
22    liff I am] witte I am T In H Ed
23    curiousely T In H Ed
24    be] ben T In
25    dronk T In
28    elumyne T
29    In] If H          *tendre*] goodly La
30    I] is Ed
32    prowes T In H

With hem also went Amphibalus;
Ther baptised bi Pope *Zepheryne*,
Left al the word and becam vertuous;                    45
Of wilfull povert folwid the doctryne,--
Bi whos techyng and gracious disciplyne
Blissid Albon (as myn auctour seith)
Was aftirward convertid to our feith.

Al this processe in ordre for to sette      50
My purpos is, yiff I have liff and space,
Yiff ignoraunce nat my stile lette,
Bi influence oonly of Goddis grace,
The trowbly mystis fro me to enchace
Off rude langage, so that I may in dede      55
To write his liff ceriously procede,

f. 97 r.      Undir support of this martir benygne
My penne directe, bi mene of his praieer,
The gracious stremys sent doun for a signe
Of his celestial goodly eyn cleer,      60
To forther my labour and teche me the maneer
Of his name to write and specifie,
So as I can, the ethymologie.

This name, "Albanus," bi interpretacioun
Compounyd is of plente and whitnesse.      65
Plente he had in high perfectioun,
And white also with lillies of clennesse,
With rosis meynt, stable in ther rednesse:

---

43  hem] he H
44  Pope] <u>partially</u> erased T      *Zepheryne*] Seueryne La
45  word] worlde T In H Ed      bycame T In
46  pover H
47  gracious] vertuous H
50  this] his T In      to:  <u>om.</u> H
51  yiff] yf T In H Ed      liff]  space H
52  nat] nott T; Nought In; not H Ed
56  and ceriously T In Ed; and curiously H
60  eyen T; Ieen H
65  plente] pleynte T; ylente H      and of whitenesse T In
66  high] grete T In H Ed
67  And] Made T In H Ed
68  With white roses T In H Ed      ther] her T In
      redenesse T H; rudenesse Ed

It was weel sene that he stable stood
For Cristes feith whan paynymes shed his blood.    70

    Which too colours did neuer fade,--
Off thes lillies and of thes rosis rede,--
In blissid Albon, but euer aliche glade,
White in his baptem the lillies did sprede;
The rosis splayed whan he did shede                75
His purpurat blood, sparid for no deth,
The storme abidyng tyl he yald vp the breth.

    Thus was his chaplet made of red and white,
Whit for his clennesse, I have so told a-forn;
To chese the red he had also delit              80
Whan fro the chaff was tried whete corn
In the holy martir that hath the bront born.
Greyn of this frument was this man Albon
In the gospel remembrid of Seynt Iohn.

f. 97 v.    This chose greyn for Crist was mortified    85
To gret encresse of his eternal glorie.
The frute grew vp, bi feith imultiplied;
Thorugh meeke suffraunce he gat the victorie,
A palme of conquest to be put in memorie,
A laureat crowne, bi triumphis manyfold          90
For his meritis set on his hed, of gold.

---

69   It] Hit T In
70   shed] shad H
72   and] nor T In H Ed
73   glade] <u>in</u> La <u>a</u> <u>marginal</u> correction <u>in</u> <u>same</u> <u>or</u> <u>similar</u>
     <u>hand</u> <u>for</u> "rede" <u>in</u> <u>text</u>.   T, In, H, <u>and</u> Ed <u>read</u>
     "glade."
74   White in] Within T In H Ed
77   yald] yold In; yelde H; yafe Ed
78   his] this H, the Ed
79   clennes T H Ed
80   had] dyd (inserted above) T; <u>om</u>. In; did H Ed
83   furment   In
84   La margin, early hand:  "Granum frumenti"
87   imultiplied] multiplied T In H Ed
88   thorough T In; thurgh H; through Ed     gat] gate T In
     Ed
90   laurat In; Laurate H; lauret Ed     trihumpes T

Now to this martir crowned high in hevene
Devoutly knelyng with humble and meeke visage,
Which sit so hih above the sterris sevene:
O blissid Albon fro the celestial stage          95
Cast doun thi liht t'enlumyne my langage,
Which of my silf am nakid and bareyn,
In this gret neede that favour may be seyn.

I haue no colours but oonli white and blak,
Gold nor asur, nor fressh vermilioun.          100
Wher ought doth faile, I mote ber the lak,
Of long, of short, wantyng proporcioun,
But with thi gracious supportacioun
I hope thou shalt conveye my penne and lede;
To write thi liff thus I wole procede.          105

Explicit Prologus

Tyme remembrid of antiquyte,
The same tyme whan Cesar Iulyus
Was passid out of Rome the Cite
Ouer th'Alpies in knyhthood ful famous,
B'assent of Fortune notable and glorious,          110
This marcial man, armyd in plate and maile,
Had ouer-riden the boundis of Itaile,

---

95   the] that T In H Ed
96   doun] downe T H; dovne In      To enlumyne T In;
        to elumyne H Ed
97   self T In H      am] I am T
98   that] thy T In Ed
99   blake and white H Ed
100, 102   lines transposed in T In H Ed
101   outh T; aught In; ought Ed      feyle T In      lak] wite
        H Ed
104   my penne convey H; I hope]   In hope H
105   om. "Explicit Prologus" H
106   olde antiquyte T In H Ed
109   the Alpeys T In Ed; the Alpeyes H.  The apostrophe is
        inserted by the editor because of the modern capital
        letter provided.      knyghthode famous T In H Ed
110   Bi assent T In H Ed
111   armed T In H Ed      in] with Ed
112   Ytalie T In

f. 98 r.        Brout the contres thorugh his high renounne
                Maugre ther myght to stonde in obeisaunce
                And been soget to them of Rome Toun;                115
                All Germanye conquerid in substaunce;
                Doun descendyng in-to the reawm of Fraunce,
                Dantid ther pride; aftir did ordeyn
                With a gret arme t'arive vp in Briteyn,

                     Twies put off, bi record of Lucan,           120
                At his arryvail bi verray force and myht,
                Bi the prowesse of Cassibalan.
                Touchyng the titil, wer it wrong or riht,
                Off seid Cesar deme euery maner wiht
                What that hem list, for in conclusioun,            125
                Cause of his entre was fals divisioun

                     Among hem silff, wher bi he gat the lond,
                Made Britouns to be tributarye
                To the Romaynes bi statute and bi bond,
                Noon so hardi to be ther-to contrarye.             130
                Cause of this conquest to writen and nat tarie
                Was divisioun (the Cronycle ye may see)
                Tween Cassiballan and Duke Androchee.

---

113   Lincoln MS <u>begins here</u>; <u>first folio tattered, with many</u>
      <u>words missing or illegible.</u>      Brout] brouht Li;
             Brought T In H Ed      high] grete H; <u>om</u>. In
114   Magre H Ed        ther] her T In; theire H; theyr Ed
115   soget] suggetes T In; subiectis H Ed        them] hem T In
             H        townn T
116   Germayne Li
117   Rewm Li; Realme T In H Ed
118   Dauntyng T H        pride and T In H Ed
119   to aryve Li T In H Ed        vp in] into T; vp in to H
120   Twies] Theis T; Twys In
121   bi] of T In H Ed        verray] verry T In H; very Ed
122   cassiblan H; Cassybylan Ed
123   titil] tale T In        right or wronge H
124   Off the seid T In Ed; thesseid H
125   hem] them T In; hym Ed        list] lust H
126   his] this T H
127   silff] self T In H; selfe Ed        the] that T In H Ed
128   Made] Made the T H Ed; Made of In
131   write H Ed        not Li T Ed; nott In; not to H
132   deuision Ed
133   Cassibilan H Ed        Androgee T In H Ed

Ouer-maystred was Brutis Albioun
Bi Iulius swerd, remembrid in scriptur;                    135
Record the gospel: wher is divisioun,
Frowarde discencioun, of cas or aventur,
Thilk region may no while endur
In prosperite, for bi discord of tweyn
To subieccioun was brouht all Briteyn.                     140

f. 98 v.    Whan Cesar was put in possessioun,
Rather bi fors than any title of riht,
Ordeyned statutis in that regioun,
And this was oon, that no maner wiht
Shold in that lond receive the ordre of knyght   145
For worthynesse, for meede, nor favour,
But bi the hondis of the emperour.

And this was doon lest, peraventur,
Sondry persones encloied with rudenesse,
Nat disposid of blood nor of natur,                        150
Shold nat presume, of rural boistousnesse,
Thouh that he had strenghe and hardynesse,
To take vpon hym, what euer that he bee,
The sacrament of knyhtly dygnyte.

Anothir cause in ordre to devise                           155
Was that non sich shuld han governance
Wher-bi he myht in many sondry wise
Catche occasioun to make purveyaunce

---

136  deuysioun Li
138  Thilk] That H Ed
139  of] and Ed
142  force Li T In H Ed        eny H; by eny T        of] or Ed
143  Ordeigned T In; Ordent H Ed
144  one what maner of wight In; if that oone maner of wight
     H
145  Sulde Ed        thordre Li T In Ed
146  Nor for favour T In
148  lest] list T In; olesse [sic] H
149  encloied] enclothid T In Ed; enclosed H.   See _Glossary_.
151  boistowisnesse T; boistewyssnesse In
152  that : om. H.        streynth T; strenght In H; strength Ed
156  that] om. H Ed        none T In; oone H        such Li; suche
     T In        han] T In H Ed

Bi fors of kynrede or strengthe of allyaunce
Thorugh newe rebellioun, in tookne, word, or sygne,
Ageyn the Romaynes proudly to malygne.

And *in* sich cas th'occasioun to eschue,
The prudent Romaynes, castyng al thyng to-forn,
For comoun profite thouht it was most dewe,                    165
Of high estat ne lowe degre i-born
No man shulde, but if that he wer sworn
To the Romaynes with hert, body and myht
Ay to be trewe, receyve the ordre of knyht,

f. 99 r.     Bi a decre concludyng, in sentence,
With feyth assured, as the statute bond,                        170
First thei shuld appere in the presence
Off the emperour, sent thidre fro eche lond,
Than take ther oth next bi touche of honde,
To-fore ther goddis assuraunce made of newe
For liff or deth to th'emperour to be trewe,                    175

This statute kept in euery regioun
Beyng soget to Rome the Cite,
Stretchyng ther lordship and domynacioun
With ther imperiall marciall dygnyte

---

159   streynth T; strenght In
161   Ageyne T; Ayenste H; Agaynst Ed
162   *in*] omitted by La, Li     occasioun Li; occasions T In
          H Ed
163   to-forn] aforn T
164   comyn T In
165   astate In     ne] nor T In Ed     i-born] born Ed
166   if] yiff Li     that] om. T In H Ed
168   receyve] that receyven T In; that receyved H; that
          shuld be made a Ed
170   bounde T; bonde In H Ed
171   Furst In
172   thidre fro] there of T In; thydder of H; thither of Ed
173   ther] her T In     nex by to touche [sic] In
174   Toforn H; Toforne Ed     ther] the T In H Ed
175   or] for In
177   soget] suggett T; subget In; subiecte H; subiect Ed
          citie Ed
178   Strechyng ther Li; Strecchyng her T In; Strechyng their
          H     domynacioun] dominioun Ed

Ouyr the boundis of many gret contre;                    180
So provided bi prudent pollicie,
To them was soget al worldly chivalrie.

Havyng al kyngdamys reedi to ther hond,
Voide of rebellioun whan thei had ouht to do,
A prynce of knyhthood thei sett in euery lond         185
For gouernaunce, a styward eeke also,
Euery regioun to be rewlyd bi them too.
In rihtwysnesse lawis did ordeyn,
Fro willfull surfetis comouns to restreyn;

First provided, of high discrecioun,                    190
As Argus eyed in ther inward entent,
To see ther were no conspiracioun
Ageyn th'emperour, nothir thouht nor ment,
To redresse all thyng bi iugement,
Thes tweyn estatis of prudence to entende             195
At pryme face all outrages to amende.

f. 99 v.       It hath be seide and wreten her-to-forn
Bi old experte poetical doctryne:
Withstond principlis, lest a-boue the corn
The weede nat wexe geyn good greyn to maligne;    200

---

180   bondes In H        many a grete T In H; many countree Ed
182   wordly In        cheualry H
183   kyngdomes T In Ed; kyngdoms H        ther] her T In H
184   when In H        to do] a do H Ed
186   steward T Ed
187   to] om. Li
189   Fro] For H; From Ed;        comouns] the comyns T In H Ed
190   of] by H
191   Entire line enclosed in parentheses Ed
192   there were no werre nor conspiracioun H Ed
193   nothir] nouthir Li; nouther T; nowther In; nether H;
        neither Ed
195   tweyn] too H; two Ed        entende] attende Ed
197   Hit T In        seyen T; seyne In H; sayn Ed        writen T
        In; written H Ed        here be forn T In H Ed
198   Bi] Be T In        Poetical] Poetry callyd T In; poysy called
        H; poesy called Ed
199   Withstond] Without Ed        lest] list T        La margin:
        "Principiis obsta"; Li margin torn : "...bsta"
200   Nat] om. Ed; doo H        geyn] ageyns T; ageyne In H;
        ageynst Ed        greyn] corn H

To late among is made a medicyne
Whan that a sore, raw, ded, and corrumpable
For lak of surgeyns is waxen vncurable.

Semblably, in *kyngdamys* and citees,
Stormy troublis for to set a-syde                    205
Mevid sodeynly a-mong the comountees,
At the begynnyng in al hast to provide
Them to reforme, no lenger to abide,
The first meveers, as lawe and riht observid,
Punysh them dewly, as thei han deseruyd,             210

Lik *ther* desertis receyve ther reward,
Cherish the trewe, robbours to represse,
The prynce of knyhtis and also the stiward
Ordeyned wer bi lawe and rihtwissnesse,
As the statute pleynly did expresse,                 215
Lik trew iugis and keperes of the lawe
Of high prudence al riot to withdrawe;

And, bi report of cronycles that been olde,
Auctorised bi gret avisement,
As a diademe or a crowne of gold                     220
Is of a kyng callid the ornement,
So to a prynce longith a garnement
Frengid with gold, that peplis hih and lowe
Bi that difference ther styward myht knowe.

---

202  sore wexith dede and T In H Ed   corumptable H
203  it waxith in curable H
204  semblable H        kyngdomes T In; Kyngdoms H; kyndamys La
205  Stormys H
207  the] om. In H
209  The] For T In H Ed
210  them] hem T In      han] haue T In H Ed
211  *ther*] her T; om. La In; theire H Ed
212  represse] redresse T In H Ed
213  The prynce] This prynce T
214  weren T In        and] of T In H Ed
216  kepars T In H
218  bi] the T In H Ed; "bi" inserted above by the correcting
     hand in T        crownicles H
222  garment In H Ed
223  Frengid] Forgid T        peplis] peple In H Ed
224  ther] her T In; theire H; theyr Ed

f. 100 r.　　The prince of knyhtis vsid a pillioun　　225
　　　　For a prerogatiff in especiall;
　　　　He and the stiward bi eleccioun
　　　　Off the emperour in party and in all
　　　　Took ther charge, pryvat and generall;
　　　　No man *so* hardy, peyn of dethe, rebelle　　230
　　　　Ageyn ther power, to vsurpe, to quarelle.

　　　　The same tyme *reynyng* in Briteyn,
　　　　Kyng Severus, a famous knyhtly man,
　　　　Cast hym fully to doon his busi peyn
　　　　To plese the Emperour Dioclician,　　235
　　　　Sent his sone namyd Bassian
　　　　With a thowsand five hundrid yong of age,
　　　　Lordis sonys, fresh, lusty of corage,

　　　　Some of this noumbre wer born in Briteyn,
　　　　Some in Walis, some in Cornewayle.　　240
　　　　Among all, if I shal nat feyne,
　　　　Ther was oon of statur and entaill,
　　　　As *ferre* as Kynde coude hir craft prevaile,
　　　　Bi hir favour gaff to his persone
　　　　A prerogatiff to be sett allone.　　245

　　　　A goodly man and but yong of age,
　　　　A princis sone of Walis, as I fynde,
　　　　Callid Amphiball, gracious of visage,

---

225　pillioun] pallion Ed
227　the] his H
229　Took ther] To her T In
230　*so*] omitted La Li
231　Against Ed　　ther] thir T; their In; theire H; theyr
　　　Ed　　to quarelle] no quarelle T In H Ed
232　The] That H Ed　　reynyg La; was reignyng Ed
234　Who cast Ed　　doon] do T H Ed
237　and five H Ed　　hundreth T; hundred In H; hondred Ed
238　fresh and lusty T In H Ed
239　nombre T H　　weren In
240　some in Cornewayle] and in Cornewayle T In; and some in
　　　Cornewayle Ed
241　And among Ed　　if] yiff Li　　nat] nott T In H Ed
243　*ferre*] for La　　coude hir] couthe her T; couthe hir In
244　gaue Ed
248　Amphibalus H

In whom ther was non errour founde in kynde;
Bi disposicioun nouht was left bi-hynde.          250
In myn auctour as it is compiled,
To alle language his tonge was i-fyled.

f. 100 v.   And for *he* was born of high kynreede,
He was sent forth with notable apparaile,
Lik his estat, with many riche weede,          255
Nat forgeten harneys of plate and maile,
Tho dayes forgid aftir most fressh entaile,
As was most likly in euery mannys siht
To them that shold receive the ordre of knyht.

And whan thei wer assemblid euerychon,          260
It was a paradis vpon hem to see;
Lik as I fynde, among hem ther was oon,
A lordis sone, excellyng of beaute,
Off Verolamye born in the cite,
Callid Albanus, riht seemely of statur,          265
To all vertu disposid bi natur,

The seide Albon, bi descent of lyne
Born to be gentil of condicioun,
Bi aspectis of grace which is divyne
Predestynat bi eleccioun          270
For to be callid of this regioun

---

249   In whom there no errour H
251   Author Ed
252   langage In; languages Ed      i-fyled] fyled T H Ed;
         a filid In
253   *he*] om. in La
255   many A riche T
256   nat] nott T; nought In; not H Ed      forgotten H;
         forgettyng Ed
257   Tho] Two In      Curiously forgid, om. tho dayes, H
         after his entaile H
258   As was] He was H
260   whan] while T In H Ed
263   of] in T H
264   Borne in the citie of Verolamy Ed
265   semyly In
267   Thesseid H      dissent T; discent In H
268   iantill H
271   this] his T H Ed

Prothomartir whan he the feith hath take
And shedde his blood for Iesu Cristis sake.

Gracious he was in euery mannys siht,
Weelbelovid and a likly man,                                        275
With his felaship took the wey riht,
Toward Rome rood with Bassian,
Cam to the presence of Dioclician.
And for thei wer so likly in shewyng,
He passyngly was glad of ther comyng,                              280

f. 101 r.  A chose peeple, out pikid for the nones,
Riht wele beseyn and manly of ther cheer,
Arraied in perle, gold, and Inde stoones,
As princes children most souereyn and enteer
Them demenyng in port and in maneer,                               285
That yiff thei shal been shortly comprehendid,
In hem was nothyng for to been amendid.

This Britoun peeple, likly for the werris,
Stood in comparisoun myd othir naciouns
As doth the sonne among hevenly sterris.                           290
Lik to ther birthe wer ther condiciouns:

---

272  when T In H
273  <u>Here</u> <u>and</u> <u>in</u> <u>most</u> <u>instances</u> <u>the</u> Lansdowne MS <u>reads</u> "Ihu"
     <u>or</u> "Ihus," <u>which</u> <u>are</u> <u>henceforth</u> <u>silently</u> <u>expanded</u> <u>to</u>
     "Iesu" <u>and</u> "Iesus."
276  feleship T; felleshyp In; felliship H; felowship Ed
     wey riht] wey of riht T In H; way aright Ed
278  Come H
279  weren Ed
281  chosen H Ed
282  manly] namely T; manerly In
283  perle, gold] gold perle H Ed        Inde] precious Ed
     stonys T In H
284  childre Li        most] om. Ed
285  in maneer] on manere In
286  yiff] if T In        thei] it H Ed        been shortly]
     shortly be T In H Ed
287  been] be T In H Ed
288  Bretoun T In
289  myd othir] amyd all Ed
290  amonge the heuenly H
291  Like to the burth T In; lik to the birth H;
     Alike to theyr birthe Ed

High blood requyreth thorugh all regiouns
To resemble, in high or low parage
Fully accordyng, lik to ther lynage.

To high kynrede longith high noblesse;            295
In high monteynes stonde cedris greene;
To princes childre apperteynyth high prowes,
As among stoonys the rubie is most sheene;
Tarage of treen bi the frute is sene;
Semblably Natur did ordeyn                        300
To make in Rome the blood knowe of Briteyn.

On the Emperour this peeple, as I told,
Weer a-waytyng as thei were of degre,
Beyng pope in the dayes old
Zepherynus, which *kept* in Rome his see,          305
And whan that he biheeld the gret beaute
Off this peple that was come of newe,
Withynne hymsilff sore he gan to rewe.

f. 101 v.     Musyng in herte, thus he gan compleyn

---

292  High] Hight H       requeyreth] om. In       thorugh]
         thorough T In; thurgh H       regiouns] naciouns T In H
         Ed
293  high] hight H       parage] patrage T In H
296  In] On Li T In H Ed       stondyn T; stande Ed       Cedres
         T; cedresse H; cedrysse Ed
297  Childeren T; children In Ed; childer H       apperteneth
         Li; apparteyneth T; apperteyneth In; perteynith H;
         perteineth Ed       prowes] prowesse Li In Ed; noblesse H
298  As] om. T In       sheene] sene H
299  The tarage of trees T Ed; The taurage of trees In;
         Tareage of treis H. See *Glossary*.       fruyte is seyne
         T; fruytes is seene In
300  did so ordayne Ed
301  There to make knowen the blood of Britaine Ed
302  On] Npon (small "u" visible through "N") H; Vpon Ed
304  pope] partially erased in T; inserted above line, In
         the] thoo In; those H Ed
305  Pope Zepherynus ("Pope" partially erased) T       kept]
         om. La Li
306  that] om. T In
307  was come] comyn T; was comyn In H; comen were Ed
308  to rewe] rewe In
309  Musing in his hert H Ed       thus] this Li; that H

Ful secrely, with sihes lamentable:                    310
"Allas," quod he, "This peeple heer of Briteyne,
In al ther port and maners most notable,
So fressh, so seemely, and so honorable;
Allas," ful oft vpon the day he seith.
"Why stant this peeple in errour from our feith?"

The Pope, of rouht and compassioun
Consideryng with merciful pite,
Gan seeke weyes to fynde occasioun
To gete leiser and oportunyte
How this peeple, excellyng in beaute,                  320
Myht bi his labour thoruh spyrituall vertu
Receyve baptem bi grace of Crist Iesu.

The Lord above, consideryng the entent
Off Zepherynus in especiall,
Sich a grace to hym he hath sent,                      325
Bi influence verray celestiall
To forther his purpose, that he hath Amphiball
Bi his doctrine from his errour drawe
And conuertid vnto Cristis lawe.

Amphibalus, as ye have herd the cas,                   330
A seemely man, God beyng than his guyde,
First bi the Pope whan he baptized was,
Left his tresour, his pompe, and al his pride,
For Cristis sake with povert chase to a-byde,

---

313   and] om. H
314   seith] sygh In
316   Pope (partially erased) T        rouht] rewthe Li; ruthe T
      In H Ed
318   seeke] finde H;       to fynde] seking H; fyndynge Ed
319   gete] grete In
321   labour] vertues H      thoruh] om. H.
322   bapteme T In; baptym H; baptisme Ed
324   Zepheryne T Ed; Zepherus H
325   Such Li T; suche In H Ed
328   In cristis faith grounded be his sawe T H Ed;
      om. entire line, In. Line in T is in correcting
      hand. Originally left blank.
332   Pope (partially erased) T
334   povertie Ed       chose T In H Ed

Forsoke the word, kept hymsilf secre,                335
Off gret perfeccioun lived in pouerte.

f. 102 r.       Othir ther wern that made no delaies,
Off Zepheryne heryng the prechyng,
To be baptised deuoutly in tho daies.
But whann the rumour and the knowlachyng          340
Cam to the Emperour, without more taryeng
Thorugh al the cite comaundid hem be souht,
To his presence bi force to be brouht.

Bi lond and see his mynystres left nouht
To serche them out, but in no maneer             345
Thei wer nat cauht. But tho cam to the thouht
Off Dioclician to werk as ye shal heer,
Them of Briteyn to make hem to apper
Vpon a morwe whan Phebus shon ful briht,
Thei of his hond to take the ordre of knyht.     350

Of antiquyte, as put is in memorye,
Whan the Emperour shuld knyhtis make,
Thei did assemble bi-side an oratorie
That reised was and bilt for Martis sake,
In whoos worship thei sholde al nyht wake;        355
The next morwe, aftir the maneer,
At Phebus vprist, thei shuld echeon appeer,--

The territorye, in compas rounde and large,

---

335  word] world Li; worlde T In H Ed
337  ther] om. In     wern] weren T
338  Zepherynus T     the] his T In H Ed
340  Remure H     knowleching Li T In H; knowlegyng
341  to] fro La Li
342  hem] he H
343  To] And to T
346  tho] than Ed
350  the] om. Ed
351  Margin of T] "the oothe youen vnto knyghtis tyme of
       their creaciounne"
355  al nyht thei shold Li; all night thei shulden T; all
       nyght they did wake In; all nyght thay shulde wake H;
       all night they shulde wake Ed
357  echeon] om. T In H Ed
358  territorye] oratorie T In; orotary H; oratory Ed

Beside a temple of Bellona the goddesse,
Wher Dioclician shold yeve first in charge          360
Of hool assuraunce t'avoide al dowbilnesse,
First to keepe ther bodies in clennesse,
For liff or deth, bothe in pes and werr,
The commoun profit of th'empire to preferre.

f. 102 v.   Next this charge the Emperour anoon riht     365
In all his most imperiall mageste
Lik ther rihtis girt hem with swerdis briht,
So as thei wern of state and of degre,
Obseruaunces kept of auctorite,
First chargyng them that thei shuld entende    370
Cheeffly ther goddis to worship and deffende,

Off ther templis to save the libertees,
Preestis of the lawe in riht to make strong,
Widwis, maydenes, poore folk in citees,
Soffre in no wise no man do hem wrong,         375
Appese debatis that have endurid long,
For comoun profit as most souereyn good
In ther deffence redy to spend ther blood;

Withdrawe ther hond from lucre and couetise,
Speciali t'eschewyn ydilnesse,                 380
Pursue armys for knyhtly excercise,
In causis *know* groundid *on rightwesnesse*
*Yef their capteynes* feith, trowth, and stabilnesse,
And in sich cas rather knyhtly deye
Than ther statutis breke or disobeye.          385

---

359   goddesse] goode H
360   in] the H Ed
361   to voide T In; so avoyde H
362   ther] her T In H
364   th'empire] the Emperour T H
367   gyrde T In H
368   of degre] <u>om.</u> "of" In H
373   the] that T In H Ed
374   Widowes T Ed; Wydoues In; Widous H
375   to do hem T In H
382-83   <u>Italics</u> <u>from</u> T.  In <u>follows</u> T, <u>as</u> <u>do</u> H <u>and</u> Ed <u>save</u> <u>for</u>
        "suche trouth" <u>for</u> "feith trowth." La <u>and</u> Li <u>run</u> <u>the</u>
        <u>lines</u> <u>into</u> <u>one</u>, "In causis groundid in feith trowth and
        stabilnesse," <u>and</u> <u>leave</u> <u>a</u> <u>blank</u> <u>line</u> <u>beneath</u>.
385   to breke Ed

        Off commoun profit devisid an ymage,
        Knyhthood callid, arme of ther deffence,
        To hold vp trowth, suffre non outrage,
        Cherissh poraill, do no violence,
        Afftir ther wagis gouerne ther dispence,                    390
        Full assuraunce maad with mouth and hond,
        Sustene trouth bothe on se and lond,

f. 103 r.   Make providence that no divisioun
        Fil vnwarly on hih or lowe estate,
        Which causid hath gret dissolucioun,                        395
        Made many a reaume to be infortunate;
        For wher-as striff *contynueth* or debate
        Bi experience of many gret cite
        The liht enclipsid of ther felicite.

        Off old custome knyhthod took no heede                      400
        Vnto ther owen syngler availe,
        Withdrow ther hond fro guerdoun and fro meede,
        Wrouht no thyng but bi wise counsaile;
        The hed of mateers peised with the taile,
        This to seyn:  ther shuld no Romayn knyht                   405
        Gynne no quarel nor ende ageyns riht.

---

386   devise T In; devised H Ed
387   Called knighthood Ed       an arme H Ed
388-89 <u>are</u> <u>inverted</u> <u>in</u> La <u>but</u> <u>corrected</u> <u>here</u> <u>in</u> <u>keeping</u> <u>with</u>
        <u>marginal</u> <u>note</u> <u>in</u> <u>that</u> <u>manuscript.</u>  <u>Other</u> <u>MSS</u> <u>not</u>
        <u>inverted.</u>
390   ther dispence] the Li; her T In; theire expence H Ed
392   on] ouer T In
393   divisioun] derision T In Ed; diuision H
394   Fil] Fall T In H Ed      or] nor T In
396   rewme Li; <u>realme</u> T; many of <u>Roialme</u> In; reame H; region
        Ed
397   wher] <u>om</u>. T      as] as a H      *contynueth*] conteyneth La
        Li; contenuyth H; continueth Ed
398   Many a gret T In
399   eclipsid Li In; is eclipsed H Ed T ("is" <u>above</u> <u>in</u>
        <u>correcting</u> <u>hand</u> <u>in</u> T)
400   old] <u>om</u>. T      no] non Li T H Ed; mon In
402   Withdrow] Withdraigh In; Withdrew H Ed
405   to] is T In H Ed
406   Gynne] Yef T In; Begyn H Ed      nor] ne T In
        ageyne] ageyn Li; a yenst T In; ayenste H; against Ed

For the Romayns in ther eleccioun
Chose to that ordre folk iust and stable,
Manly of hert and of condicioun,
Sobre, nat hasty, feythful, honorable,                    410
For comoun profit previd profitable,
Benyngne of port, nat proud, but debonaire.
That woord and werk for nothyng be contraire,

Take no quarell groundid on falsheede,
Speciali the poraill to oppresse,                         415
Flee tirannye, eschewe blood to sheede
Of innocentis bi willfull sturdynesse
(Blood crieth vengeaunce to God of rihtwissnesse:
Fals homycidis, contrarie to natur,
God soffreth hem no while to endur.)                      420

f. 103 v.    All thyng odible to euery gentil knyht,
Hatefull moordre to support or maynteene
Ther offis is as thei ar bounde of riht,
Maidenes, widwis, poore folk to susteene,
Fraud and extorcioun anoon, whil it is greene,           425
In knyhtly wise to serche out the offence
And it chastise bi marcial violence;

*Than* toonge and hert bi on accord shal drawe,
On ther promys stedefastly abyde.
Off antiquyte Romayns set a lawe                          430
To punyssh periurie, spar noon homycide,
Represse of tirauntis the vengeable pride,
Yiff nede fall, ther liff and blood dispende,
The riht of goddis and templis to deffende.

---

411  preevid Li; provide and T; provide In; previd H preued
     Ed
412  port] chere T     nat] nott T; nought In; not H
     debonaire <u>om.</u> "but" T In
413  contrarye T <u>In</u>
415  the pore not to Ed
420  for to endure H Ed
422  or] nor H Ed
423  ar] arne T In
427  and chastice it Ed
428  *Than*] Ther La Li     drawe] <u>last</u> <u>three</u> <u>letters</u> <u>added</u> <u>in</u>
     <u>other</u> <u>hand</u>, La
429  to abide H Ed
432  tyrannes In
433  dispende] to spende Ed

In tokne wherof whoo took the ordre of knyht 435
(This was the vsage of antiquyte),
He shold first be shave, of verray riht,
Tookne *to* avoide all superfluyte
Of vicious lyvyng and al dishoneste,                    440
Shave away bi vertuous diligence
All old outrages out of ther concience.

*Thei* had of custom also this maneer,
Romayn knyhtis of yeeres yong and grene,
To entre a bath of watir cristal cleer
From al ordur to wash ther bodi cleene,                  445
The whitche bath dide pleynly meene,
As bookis old notably expresse,
Vnto knyhthod longith al *clennesse*:

f. 104 r.    First *specially* bi attemperance
Voide all surfetis, lyve in sobirnesse,                  450
Bi providence in vertuous gouernaunce
Maynteyn trouth, chastise all falsnesse,
Restreyn ther corage from riotous excesse,
Dishonest speche and ribaudry to flee,
Eschew avoutre, live chast lik ther degre.               455

Clennesse longith to every gentyl knyht,
As ther bathyng dooth pleynly specifye.

---

436   of olde antiquite T In H; of olde antiquitie Ed
438   to] omitted in La only
441   consciens T; consciences Ed
442   *Thei*] The La      of custom] a Custome T      also] all
      ("so" inserted above) T
443   Romayns Knyghtes T
445   ordur] other H; ordures Ed      bodies T In H Ed
446   The] om. H Ed      which Li T In; whiche H      playnly it
      did mene H Ed
447   notably done expresse H Ed
448   clenssesse La
449   speciall La      temperaunce H
450   and live In
451   providence] prudence H Ed      in] and Li T In H Ed
452   trowght T In      chastite and all falsnesse In
454   ribaudye Li; ribaudy T In
455   avoutry T In H Ed      lik] aftre T
456   Iantille H

Though ther professioun was made to Mars of right,
Whilom Romaynis bi prudent pollicie
Hadde in custom *ther* bodies to applie                    460
To serue Dian, callid the chast goddesse,
That Venus had with hem noon interesse.

Venus to vertu is contrarious,
Causith in youthe flesshly insolence,
Yeueth gret occasioun to folk coraious              465
Off hir natur, loueth riot and dispence,
Withdrawith in knyhthod martiall diligence;
For which the bath was maad for a figure
To wassh awey of Venus all the ordur.

Yiff thei be weddid, hold them to ther wives;
Yiff thei be sengill, no woman to oppresse;
For in sich caas gan the bloody strives
Tween Troye and Grekis (the stori berith witnesse),
Causid many knyhtis deyen in distresse,
For bi th'avoutry of Paris and Eleyn                    475
Greekis, Troians ther myscheffes dide pleyn.

f. 104 v.      Aftir this bath, tokned bi chastite,

---

458  Though] Thurgh H; Thrugh Ed      perfecciounn T
        of right] aright H Ed
460  *ther*] the La; her T In H; theyr Ed
461  that called was T In H; Diana that was the cast goddesse
        Ed
462  interesse] entresse T; intresse In; intraunce Ed
463  vertues Ed
465  Yeueth] Gieueth Ed      folkes T In H      coraious]
        contrarious T; coragious In H Ed
466  hir] here T; her In; theire H; theyr Ed      loueth]
        longeth T In      dispence] expence H Ed
469  the] om. all other MSS
470  Yiff] Yef T; Yif In; Yf H; If Ed
471  "were" inserted above "be" T (possibly in other hand)
        sengill] sengle Li T In H; syngle Ed
472  gan] began(ne) H Ed      bloody sad strives In; bloody
        strides T
473  Tween] Between T; By tweene In; Betwene H Ed
474  many a knyght T In Ed; many knyght H      dien T; to dye
        Ed
475  Elyne T; Helyn In
476  and Troians Ed      mischef T In      pleyn] complaine Ed

Fully maad fair and voide of vnclennesse,
With a white shert he shold clothid be
To signyfie the cheef fondresse                    480
Of all vertu callid is meekenesse,
Cleene of entent, without whom, in certeyn,
All othir vertus stond but in veyn.

For who that list in bokis for to reede,
Cast in vertu expleitid for to be,                 485
Most redi wei his purpos for to speede,
Sette his fundacioun on humylite.
She berith vp all and hath the souereynte,
Whos bildyng evir, the ground if it be souht,
Goth euer vpward and descendith nouht.             490

As a shert the body next doth touche,
With whoos touche the bodi is nat offended,
So meekenesse (on auctours I me avouche)
Among vertues is sovereynly commendid.
She and pacience of oon stok ben descendid,        495
And in som case rekned nyh and ferre,
Pees hath conquerrid more than hath the werr.

Bi prudent wrytyng and humble pacience
Kyng Dyndymus was nat rekles
To modifie the surquedous sentence                 500
Off Alisandre, thorugh meknesse, doutles:

---

478   vnclennesse] all vnclennesse T; all clennesse In
481   vertues Li T In Ed; vertuous H        that called is H Ed
482   In] om. H Ed
483   vertuous H
484   that] so H Ed
485   Cast] Chaste T In H Ed        expleitid] expert T In H Ed
          See *Glossary*.
486   his] is In; is his H Ed
487   on] vpon H Ed
491   next the body T
492   bodi] flessh Li T In. La's agreement with H and Ed may
          be accidental.  If not it runs counter to the mass of
          the evidence.       offended] last three letters added
          by other hand, La
495   ben] is H Ed
496   and] yet H        reken H Ed
499   reccheles T In; rechelece H; recheles Ed
500   modifie] notifie T In H Ed        sentence] science H Ed

To Bragmannys meknesse brouth in pes;
Meeke langage appesid the rigour
Of this forseide famous conquerour.

f. 105 r.     Wich considerid, Romayns vndirstood          505
This noble vertu of humylite
Was in som cas nedefull to knyhthood,
More expedient to euery comounte,
Them to preserue in long prosperite.
Verray meekenesse vsid in prudent wise              510
Is nat attwytid with no cowardise.

As to knyhthood longith gentilnesse,
Thyng approprid in ther religioun,
Voide of surfetis, foundid on meekenesse,
A lamb in chaumbre, in bataill a leoun:             515
Wher place and tyme gaff iust occasioun,
Bi manly soffraunce, benygne of face and cheer,
And pley the leoun whan tyme doth requeer.

Bi the processe of ther obseruauncis,
Next this shert of meekenesse, for mor speed,       520
Thei hadde a custom with sondry circumstauncis,
Off high prowesse t'avoide from them dreed,
In a mantyl for to be clad of red,
To recompence the white shert of meeknesse
With Martis colour bi knyhtly high noblesse.        525

This red mantil, so as the mateer stood
Touchyng the colour, did pleynly signyfye
Thei shold nat dreede for to spend ther blood
For comoun profit vpon no partie,

---

502   Bragmannus T In; Brygmannus H Ed
508   More] Most T In H Ed
509   Them] Hem T In      in long] long in T In H Ed
513   in ther] in her T In; to his H Ed
514   on] of In; in H
515   As a lamb H Ed
516   place] space H         gaff] yaf T In
520   this] the H Ed
521   a custom] acustome H
522   hem H         from hem to auoide drede Ed
525   noblesse] noblenesse T In; prowesse Ed
527   signifye] specifye H Ed
529   no] any Ed

       Bi proffessioun of ther chyualrye.         530
       For this cause,-- t'avoide away all dreede,
       Thei vsid of custom a mantil of fyne red.

f. 105 v.     This colour red, tookne of high prowesse,
       To susteene and hold vp trouthe and right,
       Not entremedle of wrongis and falsnesse,    535
       For love nor hate of no maner wiht,
       For fauour to no party cast ther siht;
       Stond indefferent, egale as a lyne,
       Bi noon occasioun from trouthe to declyne.

       A thyng fer of from al knyhtly desires,    540
       Straunge and foreyn to ther professiouns
       For t'apper at cessiouns or at shyres
       Bi *meyntenaunce* of fals extorciouns,
       Or to supporte bi ther protecciouns
       Causis vnleefull, bi procurage maad to-forn   545
       To make iuroures fully to be forsworn,

       A thyng, God wote, this day to mych abusid,
       Experience in deede as yt is seene.
       Thei have no colour of riht to been excusid
       Sauf of ther clyent the partie to susteene,    550
       But if thei hadde afforn be wassh clene,--

---

531  away] <u>om</u>. H Ed
535  Not entremedle (<u>originally</u> "-id" <u>but underpointed and</u>
     <u>corrected to</u> "-e" <u>above</u> )] Not entremedle Li; Nought to
     entremett T In; Not entermet(e) H Ed    and] nor In
     Ed; T <u>not</u> <u>legible</u>
537  To no partie for no fauour T In; That no party for no
     fauour H; To no party for fauour Ed    ther] her T In
538  Indifferent stonde <u>All</u> <u>MSS</u> <u>except</u> La
539  from trouth] to wronge Ed
540  all] <u>om</u>. In Ed
543  meytenaunce La
545  procurage] procage T; parcage In; brocage H Ed.  <u>See</u>
     <u>Glossary</u>.    maad] surmuttyd T; surmytted In H Ed
     to-forn] be forn H Ed
546  fully] falcely T In H; falsly Ed
547  mych] moche Li T In Ed; muche H
548  seyn T In; saine Ed
550  of] to H
551  afforn] before H Ed     wasshen Ed

Bathid, as I seide and vertuously made fair,
To sich placis thei shuld have no repair.

It is a maner of apostasie,
A knyht in pees to pleye the leoun,                      555
Nat accordyng vnto chyualrie
To drawe his swerd vsyng extorcioun;
The poore pleyneth for oppressioun,
A thyng contrarie bi sygnes manyfold
To them that were spooris of briht gold.                560

f. 106 r.    Sporis of gold, round and sharp to ride!
So as gold is metall most souereyn,
Riht so worship to knyhthood is cheef guyde.
To high noblesse bi manhood for t'atteyne,
A swerd also Romanys did ordeyne                        565
In four causes pleynly to be drawe
Afftir the rihtis of ther panyme lawe

As I told erst: the first for *defence*
Off ther goddis, and next for *the* fraunchise
Off ther templis, that no violence                      570
Be do to them in no maner wise,
As forth ther myht and power may suffise;
And the secunde, neuyr to be present
Wher doom shal passe of fals iugement;

---

552  vertuously made fair] by vertouesnesse and made feyre T;
       in vertuesnesse made feyre In; in vertous also made
       fair H; in vertues also made faire Ed
553  sich] such Li Ed; suche T In H      have] han Li
       thei] the In
556  Na La; Nought T In; Not H
557  vsyng] vsid T In
558  power T      pleyneth] compleyne H Ed
559  briht] om. Ed
564  noblenesse T In      for] om. Ed      to atteyne T Ed
565  Romanys] overwritten in La, which originally read
       "Romayns."  Li In H Ed read "Romayns"; Romeynes T.
567  ther] the T In H Ed
568  defence T In H Ed] dispense La Li
569  ther goddis] her goddis T In H      the] ther La Li
571  do] don T In H      maner of wise In
572  As ferfoth as T In; As ferforth H; As ferre as theyr
       power and might Ed.
573  neuyr] manere In

The thrydde poynt, to-forn as it is told,          575
Widwis, maidnys to helpe them in ther riht,
Punyssh robbours and tyrantis that be bold
To spoile the peeple bi ther froward myht
(This was vsid whan Albon was maade knyht);
Ther last charge, for short conclusioun,           580
Neuyr bern armys ageyn Rome Toun.

Othir articles more than I can telle,
Told and remembrid bi Dioclician,
Notable in knyhthood bi them that did excelle,
Whan the Emperour to dubbe hem first began.        585
Among othir the Britoun Bassian,
Sone of Severus, in Bryteyn kyng,
Gan thus abraide, his conceyte declaryng:

f. 106 v.          "My Lord," quod he, "With support of your grace,
So it be plesaunce to your magnyficence,           590
As ye have shewid her present in this place
Of your emperiall famous excellence,
*Synguler* favour, roial diligence,
As grettest *lord* callid on see and lond,
To make vs knyhtis with your owen hond,            595

"Lowly besechyng to condescende and see
Of your notable prudent pollicie,
Grant vs goodly of your high mageste
The first frutes of our chyvalrie

---

575    third T In; thirde H Ed        it is] I haue Ed
576    riht] might Ed
577    be] ben T In H Ed
580    Ther] The T In H        short] a T In H Ed
581    bern] to bere T In H Ed
582    more] mo All other MSS
585    Empourer (?) T        dubbe] double T
586    Bretoun T;
587    Zepherus In; Zeferus H        Bretaigne T
588    thus] this T
589    he] om. H
590    So it be plesaunce] Sith it is plesure H Ed
593    *Synguler*] Sigulle & La; Syngule & Li.        favour]
           favourer (?) T
594    *lord*] lordis La; A grettest londe lorde H        and]
           or T
599    our] yowr [sic] T In H Ed

To Mars our patron knyhtly to dedie                    600
In your presence with iustis or tornaye
Or som othir famous marcial playe,

"To have in armys knyhtly excercise,
Our grene youthe and coragis to amende,
To lerne the maner and the Romayn guyse            605
In palestre day bi day to entende,
So that ye list of grace condescende
Grant vs fredam and a place assigne
Of your imperiall support most benygne."

The Emperour, consideryng first ther cheeris,
Kowde hem gret thank for ther knyhtly request
And comendid gretly ther deseeris,
Sett a day, heeld a roial feest,
All naciouns to come atte lest
As the Emperour freely did ordeyne,                    615
To have a-do with knyhtis of Briteyne.

f. 107 r.    With Romayn knyhtis first thei had a-doo
Bi comandement of Dioclician,
Duryng the vtas (the story tellith soo),
Among all Albon, that knyhtly man,                     620
With his cosyn callid Bassian,
Gree of the feelde yoven to them tweyn
Among Romayns and knyhtis of Briteyn.

Of Ficuluees cam many worthi knyht,
Of Spayn, of Cipre, and also of Sardyne,               625
And of Almayn, in steele armyd briht:
Mars was present the feld to enlumyne!

---

600   To] om. H Ed       dedie] magnifie H Ed
601   with] to T In      iustis] iuste T In; om. H
605   and] on H
607   to condescend H Ed
608   assigne] signe T In; to assigne H Ed
613   Sett on a day H      and held T In H Ed
615   did frely In
620   Among] Amonges T In      that] the T In
622   youe Li T In; gyuen Ed
624   Ficulnees (?) La; Ficuluyes Li; Ficulnius T In H Ed;
      source has "siculos," see Explanatory Notes.
      many a worthi T In H Ed
626   y armyd T In

But among all, to the Bryteyn lyne,
The souereyn price, abouen them euerychon,
Was bi herowdis yoven to Albon.                              630

His name worthi to be put in memorie,
He quyt hymsilf so lik a manly knyht,
Grauntid to hym the pris and the victorie,
Thorugh his desert, of verray trouthe and riht,
Callid in Rome, tho, lanterne and the liht             635
Off knyhtly prowes and Phebus souereyn
Thorugh all Itaile, and day sterr of Bryteyn.

Off blissid Albon the armys in his sheeld,
Squar on his shuldris bi antiquyte,
Of fyne asur sothly was the feeld;                          640
Ther-in of gold depicte was a sawtre;
(In whoos story at leiser who list see,
Aftir his passioun, as I afferme dare,
In his armour Kyng Offa sothly bare,

f. 107 v.        Of whoos menstre he aftir was foundour,      645
As the cronycle makith mencioun.
A manly knyht, a notable gouernour,
In his dayes thorugh many regioun
His name sprad and his high renoun;
Vndir thes armys, as put is in memorie             650
In euery feeld he hadde euyr the victorie;

---

629   prince Li        aboue Ed        them] om. all other MSS
630   heraldis H; heraldes Ed
635   Callid] To be called H        tho] the All other MSS
637   Ytalie T In Ed
639   Marginal note (Ital. hand) in La, trimmed: "Albon bore
        a field azu... a saltier."
642   leiser] leisetir Li; lecestre T; leycestre In H;
        leicester Ed. See Explanatory Notes.
643   Marginal note (Ital. hand) in La, trimmed: "Offa built
        Mynster a... Verolam."
644   In his cote Armour All other MSS
645   mynster T H Ed; mynstre In        foundre T In
646   makith] manyth H
647   notable] noble T In H Ed
648   many a regioun T In H Ed
650   put is] is put H
651   he] om. T In H Ed        euyr] ay Li T In; alwey H; alway
        Ed

A-forn providid, I trowe, of yore agoon
Bi grace of God and heuenly influence
And bi the merite of glorious Seynt Albon,
Had in knyhthood marciall excellence                          655
And for t'aquyte hym bi vertuous providence
To this martir callid Seynt Albon,
Off that monastery leide the first ston,

Afftir whos hond masones did werche,--
He bar the cost, of gret devocioun.                           660
The seid armys he left vnto the cherche,
This Kyng Offa, as made is mencioun.
And fynaly, bi myn opynyoun,
Bi thes armys ageyn that don hem wrong
With helpe of Albon thei shal be made strong.                 665

The feeld of asur tokenyth stabilnesse;
The sawtre, lik a croos of Seynt Andrew,
The heuenly colour shal yeve hem perfitnesse,
Bi the holy croos force in our Lord Iesu
Fro day to day t'encrece in all vertu.                        670
The prothomartir, ther patroun seynt, Albon,
Shal hem deffende geyn all ther mortal fon.

f. 108 r.    After *thes* iustis and famous turment
Fully accomplisshid, told heer in sentence,
Bassian disposid in his entent                                675

---

654   of the glorious H Ed
655   knyhthood] knyghtly H
658   mynstre T In H; minster Ed
660   bar] bere H
664   that doon] all that doth ("that" inserted above probably
      in correcting hand) T; all that doth In H Ed      hem]
      them Ed
665   With the helpe T In
666   betokeneth T In Ed; betokenyth H      stabulnesse T;
      stablenesse In H; stedfastnes Ed
668   colour hevenly T In H Ed      yeve] gyf T In; yf H;
      give Ed
670   to increce T In H Ed      in all] all in T In H Ed
672   geyn all] a geyne all In; ayenste H; fro Ed
      foone T
673   thes] this La Li      turment] tornament T In H Ed (see
      Glossary).

T'awaite a tyme, of enter diligence,
Off the Emperour to axe goodly licence
With all the Brytouns beyng in Rome Toun
Hom to returne to Brutis Albioun.

His request grauntid was a-noon                          680
Bi Dioclician, maade noon excepcioun,
Sauff oonly this:  he seide that Albon
Shal nat departe bi no condicioun,
To hym he hadde so gret affecioun;
For high noblesse and semelynesse, allone     685
He shuld abide and waite on his persone.

To Albon egall in fayrnesse,
With Dioclician non so gret as he,
Off manly force and hardynesse
Famous in knyghthood lik Iudas Machabe,       690
As Scipioun prudent and avisee,
Off cheer benygne, discreete, and vertuous,
Yevyng counseil sad and compendious,

Mars in armys, with Mercury eloquent
Mong Romayne knyhtis rekenyd, yong and old.  695
For which the Emperour with gret avisement
Off providence (to-forn as I yow told),
To-forn al othir Albon he hath withold
On hym t'abide and wayte day and nyht,
Of his empir as formost worthi knyht.          700

---

676  T'awaite] To awaite T In H Ed
678  all] om. T In H Ed        Brytouns] Barouns T In H Ed
680  grauntid was] was graunted Ed
682  this] thus T In H Ed
686  waite] awaite Ed
691  prudent and avisee] prudent and awise T; of prudent
        aduyse was he Ed
693  sad] right sad Ed
695  Amonge T In H Ed
696  with] by Li T In H Ed
697  yow] have H Ed
698  To-forn] By fore H; Before Ed        withold] hold T;
        wolde In
699  t'abide and wayte] to abide and waite T In; to awaite
        and abide H Ed
700  formost worthi] for most worthy Li Ed; for the most
        worthiest T In; for moste worthi H

f. 108 v.      Whan Bassian had his leve i-take
               Of Dioclician with knyhtis of Bryteyn
               The Emperour for Albonys sake
               At ther departyng list nat for to feyn
               To them there,-- and aftir in certeyn,                705
               For his plesaunce (as seith the cronycler)
               Fully compleet Albon a-bood vii yeer.

               This mene while (myn auctour writith thus)
               Was this prince comen hom in dede
               In-to his contre. A knyht, Carausyus,               710
               Greetly disposid to slen and blood to sheede,
               Of the Romayns gate licence, as I reede,
               And of the senat, bi gret auctorite,
               To be made keper of the Brittyssh Se.

               Bassianus bi iust successioun                       715
               At his home-come to Bryteyn a-noon riht
               Was crownyd knyg of that regioun,
               His fadre ded, a ful notable knyht
               Callid Severus, which in the peeplis siht
               Greet favour had.  But Bassian in th'yle,           720
               The story seith, reyned but a while.

               Bi Carausyus of whom I told a-forn
               This Bassian was slayn tretourly;
               Sceptre and crowne this yong prince hath lorn,
               Carausyus vsurpyng most falsly                      725

---

701   i-take] take H Ed
704   feyn] seyn T
705   To them there] To make them ther ("make" <u>supra</u>) T; To
         make hem chere H Ed
708   write T; writh In; writith H; writeth Ed
709   Was] was come T In H Ed
710   Carauseus T In H Ed
711   slen] kill H Ed
714   made] om. H
716   home come] home comyng T In H; comyng home Ed
719   peeplis] peple In     sightes Ed
720   th'yle] that ile T In H Ed
722   Carauseus T H Ed; Caresius In
723   traytourisly T; traytorously In; traytoursly H;
         traitrously Ed
724   lorn] born H; borne Ed
725   Careuseus In

To be crowned kyng in that partie,
Hauyng no titill to the regalie
But a fals claym of mordre and tyranny.

f. 109 r.     On Bassian thus whan he was wrooke,
Bi intrusioun the kyngdam vsurpyng,                    730
To the Romayns had his oth i-brooke
And in Bryteyn took on hym to be kyng,
The Romayn trybut which that was hangyng
The Emperour falsly he gan denye;
Grauntid also withynne Albanye                         735

To the Pictys to have a dwellyng place
The which now i-callid is Scotlond.
And fro Rome thei bood no lenger space:
A senatour cam doun with myhty hond,
Callid Allectus, the malis to withstond                740
Of Caryusyus, with Romayn chaumpiouns
Brouht,-- in noumbre fully thre legiouns.

This Caryusyus, in story as I fynde,
Which traytourly hadd moordred Bassian,
Slayn bi Allectus, his name put out of mynde,          745
Romayn knyhtis with many a manly man
For t'acomplissh ther purpos tho bigan,
Brouht Brytouns thorugh ther high renoun
Almost bi force to subieccioun.

---

726   in] of H Ed
728   claym] trayne T In H Ed        murder Ed
729   wrooke] a wrooke T In H Ed
730   kynghud Li; kyngdome T In H; kyngdom Ed
731   i-brooke] broke H Ed
732   on] vpon T In H Ed
733   which] the which T H Ed
734   The] To the T In H Ed        falsly he] he falsely T In H
            Ed     gan] canne H; can Ed
736   for to have T In H Ed
737   is now callid T; now is callid In H Ed
738   An] And All other MSS
739   with a myghty T
741   Careuseus In
746   a] om. H
747   to complessh T In; to complyssh H; to accomplisshe Ed
            tho] they Ed
748   high] om. T In H Ed
749   to] vnto H Ed

To ther socour hoopyng thei shuld availe          750
Ageyn Romayns to make resistence,
Asclepeodot, *Duk* of Cornewaile
Thei chesyn of newe to stondyn at deffence,
Which thorugh his manly knyhtly excellence
Slough Allectus of verray force and myht          755
And put his felaw Gallus to the fliht.

f. 109 v.    The proude Romayns he did so encombre,
Thei myht afforn hym a-bide in no maneer,
He slough of hem at London so gret noumbre
Thorugh his knyhthood, be-side the river,--          760
Aftir whoos name (as seith the cronycler)
Is callid yet, wher Romayns did bleede,
In-to this day Walbrok, as I reede.

In memorye of that discomfitur,
The noble Britouns, aftir that bataile,          765
Off oon assent did ther busy cur
The same day, armyd in plate and maile,
Proudly to chese the Duke of Cornewaile,
Asclepeodot, ther purpos to atteyne,
To crowne hym kyng and lord of al Briteyn.          770

This myhty duke, knowyng ther entent,
Agreed weell to ther eleccioun;

---

750  thei] that it T In; it H Ed
752  Asclepiodot T; Asclepiodeth H     *Duk*] Erle La.  <u>Source</u>
      <u>has</u> "<u>dux</u>."
753  chesyn] ches Li; chose T H Ed; chese In    stondyn]
      stonde T In; stond H; stande Ed    at her defence In
754  excellence] <u>om</u>. H
755  Slow H; Slew Ed    of] by H
756  Galles All other MSS.  See *Explanatory Notes.*
758  afore H Ed
759  a number Ed
760  the] a T In H
762  Callid is there as H; Is called there as Ed
763  In-to] Unto Ed
764  discomfuture T; discomfortune In
769  Asclepiodet T; Asclepiodeth H; Asclepeodet In
771  duke] knyght <u>struck</u> <u>through</u>, <u>and</u> <u>in</u> <u>the</u> <u>same</u> <u>line</u> <u>and</u>
      <u>hand</u>, <u>Duke</u> In
772  to] vnto T In H Ed

To be crowned yit wold he nat assent
But auctorite from Rome sent doun
Bi the Emperour to Brutis Albioun,                        775
For which cause Dioclician
To Briteyn hath sent Maximyan.

The cheeff cause, in soth, of his comyng
(With othir mateers that were collaterall)
In-to that lond was to crowne hym kyng,                   780
Ther for to regne in his estat roiall.
And Dioclician in especiall
Cauht a conseyt in the same whyle
With hym to send Albon in-to that ile;

f. 110 r.    Bothe for trust, pleynly to devise,          785
And to gouerne notably that lond,
Parcell also to gwerdoun his servise,
For trouthe in knyhthood in Albon that he found,
Ordeyned hym, made suraunce with his hond,
Prynce of knyhtis and stiward sovereyn                    790
Vndir Romayns thorugh-out al Briteyn.

He sent hym thiddir also of entent
For his wisdam and his discrecioun,
With Maximyan for to be present
At this solempne coronacioun                              795

---

773 yit] that T In H Ed      he nat] not he T; he nott In; om.
        he H
774 were sent H Ed; "were" _inserted_ above in correcting
        hand, T
776 caused H Ed
777 To] Vnto H      hath sent] om. "hath" H; to sende Ed
780 was for to H Ed
783 Cauht] Hath H Ed      same] meane H Ed
784 that] om. In
786 notable H
788 of] in T In H Ed
789 and made hym Ed      assuraunce T      with his] by H;
        in Ed
791 out] om. T In H Ed
792 all so thidder of that entent T; ther all soo of entent
        In; thidder allso for that entent H; thither allso for
        that entent Ed
793 and his] and high Li T In H Ed
795 this] his In

Of Ascopleodote, lord of that regioun,
Albon as styward in that solempnyte
And prince of knyhtis receyve his dignyte,

Bi the biddyng of Dioclician
Lik custom vsid of antiquyte,                    800
Make his oth vnto Maxymyan
As prynce and styward of most auctorite
To the Emperour in his imperial see,
As he was bounde bi statute old and newe
For liff or deth euyr to be trewe.               805

All thyng accomplisshid as I have told,
Maximyan returned is a-geyn
With a trybute, thre thousand pounde of gold,
Behynd of olde deneyed, of duodeyn,
Which was with-drawe (the story seith, certeyn) 810
To the Romayns, tyme of Caraucyus,
A fals tyrant, cruel and furious.

f. 110 v.    Tyme vnto Rome whan Maxymyan
Retorned was with al his chevalrye,
In Petris chayer sat Pope Poncian,               815
That besi was on eche partye,
In Cecile and in Lumbardie,
Bi deuout techyng (as myn auctour seith)
To turne peeple vnto Cristis feith.

In that tyme maad was non obstacle            820

---

796   Asclepeodot Li Ed; Asclepeodet In; Asclepiodet T;
        Astlyopiodeth H
801   vnto] to T In H Ed
804   statutes Ed
806   thingis H; thinges Ed        complisshed T In H        like as
        T In H Ed
808   of] in Ed
809   duodeyn] disdeyne T H Ed; dusdeyne In.  See *Glossary*.
811   To] Fro T        the tyme In H Ed
813   Tyme] Came T In H; Come Ed        vnto] in to H Ed
814   his] om. H
815   Poncion Li H; Ponccon, "Pope" partly erased, T;
        Policoon In; That tyme the pope named Poncian Ed
816   eche] the other T; other In; that other H Ed
817   Sicile Li; Cesile T In H
820   was made H        non] an (struck through) In

That ther wern, in deede as it was seene,
Bi Cristis lawe turnyd bi myracle
To the noumbre thousandis ful sixtene
To the chirche of Crist, tendre and verray greene.
Whan the Emperour hath these wondris seyn,          825
Was gretly meuyd of malice and of disdeyn.

To Cristis feith he had so gret envie
Whan that he saugh, to his confusioun,
The noumbre of Cristen encrece and multiplie,
Let calle in hast bi fals collusioun              830
All the lordis of that regioun,
And all the senat, afforn hym to apper
A certeyn day to trete of this mateer.

Eche on assemblid in his high presence
Bad cast her witt to-gidre and take heede          835
And feithfully don ther diligence
In this mateer ther purpos for to speede,
What was to done in so streite a neede,
For thyng that touchith the welthe of ther cite
Must of wis counsel take auctorite.                840

f. 111 r.    For this mateer touchid oon and all,
             A thyng expedient for to been amendid,

---

821  ther] yere T In H Ed        wern] om. H Ed        was as it was
     seene H; there was as it was sene Ed
822  Bi] Thorugh H; Thrugh Ed
823  of thousandes T In H Ed        fully H Ed
824  To] om. T In H Ed
825  these] the In        wondris] wordis H; wonders Ed
826  of disdeyn] om. "of" T In H Ed
827  he] om. All other MSS
828  that he saugh] he saugh that T
832  Sennattes T In; Senatis H; Cenates Ed        hym] for In;
     om. H
833  At a certeyn H Ed
834  high] om. H
835  Bad] Byd H Ed        wittes T In H Ed        taken T
839  thynges Ed        touches T; touched H; toucheth Ed
     ther] her T In; the H Ed
840  take first authoritie Ed
841  Two folios of MS Li missing (I, 841 to II, 24).
     touchid] toucheth T; touchinge H; touched Ed

Which to amende first thei did calle
The Pope in hast *that* hath the law offendid,
And to this poynt thei be condescendid:                    845
To dampne hym bi hasti iugement,
And all Crysten that wer of his assent,

    Banyssh al Cristen out of Rome Toun
And punyssh them bi mortal cruelte,
Nat oonly ther but in every regioun.                    850
With dyvers torment cerchid every contre,
This statute made in Rome the Cite,
Thoruh al the world a decre forth sent,
Thei to be slayn and ther bookis brent,

    Spare no place ther men did hem knowe                    855
But hem pursewe vpon eche partie,
Alle ther chirchis cast doun and ouerthrowe
Pleyn with the grounde wher men cowde hem aspie.
Thus stood our feith in mortal iupartie
Off myscreauntis, foon *to* Cristis lawe,                    860
For dreed of deth that thei have them withdrawe;

    Ageyns them the paynyms wer so strong,
Drouh hem for feer eche man to his contre;
And Amphibal, that bar non armys long
Sauff in knyhthood of willful poverte,                    865
Constreyned was with othir for to flee.

_____

843   amende] redresse T In
844   "pope" <u>partially</u> erased, T    that] <u>om</u>. La <u>only</u>
      her lawes T; her lawe In; theyr lawe Ed
845   ben all T In; be all H Ed
850   every] eche T In H Ed
851   tormentys T In H Ed
852   This] the H
854   bookis] bodies T In H Ed
858   aspie] spie T In
859   ieopertie T; ieoparte In; iuparty H; ieopardie Ed
860   foon] foone T In; foes H Ed    to] <u>om</u>. La <u>only</u>
862   Ageynst T; Ageynest In; Ageynste H; Against Ed
      them] <u>inserted</u> <u>above</u> T; <u>om</u>. H, "the" <u>inserted</u> <u>supra</u>
      In
863   for feer] to fle H    to] fro H Ed
864   long] of long Ed
865   Sauff] Saving H; saue Ed

Paciently, with trauaile and with peyn,
Passyng the see, cam hom in-to Briteyn.

f. 111 v.   Conveyed he was bi grace and bi vertu
            In his repeir homward, as I reede,                    870
            His sauff-condit strong in our Lord Iesu
            (Hoo trustith hym, a-mys he may nat speede).
            The Holygost did his brydill leede
            To Verolamye, which of antiquyte
            Was in Briteyn a famous gret cite.                    875


                         *Epilogue*

            In this place heer as now I am advertid
            Off this marter for to stynte a while
            And to procede how Albon was convertid
            To Cristis feith; the processe to compile,
            The holy martir direct shal my stile                 880
            In whoos worship first I undirtook
            The translacioun of this litil book

            *At* the request and vertuous bidding
            Off my fadre, abbot of that place
            A clerk notable, perfit of livyng,                    885
            Hauyng in costom, euery hour and space,

---

868   cam] come T In; comyng H; came Ed        hom] <u>om</u>. H Ed
      in-to] to T In
869   bi vertu] <u>om</u>. bi H Ed
871   sauff] <u>om</u>. In        conduyte T In Ed        strong] <u>om</u>. T
872   Hoo] Who so T In H Ed        trustith] truste H        he]
      <u>om</u>. H
875   famous gret] grete famous T In H Ed
876   <u>Margin</u>, H, verba auctoris; <u>between</u> <u>stanzas</u>, Ed, Verbi
      auctores [<u>sic</u>]        In] Of T In H Ed        as now I] of
      now I T In, now I H Ed
877   marter] matier T H Ed; mattere In; "for" <u>supplied</u> <u>by</u>
      <u>correcting</u> <u>hand</u> T
879   Cristis] Christen Ed
883   At] And La        and] of H
884   thabbot H Ed
885   notable] noble H Ed        perfit] and perfite H
886   euery hour and space] euere by oure and space H

T'outray slouthe and vertu to purchace,
Like an ampte al sesouns of the yeer
To gadryn greyn and stuffyn his garneer.

Bi whoos notable compilaciouns                    890
Enlumyned is nat only his librarie,
But bi diligent occupaciouns
Geyn idilnesse to all vertu contrarie
Hath sett in ordre in his famous *Garnarie*
(A book compiled, richer than gold in coffris)   895
Liff of poetes and prudent philosophris

f. 112 r.      Of his name the ethymologie,
Sayde of an hom or a stede of whete,
Of God providid, doth clerkly sygnyfie
Whete gleenes of many old poete,               900
Greyn, frute, and flour, with rethoriques swete
Of philosophres, callyng to memorie
Of his labour the laureat reportorie.

        And, as I told, bi his comaundement

---

887  Lines 887 and 888 are inverted in T but marked "B,"
     "A," by correcting hand.      T'outray] To wroth T;
     to wrath In; To avoid H Ed      slought T      to] om.
     In, inserted above (in other hand?) T
888  an] anny In; eny T H; any Ed      ampte] empte T
889  To] And T      gadre T; gader H Ed      stuffen T In Ed;
     stuf In H
890  Bi whoos] W whos T [sic] (small "b" visible next to
     initial "W")
891  his gay librarie H Ed
892  But bi diligent] But also full diligent H; By also full
     diligent Ed
894  granarie T; garnere H; grauery [sic] Ed
895  richer] rather ("richer" above in correcting hand) T
     coffers H Ed; cofurs T In
896  liffis T H      poyettis and prudent phelozyfiers H
897  ethiologie H
898  Sayde of an hom] His seide on home H; Is sayd of am [sic]
     Home Ed
899  clerkly] clerely T In H Ed
900  gleues Ed      of many old poete] the mouth of that
     famous poete T (placed in blank half-line by
     correcting hand); of mouth old poete In; of the mouth
     of the olde poyete H; of the mouthe of tholde poete Ed
902  callyng] called H
904  told] seide H; sayde Ed

I took vpon me this translacioun,                905
First to compyle in al my best entent
His famous knyhthood and his high renoun.
And now to telle of his convercioun
To Cristis lawe I cast me for to write,
Folwyng the story, his passioun to endite,     910

To procede, lik as I am bound,
For t'accomplissh, breefly, in substaunce,
This litill book, and calle in the secunde,
Off his martirdam and meeke sofferaunce,
And put afforn cleerly in remembraunce         915
How Amphibal, as the Cronycle seith,
Turnyd Albon vnto Cristis feith.

Eche of hem, bi record of writyng,
Was pleynly out of othris remembraunce,
For Albon had left the knolachyng             920
Of Amphibal and al old acqueyntaunce,
But bi the mene of Goddis ordynaunce
I wil declar, as I am bounde of dette,
In Verolamye to telle how thei mette,

f. 112 v.    Pleynly procede, as I first undirtook,     925
The residewe t'accomplissh for his sake.
Make her an ende of the first booke!
But now in soth my penne I feele quake,
Voide of al colours sauff rude colours blake,

---

908  convercioun] conversacioun T In H Ed (T has "conuersion"
        in margin, in other hand)
909  lawe] feith H
912  to complessh T In; to accomplissh H Ed
913  in] it T In H Ed
919  out of othris] oute ("of" above, possibly in other hand)
        T; oute others In; with oute others H Ed
921  Amphabell Ed
925  procede] to procede T      first] om. H
927  the] this H
928  in soth] forsothe H Ed
929  colour T Ed; coloure In H      rude colours] of lettres
        (doubtful abbrev.) T; of letters In H Ed

In this processe my dulnesse to acquyte,                    930
The martirdam of Albon for to endite.

*End of Book I*

---

931   Seinte Albon H

Rubrics <u>following</u> <u>1</u>. <u>931</u>:  Here endith the furst boke T
   In H; Here endeth the first boke which treateth of the
   lyfe of Albon before he was conuerted to the faythe.
   Ed.

And here begynnyth the Prolog of the secunde boke of the
   conuercioun and conuertyng of the blessid Martyr Seint
   Alboon.  T In; H <u>omits</u> "boke," "here," "and
   conuertyng," <u>and</u> <u>concludes</u> "prothomartir of all
   Englond Seint Albone."  Here begynneth the prologue of
   the secunde boke / treatynge of the conuersion of the
   blessed prothomaþtr [<u>sic</u>] of Englande called Sainct
   Albon. Ed

*Book II*

*Prologue*

So as Aurora partith the derk nyht
Toward the tyme of Phebus vprysyng
And Lucifer with agreable liht
Bryngith kalendis of a glad morwenyng,
So bi exaumple the trewe just lyvyng          5
Of old tyme in Seynt Albon vsid
Causid the Lord which gwerdoneth euery thyng
That his meritis of Hym was not refusid.

Euery thyng drawith to his nature
Lik as Kynde yeueeth heuenly influence        10
To disposen euery creatur,
Somme to profite, somme to offence,
Somme to encrece, bi parfit providence.
Wher vertu hath the domynacioun,
Of God ordeyned, bi enteer diligennce,        15
*That* sensualite be bridelid bi resoun,

Among paynymys and Iewis hath be seyn
That vertu hath many of hem governyd;
Tauth bi natur, wrouht no thyng in veyn,

_____

1   Liber 2 La <u>in left margin</u>      partieth T In
4   kalendis] Canduls H      mornyng T In H; mornynge Ed
5   ensample T In H Ed      trewe just] juste true H; <u>om.</u>
    "just" Ed
8   his] the H Ed      was] were T In H Ed
10  yeueeth] yevith T In H; gyueth Ed
11  To] For to H Ed
12  som to do T H Ed; and som to do In
16  *That*] The La      brydely In      bi] be T; with H Ed
17  hath] haue Ed
19  Tauth] Thought T; Taught In H Ed      bi] that T      in]
    <u>om.</u> In

But as kynde and resoun hath them lernyd,        20
Good greyn from chaff among hem was concernyd.
This hath be *provid* in many sondry cas,
Good from evil bi them trewly discernyd,--
Record of Cornelie and of Seynt Ewstas.

f. 113 r.     Whoo thauht Traian whilom to do riht        25
Whan the widwe compleyned hir greuaunce?
To hir offence the emperour cast his siht;
Resoun tauht hym, for al his gret puyssaunce,
To hir request to holden the balaunce
Of rihtwissnesse, to seen, though he wer strong,  30
In her povert, to asswage hir perturbaunce,
Bi egal doom he to redresse hir wrong.

This storye is of old put in memorie
For rihtwisnesse in especiall,
How that Traian bi praier of Gregorie        35
Was preseruyd from peynes eternall,

---

20   as] a In
21   among hem] om. H Ed        concernyd] conserned T; conservid
       In; discerned H Ed.    The late Latin meaning of
       "concernere," "separate," seems to justify acceptance
       of La reading.    See *Glossary.*
22   This] Thus T In H Ed        be] he H Ed        *provid*] providid
       La T In        many] many a T In H Ed        cas] place H Ed
       Lines 22 and 23 are inverted in T but marked "b" and
          "a" respectively in margin.
23   discernyd] "disceruyd" may be La reading; deser=nyd [sic,
       over erasure] T; deservid In; conserved H; conserned
       Ed.    See n. to l. 21 above.
24   of Cornelie] vpon Cornelie T In Ed; on Cornelie H
       of seynt] on seynt T In H
25   MS Li resumes from Book I, l. 840        thauht] tauht Li;
       taught T In; tawght H; taughte Ed        Troian T In H Ed
       do] done Ed
27   offence] greuf H; grefe Ed
28   hym] om. H
29   hir] his In        holde T In H Ed
30   seen] see H Ed
31   asswage] perswade Ed
33   This] The T In H Ed        is] om. H Ed        put] it put H Ed
35   Troian T In H Ed        prayers T In H Ed
36   fro the T In H Ed

> Fro dampnac;ious and cloistres infernall,
> T'exemplifie how God, who takith heede,
> Of his power most imperiall,
> Off riht and mercy acquytith eche good deede.          40
>
> And to purpos now of my mateer:
> Duryng his liff of gret poweer and myht,
> This blissid Albon, who so list to leer,
> *Though* lik a prynce his power gaf gret liht,
> Fostrid trowthe, did wrong to no wiht.          45
> For which the Lord hath nat his hand withdrawe
> To calle and clepe his owen chosen knyht
> To be convertid and turned to his lawe.
>
> His trouthe, his vertu, his natiff gentilnesse,
> Off custom stable, groundid in many wise,          50
> Causid God of mercifull goodnesse
> To chese this prynce vnto his servise,
> All fals ydolis manly to despise,
> This chose chaumpion, born of Briteyn lyne,
> This newe Titan, whoos bemys dide arise          55
> Out of th'orient this lond to enlumyne.

f. 113 v.
> Now hens forth shal be my processe,
> With· Goddis helpe, my penne to applie
> How in his tyme he kept rihtwisnesse
> And lik a prince how he did hym guye          60
> To sette his cite vpon eche partie
> In gouernaunce, fro riht that thei nat twynne,

---

37    damnacioun T In H Ed          cloistres] cloister H Ed
38    who] om. T In H Ed
39    his grettest power H Ed
40    Off] How T
41    to purpos] "the" above the line, T; to the purpose H Ed
       now] om. T In H          mateer] nature In
43    Albon] om. In          leer] here T In H Ed
44    *Though*] Thouht La Li
46    hath nat his hand] his hand had nat Li; his hond hath
       nott T In H Ed
47    clepe him] clepe him his H
51    of his merciful T H Ed; of his high merciful In
52    chese] the H          vnto] to T In; into H Ed
54    born] om. H          of] of the Li H
56    th'orient] the Orient T In; orient H Ed
62    that] om. H Ed

Undir the reynes of prudent pollicie.
Which to rehers thus I wole begynne:

*End of the Prologue*

Wndir the Romayns, cheef and principall 65
(With greet avis it liked them ordeyn
Bi comyssioun and title imperiall,
Prynce and stiward thorugh out al Briteyn.)
Albon was chose, which did first his peyn
Lik a prynce, nat slaw nor rekeles, 70
To voide all trouble and rewle the peeple in pees.

Bi pollicie he hath so providid,
Set statutis so myhti and so strong,
And his lawis so *vertuously* devidid,
For comoun profit to endur long, 75
That no man shold do to othir wrong,
And wher he saw innocentis opre[ssi]d,
Set a peyn in hast to be redressid.

The riche he made live lik ther estate,
Withoute extorcioun doon to the poraile, 80

---

63  reynes] Regons H; reignes Ed
64  rehers] were H    Rubrics: Li marg. (torn) "...logus...
ps"; Here endith the Prolog T H; Here endith the
Prolog of the Secunde Boke In H
65  Large decorated cap., La. Here begynnyth the Secunde Boke
of the gloriouse Albon. How he was made gouernowre of
Verolamye, T. In, H, and Ed correspond substantially
to T.
66  avis] avice T; advise In; advice H; auise Ed    liked]
likith H    them to orden H Ed
68  out] om. H    al] al the In
69  Albon was chose] To chese Albon H Ed    first his peyn]
his besy peyne H
70  slaw] slouh Li; slough T In; slow H; slowe Ed
71  voide] avoide T In H
72  he] om. H
73  mightily T
74  *vertuously*] vetuously La
76  to] om. In
77  Bracketed letters blotted in La, but confirmed by other
MSS.
79  made he to lyue H; he made leve In    lik] to T In H Ed
80  doon] do T In H Ed    the] om. T

Repressid riot, soffred no debate,
Idill peeple constreyned to travaile;
Aforn providid for plente of vitaile,
Lik his office, with vertuous diligence.
Bi suffisaunce ther wer noon indigence.                    85

f. 114 r.      Bilovid and dred of high and lowe degre,
For frende nor foe declyned nat from trouthe.
The goode hym lovid for his benygnyte;
The riche drad hym; on poore he hadde ay routhe.
Wrong to redresse, ther was in hym no slouthe;    90
In his domys stedfast as a wall,
Nat syngler founde, nothir parciall.

Natur tauht hym all vices for to flee,
Lik, the lawis to which he was bounde.
A chastiser of al dishoneste,                                  95
Gaff nevir doom til trewthe wer out founde;
Neuyr to hevy, nevir to iocounde,
As tyme and mateer gaaf hym occasioun,
So was demenyd his disposicioun.

He hadde also of his acqueyntaunce              100
Four verteus callid cardynall:
Reyn of his bridill led attemperaunce;
Rihtwysnesse with mercy rewlid all,
Trouth to deffende and manhood marciall.
Bi force also thorugh his high prowesse              105
Sparid nat to chastise all falsnesse.

---

81     riot] no H
86     of] with T In H Ed
89     on poore] on the power T In H; on the pore Ed
         routhe] reuth T; reught In      ay] om. T In H Ed
90     in him ther was H
91     domys] dome H
92     nothir] ne T In; nor yet H Ed
94     which] which that Li T In
97     Neuyr to hevy] Nother to hevy H Ed      nevir] nor never
         T; nother H Ed
98     And as time H; But as time Ed      mateer] nature H
99     demenyd] demyd Li
101    verteus] vertues T In Ed; vertuous H
102    The reyne T In H Ed      temperaunce H Ed
105    his] om. In H Ed; this Li
         high] om. T

He coude appese folk that list debate,
Reforme old rancour wher he coude it spie;
Lik a prynce knyhtly he did hate
Sich as coude falsly forge and lie                    110
Stoppid his eeris from al flatrye,
To foreyn quarell list yiff no credence
Til the party come to audience.

f. 114 v.     Envious slandre *punysshid* rigerously,
Compassed of malis, hattreede, and diffame;           115
To dowble tongis evir he was enmye,
Which to seyn evil of custom haue no shame,
And bakbiters that han ther lippis lame
To sey weele; this prince, yonge and olde,
Voidid al sich out of his howsolde.                    120

Bi discrecioun he coude punyssh and spar,
His hert ay voide of all duplicite,
Large of custom, *to* nakid folk and bar
His gate ay open for hospitalite,
That yiff his vertews shuld rekned be                  125
Heer in this book, told from his yong age,
I have ther-to no kunnyng nor langage.

Nat withstandyng, as I have be-hiht,
I wil procede and nat excuse me
To declare how God saw to his knyht,                   130
The tyme rehersid, the date also, parde,
Whan Amphibalus entryd the cite
Off Verolamye, told eke the occasioun
How he and Albon mettyn in the toun.

---

108  old] all H Ed        spie] espie T In Ed; aspye H
111  flaterye T
112  quarellis H Ed        yiff] yeve Ed
113  come to] came vnto T In H; come unto Ed
114  *punysshid*] ponyssh La; be punysshed In        rigerously]
         rygouresly T
116  enemye In
117  evil] well H
122  ay voide] avoided H        of] om. H
123  *to*] of La Li T In
125  reken H
126  his] om. T H
130  how] of how H
134  mettyn] mett T In; met H Ed

                    Amphibalus, entryng the cite                     135
                    Off aventur to seke his herbergage,
                    Bi the stretis vp and doun went he
                    Lik a pilgrym of cheer and of visage,
                    Til it fell so he mett in his passage
                    The noble prynce (pleynly to conclude),          140
                    Blissid Albon, with a gret multitude.

f. 115 r.           This myhty prince, bi grace fortunat,
                    Afftir custom vsid that tyme of olde,
                    Amyd the cite walkyng in his estat
                    In a garnement freengid al with gold,            145
                    Amphibalus vertuously maad bold,
                    With humble cheer and meke visage
                    Besouht hym lowly graunte hym herbergage.

                    For whan that he on Albon cast his look
                    And hym bi-heeld with every circumstance,         150
                    Bi long avis good heede of hym he took;
                    It fil anoon in-to his remembraunce,
                    Ful yoore a-goon of ther acqueyntaunce:
                    How thei in oon, as fortune dide assent,
                    Out of Briteyn in-to Rome went.                   155

                    For Goddis sake this Amphibalus
                    Off herbergage gan lowly hym requeer,
                    To be receyvid and take in to his hows.
                    Albon anoon (the story doth vs ler)

---

135   entryng] entred Ed
136   his] om. T In H Ed
138   of visage] om. "of" T In H Ed
139   fell] befell H        his] om. H Ed
142   grace fortunat] great fortune Ed
144   walkyng] walked Ed        his] om. H
145   garment T H Ed; garnament In        freengid] frengid T In;
          frenged H Ed
148   lowly] mekely H        to graunte T In H Ed
149   that] om. T H        cast] had cast T; gan cast H
151   of hym good heed All other MSS
153   ther] his T In H Ed
154   as] of T In H Ed
155   in-to] he into Li; then vnto T; thei in to In; and vnto
          H Ed
157   gan] can Ed
159   the story : as the story In H Ed; as story, "the"
          inserted above, T

Was in sich cas straunge in no maneer,                    160
Havyng a custom *to* high and lowe degre
Freely to graunte hospitalite.

   In-to his hous he goodly hath receyvid
This symple clerk, list no lenger tarye,
His port, his cheer *benygnely* conceyvid,                    165
Mynystred hym al that was necessarie;
Fro Cristis lawe though Albon did varie,
Lik a prynce benygne and vertuous
Received hym ful goodly in his hous.

f. 115 v.   Not aftir long, oonly bi Goddis grace                    170
Of knyhtly favour souht oportunyte
To gete a tyme, a leyser, and a space
T'avoide fro hym his peeple and his mene,
With this pilgryme allone for to be,
And secretly, whan thei wer mett in fer,                    175
To hym he seide anoon as ye shal heer:

   "By many syngnes and toknes that I can,
Dyvers daungers, straunge to recur,--
In soth, that ye ben a Cristen man.
Off hardynesse durst your silff assur;                    180
Put your body and liff in aventur,
Amonge paynyms your persone to iuparte!
Withoute deth how myht ye departe?"

   Quod Amphibalus, "Crist Iesu of his grace,
Of his mercy, bet than I have deseruyd,                    185
From al daunger and euery *perilous* place,
Crist, Goddis sone, my bodie hath concervid,

---

161   to] of La <u>only</u>
163   he goodly] hym goodly T H Ed; hym goodly he In
165   benygly La       conceyvid] received Ed
166   hym] to hym T In H Ed
167   Fro] For T In; From H Ed
169   in] in to T In H Ed
173   meyne Li T In; mayne H Ed
180   And of H Ed      "hou" <u>above the line in other hand</u>
      <u>before</u> "durst," T
181   To put H
185   bet than] be hit than T In; be hit that H; be it that
      Ed
186   perlious La; perlous T In; peryllous Ed
187   concervid] preservid T In H Ed

Be my guyde, and my liff preseruyd,
To this cite brouht me sauff to preche
His glorious lawe, and his feith to teche."          190

Quod Albon than, "How may this be trewe?
What that he is I wold fayn ler,
This sone of God! A straunge thyng and newe!
Had God a sone? Declar this mateer."
Quod Amphibal, "So that ye list heer,               195
Paciently, for no thyng I wil spar
Ceriously the trouth to declar."

f. 116 r.     Amphibalus is entrid of resoun
On the Gospel to groundyn his processe
And to conferme his disputacioun.                   200
Off Hooly Writ he took iustly witnesse
How our bileve recordith in sothnesse
Of God the Fadre and God the Soone also:
"This our beleeve, tak good heed herto!

"The Soone, in soth, most perfyt and most good,
For mannys help and savacioun
Was incarnate and took flessh and blood,
And semblably, for short conclusioun,
Of his benygne consolacioun,

---

188  preseruyd] conseruid T In H Ed.   T has "preservid" can-
     celled before "conseruid."
190  His] The In
193  This] The T In H Ed     and a newe T In H Ed
195  Amphibalus H     So that ye] To so I La     that] om. H
     list] list to H Ed
196  I wil] woll I T In H; wyll I Ed
197  Ceriously] Curiously In H Ed.  T's "curiously"
     corrected to conform to La.
198  entrid] entretyd In Ed     of] by T In H Ed
204  This is T In H Ed     herto] thertoo T In H Ed
205-211  This entire stanza is underscored in La. only.
205-213  MS Li has a long hole through middle part of each
         line.
205  in soth] om. T H Ed; in the In     most perfyt] parfite
     H
206  help] helth T In H Ed
208, 210, 209, 211  appear in that order in T, but marginally
                    corrected by letters a, c, b, d.
209  his moste benygne H Ed

Rith so as he made man in deede,                                210
So cam he doun to taken our manheede.

"And as hym list, of grace and of mercy,
Bi his power which that is devyne
Ordeyned maidenys to live heer perfitly,
So he *ageynward*, pleynly to termyne,          215
Took flessh and blood of a pur virgyne;
The tyme cam, ther was maad non obstacle,
But that he wrouht this merveilous myracle.

"The tyme aprochid of grace and of gladnesse,
Toward somer, whan the lusty queene                220
Callid Flora with motles of swetnesse
Clad the soil al in newe grene,
And amerous Ver ageyn the sonne sheene
Bi the cherisshyng of Aprill with his shours
Bryngeth kalendis of May and of his flours.        225

f. 116 v.      "So in that sesoun heuenly and dyvyne,
Off wyntir stormys *was* past al the outrage,
And in the Rame Phebus gan to shyne;
The same tyme, to our gret avauntage,

---

210  made] first made T In Ed
211  So cam he doun] Cam doune T; So came he doune In H; So
        come he doune Ed
212  list] self In
214  ordent maydens H
215  ageyward La          termyne] determyne Ed
216  Took] To In
217  maad] <u>om</u>. T In H Ed
218  this] his T H Ed
219  of gladnesse] <u>om</u>. "of" T In H Ed
221  motles of] mottles and T In; motleis H; motleis of Ed
222  Clad] Cladde In; Clothed H Ed
223  Ver] were T In H; Veer Ed. <u>This, together with</u> l. 221
        (<u>see note above</u>) <u>is the first clear evidence of</u> utili-
        <u>zation by</u> Ed <u>of a second</u> MS, <u>more closely affiliated</u>
        <u>with</u> La <u>and</u> Li.    sheene] shyne In Ed
225  Bryngyth inne In          of his] his T In
226  that] the T In H Ed
227  *was*] wast La <u>only</u>          past al the outrage] passid all
        outrage <u>All other</u> MSS
228  La <u>and</u> H <u>possibly read</u> "Raine"; Ram Li T; Raam In;
        rayne Ed

Doun from heuene was sent a massage                    230
Which concludid, for our felicite
A branche shold spryng out of Iesse.

"This newe tydyng to Nazareth was sent,
And Gabriel cam on this massage,
The Trynyte hool beyng of assent,                      235
For to accomplissh this gracious viage,
The Holygost holdyng his passage,
Doun descendyng, riht as any lyne,
Into the breste of a pur virgyne.

"Lik as Lucas in his gospel seide,                     240
As is remembrid in the same place,
Whan Gabryel lowly gan a-breide,
Meekly saide, 'Heil Mary, ful of grace,
Thou chose of God, euery hour and space
A tabernacle of the Trynyte,                           245
Among all women blissid mote thou be!'

"Whan she had herd the angell thus expresse,
Troublid in his worde, of femynyte,
Thouht in hir silff of verray chast clennesse,
This chose myrrour of humylite,                        250
This salutacioun what it myht be.
The angel, seeyng hir fer of womanheed,
Seyde, 'O Mary, have her-of no dreede;

f. 117 r.      "'Afforn God thou hast founde grace;

---

230  massage] massenger In; message H Ed
231  concludid] concludith In      for] all T
233-42  MS Li has hole through middle part of each line
234  this] his In H Ed
235  of] in oone T In H Ed
236  complyssh H
237  holdyng] hodyng In      his] this H
240  Lucas] Luke T In H Ed      seide] seith H; sayth Ed
244  chose] chosin T In H Ed
245  A] As Li; The T In H Ed
247  thus] this T In
248  worde] wordis H Ed
251  myght it H
252  fer] aferd T In H Ed
254  Ms Li missing folio 18, ll. 254-309

Thou shalt conceyve a chyld in clennesse,                    255
Of whoos birthe Bedleem shal be the place,
As the gospel can ber her-of witnesse,
And his name pleynly to expresse,
Thou shalt hym name name of most vertu;
Whan he is born calle hym Iesu.'                             260


   "'How may this be?' quod this glorious maide
That knowe no man in deede, wil, nor thouht.
The angell than vnto Mary saide,
'As I to-forn to the have tydyng brouht,
Bi the Holigost this myracle shal be wrouht;               265
The vertu also of hym that sitt hyhest
Shal ovir-shadwe and liten in thi brest;


   "'For thilk Lord that shal of the be born,
As thyng most holy men shal hym also calle
The Sone of God,-- prophetis wroot be-forn,--           270
Sich hevenly grace is vpon the falle
Bi a prerogatiff a-boue women alle,
With liht surmountyng the briht sterris sevene;
This massage I have the brouht from hevene.'


   "Quod Maria, 'Fulfillid be thi will                       275
Afftir the worde which thou hast brouht to me.
Behold his handmaide and his humble ancille!'

---

255  in] in all T In H Ed
257  her-of] om. H
260  calle] and call H Ed
261  quod] seide H Ed        this] the T In
262  will dede H
264  to the have tyding] have tyding T; tyding have tyding
       [sic] In; have thee tyding H; have thee tydinges Ed
266  of] om. H      sitteth T In
267  liten] light T In H Ed      in] in to T H Ed; vnto In
       thi] the H
268  thilk] that H Ed
269  also] om. T In H Ed
270  as Prophetes T In H Ed        wroot] write In
273  the] aboue the H Ed
274  the brouht] brought the H Ed
276  to] vnto H Ed
277  his handmaide] this handmaide T In H Ed      his humble]
       this humble H Ed

This was hir answer with al humylite.
Though God was plesid with hir virgynyte,
Yit was the Lord, doctours ber witnesse,                    280
I-plesid more with hir devout meekenesse.

f. 117 v.     "Thus hath a maide thoruh hir parfitnesse
To bere hir Lord graciously deservid,
A chose douhtir, bi hir pur clennesse
To bern hir fadir, hir chastite concervid.                  285
Bi hir meritis, that wer to hir reservid,
As I seide erst, bi a prerogatiff,
She a-mong women was maide, modir, and wiff.

        "To God a maide to fulfille his will
And to the Lord seruant bi mekenesse,                       290
Douhtir and modre and feithful eeke ancill,
Which to remembre hath brouht gostly gladnesse
Of all weelfar, our damages to redresse
(Afforn record bi prophetis in substaunce),                 295
Vs to deffende geyn al mortal grevaunce.

        "For which, deer host, sith it may availe,
To my doctryne yeuyth hertly credence.
God hath me sent to tech yow and counsaile,
So that ye list with humble diligence
Become his knyht and do hym reuerence,                      300
Obey his lawe and his preceptis all.
Takith good heed to yow what shal be-fall!

        "His feith to yow shal yeve so gret vertu
That ye shal make blynd folk to see

---

278   hir answer] he answerde H
279   In La, "hir" is followed by "hi," apparently meaning-
        less.
281   I-plesid] om. "I" H Ed
290   Lord a H Ed
291   feithful eeke] eke feithfull T In H Ed
293   weelfar] daungeres H     damages] daungers T In Ed;
        welfare H          redresse] represse H Ed
294   Afforn record] And forn recordyd T; Aforn by recorde H Ed
        bi] of H Ed
295   geyn] ageyne T In H; Agayne Ed
302   be] om. H
304   ye shal make blynd folk] blynd folk ye shal make H Ed
        to] for to H Ed

Bi invocacioun oonly of Crist Iesu, 305
Deliver the peeple from all adversite,
Leprous folk and thei that lame be
To be maade cleene and make hem gon vp riht,
And euery siknesse recur thorugh his myht.

f. 118 r. "Ye shal escape bi his providence 310
All myscheevis which been to yow contrarye,
Live long tyme, go fre from pestilence.
Fro Cristis feith yif that ye nat varie
To graunte your askyng the Lord shal nat tarie,
But atte last, or ye hens weende, 315
Bi martirdam ye shal make an eende.

"Bi martirdam ye eende shal your liff,
And blissidly ye from this world shal passe
Out of trouble and transitorie striff,
Which day bi day do yow her manace. 320
Thoruh Cristis myht and influence of grace
Ye shal to God, to your gret avauntage,
Bi meeke sofraunce make your passage.

"This was cheef cause and gronde of my comyng,
Sent bi Iesu in-to this roial toun 325
As a bedill to bryng yow tidyng

---

305  Bi the T
307  lepours H       thei] thoo H Ed
309  recur] recouer T In H Ed
310  MS Li resumes from II, 253.
311  which been to yow] om. "been" In; to youe that been H;
       to yow that ben Ed
313  Fro] For T (corrected above) "fro" T; for In; from Ed
       that ye] ye that T In
314  nat] not T (inserted in correcting hand); will not verrye
       H Ed
315  atte] at T H Ed
317  eende shal] shall ende H Ed
318  ye] om. T In H Ed
319  of] of all T In H Ed
320  do] doth T In H Ed      yow her] here yow In
324  Three long horizontal lines divide this line from the
       preceding one in La.
324-30  This entire stanza is underscored in MS La only.
325  in-to] vnto H       roial] om. T In H Ed
326  bidell T In

How bi his myhty visitacioun
Ye shal endur peyn and passioun
For Cristis feith in most pacient wise,
As knyht and martir chose to his servise.                    330

"That *is* his wil, as ye shal fynde in deede,
To recompense the gret humanyte
Which ye han vsid, of fredam in manheede,
To indigent folk and peeple in pouerte,
And, specialy, for hospitalite,                              335
With othir deedis in noumbre callid seuene,
Deedis of mercy regestrid now in heuene:

f. 118 v.        "To feede the pore which had no vitaile,
And to visite folk in prysoun;
Receive them that herberwe did faile;                        340
Comfort the seke, mynystre them foisoun;
Bedreede folk that lay in myscheef doun,
Part with hem of that thei had neede;
And bury them that lay in myscheef dede.

"To his seruauntis *all* that ye han mynystred 345
Cronicled been in the heuenly consistorie,
In his bookis perpetualy regestryd;
Eche good deede the Lord hath in memorie,
It to guerdoun with a palme of glorie,
Perpetuali with hym to regne in ioie,--                      350
Gretter conquest than was the siege of Troie.

"Sith ye have your hondis nat withdrawe
From hospitalite, poore folk to feede,

---

331  *is*] he La <u>only</u>      as] <u>om</u>. H Ed
333  in] and <u>All other MSS</u>
334  To] The H
339  folkes T In Ed; folkis H
340  harborough T
341-42  <u>Lines inverted in</u> T In H Ed
342  Bedreede] Bi dredde T In
343  of] <u>om</u>. H
345  <u>All MSS read</u> "& all." <u>See Explanatory Notes</u>.
348  hath] <u>om</u>. In
349  glorie] victory H Ed
352  sith] suche In      have] <u>before</u> "not" <u>in</u> H Ed
        hondis] hondy In; handes Ed
353  folkis H      to] for to H Ed

Whil ye have lived in the panym lawe,
Causes of poore to promote and speede,                    355
God forget nat to quyte yow your meede:
Yiff ye thus doon aftir ye be baptised,
A double palme for yow shal be devised."

Lik a prynce in most knyhtly wise
Albon obeied with enteer diligence;                       360
All these wordis gan wisly aduertise,
Answeryng these woordis in sentence:
"What maner worship, what maner reuerence,
Shal I do than, whan I am with-drawe
From ydolatrie, turned to Cristis lawe?"                  365

f. 119 r.    Amphibalus gaff answer to Albon:
"Ye mote bileve and in no doute be,
Ther is no God in this world but oon,
The Fadir, the Sone, the Holigost, thes thre,
Ioyned in oon bi perfite vnite,                           370
The fundacioun, as I can weel preve,
First article and *grounde of* our bileve.

"This feith in soth shal cleerly yow direct
Yiff that ye list yeve ther-to credence,
All odir errours t'avoiden and correct.                   375
Yiff ye so doon with humble reuerence,
I dar afferme and conclude in sentence

---

354  Whil ye have lived] Which (corrected to "with" above)
     ye have lived T; Which ye lived In       the] this T In
     H Ed
355  Cause T       the poore T In H Ed        to speede H Ed
356  forget nat] foryete nought T In; foryeteth not H;
     forgetteth not Ed       quyte] acquyte H       yow] om. T
     In H Ed
357  ye thus] this be T In H Ed
361  gan] can H
362  worde In
365  and turned T In H Ed
367  in no] "in" added above, T; "no" added above, H
372  *grounde of*] growndid on La; growndid of Li; "is" added
     by correcting hand above "and" T
374  yeve] yf H       ther-to] "ther" inserted supra; "to" in
     text T
375  odir] olde All other MSS.       t'avoiden] to avoide T In H
     Ed

That your gynnyng to God is acceptable
And to your silf tresour most profitable.

"Of the Fadir the power eternall,                      380
Off the Sone the sovereyn sapience,
Of the Holigost in especiall,
Grace doth procede bi vertuous providence.
And to descrive the magnyficence
Of all these .iii. callid .iii. and .ii. and oon,
Vndevided thei neuer a-sondre gon.

"And if ye list vnto his lawe turne,
Off his most digne imperial mageste
He shal yow make with hym to soiourne,
This blissed Lord, this glorious Trinyte,               390
Wher ioie is evir and al felicite,
To-forn whoos face eternalli lastyng
Thre ierarchies doon osanna syng.

f. 119 v.    "Off this mateer beeth no thyng in dowte;
Settith a-side al ambiguyte;                            395
Forsake your mametis and all that fals rowte,
For *thei* be made of metal, ston, and tree
Which may nat help nor forther in no degre,--
Satorn, Iubiter, Mars, and Appollo,
With fals goddessis Dian and Iuno.                      400

"Thouh thei have eris in soth thei may nat her;
With yen grete of lookyng thei do faile;

---

378  gynnyng] "be" inserted supra, T; begynnyng Ed
379  silf] sowle T In H Ed
381  the sovereyn] om. "the" H Ed
382  speciall In
383  vertues H
385  these] the Ed      ii and iii and oon Li; two thre and
        oone T In; thre in oon H; thre and one Ed
387  if] om. H       his] this T In H Ed
390  glorious] blessed H Ed
393  doon] one Ed
395  Settith] Settyng In; Sittyng H
397  *thei*] the La only
398  help] helpen T In      forther] fortheren T In
400  the falce T In H      Iuno] Iune Ed
401  soth] trouth H Ed

Thei be forgid of gold and stonys cleer;
Who callith to them, *thei* may nat availe.
Now, *dere* oost, forsake *al* this rascaile,                405
As I have seide, and doth in Crist delite,
And he bi grace shal make yow to profite."

A large space Albon kept hym cloos,
Feyned in maner as he hadde had disdeyn.
From his place in gret hast he aroos;                410
Yit or he went, thus he gan to seyn:
"Ye be nat wys, your doctryne is in veyn;
Yiff it wer wist ye wer in this cite,
Ye shold endur ful gret adversite.

"For your sake ther shuld be practised                415
Dyvers tormentis, to your destructioun;
For your blaspheme cruely chastised
Without favour or remyssioun,
Atte last, with short conclusioun,
Your hed smet of withouten any grace,                420
Yiff ye wer knowe or foundyn in this place.

f. 120 r.      "In this mateer I can non othir feele;
For your persone som-what I stonde in dreede.
Your beyng her yit shal I conceele,

---

403   of] in T In H Ed
404   who] who that T In       *thei*] the La *only*       nat]
            nothyng All other MSS
405   *dere*] her La Li       *al*] & al La Li
406   doth] do Ed
407   to] om. H Ed       profite] profith T; perfyte H Ed
408   A] om. H
409   hadde had] had hadde T; had In H Ed
410   he] om. H       aroos] ros Li; roos T; rose In; arose Ed
411   gan] canne H
412   in] om. H
417   blassemye H; blasphemye Ed
418   or] of T In
419   with] for T In H Ed
420   smet] smeten T; smytten In; smetten H; smyten Ed
            any] om. T In H Ed
423   dreede] doute H Ed
424   Your beyng] You ben Ed       shal I] I shall T In H Ed
            conceele] connceill T In; counsayle Ed

And yow preserve that no man shal take heede        425
Of your conceite nor what ye mene in deede."
And with that woord out of the place he goth,
Shewyng a cheer lik as he wer wroth.

Bi grace of God and fauour of Fortune,
All that he seide was doon with reverence;           430
Off gentilnesse he was nat inportune,
Suffryd all thyng with humble pacience,
Al be it so he gaff nat ful credence
To his doctryne,-- of thynges which he tolde
Stood in doute what party he shal holde.             435

Albon in hast thouht for the best,
Whan Lucyna shoon ful cleer and briht,
With slep oppressid, for to take his rest.
Amphibalus sat al that longe nyht
Vpon his knees lik Goddis owne knyht,                440
For love of Albon with gret devocioun
Makyng to God meekly his orysoun.

To whoos praier of grace God took keep,
List to considre his trewe affeccioun,
And in this while as Alboun lay and sleep,           445
The same nyht he had a visioun,
Straunge and dyuers bi manyfold resoun,
And wondir fer from his intelligence
What it menyth or what was the sentence.

---

428    Shewyng] Sheweth Ed     wer] had been Ed
429    By the grace T      "God" inserted above, La
433    nat] no T In H Ed
434    thynge In
435    shal] shulde H Ed
437    cleer] shene H Ed
438    slep] La seems to have written "h" for "l" and covered
          error with his "e."
438-49  Increasing portions of each line missing in Li because
          of diagonal tear.
440    lik] as H Ed
442    to God] om. T In; full H Ed
444    And list H      trewe] om. T In H Ed
445    lay] leyde H
446    a visioun] avisioun H
448    fer] ferne T; ferre In
449    menyth] ment T In H Ed

f. 120 v.  Toward morwe as Albon did abraide                    450
  Out of his sleep and Phebus shon ful *sheene*,
Gan to merveile and no word he seide
Touchyng his dreem newe, tendre and grene,
Vndirstood nat what it shold mene,
Roos vp in hast and to the pylgryme went,        455
Besechyng hym declar what *it* ment.

  "My freend," quod he, "Yif al the thyng be trewe
Which ye have prechid of Crist and of his lawe,
Dyvers *mervailes* vncouth straunge and newe
Shewid to me to-nyht ar it gan dawe              460
I yow biseche your vois nat to withdrawe
For to declar the exposicioun
Whan I have told yow my avisioun,

  "The which, trewly as I reherse can,--
Lokyng vpward to the heuenly mansioun,           465
Me thought sothly that I saw a man
Fro that paleys to this world cam doun,
Off whos beaute was no comparisoun.
Eeke, as me thouht, of boistous folk and rude
He was be-sett with a gret multitude.           470

  "This peeple, envious, and froward of entent,
As it sempt, of malis and haterede,
With many sondry cruel fel torment,

---

450  as] when H Ed
451  *sheene*] cleer La only
453  tendre] fressh H Ed
456  to declare T In H Ed     *it*] he La; it s [sic] T
457  the] om. T In H Ed
459  *mervailes* vncouth] mervaile vncouth La; mervaill
    vncouth Li; mervailes unknow T In H; meruayles
    unknowne Ed
460  to-nyht] this nyht All other MSS    ar] or T In Ed
    gan] can T In H Ed
461  vois] voice T In H; witte Ed    nat to] ye nott T In H;
    ye nat Ed
467-77  Increasing portions of each line missing in Li
    because of diagonal tear.
467  paleys] place H Ed; palis T In
469  as] om. H Ed
472  sempt] semyd T In; semed H Ed
473  many a sondry H Ed    cruel] om. T In H Ed

With sharpe scoorges made his sydes bleede,
Bounde his handis (I took ther-of good heede),    475
And on a cros thei heng hym vp ful blyve;
With sper and nailes thei gaf hym woundis five.

f. 121 r.    "Nakid he was, body, feet, and hondis,
On lengthe and brede drawen with gret peyn
Bi the constreynt of myhty strong bondis.          480
Draw a-sondre was every nerve and veyn,
With a sharp sper his hert clove on tweyn:
Percid he was so deepe and so profounde
That blood and watir ran out of that wounde.

"With a red sper thei rauht (I took good heede),
Gaf hym drynk, eseil meynt with galle,
A crowne of thornes set vpon his hed;
A-mong his cruel peynes alle,
Kyng of Iewis of malice thei hym calle,
And in scorne maliciously cryeng,                  490
Of Iewry salued hym as kyng.

"As me thouht, thei gretly did offende
To maken hym al his blood to bleede,
And fro the cros bad hym doun descende
Yiff that he wer Goddis sone in deede.             495
His skyn to-rent, al blody was his weede,

---

476   heng] hynge T Ed; hing H
478   Nakid] Makid Li      feet] foot T In H
480   the] om. La only      bondis] hondis La Li
481   Draw] Drawen T In H Ed      nerve] Narf T H Ed; nerf In
482   his hert] is, om. "hert" H      cloven H Ed      on tweyn]
      a tweyne T H; in tweyn Ed
483   so profounde] om. "so" Ed
485   red] reed Li; reede T In H Ed      thei rauht] therof H
      good] om. H Ed
486   Gan yef hym drynk H; To gyue hym drynke Ed      meynt]
      mengled Ed
487   thorne Ed
488   And among T
489   of malice] in scorn H Ed
490   scorne] despite H Ed
491   saluted H Ed
493   maken hym] make T In H Ed      blood] body T In H Ed
      to bleede] so for to bleede H
494   bad] had In; doune bad hym Ed

Lik a meke lamb offred in sacryfise,
Which to be-hold myn hert did agryse.

"Aftir these peynes, grevous and importable,
And al his hydous mortall tormentrie,                    500
With a gret vois, pitous and lamentable,
Vpon the poynt whan he shold dye,
To his Fadir thus he gan to crye:
"In-to thyn handis, Fadir, I comende
My goost, my spiryt," and thus he made an eende.

f. 121 v.     "And with that cry, as he yaff vp the gost,
Fro the cros his body take doun,
Lik welle-streemys vpon euery cost
His grene woundis shad out gret foisoun
Of bloody dropis, and for conclusioun                   510
Off all his peynes the body was anon
Closid and aselid vndir a large ston.

"And whil that he with strong hond was kept cloos
(Merueyl of merueyl, most I gan merueile!),
The ded body to live ageyn he ros,                      515
Maugre the knyhtis with al ther plate or maile.
A sodeyn slombir ther hedis did assaile;
An angel aftir, most sovereyn of delite,

---

497-98  T:  (497 placed by correcting hand in space left for
        the purpose)
                To se hym tormented in so crewelle wise
                Lyke a meke lombe myn herte did agryse
        In:  Like a meke lombe myn hert did agrise (only one
        line)
            H and Ed:  497 corresponds to T's 498;  498 to T's 497;
        "turment" for T's "tormented."
499     peynes] payimes (?) H        inportable] intollerable Ed
503     thus] this H
507     take] thei toke T H Ed;  he toke In
509     fusion H
510     a conclusioun T In H Ed
512     aselid] ensealid T H Ed;  inseayled In        large] grete
            T In H Ed
513     was] om. In
514     of mervailes T In H Ed        gan] canne T;  can In H Ed
515     he] vp T In;  om. H Ed
516     ther] om. H Ed        or] and T In H Ed
518     aftir] om. Ed

I sauh apper, and he was clad in white.

"Among othir merveyl this was oon                    520
Which I be-heeld in myn avisioun:
Out of his grave closid with a stoon
He roos vp lik a strong chaumpioun,--
With open eye I hadde inspectioun
Of al this thyng, no parte left bi-hynde,         525
Fro poynt to poynt al marked in my mynde.

"Red nor song a-mong the Briton layes
Was neuer herd so swete an heuenly soun
Aftir the noumbre of ful fourty dayes
Folwyng aftir his resurrectioun,                    530
To the tyme of his ascencioun,
Whan the multitude of *angelis* all in feer
Conveied hym a-bove the sterrys cleere.

f. 122 r.   "I sauh this thyng and knew it wele inow
Bi a maner vncouth apparence,--                      535
The garnementis whitter than mylk or snow
Of all the *angelis* that did hym reverence;
This was ther song and refreyte in sentence:
'Blessid be the Fadre, and blessid mote he be,

---

519   was clad] clothed H; was clothid T In Ed
520   mervailes T In H Ed      this] there Ed
523   vp] hym up Li T In H; hym, om. "up" Ed
524   eye] eyen T In H Ed      inspectioun] aspeccion H;
        aspection Ed
527   songen T Ed; songe H      Breton Li; Brytaignes T;
        Briteygnes In; Bryttone H; Brytons Ed      layes] lawis
        H
528-29   In reverse order, corrected in margin H
529   of ful] full of T H Ed; full In
530   Folowed H Ed      his] the T In H Ed
532   Whan] That H      the] om. Li In H      *angelis*] Angel
        La Li, with an "e" hook or flourish which may be a
        mistake for an "is" contraction; Aungellis T; all
        Aungellis In; Aungeles H; angels Ed
534-89   One folio of MS Li is missing.
534   I] A T
536   garmentis T H Ed; garnamentes In
537   *angelis*] Angel La Li (see n. to 532); Angellis T In;
        Aungellis H; thangels Ed
539   Blessid be] Blessid T In      and] om. H Ed

The Sone, eek blissid in his humanyte.'          540

"These vncouth tidynges I saugh hem in my sleep,
And many othir tidynges mo with-all,
Secre thynges,-- I took of them good keep,--
Not to be shewid no man mortall."
And all he told vnto Amphiball          545
Whan he a-wook, and with ful humble entent,
Be-sechyng hym declare what it ment.

Which thyng to her he gretly was delited
Withynne hym silf of spiritual gladnesse,
Sauh his hert was of God visited,          550
And ful deuoutly a cros he gan forth dresse.
"Loo her," quod he, "This token berith witnesse
Of all the sygnes, cler as the sonne bem,
That wer to yow shewid in your drem.

"The man the which to yow did apper,          555
Sent from heuene, so fair and glorious,
He was the same as I shal yow lere,
My blissid Lord, my owen Lord Iesus,
Most benygne, most meeke, most vertuous,
Which on a cros sofred passioun          560
As ye sauh cleerly in your avisioun.

f. 122 v.     "Only bi mercy, bi his gracious avis,

---

541  These] Thes T; This In        saugh] saw H; sawe Ed
542  many othir] other many H      tidynges] thynges T In H
     Ed                                                    Ed
543  Secrete T H Ed; Secret In
544  shewid] shewid to T In H Ed
545  Indentation omitted in T In H Ed        all] om. after
     "And"; insert after "Amphiball" T In H Ed        to]
     unto T H
546  and with] in T In H Ed
547  declare] to declare T In H Ed
548  thinges H Ed        he] om. T In H Ed
550  Sauh] Saugh that T In H; Saw that Ed
554  to] vnto T In H Ed
555  the which] om. "the" T In H Ed
558  My lord blessid be he myn ("owne" above) lord Iesus T
     Lord] lord Criste H Ed
559  most meeke] meeke and T In; most meeke and H Ed
562  bi his] and by his T In

Off the trespace to make redempcioun,
Touchyng the appil which in paradis
Adam eete of bi fals suggestioun                              565
Of a serpent, to gret confusioun,
First of hymsilf, next of all his lyne,
Til Cristis passioun was our cheef medicyne.

"Ageyn Adam the serpent was so wood,
To stanche his venym was fonde no obstacle                    570
Til on the cros Crist Iesu spent his blood
As medicyne, bawme, and cheef triacle,
Licour of licours, distillyng bi myracle
Fro the condutis of Cristis woundis . v .
Man to restore ageyn from deth to live.                       575

"Whos blissid passion is our restoratiff,
Helthe and diffence of most excellence
T'asswage the bollyng of al our mortal striff,
Bawme imperiall geyn feendis violence,
Off philosophres celestial quynt essence,                    580
To all weelfare *mankynde* to restore,
Helpith al seeknesse whan lechis can no more,

"Our leche, our Galian, our gostly Ypocras,
Our Sampson callid, that venquysshid the leoun,
Our myhti chaumpioun, the famous strong Athlas,  585
That bar vp heuen for our salvacioun,
High on the cros makyng our raunsoun.

---

565   of] om. In
567   First] For first In
568   was] that was T In H Ed        cheef] om. H Ed
570   no] non T H; none Ed
571   spent] spende Ed
572   As] A T In H Ed
576   is] om. H
578   bollyng] bulyng T; buluyng In; boluyng H; bolynge Ed
        al] om. T In H Ed
580   Off] The T In H Ed         philosophres] philosopher H;
        philosophre Ed        quynt] queynt T In Ed
581   *mankynde*] makyng La only
582   seeknesse] syknessis H Ed
583   Galian] Galien T; Ypocras H Ed        Ypocras] Galyen H Ed
584   that] of In
585   Athlas] Atthellas T In; Achilles H Ed

He that ye saugh was the same man,
In your avisioun, that ovircam Sathan.

f. 123 r.      "The multitude that aboute hym stood            590
Was fals Iewis, his deth ymagynyng.
Of cursid malis nayled hym to the roode;
List nat receyve his gracious comyng;
Off ther prophetis refusid the wrytyng,
Knew nat ther Lord, but as folk adversarie,       595
For his goodnesse wer to hym ay contrarie.

     "Mercifull Iesu, geyn deth to stynt our striff
List sofre deth fro deth to make vs free,
Venquysshid deth, with deth to bryng in lyff
Whan liff was slayn, heng vpon a tree.            600
Forbode frute brouht in mortalite;
Bi a rounde appil was causid al this losse,
Bi frute reformed that heng vpon a crosse.

     "Adam ete frute, fair, fressh, and delicate,
Wherbi cam in the venym serpentyne               605
Which made God with man first atte debat,
But ther-ageyn the heuenly frute dyvyne
Which that sprang out of a pur virgyne,
This frute of frutis, our cheef repast and foode,
Gat the tryumphe of deth vp-on the roode.        610

---

588  ye] youe H
590  MS Li resumes from 1. 533       aboute] above Ed
591  Was] Were T In H Ed
592  hym] om. H
596  ay] om. T In H Ed
597  geyn] ageyne T; ageyn In
600  heng] heeng hih Li; an high T In H Ed
601  in mortalite] immortalyte Ed
603  a] the Li T In H Ed
604-73  Lines missing in Ed. Although Ed itself is printed
     four stanzas to the page, this portion of Ed was probably
     set up from a manuscript with five to the side (like T,
     In, and H). If a leaf were missing from this hypothet-
     ical manuscript, the absence of seventy lines would be
     explained. It may, on the other hand, be an editorial
     abridgment.
604  fressh] om. H
605  venym] venemous T; venemys In
606  atte] at Li T In H Ed

"This blissid frute, Iesu, to stynte our peyn
Outraied deth: first with his passioun
He slough Satan and bonde hym in a cheyn,
Brak the gatis of the infernal doungoun,
And his seruauntis that lay ther in prisoun,      615
Of his imperial power most enteer
He lad hem vp a-bove the sterris cleer.

f. 123 v.     "Thus with the pris of his precious blood,
And bi his deth of deth he gat the victorie;
On Good Fryday, hangyng on the roode,             620
Drough to hym all (the gospel makith memorie).
To helle he went to bryng Adam to glorie,
Free from al myschiff of the infernal boundis,
Bi the conquest of his precious woundis.

"Cam from Edom and did his baner spreede,         625
Clad in purpil as champioun and kyng,
Shet vp Sathan among the flawmys rede,
Made Cerberus to levyn his berkyng,
And with his sote melodious syngyng,
As Orpheus fett Eridice his wiff,                 630
So he fro deth restored man to liff.

"Thus hath this lamb slayn this leoun,
Outraied the wolff the sheep with his meekenesse,
Our olifant venquysshid the dragoun,
Olofern ded with Iudittis clennesse,             635
And Crist Iesu, our Hercules in prowesse,

---

612  Outraied] Outeraged T In H
613  bounde] T H
614  Brak the] Brak iii H        gatis] yatis T H; yates In
615  lay ther] layn, om. "ther," T In; lay, om. "ther," H
616  Of] And In
618  Thus] This T In        with] is In
621  And as the gospell to us makith memorye H        all] as T
        In
624  his] om. Li
625  did] om. T In; his banner did spede H
626  Clad] Clothid T In H        and] or In; or a H
630  fett] sett T In        Erudyce Li; Ereudes T; Ereudys In H
632  this leoun] the leoun T In H
633  Outraied] Outraged T In H
635  Olifernus T In; Olifernes H        ded] slayn H
        clennesse] chast clennesse T In H

Ravisshid hath, the chaumpion most prudent,
The applis of gold awey fro the serpent.

    "This goldene appil (bi a simylitude)
Which surmountid in beaute and richesse          640
(Bi resemblaunce pleynly to conclude),
Was mannys sowle, bounden in distresse
Bi a fals dragoun, til Crist thorugh his mekenesse
And bi his suffraunce made hym go fre
From al daunger of infernall pouste.          645

f. 124 r.    "The sowle of man, Cristis spouse enteer,
Most acceptable in the Lordis siht
With Cristis blood for it was bouht so deer,
Is of more pris than gold that shyneth briht;
And in your drem, so as ye saugh tonyht,          650
To save man Crist sofred woundis felle;
So bi his passioun Sathan lyth bounde in helle."

    Amphibal bad hym take heed her-to,
Alle these wordis emprente *hem* in his mynde.
"Certis," quod Albon, "Of hert so I do;          655
Ther shal no word ther-of be left bi-hynde.
I sauh my silff,-- myn eyen wer nat blynde,--
How Crist Iesu with his most myhti honde,
Deepe in helle how he the serpent bonde,

    "And bi ful cleer notable euydence,          660
Lik as ye seyn, accordyng to my drem,
I saugh al thyng in experience,
Bryht, in effect, as is the sonne bem
That cast his stremys ovir many rewm,
Riht so I knowe, bi tookenys old and newe,          665
All that ye telle how it is verray trewe,

---

637   the] this T In H
640   and] in H
647   the] <u>om.</u> T In H
650   tonyht] this night Li T In H
652   <u>undecipherable mark in</u> La <u>between</u> "bi" <u>and</u> "his," <u>om. by</u>
      <u>other</u> MSS.     lyth] lieth T In H
653   Amphibalus T In H
654   *hem*] hym La; them H    his] youre H
664   stremys] bemys H    rewm] a realme T In H

"Makyng promys with feithful obeisaunce,
Sey what ye list, I shal yeve audience
To your techyng, feith and attendaunce,
With hert, body, mynde, and al credence,          670
As your disciple, vndir obedience.
That I sey now, be it seid for evir,
Fro your doctryne nevir to dissevir.

f. 124 v.     "Lat me, I prey yow, have verray knowlechyng
Bi your discret feithful dilligence               675
As ye that ben expert in many thyng,
What obseruaunce, what dewe reverence
Vnto the Fadir and his magnyficence,
To the Holigost,-- telle on first of thes too,--
And to the Sone, what servise shal I doo?"        680

Whan Amphiball gan pleynly advertise
His feithful askyng with all humylite,
Gan reioish in many sondry wise
That this Albon, wher-as he stood fre,
Was goodly mevid to askyn of tho Thre,            685
Bi God enspired.  Conceivid of resoun,
Oonly of grace cam this questioun.

Thankid God and goodly gan hym dresse
To comfort the trewe affeccioun
Off blissid Albon, and trewly to expresse,        690
Hym to quyte, for short conclusioun,
Of his demande made a solucioun;

---

667   obeisaunce] obseruaunce T In H
670   al] ful Li T In H
673   to] for to T
674   Ed resumes from II, 603; the numbering of the present
        edition from line 603 no longer corresponds to
        Horstmann's line numbering for the remainder of Book
        II.        knowlechyng] knowleche T; knowlege H;
        knowlegyng Ed
676   many] many A T In H Ed
678   and his] and to his H
681   Amphabell Ed        gan] can In        advertise] to
        advertise T In H Ed
684   That this] There this In; That his H; This Ed
685   Was] Has In        tho] these T In Ed
688   hym] his T

His conceitis discretly to appese
Thus he seide to sett his hert in ese:

"These thre persones which ye have named her,
The Fadir, the Sone, the Holigost, these thre,
Be sothfastly,-- lik as ye shal leer,
Trust me riht weel,-- oo God in Trynyte,
Ioyned in oon bi perfit vnite.
Beleeve this iustly and all your wittis dresse    700
For liff or deth these articles to confesse."

f. 125 r.    "This is my feith and I beleve thus,"
Quod blissid Albon with al humylite;
"Ther is no God but my lord Iesus,
Which that cam doun from his Fadres se,           705
Meekly to take our humanyte;
For our helthe and our salvacioun
List of his mercy suffre passioun."

"He with the Fadir, the Holigost, thes thre"
(Amphibal rehersyng to Albon)                     710
"Been al oo God bi perfit vnyte,
And othir God in al this world is noon;
Fro this beleve loke that ye nat goon."
Thes wordis often rehersid in sentence,
Albon fill doun with devout reuerence             715

To-fore the cros and with gret repentaunce
Saide, "O Lord, mercy of my mysdede;

---

694   in] att T H
697   leer] here T In H Ed
700   all] om. T In H Ed
701   these articles] this article T In H Ed
702   my] om. H
705   from] om. H
708   suffre] to suffre T In H Ed
710   Amphibalus T In H Ed       to] vnto T In H Ed
711   Been] thei ben T In H; they be Ed
712   And othir] A nother T H       this] the T In H Ed       is]
         is ther In
713   Fro] And T In Ed; As H       that] om. Ed       goon]
         forgone T In H Ed
714   Thes wordis often] This word ofte T H Ed; this word
         oost In
717   Saide] And saide Ed       mercy of] Iesu on T In H Ed

O Iesu, mercy, receyve my penaunce,
Which on the cros list for my sake bleede."
And on his knees fast he gan hym speede          720
With contrite hert erect to God a-loft.
With wepyng eyen the cros he kissid oft;

With all his membris hath hym silf applied.
As on the cros Crist had be present,
And he with hym wher he was crucified,           725
So of hool will Albon was dilligent;
His face, his eyen, with teeris al be-sprent,
This penytant, his langour for to lisse,
Was evir besi Cristis feet to kysse.

f. 125 v.    The bittir teeris from his eyen tweyn      730
Lik cristal wellis encresyng as a flood,
Albon ay besy to make the watir reyn,
To medle his weepyng with Cristis owen blood,--
I meene the woundis graven on the rood,
Vpon the cros that was vnto hym shewid,          735
Of dreery sobbyng the carectis al be-dewid.

Bi grace enspired thus, Albon gan hym drawe
To take the ordre and the religioun
Off Cristis feith and bynde hym to that lawe

719   bleede] to bleede Ed
721   erect] grete T In H Ed
722   eyen] terys T In H Ed
723   his] <u>om</u>. In        silf] <u>om</u>. T In H Ed
724   the] a T H
725   wher] whe [sic] H; whan Ed        was] were T In H
726   will Albon] hert with Albon T H; with Albon In; herte
        Albon Ed
727   bespernt In
728   penytant] penitaunce H
729   feet] Crosse T H; foot In Ed        to] for to T In H
730   The] His T H Ed
731   cristal wellis] crystal well Li; cristall a well T In H;
        a christall well Ed
733   medle] medull H; myngle Ed
734   I] In T In H        woundis] wounde In Ed
735   cros] rode crosse In        vnto hym shewid] to hym i
        shewid T H; to hym showed In Ed
736   dreery] dere T H        be-dewid] he dewid In
738   and the] of T In H Ed

With will and hert and hool affeccioun,                 740
And secrely made his professioun
To Crist Iesu, tyme and hour devised,
Bi Amphibalus whan he was baptised.

  Thus in the name of the holy Trinyte
Amphibalus baptised hath Albon,
Made hym stable bi perfit charite,                      745
Bi cler instructioun with the articles everychoun
Of Cristis feith, and aftir that, a-noun,
This chose of God, bi the Hooligost devised,
These wordis seide whan he was baptised;                750

  With humble hert this was the langage
Off holy Albon:  Quod he,"I heer for-sake
The pompe of Sathan with al his baronage
And al the poweer of ougly feendis blake;
Sowle and body to Iesu I betake,                        755
Which for mankynde deyed (it is no nay,--
Thus I beleeve) and roos the thrydde day."

f. 126 r.    Quod Amphibal with a glad visage,
"Be strong of feith, our Lord is hool with the,
Wil nat faile to conferme your corage                   760
Bi tooknys shewid of his *benignitee*.
In especial reportith this of me:
Othir affor yow, as I rehers can,
That thei wer tauht, thei lernyd it of man,

  "But your lernyng excellyng in vertu,                 765

---

741   secretly T In H Ed
744-50   <u>These lines are omitted in</u> Ed.
744   Thus] <u>om</u>. T In H
750   whan] He when T In H
752   I heer] here I H
755   Sowle] My sowle Ed
757   Thus] This T In H       roos] a roos T; arois In; aroos H
758   Amphibalus T In H Ed
759   hool] holde Ed
760   Wil] He wil Ed       faile] feine T       conferme] conserue
         T In H; confyrme Ed
761   *benignitee*] humylite La Li
762   reportith] report In
763   Othir] To other Ed
765   lernyng] langage T In H Ed

Experience hath yove yow, knolechyng
Bi revelacioun of our lord Iesu,
Which hath to yow declared every thyng--
His birthe, his passioun and his vp-risyng,--
Off al this thyng lik as ye had a siht,                    770
To calle yow to hym to been his chose knyht,

    "Which, me seemyth, ouht i-now suffise,
With the surpluse of your avisioun,--
To yow expounned the maner and the guyse
Of Cristis feith with ful instructioun,--          775
Meekely of hert, with supportacioun
That my request your bryhtnesse nat ne greve,
For to depart goodly to yeeve me leve.

    "I am meeuyd of verray concience
In othir contres to preche Cristis *lawe*.           780
I hope to yow it shal be non offence
For a sesoun though I me with-drawe;
It is a biwoord and a ful old sawe
Which hath be seide sith go many yeer,
Freendis al wey may nat be in feer."                 785

f. 126 v.    "Freendis," quod Albon, "nevir depart a-sondir,
Ioyned in vertu and i-knyt bi grace;
Thouh oon be her and a-nothir yondir,
Ther hert is oon euery hour and space.

---

768  hath to yow] to you hath Ed
769  and] om. In Ed
770  this thyng] this thynges T; thingis In; the thyngis H
     a] in T In H Ed
772  me] be H        i-now] i nouh Li; i nowgh to T H; i nought
     In; ynough Ed        to suffise T H
774  maner] matier H
777  That] Att T H Ed; Hat In        bryhtnesse] highnesse T In
     H Ed        nat ne greve] nott ne greve T; nough to greve
     In H; not ye greue Ed
779  am] om. H
780  In] om. T In H Ed        lawe] law^eye [sic] La
781  be] do Ed
784  go] gone Ed        many yeer] many a yeer In H Ed
785  be] ben T In Ed
787  i-knyt] knyt Ed
788  her] yonder H        and] om. In        yondir] here H
789  Ther] Her T In        hert] hertes Ed        is] ben Ed

In God convived, ther partith hem no place;  790
Of oo wil ay what thei ha to done.
For which I pray, departith nat so sone.

"T'abide a wike ye may do me gret ese,
Bi your doctrine to have instructioun
My lord Iesu how I shal hym plese  795
With riht hool hert and trewe affeccioun,
To serve hym dewly lik my professioun,
And in his feith wher-in I most delite,
With your techyng that I may profite."

Amphibalus, knowyng his entent,  800
List in no wise denyen his axyng.
The long nyht thei to-gidre spent
Oonly in prayer and devout praysyng,
For out of siht thei chose ther abydyng;
Fro noise of folk thei gan hem silf withdrawe.  805
Al this while thei spak of Cristis lawe.

Off Cristis feith and his religioun
Was ther talkyng and ther daliaunce;
Among, to God thei made ther orisoun
Them to preserve from feendis encombraunce.  810
In this while,-- God giff hym sory chance,--
A cursid paynym, of malice and envie,
Wher thei mett the place he did aspie.

---

790  convived] conbyned All other MSS.  See *Glossary*.
791  what] that T In H Ed      ha] haue T In H Ed
792  pray] pray youe H
793  wike] woke T; wooke In; weke H Ed
794  have] have youre H
795  My] of my H      I shal] shall I T In Ed
798  his] om. H
800  Stanza beginning at this line and that beginning at l.
      807 are inverted in La, but corrected by "b" and "a"
      in margin.
801  in] om. H
802  nyht] myght H
805  Fro] For T In H
806  Al this] And al this T In H; And al that Ed
807  and] and of T In H Ed
808  talkyng] fayth Ed      ther daliaunce] her daliaunce T In;
      daliaunce H
810  preserve] defende Ed      from] om. In      encombraunce]
      accombrance Ed
811  giff] yef T In; yeue H; yafe Ed      hym] them Ed

f. 127 r.       To a-voide hem of comfort and refuge
                This saide paynym of malis list nat spar        815
                To accuse them bothe to the iuge,
                Of ther metyng the maner to declare,
                And more-ovir,-- euyl mote he fare,--
                Of malicious froward cursidnesse
                The iuge he set affir with woodnesse.           820

                With envious sturdy violence
                Thoruh the cite thei serchid wer and souht
                And comandid t'apper in the presence,
                To-fore the iuge bothe to be brouht.
                The toun cerchid, but thei fonde hem nouht.     825
                Blissid Albon, meeuyd of corage
                To keepe his maistir and save hym fro damage;

                Vpon a nyht, to-forn the dawnyng,
                This blissed Albon his maistir gan conveie;
                With hevy cheer, most pitously weepyng,         830
                Out of the cite brouht hym on his weye;
                At the departyng ferd as thei wold deye.
                So wer ther hertis ioyned in oo cheyne,
                Nat lik to twyn til deth depart them tweyn.

                O feithful love, stondyng in sich cas          835
                Bi remembraunce in comparisoun
                As whilom did David and Ionathas
                (Maugre Kyng Saulis persecucioun,
                Feynyng was non nor *symulacioun*),

---

814-925  Two leaves missing from this point in MS Li
815   saide paynym] peyneme a fore seid T In H Ed      spar]
        to spare H
816   To accuse] For to accuse T In H Ed       to the] vnto the
        T In H Ed
817   maner] trouth H
820   affir] on fir T In H; a fyre Ed
824   to be] two to be T H Ed; two he In
828   to-forn] to fore T In H; before Ed
829   gan] he can T H; he gan In
833   ther] "her" added above, T; her In; om. H
834   tweyn] in twaine Ed
835   cas] estate T In H ("cace" in other hand in margin, T)
        a state Ed
836   remembraunce] resemblaunce T In H Ed
839   *symulacioun*] silmacioun La; dissimulation Ed

Lik to perseuere, playnly to termyne,                840
Til Antropos ther livis threed vntwyne.

f. 127 v.    Ther love more sad, stable, and vertuous
In comparisoun than that poetes made
Off Pirothe othir of Theseus,
Of Horestes othir of Pilade,                845
Fressh for a sesoun, that wil so fade
As whilom did the love of Achilles
And Patroclus, slayn amyd the pres

Whan that Ector, the Troian chaumpioun,
Slough Patroclus for his frowardnesse,                850
Maugre Achilles, for al his high renoun,
T'exemplifie ther is no stabilnesse
In wordly love, but chaunge and doubilnesse,
Be it of blood, kynreede, or allye.
Without vertu al stant in iupartie!                855

Of these tweyn the love was al a-nothir;
Bi *entrechaungyng* attween hem set a lawe:
*Albon* t'abide and dien for his brothir,
Amphibal his presence to with-drawe.
In ther hertis the fervence did a-dawe                860
Off parfit love, for t'endur long,
As Salomoun seith how love as deth is strong.

---

840    perseuere] perserue T In; preserue H; endure Ed
841    threed vntwyne] tred atweyne T; tryed a twynne In; tryed
          atweyne H; tryed atwyne Ed
843    than] om. H        that] the T In Ed        poete T H
844    Theseus] Thedeus T H Ed; Tideus In
845    Pilade] Pallade T; Palade H
846    wil so] woll soone T In; wolde sone Ed; wil sone H
849    Troiayns T; Troians H
851    high] om. In
853    chaunge] chance H
854    kynreede] kynde T In; kynne H Ed
856    al] om. T In H Ed
857    *entrechaungyng*] entirchauntyng La only        attween]
          betwene T In H
858    *Albo* La only
859    Amphibalus T In H Ed        his] om. T In H
861    for t'endur] to endure T In H Ed
862    seith] writte T; write In H; writeth Ed        as] and T In
          H

In all sich cas that love makith hertis bold.
And bi exaumple that love *avoidith* dreed,
Albon for love tooke his cloth of gold,                    865
Lik a prince list knyhtly chaunge his weede;
Off enteer hert he gan it for to spreede
Ovir the shuldres of *Amphiball* a-noon,
Hour whan thei tweyn a-sondir shuld gon.

f. 128 r.    From all his foon he iustly was assured,       870
Who that evyr hadde on this cloth of gold,
Tyl he the place fully hath recured,
To stond at large, afforn as I have tolde.
Thus with sobbyng and weepyng many fold
God soffred them assondre to devide,                      875
For-sooke hem nouthir, but was her bothe guyde.

A symple sclaveyn, to-torn and thredbare,
Off Amphibal a ful old garlement,
This noble prince Albon list nat spar
To cast vpon, thouh it wer al to-rent,                    880
So hool to Crist was sett al his entent,
And in his povert to shewe that he was pleyn,
To his tugurrye he torned hom a-geyn.

Amphibalus northward took his passage;
Chose of hert God to been his guyde,                      885

---

863   that] the T In Ed
864   exaumple] ensample Ed        avoided La <u>only</u>
865   Albon] And Albon T H
866   Lik] And like Ed        knyhtly] <u>om.</u> Ed        chaunge] g
        chaunge [<u>sic</u>] In; to chaunge Ed
868   *Amphiball*] Al_____ (space <u>left blank</u>) La
869   Hour] The hour T In H Ed        tweyn a-sondir] a tweynne
        T In H; atwynne Ed
872   the] <u>om.</u> In
875   them] hem T H; hym In        to] for to T H        asondry
        T H
876   nouthir] nott T In H        bothe] bothes Ed
877   sclaveyn] slaven H; sclauenne Ed        to-torn] to toryn
        T H; for torne Ed
878   garlement] garment T H Ed; garnement In
880   vpon] vpon hym T In H Ed
883   tugurrye] Tigurry T In Ed        he torned] returned T In
        H Ed
884   took] to T In H Ed
885   Chose] Chere Ed

For a tyme eschewe the cruel rage
Of paynymes, as Fortune list provide,
But holy Albon did the bront a-bide,
To live and deye as Goddis chaumpioun.
Crist bar his standard; the cros was his penoun.

This sodeyn chaunge he helde was no los,
For-soke richesse, tok hym to poverte;
His tresour was to kneele affore the cros,
His hertly ioie and his felicite.
And for a while thus I lete hym be                    895
In his praier and telle wil in deede
How his enmyes ageyns hym procede:

f. 128 v.    Ther was a statute proclamyd in the toun
Who that wold do no reverence
To ther goddis, nor meekely knele doun,               900
In-to ther feeris for to cast encence,
He shold anon bi cruel violence
Be take and leid vpon an auteer, bounde,
To-fore ther goddis and slayn with many a wounde,

Of his body to make sacrifise.                        905
Supersticious was this oblatioun,
Which of newe paynymes gan practise
Ageyn the doctrine and predicatioun
Bi Amphibalus brouht in-to the toun,
Bi the iuge set in ordynaunce,                        910
On hym and Albon first to do vengeaunce,

---

886    eschewe] to eschewe T In H Ed
889    live] loue In
891    chaunge] chaunce Ed       helde] held it T In H Ed
892    tok] to H
893    affore] aforn T In; aforne H Ed
894    hertly] herty H Ed
896    praier] prayers T In H Ed       wil] I woll T; I wil H;
          I wyll Ed
899    do] nott do T In H Ed
900    To ther] Vnto her T In H; Vnto theyr Ed       nor] ne T
          In; and H; nor Ed
901    ther feeris] her fires T In H; theyr fyre Ed
903    Be take] To be take T In H
907    gan] can T In H
910    in] an T H

So to punyssh, oon and oon bi rowe,
Without mersy or long avisement.
To blissid Albon this statute was weel knowe,
Bothe of ther doom and cruel iugement,                    915
And ay this prince, stable in his entent,
Maad strong in God for liff or deth, t'endur
The Lordis sonde and take his aventur.

Whan somer floures blew, whiht, and rede,
Wer in the hyhest lusty fressh sesoun,                    920
And fyry Phebus from the Crabbis hede
Took his passage toward the Leoun,
At Verolamye, into the roial toun,
The same tyme, paynymes had advertid
To Cristis faithe how Albon was *convertid*.             925

f. 129 r.    For which a-geyn hym so obstynat thei stoode,
Lik wilde boris or tigris in ther rage
Wengeable of hert, furious, and woode,
Malencolik, pale of ther visage.
And al the nyht with cursed fel langage                   930
Gan to manace, lik wolvis ravynous,
This blissed Albon and Amphibalus.

The dirk tydes of the clowdy nyht
Withdrough ther shadwis and ther skies blake,
And Lucifer gan shewe his stremys briht                   935
Whan Aurora hath the bed for-sake

---

918   sonde] honde T In H; hande Ed.  See *Glossary*.      take]
      om. T In H Ed
919   blew] blowid T; bloued In; blowed Ed
920   Wer] And were T In H Ed      the] her T In H; theyr Ed
921   Crabbis] Crabbe his T; crabbe is H
922   Took] To H
923   into the] in that T H; in the In.  See *Glossary*.
924   had] haue T In H Ed      advertid] auertyd T In H Ed
925   faithe] inserted into La text by later hand in space
      erased or blank.  T, In, H, and Ed all read "faith."
      covertid La
926   Lincoln Manuscript resumes here after two missing folios
      of fifty-six lines each.
929   pale] and pale Ed
934   shadowes T In H Ed
935   shewe] to shewe T H      stremys] beames Ed
936   Whan] And T In H Ed

Off fyry Titan and hir leve take,
And Phebus chariete, drawith vp with Flegonte,
Gan enlumyne al our orizonte.

The holsom bawme gan in *meedwis* fleete        940
Among the flours and holsom levis grene;
The sylver dew gan eek the soil to weete,
Lik perlis rounde, as any cristal shene,
Whan Natur, of worldly thynges queene,
Ordeyned a day of fresshnes plentevous        945
Whan Albon was besegid in his hous.

The paynymes gan make hem silf strong
This noble prince Albon to pirsewe,
Vpon the hour whan the lark song,
In hir ledne gan the day salewe;        950
Ther *purpos* was speciali to sewe
Amphibalus, but for that he was gon,
In stede of hym thei fil vpon Albon.

f. 129 v.    Affor the cros thei fonden hym knelyng
In his praier and thei vpon hym went;        955
Roos with his cros, made no taryeng;

---

937  take] i take T H
938  Flegonte] Flegetonte T H; flegoute Ed
939  Gan] Gan to T In H; And gan Ed        our] the Ed
940  La reads m  dwis with space for two letters erased;
     medowes T In; medewes H; meddowes Ed
941  flours] leueys H        holsom] om. H        levis] flours H
942  eek] om. Ed
944  queene] the queene Ed
945  plentevous] plentuous T In; plentous H Ed
947  hem silf] theyr selfe Ed
948  prince] Evidence of erasure at second letter La
949  the hour] that hour Ed        lark] larkes Ed
950  gan] and gan Ed        salewe] to salue T; to salew H
951  *purpos*] blot in La covering second and third letters;
     supplied from all other MSS.
952  for] om. T In H Ed
955  prayers H        thei vpon hym went] ther vpon hym they
     went T H
956  He a rose up with his cros and made ("no" added above in
     correcting hand, T) tarying T H; Arose vp with his
     cros and made no tarying In; He rose up and made no
     tarrying Ed

Gret multitude that the iuge sent
Fel vpon hym, lik wolvis thei hym rent.
In ther furious mortal fel deluge
Thei hym present affor the cruel iuge.            960

    Meek as a lamb, of port and cheer benygne,
To doon his bataile lik Goddis owen knyht,
His baner was, his standard and his sygne,
The cros of Iesu, which he bar vp-riht,
Maugre paynymes in ther alder siht,              965
Lik a chanpioun vpon hem to werreye;
Vndir that penoun cast hym live and deye.

    God was with hym to susteene his partie;
Steedfast of hert, hardy as leoun,
Put his liff for Crist in iupartie.               970
Off body *naked, trought was* his habirioun,
His sheeld was feith, his swerd and his burdoun,
His sper, his pollex, surer than steel t'endur,
Was oonly hope victory to recur.

    His sabatouns set on a ground of trouthe    975
And his grevis forgid with stabilnesse
And his poleynys, pliant without slouthe,
And his cusshewis, born vp with high prowesse,
A peyr curas closid with rihtwisnesse,
And his vmbras was trust that went be-forn,      980
Rerbras of charite which myht nat be forlorn;

---

957   Gret] And the great Ed
960   affor] anon afore Ed       cruel] <u>om</u>. T In H Ed
962   Goddis] Christis Ed
966   vpon] ageyne T In H Ed
967   live] to live T In H Ed
968   with] <u>om</u>. In H
969   leoun] a leoun T In H Ed
971   *naked, trought was*] makid thorugh La Li; <u>italics from</u> T.
    habirioun] haburgeoun T In; haburchon H; <u>habergon Ed</u>
973   pollex] pollax T In H Ed
974   victory] the victory Ed
975   a] <u>om</u>. In H Ed; T <u>not</u> <u>visible</u> <u>because</u> <u>of</u> <u>crease</u>.
977   poleynys] polynes In; poleynes H; polayns Ed
978   cusshewis] kussheus T In H; quisshews Ed
979   peyr] payre of T H Ed
980   vmbras] wambras T In H; vauntbrace Ed      be-forn] a
    forn T H Ed
981   Rerbras] The Rerebrace T H      forlorn] forborn T In H;
    forlorne Ed

f. 130 r.      Gloves of plate, to bern of and deffende,
               Was trewe affectioun meedlid with the deede,
               A large pavis, gretly to comende,
               Of trewe mevyng, t'avoide a-way al dreede,          985
               And thus in trouthe, whoso list take heede,
               All in vertews enarmyd for deffence,
               With a cote armewr a-bove, of pacience.

               Charite was cheef of his consaile,
               Tauht hym the maner a-geyn his cruel foon           990
               How that he shold to his gret availe
               Entre the feeld and knyhtly for to gon,
               Though it so wer that he was but allon;
               His baner splaied ful erly on a morwe,
               Grace was his guyde, with Seyn Iohn to borwe.       995

               First he was lad bi mortal violence,
               Drawe and to-torn in most cruel wise,
               The holly cros vp born for his diffence,
               And brouht he was for to do sacrifise
               To ther ydolis, but he did them despise,            1000
               Asclipiodot the iuge ther present,
               And al the cite gadrid of entent.

               This Goddis knyht, holdyng the cros in honde,
               Invyncible bi vertu of that sygne,
               And paynymys that about hym stoond,                 1005
               Cruel, cursid, ageyn hym did maligne,

---

982    bern of] beren T In H; beare of Ed
984    pavis] _paveis_ T In; pavays H; pauice Ed
985    mevyng] meenyng Li; menyng T In H; meanyng Ed; _see_
           _Glossary_.
986    thus] _om._ In; this H
990    thaught T In
991    Entre] Enter in to Ed      to] do to T In H Ed
992    for] _om._ T In H Ed      gon] done T In H
993    Though it] All that it T In H Ed      allon] oon alone H
994    splaied] sprayd In      a] the T In H Ed
997    to-] _om._ Ed
1000   To] Vnto T In Ed
1002   entent] oon entent T In H
1004   Invinsible T; Invisible In H Ed
1006   Cruel] Cruel and T In H Ed      did] gan _All_ _other_ _MSS_

Thouh thei and he wer born bothe of o lyne.
The iuge troublid whan that he took heed
Of Cristis cros *and had a manere dreede!*

f. 130 v.    Albon alwey, this prince ful notable,        1010
Stood ay vpriht with look most coraious,
Euer of on hert, as any *centre* stable,
The cros afforn, baner most glorious,
Most agreable, and most victorious.
And first of all (the story doth vs leer),        1015
Of his maistir the iuge did hym enqueer,

Axed of hym what partye he was gon
Bi his sleihte and his vncouth wile,
Which despised ther goddis euerychon,
Cam of newe ther cite to beguyle.        1020
At whoos wordis Albon stynt a while,
Saide atte last with sobre countenaunce,
He was departid bi Goddis ordynaunce.

Quod the iuge, "Wher-evir that he be,
Outhir besiled or i-sett a-side,        1025
Touchyng the feith which he hath tauht to the
And theryn be thi maistir and thi guyde,
And is now fled, and durst nat abide
Bi his doctryne, a reson ful notable,--
His prechyng nouht othir,-- he is nat stable;        1030

---

1007   Thouh] Thought H      and he] here T In; *om.* H Ed
       wer] were there Ed      bothe] *om.* T In H Ed
1009   and had a maner of drede T H; La repeats "whan that he
       took heed" from previous line; reading above is from
       Li.
1010   ful] *om.* In
1012   *centre*] hert La Li
1016   did hym] of him ded T H Ed; dide of him In
1017   Axed] And axed T In H Ed      what] to what T In H Ed
1018   sleihte] flyght In
1022   Saide] And saide T In H Ed
1025   besiled] embesyled Ed      or i-sett] or sett T In H;
       orels set Ed
1026   which] that T In H Ed      to] *om.* T H
1028   is now] now is T H
1030   nouht] is nought T In H Ed      other] or Ed

"I trowe he wold have come to presence
Yiff in his feith had be no variaunce,--
Or som remors of his conscience
Hath cast his hert in newe repentaunce!
Yiff *he* had hadde in his feith constaunce,          1035
Lik a maistir, he shuld nat agon,
And his disciple in myscheef left allon.

f. 131 r.       "In his doctrine, as to myn entent,
Ther is deceite outhir som falsnesse,
Or in his techyng he is fraudulent             1040
Which hath the brouht in-to so gret woodnesse,
To forsake thi tresour and richesse,
All our goddis in so froward wise
Off wilfulnesse and malice to despise.

"Thou stondist now in ful *perilous* poynt.    1045
The clerk hath brouht the in so streiht a chaar,
Set thi reson so fer out of ioynt
And made thi witt so nakid and so bar
That thou art sett, pleynly to declar,
In Cristis cause so from our feith to erre,      1050
Geyn al our goddis to gynne a mortal werre

---

1031   I trowe] In trouth H
1032   be] he H
1033   Or] Outher T In H; Other Ed
1035   *he*] om. La *only*      had hadde] In La marked thus: ⟨had
       ⟨hadde; he hadde had Li T; he had hadde In; he had had
       Ed
1036   agon] haue gone T In Ed. See *Glossary.*
1037   left] leue T In; leaue Ed
1038   his] this In Ed
1041   to] om. T In H Ed
1042   ryches Ed
1043   All] Of all T In H Ed
1044   to despise] hem to despise T In; them to despise H Ed
1045   ful] a ful T In H Ed      *perilous*] perlious La;
       perilous Li; perlous T In H Ed
1046   hath] om. In      the] om. H      streiht] grete T In H
       Ed      chaar] share T In H; snare Ed
1047   Set] And set T In H Ed
1049   sett] om. T In H Ed
1050   so] and so T In H Ed
1051   Geyn] Ageyne T In H Ed      gynne] begyn Ed

"Which thyng considrid, as it is skil and riht,
And egally peised in balaunce,
Wrong doon to them bi any maner wiht
Nouthir be favour, frendship, nor suffraunce    1055
May nat passe without gret vengeaunce;
Vpon blaspheme, the lawe doth ordeyne,
A-geyn goddis, deth to be ther peyne.

"Vn-to a fool thou gaff hasty credence,
And bi his foly he hath the be-guyled;          1060
First, to goddis thou dost no reverence,
Of despite wilnat be reconsiled,
Farist lik a man which is vnhabiled,
Stondyng as now fro grace desolat,
Vil and abiect, out of thyn old estat.          1065

f. 131 v.    "In sich cas eche man may be deceivid
Bi sich fals foreyn informacioun,
But now thyn errour is cleerly apparceivid.
Do bi consail for thi saluacioun.
Or thou incurre the indignacioun,             1070
And or iugement bi rigour the manace,
Forsake that secte, fal doun, and axe grace.

"To thyn estat thou maist thus be restorid;
With humble hert do to them sacrifise,
And *thi tresour* and richesse shal be morid    1075
And encrece in many sondry wise.

---

1052   it] om. H
1053   in] in a T H
1054   doon to them] to do them T In H Ed
1057   blaspheme] bassume (?) H; blasphemy Ed
1058   goddis] the goddis T In H Ed
1059   Vn-to] Into T
1061   to] to the T In Ed; to thy H      dost no] most do T H
1062   wilnat] wilt nat Li H; woolt nott T In; wylte not Ed
1063   Farist] Thou farist T In H Ed      lik] as Ed
1068   perseyued T H
1071   or] or in H
1074   to] om. T In H Ed
1075   *thi tresour*] thoesour [sic] La; thi tresour Li; thi
          trosour T; tresoure In; thy tresoure H; thy treasure
          Ed      richesse] thi richesse T In; thy riches Ed
1076   encrece] encresid T In H Ed      in] by T H      many]
          many a Ed

To gret worship sodeynly arrise;
Of townes, *castellis*, lord we shal the make,
So thou wilt thi feith of Crist fo-sake."

Off hert and wil verray indivisible,                    1080
Albon al hol kept his ground and place;
The iugis promys, flatryng and fallible,
Boistous thretis with which he gan manace,
Void of dreed, off oo cher and oo face,
This manly prynce, this hardy knyht Albon,              1085
Stood atwene bothe, stable as any ston,

To the iuge seide as ye shal here:
"These manacis nor promyss of plesaunce,
Thi froward speche nor thi frownyng cheer
Shal me nat meve o poynt fro my constaunce;             1090
In Crist Iesu is hol my suffisaunce,
For me list nat long processe her devise:
Thi gold, thi tresour, thi goddis I despise.

f. 132 r.    "And wher thou hast my maistir eeke accusid
Of in-constance and duplicite,                          1095
Be riht wele sur God hath hym excusid;
That he did, the counseil come of me;

---

1077  sodeynly] and sodeynly T In H Ed
1078  *castellis*] castell La Li (see n. to II, 532); castelles
        T In; castels H Ed
1079  thi] the T In Ed
1080  wil] thought T In H Ed      verray] were H
1081  al hol] stode hole and T In H Ed
1082  fallybel Ed
1083  thretis] thretenynges T In Ed; threting H
1084  oo face] of oo face T In; of oon face H
1085  knyht] prynce H
1086  atwene] atwynne T; betwene Ed      bothe] as In; bothe
        as H
1088  These] Thy T In H Ed
1089  Thi froward] ne froward T H; In froward In Ed
1090  o] a Li; one T; on Ed
1091  hol] hol all T In; all H
1092  nat] nat here Ed      her to Ed
1094  eke my mastre T
1095  in-constance] my constance H
1096  hath] om. H
1097  of] fro In

He fledde nat, God wot, for fer of the;
I was concentid to kepe hym in absence,
And ellis had he come to audience.              1100

　　"Fro the trewth me list nat declyne;
Alle thi wordis be seid but in veyn.
Of my maistir I confesse the doctryne,
For liff or deth nevir to turne ageyn
Fro Cristis feith, which stondith in certeyn, 1105
For it causith folk lame to gon vp-riht
And folk blynd for to recur ther siht.

　　"This feith so hool is fitchid in my mynde,
On-to me more precious and more deer
Than all the stonys that comen out of Ynde,   1110
Or all the richesse that thou rehersist heer,
Gold or tresour if reknyd al in feer;
Wordly worship, pompe, or veynglorie,
To feith *comparid*, be thynges transitorie.

　　"This feith in God makith me so riche and strong,
Al wordly good for it I do despise.
What shold I lenger draw the a-long?
To fals goddis in no maner wise
I wil nat do worship nor sacrifise.
Eche on be fals, have no wit nor mynde;       1120
Ye that serve hem be verray mad and blynde.

---

1098　God wot] wote H
1099　concentid] assentid T In H Ed　　in] om. T In H Ed
1103　maistir] maistry H
1107　folkes T In H Ed　　for] om. T In H Ed
1108　is fitchid] is ficchid Li; is ficched T In H; infyxed
　　　is Ed
1112　if] om. T In H Ed　　in feer] i feer Li
1113　worship] worshipis All other MSS　　or] and T H
1114　To] The H　　*comparid*] comparith La only. There are
　　　traces of change from "t" to "d" in La. See II, 938.
1116　Al] And T H
1117　shold] shal In
1118　To] The H　　wise] of wise T In Ed
1120　Eche on] Euerychone T In H　　be] by H　　have] and
　　　have T H Ed; and hath In　　no] nother T H Ed; nothe
　　　nother [sic] In　　nor] ne T
1121　Ye] He H

f. 132 v.        "Most disceyvable whan a man hath neede
                 Been your goddis, with al your mawmetrie;
                 It hath be provid afforn in my kynreede
                 And many othir born of my allye.                    1125
                 All sich rascail of purpos I defie!
                 Fals and failyng, of old tyme and newe,
                 To all ther servantis of custom most ontrewe.

                 "I cast neuyr with hem to have a-do
                 Nor make fyr vpon ther auters                       1130
                 (This my answer, take good heed herto),
                 Nor no *rechelis* cast in ther sensers,
                 Kneele afforn them this hundrid thousond yeers;
                 This is in som, for oo woord and all,
                 Myn last wil and myn answer fynall."                 1135

                 With this answer ther roos a *sodeyn* cry,
                 Noise in the peepil, clamour, and wepyng.
                 Aboute the martir thei went besily,
                 Lik woodmen vpon hym gawryng.
                 Herd al the speche, spak a-geyn no thyng,--          1140
                 The iuges manacis, the peeplis violence,--
                 Sofred al and kept his pacience.

                 The peeple, a-geyn hym vengeable and cruell,
                 To ther templis brouht hym anon riht;
                 Bi violence thei gan hym compelle                    1145

---

1130   fyr] a fire H
1131   This] This is T In H Ed
1132   *rechelis* is Li reading; rechelers La; recheles In;
          ensence T H Ed.   Ed here follows T and H.  Cf. II,
          1191.     ther] her T In H
1133   Kneele] Nor kneele T In H Ed        them] hem T In; theyme
          H
1134   and all] all & all In
1135   myn answer] my answer Li T; answer Ed
1136   roos] rose up Ed        sodey La only
1137   Noise in] Noise of Ed
1139   gawryng] gamyng In
1140   Herd al the speche] He herd of her speche T H; He herd
          all her speche In; He herd all theyr speche Ed
1141   manacis] manasse T H; manace In Ed
1142   Sofred] He suffred T In H Ed
1145   compelle] to compelle T In H Ed

To ther goddis to offre and set vp liht.
Blissed Albon, as Goddis owen knyht,
Stable of hert and hool in his entent,
To sacrifise wold neuyr assent.

f. 133 r.      The peeple than in ther furious heete          1150
Bi the iugis cruel comaundement
Thei stript hym first and with scoorgis beete
Til his body and skyn was al to-rent.
He with glad cheer suffryd his torment;
His eyen vp lift, to God began a-braide,          1155
And to the Lord devoutly thus he saide:

    "Lord God," quod he, "Keepe myn inward thouht;
Grant of thi grace in my grevous peyn
Pacience, that I ne grutche noht.
Off thi mercy, O Iesu, nat disdeyn          1160
My freel flessh fro murmour to restreyn,
Sith that my wil stant hoole, withouten striff,
To the to offren bodi, sowle, and lyff.

    "Remembre, Lord, on thi seruant Albon,
For nouthir floodis, stormys, wynd, nor reyn          1165
May hurt that hous bilt on a stable ston.

---

1146   set] to set T Ed
1148   Stable of] Stable in H
1149   wold] he wolde T H
1151   iugis] iewes Ed
1152   hym] hem In
1153   skyn] his skynne H
1154   He] But he T In H Ed
1155   began] and began T In H
1156   thus] this H
1157   MS H is misbound; the text in correct sequence jumps
           from f. 30 v. to f. 47 r. as presently bound.
1159   grutche] gruch Li; grocche T; grucche In; grouche H;
           grudge Ed
1163   to] om. La Li      bodi] my T In H Ed      and lyff] and
           eke my lyfe Ed
1164   Lord] the lord T In H Ed
1165   floodis] flody T In H Ed
1166   May] My La; May not T H (in T "not" inserted by
           correcting hand)      a] om. Ed

And semblably it is but seldom seyn,
Who bildith in Crist bildith nat in veyn;
Sith my bildyng stant holly in thi grace,
Suffre nat my will remeve from his place.          1170

"My vois, my tonge, my will fully recorde;
All of assent, without excepcioun,
For liff nor deth, thei nevir shal discorde.
But thou, Iesu, madist my redempcioun;
Now bi the vertu of thi passioun,                1175
O blissid Lord, graunt me constaunce
Among my peynes, hool will and meeke soffraunce."

f. 133 v.   Whil the martir was scorgid and bete,
This was his vois, on Crist Iesu to crye;
To calle his helpe wolde neuer lete,             1180
Nouthir for smert nor peynful tormentrye.
To paynym lawe he wold nevir applie,
Nouthir for manace, rebuke, nor rigour,
For fair speche, for promys, nor favour.

Lik a diamant, he wold nat be brooke          1185
Nor restreyned from his old constaunce;
Fro Cristis feith thei myht hym nat revoke
With all ther feyned woordis of plesaunce.
Than was he put vndir gouernaunce
Of the iuge, as a lamb among houndis,            1190
Ful sixe wikes nat to passe his boundis.

---

1167   See *Explanatory Notes*.  semblable H       but] ful All
       other MSS       Seldom] seld T H Ed; sylde In
1168   Who] Who that T In H      in Crist] on Crist T In H;
       bildith] he bildith T In H
1170   his] this T In H Ed
1171   my tonge, my will] my will my tounge H
1172   without] withouten T In; withouten eny H
1173   nor] for T In H Ed
1174   my] our Ed
1177   my] the Ed
1180   See *Explanatory Notes*.
1181   nor] om. T In H
1182   To paynym] Vnto peynems
1183   nor] or T In H
1185   he] yt H
1186   restreyned] receyued H      old] wilde H
1187   hym nat] nott hym T In H; not Ed
1190   Of] As H      as] om. H
1191   See *Explanatory Notes*.  wikes] monthes T In H; wekes Ed

Duryng this tyme (the book makith mencioun),
He, streyhtly kept of more than oon or tweyn,
Lik a martir hold in streiht prisoun,
Myht nat reche ferther than his cheyn.                    1195
The elementis his wrongis gan compleyn
In ther maner, a-geyn naturis lawe,
Ther benefises of kynde to with-drawe.

Vpon the erthe on herbe, gras, or flour,
All this tyme was no dewe i-seene;                        1200
The grounde to cherissh cam nothir reyn nor shour,
Nor no moistour fil vpon the greene.
Flora slept, that is of flours queene;
Eolus the smyth with his wyndis soft
Al this while enspired nat a-loft.                        1205

f. 134 r.    The erthe scaldid with fervence of the sonne,
Heete on nyhtis was intollerable;
Ther grew no frute; schyes wer al donne;
Greyn cam non vp; lond was nat arrable.
Thus, bi a *maner* compleynt lamentable,                 1210
Heuen and erthe compleynedyn of riht
The gret iniurie doon to Goddis knyht.

---

1196  gan] gan to T In H Ed
1197  ther] a In
1198  benefettes T; benefites In; benefettis H; benefytes Ed
1199  or] ne T In; nor Ed
1200  All this tyme] on al thes T In; On these H; On all
         these thre Ed      i-seene] seyne H; sene Ed
1202  Nor] For T In H Ed      moistour] moystre T In; moyste H;
         moisture Ed
1203  of] the T In Ed; om. H      flours] *floras* H
1204  smyth] smothe T In H Ed. See *Glossary*. with his] om.
         T In H Ed
1206  scaldid] scalled H; scaldeth Ed      with] with the T In
         H Ed
1207  on tollerable H
1208  schyes] skyes Li; the skyes T In H Ed
1209  Greynes come non / vplande was not erable Ed      lond]
         the lond H      was] om. H      nat] noon Ed; nott T;
         not H Ed
1210  a] om. H      *maner*] man La Li In; maner of T
1211  compleynedyn] compleyned hem T H; compleynen In;
         complayned them Ed
1212  gret] om. T In H Ed      Goddis] goddis owne H

The peeple playned lakkyng of vitaile,
Dempt it causid bi som sorcerie
That elementis list holden a bataile 1215
For Cristis knyht, to holden vp his partie
Geyn myscreauntis with ther turmentrie,
Maugre ther malis to make the martir strong,
To shewe bi signes paynyms did hym wrong.

Asclepeodot, sittyng as iuge than, 1220
Though he to Albon had gret hatereede,
Yit bi-cause of Dioclician
To slee the martir durst nat proceede
Til he had sent lettres, as I reede,
Vp to the Emperour, rehersyng how Albon 1225
For-saken hadde ther goddis euerychon,

Enfourmyng hym of his obstynacye,
How all ther goddis he sett al-so at nouht,
And how ther power he pleynly dooth defye;
Was maade Cristen of hert, will, and thouht, 1230
And hath al-so sotil weyes souht
The peeplis hert fro goddis to withdrawe,
In ther despite, to folwe a newe lawe.

f. 134 v.    But, for the gret famyliarite
Which Albon had with the Emperour, 1235
Bi-cause also of his gret dignyte,--

---

1213  lakkyng] for lak T H; for lackyng Ed
1214  it causid bi] cause of T In H; it cause of Ed
1215  elementis] the elementis T In H; Thelementis Ed
        holden] to holde Ed
1216  holde Li; hold Ed
1217  Ageyne T In H Ed
1218  martir] matier H
1219  paynyms] that the peynems T In H
1220  iuge] a iuge H
1223  durst] he durst T H
1225  Vp to] Vnto T In H; To Ed
1228  al-so] om. T H
1229  he pleynly dooth] he doth pleynly T In H; pleynly he
        doth Ed
1230  Was] And was T In H Ed
1231  sotil] sotelly T In H; subtylly Ed      weyes] wyse H
        ·souht] thought Ed
1232  peeplis hert] peple hertis T In H; peoples hertes Ed
        fro] from our T In H      to] om. Ed
1234  gret] great and kynde Ed

And of his kyn had so gret favour,--
The iuge drad for to do rigour
Vpon this prynce of deth bi cruelte
Til fro the Emperour he had auctorite,                    1240

    And ther be doon execucioun
Bi high avis of al the hool empir,
To punyssh all thoo for fals rebellioun
Which to distroie your goddis so desir.
With which lettres the emperour, set a-fire,    1245
Bood no lenger, in al hast gan ordeyne
To send his felaw doun into Briteyne.

    And in gret hast (the story tellith vs)
Dioclician hath sent a gret power
With *Maxymyan*, callid Herculyus,                    1250
In-to Briteyn to cerche out the maner;
Wher that any wer founde ferr or neer,
Of Cristis feith, to sleen hem evirychon
Without mercy, except *only* Albon,--

    His liff to save bi a condicioun:                    1255
Yiff to ther sect he wold a-geyn resorte,
Fro Cristis lawe turne his opynyoun,
Off ther goddis the statutis to supporte,

---

1238  The] And the T In H; That the Ed
1239  bi] or T In H Ed
1241  And] And but T In H Ed        be] om. Ed        doon] done by
      In; done great Ed
1242  avis] avice T; avise In H; aduise Ed
1243  for] fro T In H; from Ed
1244  so] do H
1246  Bood] Abode T In H Ed        in al hast] but in all hast T
      In H; but hastyly Ed
1247  felaw] felow Maximian In
1248  vs] thus T In H; expresse Ed
1250  *Maxymyan*] Maxynyyan La        Herculyus] hercules T In;
      Herculesse Ed
1251  maner] manace In; mattier Ed
1253  hem] om. T In H Ed
1254  *only*] om. La Li
1256  sect] sectes Ed        resorte] restore Ed
1257  lawe] feith H; loore Ed
1258  statutis] statute In

To Dioclician that thei may reporte
How that Albon sore doth repent                          1260
To Cristis feith that evir he did assent.

f. 135 r.    Made hym promys, so that he wole tourne
To ther ydolis with feyned fair language;
Among with thretis thei daily hym adiorne
To pervert his hert and his corage.                      1265
But evir i-lik of cheer and of visage,
Tween fire and watir, now hard, now blandisshyng,
From his constaunce thei myht hym nevir bryng.

Lik a strong tour bilt on an high mounteyn,
Took non heed of ther *monyciouns*,                      1270
Stood in our feith so stable and so certeyn
That riche promys of castellis and of touns
With many *lordshipis* in dyvers regiouns
He set at nouht, bi grace and bi vertu
His ground so stable a-bod in Crist Iesu.                1275

Than bi precepte of Dioclician,
Yiff he nat chaunge for fairnesse nor for dreede,

---

1259   thei] he T H
1260   sore doth] dooth sore him T In H; doth hym sore Ed
1261   evir] om. In Ed
1262   tourne] tornyn T; turned In; termyne H; turnen Ed
1264   thretis] thretenynges T H; thretynges In; thretninges
       Ed        adiorne] adiuren T In Ed; aiuryen H
1266   of visage] visage T In H
1267   Tween] Betwene T In H Ed
1268   hym] om. H
1269   an] a In        high] om. H
1270-71  These lines reversed in T, In, and H.
1270   mocions La; monyciouns certeyne ("certeyne" in
       different ink) T
1271   Stood] He stood ("He" in margin) T        so certeyn]
       victorious (other ink and hand, erased word beneath)
       T; ee certeyne [sic] In
1272   That] Their T In H Ed        of touns] om. "of" T In;
       towrs H
1273   *lordshipis*] lordship La; see note to II, 532; cf. II,
       1078.
1275   so] to In        a-bod] a bove In
1277   fairnesse] fere H        nor] ne In

The charge was yove to Maxymyan
Bi iugement and doome to takyn heede
To assygne a knyht to smyten of his hede;                    1280
Sich oon that had in knyhthod gret renoun
Shuld on this prince doon excecucioun.

It was also comandid in sentence
Off the Emperour that Amphibalus,
Yiff he wer take, bi mortal violence,                    1285
Withoute mercy shuld be servid thus
Bi iugement cruel and furious:
Made nakid first and to a stak bounde,
At his navil made a large wounde,

f. 135 v.   He compellid among that *cruel* route,                    1290
At the navil his bowelis to be take
And his roppis cerclid rond a-boute
Lyk a long rope teyd vnto a stake,
And of his liff an ende for to make;
Aldir-last thei, voide of al pite,                    1295
Smyte of his hed bi furious cruelte.

This was the doom touchyng the tormentis
Off blissid Albon and Amphibalus,
Falsly concludid in the iugementis
Of Maximyan (myn auctour tellith thus).                    1300
With Asclepeodot, wood and contrarious,

---

1278   yove] yeven T H Ed; yeve In       to] fro H
1280   smyten] smyte T In H
1281   that] as Ed       gret] high T In Ed
1283   It was also] This was so T In H Ed       in] by T In
       H Ed
1285   mortal] notable T In H Ed
1288   stak] stok T H; stoke In; stake Ed
1289   At] And at T H
1290   that] the T In H Ed       cruel] crue La
1292   roppis] guttis T In H Ed       cerclid] serchid T In H Ed
       rond] round Li; rowde [sic] T; rounde In H Ed
1293   vnto] to H Ed       a stake] that stake Li
1294   an] so an T In H Ed       for] om. T In H Ed
1295   Aldir] And att T In Ed; And at the H       thei] om. T In
       H Ed
1296   Smyte] Smyten T In H
1297   This] Thus H
1299   concludid] concluding H       the] their T; her H

In that cite, bothe to present,
Of Verolamye, which gaff this iugement.

The citeceynes gadrid enviroun
For this mateer with gret diligence,                    1305
Bothe of Londoun and many othir toun,
Of iugement to heeryn the sentence
Yove on Albon in opyn audience
Vndir these wordis put in remembraunce,
As ye shal her rehersid in substaunce:                  1310

Tyme of the Emperour Dioclician
Whan he stood hihest in his mageste,
At Verolamye (the stori telle can),
Whan Albon was lord of that cite,
Callid tho daies for his dygnyte                        1315
(Record on cronyclis which that lyst nat feyn),
Prynce of knyhtis and stiward of Breteyn,

f. 136 r.      Duryng his liff to have possessioun
As his power afforn hath be practised,
But now for he bi fals rebellioun                       1320
Off wilfulnesse and malis hath despised,
Affor thes daies bi antiquyte divised,
The olde worshepis, notable and famous,
Doon to Iubiter, Appollo, and Venus,

---

1302  to] two there T In H Ed
1303  Of] In T In H Ed
1304  enviroun] euerychone H
1306  of] at T In
1307  here T Ed
1308  Yove] Yf H; Yoven Ed      on] vpon T In H Ed
1309  these] this T
1312  hihest in his mageste] in his hihest maieste T; in high
        mageste H
1313  the] as the In
1315  Callid tho daies] Tho dayes callid T In Ed; Two dayes
        called H
1316  Record on] Recordyd in T In; Recorde in H; Recorde of
        Ed      that] om. H
1319  As his] All his T In Ed; All this H      afforn] beforn
        In
1320  bi] bee H
1322  Affor] A forn T In H; Beforne Ed      bi] of (under-
        pointed, bi inserted in margin in similar hand) La;
        bi All other MSS.
1323  worship H

For which cause, lat every man tak heed,      1325
Lik as the lawe concludid hath of riht,
Bi iugement in hast he to be dede,
His hed smet of first in the peeplis siht
Bi the hondis of som old worthi knyht,--
Cause the martir *was of* high renoun          1330
Ther shuld a knyht doon excecucioun.

Bi doom also aftir whan he wer ded,
The place assygned bi sort or aventur,
Fro the body whan partid is the hed,
The coors ther shuld have his sepultur        1335
Passyng a-nothir, pryvat, creature;
Ther-to, bi grace, the body with the hed
Ioyned to-gidre in a gret chest of led,

With hym buried his cros and his sclaveyn,
A large tombe for a memoriall.                 1340
This was the doom of the iugis tweyn
In Verolamye, a cite roiall,
For to avenge ther goddis infernall,
Vpon Albon whom thei did deeme
Geyn ther lawis for a fals blaspheeme.         1345

f. 136 v.    Dempte he was cause of the mysaventur,
That her londis brouht forth no greyn,
The benefetis with-drawen of natur.
To cherissh ther frute cam ther no dew nor reyn;

---

1326   concludid hath] concludith T In H Ed
1328   smet] smyt Li; smeten T H; smyten In Ed
1329   handes Ed      old] wolde H
1330   Cause] Bicause T In H Ed      *was of*] of his La only
1332   aftir] that aftir H; aftir that T In
1334   is] was All other MSS
1335   coors] crosse Li T In H; corps Ed
1337   bi grace] be grave Li T In H; be grauen Ed
1339   his cros] was his crosse T H
1342   a cite] a Cite ful Li; Cite full T In H Ed
1343   For] om. T In H Ed
1345   Geyn] Ageyne T In H Ed
1346   the] om. T In H Ed
1347   greynes In
1348   The] Ther T H
1349   ther no] nether T In H; noder Ed      reyn] reynes In

Bi sodeyn vengeaunce, as ye han herd seyn,          1350
Dyversly sorwis wer made double.
To fynde the ground that causid al this trouble,--

Outhir it cam bi som froward fortune,
Bi witche-craft, or bi som sorcerie,
Which so long doth vpon hem contune,--          1355
Outhir bi magik or bi fals nygromancie,--
Eche man dempte aftir his fantasie;
Withynne the cite ther seid eek many oon
It come for vengeaunce doon to Seynt Albon.

With this vnwar sodeyn aduersite          1360
I-troublid was al that regioun.
In Verolamye grettest of that cite
Made among hem a convocacioun.
In all the contres, of cite, borugh, and toun
The wisest cam doun from eche partie          1365
Geyn this myscheff to shape a remedie;

Among hem silff cast a providence.
Wrong that was doon to Alboun in that toun
Ageyn trouthe and good concience
Off this myscheef was cheef occasioun,          1370

---

1350  herd] herd me Li T Ed; me In
1351  sorwis] their sorowes T In Ed; her sorow H
1352  ground] cause Ed          that] what T In H Ed          causid]
         made Ed
1353  froward] soden In          fortune] auenture Ed
1354  som] om. Ed
1355  doth vpon hem contune] vpon them doth continue T; vpon
         them continuee In; vpon them did continue H; vpon
         them doth endure Ed.  See rime above and Glossary
         s.v. "contune."  See Note to II, 612.
1356  magik] Artmagik T In H Ed          fals] om. T In H Ed
1357  man] om. T In H Ed
1358  ther] they Ed          eek] om. In          many] may T
1359  doon to] of T In H Ed
1360  vnwar sodeyn] unwar and soden H; sodeyn unware Ed
1361  that] the Ed
1362  In] Of T In H Ed          grettest] the grettest T In H Ed
1364  In] Of T In H Ed          contres] countre Ed          of] om. H
         and] or Li T In H
1367  cast] they cast H          a] of Li; see Glossary.
1369  Ageyn] and ageyne T          and] of T In H

And, bi assent, to relece his persoun;
Ther aduersite so myht ben amendid--
Bi mene of hym to whom thei had offendid.

f. 137 r.    Bare foot and bare *hed* whan that he was take,
Lik a prisoner brouht to ther presence,                 1375
On this mater a counceil thei did make,
Dempt of resoun in hym was noon offence,
For at *them* silf began this violence,
And he stood quyte in ther opynyoun,
Of his iniurie havyng compassioun.                      1380

Thei considred his blood and his kynreede,
His alliaunce, and his high noblesse,
For whiche thei stood a parcel in gret dreede,
All the cite trowblid with hevynesse
To seen ther lord brouht in sich distresse,             1385
Causyng that cite and that famous toun
To stond in rumour and gret discencioun,

Seeyng ther stiward that was so noble a knyht
And a free man born of that cite,
His famous lyne doun descendid riht                     1390
Fro the Romayns of old antiquyte:
Bi comparisouns cronycles, who lyst, see
The stok conveied of hym, that was so good,
First from Troianys, and from the Romayn blood.

---

1371  persoun] prison Ed
1372  aduersiteis H        so myht ben] myght soo be H
1374  *hed*] <u>om</u>. La Li Ed
1376  On] Of T In H Ed        did] canne T; gan In H Ed
1378  *them*] hym La; hem T In H
1382  high] <u>om</u>. In        noblesse] noblenesse T In H
1383  thei] <u>the</u> In
1384  hevynesse] grete hevynesse H
1385  seen] sye H; se Ed
1386  Causyng] Caused H
1389  a free man born of] a man fre born of T In H; a man fre
       fre born in H
1390  descendid] descendith T H; descendyng of In; descendyng
       Ed
1392  comparisoun T In H Ed        cronycles] corownycles H; the
       cronycle Ed        see] here or see H
1394  the] <u>om</u>. T In H Ed

First fro the party for to speke of Troie,   1395
He hadde with Ector magnanymyte,
Off whoos nobles al Bryteyn may have ioie,
Sad as Scipioun, voide of duplicite,
An Verolamye, that famous old cite,
May weel reioissh, renewid ever i-liche,          1400
With his reliques that thei be made so riche.

f. 137 v.      And to reherse of his condiciouns,
A rihtful prynce in al his governaunce
In whom wer nevir founde occasiouns
Off froward mevyng nor double variaunce,          1405
Nevir ment to no man displesaunce.
Peised al *this, allas, voide of* refuge,
Now, lik a theeff, he stant be-forn a iuge.

But to refourme of birth his liberte
Cheef of the cite did *her* besy peyn             1410
This noble prynce a-mong hem to go fre
Fro bonde of fetris and noise of any cheyn,
But ther-vpon the martir gan compleyn
Withynne hym silf lest siche noise and soun
In any wise shuld lett his passioun.              1415

---

1395   fro] for T H
1397   nobles] noblesse T In Ed; noblenesse H       have] o̲m̲. T
       H
1398   as] a Ed
1399   And All other MSS
1401   thei be] it is Ed
1402   And to] And so to T In; And so H
1403   his] o̲m̲. In
1404   wer] was T In H Ed
1405   mevyng] meeuyng (meenyng ?) Li T In; meanyng Ed.   C̲f̲. II,
       985 a̲n̲d̲ n̲.     nor] no Li
1407   *this allas voide of* A̲l̲l̲ other M̲S̲S̲] thyng voide of al La
1408   be-forn] a fore T In; be fore H; aforne Ed       a] the
       A̲l̲l̲ other M̲S̲S̲
1409   of birth his liberte] his birth and liberte T In H Ed
1410   Cheef] The cheef T In H Ed      *her*] his La; theyr Ed
1411   to] o̲m̲. T
1412   of fetris] and F̲e̲t̲r̲e̲s̲ T In; or fetris H Ed       and
       noise] or noise T In H Ed
1414   hym] o̲m̲. T      and] or T In H      soun] foysoun H

That kynde of mercy which thei did hym shewe
Of his peynes bi a maner of allegeaunce
The martir dempte, to speke in wordis fewe,
It was to hym most odyous vengeaunce,
For his desir and his hertly plesaunce          1420
Was oonly this, short processe for to make,
To suffre deth only for Cristis sake.

f. 138 v.   With *hertly* sobbyng and profound science deepe,
Toward heuen meekely he cast his siht,
Of inward constreynt pitously gann weepe,        1425
The cros afforn hym deuoutly held vpriht,
Cryeng to Iesu, "Have mercy on thi knyht;
Lat nat the feende bi no collusioun
Ster the peeple to let my passioun."

f. 139 r.   To the peeple turnyng his knyhtly face,     1430
A-braide to them of hert and hool corage:
"Your feyned favour, your dissimyled grace
May in this cas do me non auauntage,
Fully disposid to perfourme my viage,

---

1416   thei] he In       shewe] suche was In
1417   peyne H       bi a maner of] bamaner Li
1419   to] om. In
1420   hertly] hasty H; herty Ed
1421   oonly this] This only In; only thus H
1422   After this line there occurs in La a stanza which
          belongs at l. 1451 and is there repeated in the
          manuscript, in substantially the same form (see n.
          to 1451-73). At l. 1422, the stanza is cancelled by
          'va...cat' in right margin at beginning and end of
          the stanza.
1423-29  This short folio in La, one quarter as tall as the
          rest, and blank on recto, is so inserted as to cover
          and replace misplaced stanza discussed in note to l.
          1422. It is in the La hand.
1423   herly La; hertly Li T In; hertty H Ed      and profound
          science deepe] and profound science T In; and profound
          science eke H; profound and depe Ed
1424   meekely he] meekely T; he meekely H
1425   gann] can Ed
1428   collusioun] conclusion H
1430   To the] To this prince the H      his knyhtly] there H
1431   To] vnto T In H Ed
1432   dissimyled] dissemely H; dissymuled Ed

For to complissh lik as I have be-gonne.                1435
In Crist Iesu my tryumphe may be wonne.

"Sith I am reedy to endur peyn
Of my free wil, whi sofre ye so long?
Of my desires desyr most sovereyn,
For Cristis sake t'endur peynes strong,                1440
My martirdam whi do ye so prolong?
In your entent ageyn me ye don erre,
That I coveite, so *long* to differr.

"I mervayl moche how that ye may susteene
Of necligence so long for t'abyde,                1445
Whil the mateer is newe, fressh and greene,
Excecucioun for to set a-side.
Look your statutis and ther-on doth provide;
Vn-to your goddis reportith how that I
Of al this world am the most enmye.                1450

"Sith thei be wrouht *of* men that ben mortall,
Vnworthi preevid to any dignyte,
Forgid ydolis of stoon and of metall

---

1435  accomplysshe Ed      I] om. In
1437  Sith] Sith that T In
1439  desires] desyre Ed      desyr] I desyr T In H Ed
1441  My] By H      so] so longe H
1443  I] I do T In H Ed      long] long to long La; long ye
       do In      to differr] om. "to" In
1444  moche] om. T In H Ed      that] om. T In Ed
1445  for] om. T In H Ed
1446  mateer] martyr T In H Ed      newe] now In
1447  to] om. H
1448  ther-on] thervpon T In H Ed      doth] so T H; do In;
       om. Ed
1449  reporth In
1450  the] her T In H; ther Ed      enmye] envy H
1451-57  also appear earlier in La; cf. 1. 1422, n. The
       variants of this earlier form are recorded as "La2."
       Both passages are in the same hand. The variants
       suggest the degree of liberty a scribe might take with
       his text.
1451  wrouht] wroth In; worthy H      of] bi La only (La2 reads
       "of")      ben] be La2
1452  preevid] previd La2      to any] to my T In; in any H;
       to beare Any Ed
1453  Forgid] But forged Ed      of metall] om. "of" H Ed

Vn-to whoos froward *vsurpid* deite
Foolis do wrong to kneele vpon ther kne;                   1455
Who callith to them thei yeve non audience,
Dombe as a stok, voide of al intelligence.

f. 139 v.     "A fool is he among foolis alle
To a blynd stok that kneleeth to ha siht,
And so is he that dooth for strenghe calle             1460
To hym that hath no power nor no myht,
Can nat discerne atweene derknesse and liht.
Large-lippid, but wordis have thei non;
Of tong mewet and dul as stok or ston.

"O fruteles hope!  O fals hope disespeired!
O vanite!  O rudnesse detestable!
O apparence with wanhope foul appeired!
O ygnoraunce passyng abhomynable!
O ydalatres of corage most vnstable,
Whi worship ye in your conceites blynd                 1470
Cursid mawmetis that nouthir ha wit nor mynde?

"Thei be provid wors of condicioun,
Lasse of power, sothly, than be ye.
Of wordly thynges ye have inspeccioun;
Thei have gret eyen, yit thei may nat see,             1475

---

1454   *vsurpid*] om. La; deite vsurpid [sic] T; vsurpid deite
       In H; Falsely usurped agayne the deyte Ed
1456   Who] For who Ed      yeve] give La²; yef T; yeve Ed
1457   al] all La²; om. Ed
1459   ha] haue T In H Ed
1461   hath] om. H      nor no] ne H
1462   atweene] betweene T In Ed; by twene H
1463   but] om. T In H Ed      worthis H
1464   mewet] mwet Li; meut H; meued Ed      and dul as] as any
       T H Ed; as In
1465   o fals] of fals H      hope] trust All other MSS
       disepeyred In; dishoperyd H; dispayred Ed
1471   "that" is followed by "h" diagonally cancelled in La.
       nouthir] nothe T; nother In Ed; never H      ha] han
       (or "hau") Li; haue T In Ed; had H; have Ed
1472   of] in H
1475   may] mow Li T In

Boistous hondis, felyng no thyng, parde!
Ther armys long may make no deffence;
With ther deffe eris may yiff non audience.

"What thyng is wors than yeve the souereynte
Of your handwerk to forged fals ymages,          1480
Deff, blynd, and domb, vnto whos deite,
Though ye calle ay to-fore ther ded visages,
Thei knowe no thyng th'entent of your langages,
Of all five wittis thei been so defectiff.
What causith this but lak of sowles and liff?  1485

f. 140 r.          "For how myht he verrayly in deede
Without feelyng of ioie or hevynesse
Restore to liff folk that been dede
Or make hem hool that pleyn on her siknesse?
For al deceite, trouble, and doublenesse          1490
Of wordly myscheevis, souht on eche partie
Was first brouht in bi fals ydolatrye.

"A man that hath memorie and resoun,
Whom God hath made lik to his ymage,
Is foule blent in his discrecioun          1495
To fals ydoles to knele or doon homage.
Woo be to them, ruyne, and damage
Trouble, myscheeff, vn-to on and all,

---

1476   felyng] feele Li; thei fele T In H Ed
1477   may] thei may T In H; they Ed
1478   yiff] yeve T In H; haue Ed
1480   handwerk] owne honde H          forged] forge ("d" added
          above in T) T In H
1482   ye] they H          ay] all H          to-fore] afore H; afforne
          Ed          ded] om. T In H Ed
1484   all] all the H          defectiff] detectyfe H
1485   this] thus H          sowles] sowle T In H Ed
1488   folk] folkes T In H Ed          that] om. H
1489   on] of T H Ed
1490   al] al his H          deceite, trouble, and] distresse
          disceyte or Ed
1491   on] in T H
1493   memorie] wit memory H          and] of T In Ed
1494   Whom] When H          lik] the lik H
1495   Is] His H
1497   Woo] Who La

To sich mawmettis that for helpe call!"

Whan the paynymes herd and vndirstood 1500
That thei nat myht remeve his conscience
From Crist Iesu that deide vpon the roode
For fair nor foule, favour nor violence,
Took her conceil and all of oo sentence
A place assygned lik ther oppynyoun: 1505
Schuld at Holmerste suffre passioun.

In ther oppynyoun bi contraversie
Stood atte debate as thei wer applied,
What maner deth Albon schold dye,
Which hath ther goddis and ther sect denyed. 1510
Som on a cros wold han hym crucified;
Othir ther wer, which did in malis rave,
Wold have hym quyk buried in his grave.

f. 140 v.     Som also afforn ar he wer ded,
Of fals envie and furious woodnesse, 1515
Wold have his eyn rent out of his hed,
That he sholde in myscheff of blyndnesse,
Al desolat and abiect in derknesse,
Folwe his maistir with his eyen blynde,
Of aventur til he myht hym fynde, 1520

Eche on concludyng that he shal be ded,
And fynally, this was ther iugement,

---

1499  mawmettis] mawmettri T In Ed; mawmentry H
1501  nat myht] <u>reversed</u>, T In H Ed
1502  the] a In
1503  favour] for favour T In H Ed
1504  Took] To do be T; To be In; To do by H Ed
1506  holmeherst T; holmhurst In H; Holmehurst Ed
       passioun] his passioun Ed
1509  maner] maner of T In H
1510  ther goddis] her goddes T H; <u>om</u>. "ther" In
1512  which] that Ed
1513  buried] karued Ed
1514  ar] or Li In Ed; <u>om</u>. T H
1515  and] <u>om</u>. T In H
1516  rent] <u>om</u>. T In H Ed
1517  of] and T H
1521  shal] shulde T In H

Lad to Holmerst, and ther smet of his hed,--
The iuge cruel with paynymes of assent.
And lik a lamb mong wolvis al to-rent,                1525
To-ward his deth and pitous passioun,
In cheynes bounde, lad hym thorugh the toun.

No favour shewid, lettyng, nor obstacle,
But cruel rigour voide of al pite.
Lik as men gon to some vncouth spectacle,             1530
Peeple cam doun his martirdam to see,
The iuge allone left in the cite.
Lik tormentours this was ther furious cry:
"Out of this toun drawith forth our enmy.

"B'experience at eye ye may deeme,                    1535
Lik his desert, so folwith hym his chaunce,
To our goddis most odious blaspheeme,
Ground and gynnyng of our sodeyn grevaunce."
On whom thei list to shewe ther *vengance*,
This was ther noise, ferr from al resoun,             1540
As thei hym ladde toward his passioun.

f. 141 r.     Ther was so gret concours of folk aboute,
The multitude gan al-way multiplie;
Of paynymes contrarious was the route;
The grond so ful vpon eche partie,                    1545
Men myht vnethe any space espie
To stonde vpon, myn auctour list nat feyn,
Whan blissid Albon was lad on-to his peyn.

---

1523  to] vnto T In H      smet] to smyte T In; smote H;
      smyte Ed
1524  iuge cruel] cruell iuge T In H; cruell iuges Ed
      of] of on In
1525  And] om. T In H Ed
1530  gon] goth H
1534  this] the In      drawith] drawe Ed
1535  at] at the In
1536  desert] diffectyfe (?) H
1538  gynnyng] begynning H
1539  *vengance*] grevaunce La
1542  concours] prece H
1543  multiplie] to multiplie T In H Ed
1544  contrarious] contagious T In H Ed
1545  vpon] of T H; on In Ed      eche] euery Ed
1548  blissid] om. T H      on-to] toward All other MSS

The fervent heete of the somers sonne
Hath with his stremys the soile so clad and brent,
Vpon the Leon as he is cours hath ronne,
With his brennyng the ground was al—most shent.
Vndir ther feete, as the peeple went,
The soile so hot, of sodeyn aventur,
For eschaufyng thei myht nat endure.                    1555

*Lastyng* this heete, that Phebus schoon so cleer,
The peeple in noumbre wex rather more than lasse,
Til that thei cam to a gret ryveer
Whos sturdy wawis wold nat suffre hem passe;
The gret depnes gan hem to manasse,                     1560
The brigge streite, the prees so gret and huge,
That many oon was dreynt in that deluge.

Gret prees of peeple doun to the watir cam,
The ryver deepe, the brigge narwe and small;
Thei that coude, ouyr the ryver swam;                   1565
Who coude nat swymme turnyd ovir as a ball.
The comberous prees caused many a fall;
The noise was gret, the rumour and compleynt,
In this passage, of peeple that was dreynt.

f. 141 v.    Favour was non of brothir vn-to brothir,  1570
Thei *wer* so besy to passe the ryver;

---

1549  fervent] firment H      heete] hote H      somers] somer
         All other MSS
1550  soile] solis H
1551  Vpon] Vp in T In H Ed      he is] his All other MSS.
         See *Explanatory Notes*.
1553  ther] the T In H Ed      as] wher as All other MSS
         the] om. H
1555  eschaufyng] enchaufyng T In H Ed
1556  *Lastyng*] Hastyng La      that] whan In Ed
1557  wex] waxid T In H Ed
1561  brigge] bruge In; brydge Ed      prees] peple T In H Ed
1562  was] were Ed      deluge] flouge H
1563  to] in H
1565  coude] om. H      swam] swyme In
1566  Who] who that T In H Ed      swymme] swymmen In; om. Ed
1567  comberous] cummerment of H
1569  this] his T In      a] om. H
1570  was] was ther In
1571  *wer*] was La      passe] passe ouere H

In that gret prees eche man oppressid othir;
To passe the brygge ther was so gret daunger.
The heete, inportable that tyme of the yeer,
Causid manyon which at the brygge stood,          1575
For gret feyntnesse to fallen in the flood.

This gret myscheeff whan Albon gan behold,
Mevid of mercy and compassioun,
With wepyng eyen, as he to watir wold,
Vn-to the erthe fil on knees doun.          1580
His look vp cast with gret devocioun,
Toward heuen makyng his praieer,
To Iesu Crist seide as ye shal heer:

"O Lord Iesu, from whos blissid side,
Whan thou for man wer nailed on the rood,          1585
Thorugh whoos hert ther did a sper glide,
At which wounde ran watir out and blood,
O blissid Lord, mercyfull and good,
So as I saugh in myn avisioun
Out of thyn hert too licours ren doun,          1590

"That is to seyn, red blood and watir cleer,
The too licours of our redempcioun,
At my request drye vp this riveer,
Staunche the flood and her myn orysoun,
And take this peeple vndir proteccioun.          1595
Suffre that thei with drye feet may weende

---

1572   prees] pride T In Ed      man] om. H
1573   To] Soo H      brygge] brugge T; bruge In; byrgge H;
          brydge Ed
1576   feyntnesse] feyntise In      in] in to H Ed
1578   and] and of Ed
1579   he] thei T Ed; the In H      to] om. T In H Ed
1580   on] on his All other MSS
1583   Crist Iesu All other MSS
1584   from whos] owte of whos T In H Ed
1585   on] or H
1587   At] And H
1590   ren doun] ranne oute ("oute" struck out, "adowne" in
          margin, different hand and ink) T; ranne doune In;
          oute ronne H; ranne adown Ed
1592   The] Thei T In H; Those Ed
1595   this] these H      vndir] vndir thi T In H Ed

Of my passioun for to seen an eende."

f. 142 r.    And whil the teeris from his eyn ran,
Doun bi his cheekis vpon eche partie,
Bi devout praier of this holy man            1600
All sodeynly the river was maad drye,
The floodis, staunchid, vanysshid lik a skye.
It nedith nat the maner out to cerche
Whan God bi grace list any thyng werche.

For he that made, maugre Pharaoo,        1605
His peeple of Israel to passe the Red See
With drye foot, the same Lord also,
Whil that Albon kneelid on his knee,
Prayeng, the Lord of grace and of pite
Grauntid the peeple to have inspeccioun     1610
And passe the river to seen his passioun.

An vncouth mervaile, a gracious myracle!
Folk drowned, lowe at the botme seyn
(With Goddis myht wher may be non obstacle),
The river drye, founde wer a-geyn;       1615
Void of moistour, smothe was the pleyn.
Of the holy martir the merite alwey morid;
Folk afforn drowned to liff wer restorid.

---

1597   for] <u>om</u>. T In H Ed     seen] se H Ed
1598   whyls Ed
1599   vpon] on T In H Ed
1602   flode T H Ed     lik] as Ed
1603   It nedith] He nedid T H Ed; hit nedyd In
1604   werche] to werche T In H Ed
1605   maugre] this H
1606   His] The T In H Ed     to] <u>om</u>. T In H Ed
1607   foot] feet T In H Ed     also] euen so Ed
1608   Whil] Was Ed     on] vpon T In H Ed
1609   of pite] <u>om</u>. "of" Ed
1610   Grauntid] Graunt T In H Ed
1613   Folkes T In H Ed     at] in H     the] <u>om</u>. In
1614   wher] So <u>all</u> <u>MSS</u>, <u>although</u> "<u>ther</u>" <u>seems</u> <u>necessary</u> <u>to</u>
       the <u>sense</u>.
1615   wer] was T H Ed
1616   the] and Ed
1617   merite] martir Li; vertu T In H Ed
1618   wer] was H

No tokne of deth was in ther face seyn,
Quyk and liffly to every mannys siht.          1620
Thes grete myracles, notable in certeyn,
First of the river dryed bi Goddis myht,
All this considred, the silue same knyht
Which was assygned for to do vengeance
On blissed Albon fil in repentaunce.          1625

f. 142 v.    The same knyht, a-stoned and a-ferd,
Which drouh Albon toward his passioun,
Of God visitid, cast a-wey his swerd,
Affor the martir meekely kneelid doun,
And vnto God made his confessioun,          1630
Besechyng Albon of comfort and socour,
In humble wise beknowyng his errour:

"Seruant of God, O blissid man Albon,
This God oonly is verray God certeyn;
Ther is no God sothly but he allon;          1635
Alle othir goddis ber the name in veyn.
For bi myracles which that I have seyn,
I dar afferme the trouthe doth weel preve,
He is verray God on whom that I beleve.

"I wot riht weele he is myhti and he is good,
For in a moment, thorugh his magnyficence
At thi request he voidid al the flood
As Lord of Lordis, most dygne of reuerence,
Non lik to hym of power nor potence,

---

1619   facis T In H Ed
1620   Quyk] But quicke Ed
1624   for] om. T In H
1627   drouh] thorough T In H; through Ed
1629   meekely] meekely he H          doun] adoun T In Ed
1632   beknowyng] bi knowyng Li T; be knowing In; knowing H
1634   This] Thi T In H Ed
1636   the] her T In H Ed
1637   For bi] Bi the T In H Ed
1638   doth] it doth T In H Ed
1639   on] of In
1640   and] om. H
1642   he] om. T In H Ed          al] hath All other MSS
1643   As] As a H
1644   nor] ne H; and Ed

Which on this erthe as sovereyn Lord and Kyng, 1645
Passyng all othir, doth merveilis in werkyng.

"Sett al a-side, the deede berith wittnesse
Of no collusioun nor fals apparence
Of Godly myht, shewing his gretnesse,
Riht as it is, in verray existence,                1650
For which I axe of al old necligence
Mercy of hym, and pray for my trespace,
O glorious martir, that Lord to do me grace.

f. 143 r.   "Ther is no Lord but only Crist Iesus;
He is my Lord, and I wil been his knyht,            1655
Which made this strem to depart thus,
A gret myracle wrouht in the peeplis siht.
His power gret and he is most of myht.
All fals goddis her I do for-sake
And to his mercy al hool I me betake."             1660

This knyht bi grace thus sodeynly convertid,
The name of whom was Araclyus,
The which thyng whan paynymes had advertid,
Thei fil vpon hym lik wolvis dispitous.
Touchyng the river, said it was nat thus;           1665
It wer ther goddis and non othir wiht
That wrouht this myracle bi ther gret myht.

"Our myhty goddis, most famous and most goode,
Of ther benyngne gracious influence,

---

1646  in] om. T In H      doth] doth very H
1648  nor] nor no Li; nor of no T In H Ed
1650  existence] recistaunce H
1651  neglygence In Ed
1652  of hym] om. H Ed; "of" cancelled, "hym" omitted, T
1655  been] be T In H Ed
1656  this strem] thes stremis T H Ed
1658  power] power is T In H Ed
1660  al hool] om. H; holy Ed      betake] take T In H Ed
1661  thus] this H
1663  The] om. Ed      thyng] thyngis H      had] han Li; haue
       T In H Ed      auertyd In
1664  fil] fyllen T In; fell Ed      lik] as T In H Ed
       dispitous] most spitious H
1666  It wer ther] Hit weren her T In; Hit were her H; It
       weren theyr Ed

Thei have a-voidid this river and this floode,    1670
Of whoos secretis we have experience,
And in effect ful notable evidence,
Which for our sake, yif it wele be souht,
For our passage, this myracle thei han wrouht

"For to accomplissh that thei have begonne    1675
Geyn ther most enmye, lik our entencioun.
Our god most myhti, the firy fervent sonne,
With his gret heete and bemys that come doun,
Hath ravisshid, for short conclusioun,
This glorious Phebus with his stremys cleer,    1680
The watry mostour of this gret ryver.

f. 143 v.       "Thei have considrid our gret devocioun
Which we have to-ward ther deite,
How we labour for execucioun
Geyn ther most enmy found in this cite.    1685
But, for to hyndre ther magnanymyte,
Thou, in contrarie, accordid with Albon,
Hast an opynyoun ageynst vs everichon."

This was *ther* language and ther daliaunce
Off hateful malis a-geyn this trew knyht,    1690
With gret rebukes for his repentaunce.
Fil vpon hym lik wolvis anoon riht

---

1673   wele be] be wel <u>All</u> <u>other</u> <u>MSS</u>
1674   thei han] thei haue T In H; haue we Ed
1675   thei] we T In H Ed
1676   Geyn ther] Ageyn our T In H Ed        lik] lik to T In H
         Ed
1677   fyre H
1678   come doun] coon [<u>sic</u>] doun T; came doun In H; yuyronne
         [<u>sic</u>] Ed
1679   for] for a T In H; with a Ed
1681   moystere T; moystur In; moystery H; moysture Ed
1683   ther] her T In; oure H; theyr Ed
1685   enmy] <u>om.</u> In; envy H; ennemy Ed        this] the Ed
1686   to] <u>added</u> <u>above</u> T; <u>om.</u> In Ed
1687   Thou] Though thou T In H Ed        accordid] accordist T
         In H Ed
1689   *ther*] the La Li; her T In H; theyr Ed        ther] her T
         In H
1691   his] his grete H

And callid hym in al the peeples siht,--
To ther goddis he was a fals blaspheeme
Worthi to deye, of malis thus thei deeme.          1695

Ran vpon hym with peynes ful vncouth,
Of gret envie thei hadden to Albon.
First thei smyte the teeth out of his mouth;
Aftir, thei brak his bonys euerychoun;
Without wounde membre was left non.                1700
Of mynde and hert alway hool he stood,
For in his breest the feith of Crist a-bood.

Oonly, bi grace, he had this avauntage:
In his beleve so hool he did stonde,
Which of his feith myht sofre no damage.           1705
Kept his promys which he took on honde,
He left halff ded liggyng on the stronde.
From wikke to wers, fro cryme to cryme in deede,
Lik homycides the paynymes gan proceede.

f. 144 r.     With broke bonys this pitous woundid knyht   1710
Was on the strond left with dedly cheer,
Pale of hewe, myht nat sitt vp-riht,
As the story in ordre doth vs leer.
Bi many stubbis and many sharp breer
Bar foot thei lad hym, void of compassioun,        1715
This blissed Albon, toward his passioun.

---

1693  callid] callid in H
1694  ther] their T; her H; theyr Ed
1696  with] om. In
1697  Of] A H      envie] malice T In H Ed      hadden] had Ed
      to] vnto T In H Ed
1698  smyte] smytten T In H; smyten Ed      mouth] hede H
1699  Aftir] And ther T In H Ed
1700  membre] memb [sic] H
1701  and] of T In H Ed
1704  he did] dyd he Ed
1705  of] for T In H Ed
1706  on] in T In H Ed
1707  liggyng] lying H; lyeng Ed
1708  Fro] For In H      to wers] or wors T In H Ed
1709  Li breaks off at this point and does not resume until
      II, 1836; however, see textual note to II, 1801-14.
1714  stubbis] a stubbe T In H Ed

*That he was* bare the tracis wer weel seyn,
For with his blood the soile was died red.
Made his passage to-ward an high mountayn,
Thorugh sharpe stonys squar as speris hed.          1720
Thus entretid to-forn or he was ded,
*Withoute wepyng* what erthely creatur
Myht seen a prince sich dedly peyn endur?

Stedfast of hert, his trust wold neuyr faile.
Groundid in God and in his feith so stable,          1725
Goth vp the hil t'accomplissh his bataile.
And ther was peeple verray innumerable,
The sonne was hoot, the heete was inportable,
In poynt almost, with fervence and with dust,
To sle the peeple with a sodeyn thrust.              1730

Constreyned with heete, gan to crye echon
Of cursid malis and fals malencolie,
Vpon the martir made a-saute anon,
Seyde thorugh his magik and his sorcerie
That thei wer lik of mortal thrust to dye,           1735
Ageyn whoos dedly furious cruelte
Blissid Albon gan shewe his charite.

f. 144 v.     To pray for them that did hym most torment,
This was his custom and his old vsage.
With hool hert and humble trewe entent              1740

---

1717    *That he was* bare] This was ther bare La
1720    as speris] as A <u>spere</u> is T; as a speris In
1721    to-forn] a-forn T In H Ed       entretid] entered H
1722    *Withoute wepyng*] With wepyng eyen La
1723    dedly] erthely H
1727    was] were Ed       verray] verely T In H Ed
        vn nemurable H
1728    the heete] and also H       was inportable] <u>om</u>. "was" H
        Ed
1730    thrust] thurst T In H Ed
1731    to] <u>om</u>. Ed
1734    Seyde] And seyden T In Ed; And seid H
1735    of] thorough T In H Ed       thrust] thurst T In H Ed.
        See II, 1730 <u>and</u> <u>n</u>.
1736    Agaynst Ed
1737    <u>Cheritee</u> T
1738    La <u>top margin</u>] "And from hens ye world" <u>in</u> <u>later</u> <u>hand</u>
        torment] tormentrye H

Prayed God, with teeris in his visage,
Of this myscheef stynte the gret rage,
That the peeple shuld in no degre
Bi cause of hym suffre non aduersite.

"O Lord," quod he, "*Fro* thyn heuenly empire,
Lik as thou art most myhti of puyssaunce,
Thi smothe wynd bi grace late enspire,
Callid Zephirus, to doon hem allegeaunce.
This rigorus ayer with dew attemperaunce,--
Tween hoot and cold set a mene indeede;                    1750
Or thou do vengeance mercy may proceede.

"Of this myscheeff ordeyn a relece;
Without vengeaunce sofre this peeple gon,
That whilom madist thi seruant Moises
With the yerde to smyte a drye ston,                       1755
At whoos touchyng cam watir out a-non.
Now gracious Lord, with newe stremys fressh
On this dry hil this peeple do refressh;

Thi gracious mercy fro them do nat appelle."
Off blissid Albon rehersid this praier,                    1760
At his feet a-non sprang vp a welle,
Ful plentevous, with cristal stremys cleer.
A wondir thyng and merveilous to heer,
From a drye hil, of moistour voide at all,

---

1742  stynte] stynten T In; to stynt Ed
1744  suffre non] suffred non H; to suffre Ed
1745  *Fro*] for La Li Ed
1746  of] and H        pusaunte H; pusance Ed
1747  bi grace late] bi grace let T In Ed; be let H
1749  rigorus] rigours T In; rygours Ed        dew] dew of T In
      H Ed
1750  Tween] Betwene T In H Ed        hot] hete H        mene]
      mede H
1755  the] his T In H Ed        smyte] smyte vpon T In H Ed
1756  watir] om. H
1758  this] these H Ed
1759  appelle] epelle T In; excelle H; expelle Ed
1760  this] was this In
1762  plentevous] plentous T In Ed
1763  wondir] wonders T Ed; wondres In; wonderus H        and]
      and a Ed
1764  of moistour] of moistre T In; amoystre H; of moystyr Ed

      Seen spryng a welle, cleerer than cristall!    1765

f. 145 r.     Of which watir *ther* was so gret foisoun,
      And of that spryng so gracious habundaunce,
      That from a-bove ther cam a riveer doon.
      The holsom streem was of so gret plesaunce,
      To staunche the thurst fond ther suffisaunce,   1770
      The heete asswagid, the peeple out of dispeir,
      Bi Goddis grace so tempre was the eyr.

      Thus was the peeple refresshid at ther lust
      Bi the holy martir merciful and good;
      Yit of fals malis thei had a froward thurst    1775
      In ther corages, lik furious folk and wood,
      A-geyn nature for to sheede blood,--
      The blood of hym which in ther disese
      Bi his prayer the mysscheeff did appese.

      Ther thurst was staunchid, thei wer refresshid
                                       weel,
      But a fals thurst of malis and haterede
      In ther desires was stanchid neuyradeele.
      Thei wer besi the blisful blood to sheede
      Of hym that halpe hem in ther gret neede;
      Lyk blasphemes makyng a fals obstacle,     1785
      Gaff to the sonne thank of this myracle.

      With vois vp reised falsly thei begonne;
      Thus thei seide of outrageous clamour:
      "Preysyng and laude be yove vn-to the sonne

---

1765  Seen] To seen T; To see In H Ed
1766  *ther*] the La
1767  of] at H
1769  The] This T In H Ed     was] it was T In H
1770  the] her T In H; theyr Ed
1772  tempre] tempered H; temperate Ed
1774  merciful] merciable T In H; mercyfull Ed
1776  corages] coragious H
1779  the] their T In Ed; her H
1780  refresshid] afresshed H
1782  desire H
1734  gret] moste H
1786  of] for Ed    this] his In
1789  vn-to] to T In H; to you Ed

Which in this myscheeff hath been our saviour, 1790
Stanchid our thurst with his gracious licour,
Bi his beemys most fressh and cleer shynyng
Vs to releve made a welle vp spryng."

*verba translatoris*

f. 145 v.      O peeple blyndid with fals errour,
O froward peeple, dul, rude, and obstynat,      1795
O bestial folk, ferthest from favour
Off grace and vertu, O peeple infortunat,
In your conceite, O folk most indurat,
That God hath shewid for love of Albon
Ye yeve the thank to ymagis made of ston.      1800

Li f.        *O most vnhappy, O peeple vngracious,*
43 r.        *Wers than beestis, O void of al resoun,*
            *O cruel tigris, O woluys furious,*
            *O foltissh assis, dul of discrecioun,*
            *Falsly to deeme in your oppynyoun,*      1805
            *Thyng that Albon bi grace of God hath wonne*

---

1790   saviour] socoure H
1791   Stanchid] Staunching H
1793   vp] to H
1794   O] om. H        peeple] peeple vnkynde T In H Ed
        *verba translatoris* in margin T In; between lines of
        text Ed.   Different hand in T [?] Om. La Li H
1795   dul rude] rude dull Ed
1796   ferthest] ferther H; forthest Ed      favour] all savour
        T H Ed
1800   yeve] yef T; gyfe Ed      the] om. H Ed      ymagis] an
        ymage In; thingis H
1801-14  These lines are omitted in La. They occur in all
        other MSS. The text above is from Li; there the lines
        are apparently not in proper order.  Though the folio
        on which they would occur in Li is lost, one can assume
        from the number of stanzas missing that they were never
        correctly inserted in Li. They do occur after 1. 2017
        (Li f. 43 r.) and are crossed out, with "va---cat"
        appearing in both margins.  In the remaining manuscripts
        both stanzas occur as placed here. The style is unmis-
        takeably genuine. The lines appear in situ in T, In, H
        and Ed.
1802   O] om. H
1804   *foltissh*] folyssh H Ed      asshes H
1806   *Thyng*] A thyng In; Think H

*To yeue the laude othir to sterr or sonne.*

*Ye sette a-side the sothfast sonne of lyff,*
*The sonne of grace that al this world doth guye,*
*Which may you save ageyn al mortal striff,*        1810
*To all your soris best do remedye.*
*Ye do gret wrong for to deyfye*
*This wordly sonne for temporal lihtnesse*
*And to forsake the sonne of rihtwisnesse.*

La f.        Lik fals blasphemys forsook your *Creatour*    1815
145 v.       And do worship vnto a creatur.
(cont.)      The sonne of liff may clipse no *shour*,
             Whoos hevenly bemys, bi recorde of scripture,
             Yeuyth lyht of grace to euery creatur.
             But ye are froward his influence to take,      1820
             And for ydolis his lordship to for-sake.

             What may availe Iubiter or Satourne,
             Or cruel Mars that causith striff and werr?
             Your werdly Phebus a day doth her soiourne;
             *The nyght* comyth *on*, his liht is from you ferr,--
             And eke your Venus, callid the day sterr!
             All these rekenyd, in your mad woodnesse

---

1807  *To yeue*] ye yef T H Ed;     *or*] or to T
1809  *that*] that doth T In H Ed    *this*] the Ed      *doth*]
      <u>om</u>. T In H Ed
1811  *your*] our T H Ed      *best do*] best may do T In H; may
      do best Ed
1812  *deyfye*] defye H Ed
1813  *lihtnesse*] bryghtnesse T In H Ed
1815  forsook] forsake In H      *Creatour*] creatouris La;
      creature H Ed. <u>See</u> II, 1817 <u>and</u> II, 532.
1816  vnto] to T In H Ed
1817  clipse] enclypse T In H; clyppis Ed      no] youre H
      *shour*] shouris La; shoues T In H (T <u>corrected to</u>
      "shoure" <u>in later hand</u>); shoure Ed. <u>See</u> II, 1815
      <u>and</u> <u>n</u>.
1820  are] arn T In Ed
1821  for] for yowre T In Ed      his] his good H
      lordship] lordshyps Ed
1823  and] or T H Ed
1824  Your] Or H      a] o T In; Yt one Ed
1825  *The nyght* comyth *on*] ther comyth oon La; the nyght
      comyth and In      his] the Ed

Calle hem of costom your goddis and your goddesse.

God hath this day myraclis shewid her
To magnyfie his glorious knyht Albon                          1830
With a fressh welle, and dryed vp the riveer.
Rekne vp your goddis and for-yete neuer oon
Off these myraclis; in soth ther part is noon.
A fool is he that of hem doth retche
Sith to sich thyng ther power may nat stretche.

f. 146 r.     Of ther power me list no more t'entrete,
Which ledith men to ther dampnacioun.
Mars nor Iubiter nor Phebus with his heete
May do no favour nor mycigacioun
Geyn no myscheeff, lik your opynyoun;                         1840
These seide myracles wer wrouht thoruh vertu
For love of Albon bi grace of Crist Iesu.

Your discreciouns been to fowle blent,
Your conceyte dirk, fals your professioun.
Maugre your maumetis, in al my best entent,                  1845
I wole procede with hool affeccioun
T'accomplissh vp the hooly passioun
Of Seynt Albon, bi grace of his favour,

---

1828  Calle hem] Called T H Ed        costom] your custome Ed
      your goddis] om. "your" Ed       your goddesse] om.
      "your" T In H Ed
1829  hath] that T H Ed, corrected to "hath" in T
      myraclis] om. T In H Ed
1831  welle] wyre H       vp] om. T In H Ed
1833  ther] her T In H; his Ed       part] partie T In H; parte
      Ed
1835  to] vnto T In H Ed
1836  Li resumes from II, 1709       more] lenger H
      t'entrete] to entrete T In Ed; ontrete H
1837  to] vnto T Ed; into In
1840  Geyn no] Ageyne the T In H Ed
1841  thoruh] by T In H Ed
1842  grace] vertu H
1843  to] so All other MSS
1844  dirk] derk and T H; derk In; derke and Ed       fals]
      falce in In; and fals in T H Ed       professioun]
      opynioun T H Ed

In this translacioun to folwe myn auctour.

Aftir this myracle shewid of the welle,          1850
A gracious gifte, a tresour of gret pris
(Lik her-to-forn as ye have herd me telle),
Yit, for al that, folwyng ther old avis,
The peeple abode stylle in ther malis,
Fro the mounteyn cast hem nat to weende,          1855
Of the martir til thei have made an eende.

First his lokkys, that wer longe and large,
*Maliciously* the bounde hem to a stake,
Chose out a knyht, and leide on hym the charge
That in all hast *he* shuld hym redy make          1860
And a sharpe swerd in *his* hondis take
As thei hym bad, havyng of God no dreede,
With a gret strok smet of his hooly hede.

f. 146 v.     The hed heng stille, the body fil to grounde,
His crosse also, al be-spreynt with blood,          1865

---

1849  this] his T In H Ed     to folwe] to folwen Li; folowen
      of T In H; folowyng Ed     MS T, <u>foot</u> <u>of</u> f. 40 v.,
      "Here endith the secund boke and begynnyth the
      prologe of the iii boke." <u>This</u> <u>seems</u> <u>to</u> <u>be</u> <u>in</u> <u>another</u>
      <u>hand</u>; <u>there</u> <u>is</u> <u>a</u> <u>large</u> <u>initial</u> <u>in</u> T <u>at</u> <u>first</u> <u>line</u> <u>of</u>
      <u>Book</u> <u>III</u> <u>according</u> <u>to</u> <u>other</u> <u>manuscripts</u>.
1850-1919  <u>One</u> <u>folio</u> <u>of</u> MS In <u>is</u> <u>missing</u>
1850  Aftir] Afore H     this myracle] thes miracles T H Ed
      of] at T H Ed
1851  gifte] yefte T; treasure Ed     tresour] yefte Ed
1854  abode] bode H
1855  hem] <u>om</u>. Ed     to] for to Ed
1857  First] First hent T H Ed     longe and large] large and
      longe H
1858  Malciously La     the] thei Li T; <u>om</u>. Ed     hem] them
      Ed
1859  leide on hym the charge] on hym leyd the charge T Ed;
      that myghty and stronge H
1860  *he*] thei La Li In T
1861  sharpe swerd] swerd sharpe T Ed     *his*] her La
      hondis] honde T H; hande Ed
1862  As] And T H Ed
1863  smet] to smyte T H Ed     hooly] <u>om</u>. H Ed
1865  La: "His crosse also     also al be-spreynt with blood"

Kept for a relik wan it was aftir founde,
Maugre paynymys contrarious and wood,
For a-monge hem secrely ther stood
A Cristen man, which that took keepe
The seide cros devoutly for to keepe.                      1870

This tormentour, this cursid paynym knyht,
He that smot of the hed of Seynt Albon,
Bi vengeance he hath lost his siht:
Bothen his eyen fil from his hed anon.
Without recur his wordly ioie is gon.                      1875
Which first was glad to make the martir bleede,
Lik his desert receyved hath his meede.

The woundid knyht, which in the vale abod,
Araclyus, as ye have herd devise,
The deth of Albon whan he vndirstood,                      1880
Which for febilnesse myht nat a-rise,
Gan peyn hymsilf in ful pitous wise,
A-mong paynymys as he myht hym keepe,
With hond and foote vpon the hyll to kreepe.

Vpon the mounte as the same knyht                          1885
Afforcid hym silf on hond and foot to gon
The iuge hym mett, spak to hym a-non riht:
"Thou that hast so many a broken bon,
Clymb vp fast and pray to thyn Albon;
Cese nat, but crye *upon* hym sore                         1890

---

1866   wan] whan <u>All</u> other <u>MSS</u>.  See <u>*Glossary*</u>.
1867   magry H        contrarious] contagious Ed
1869   which that] which T H; the which Ed
1871   this cursid] the cursid Li T H
1873   his] her H
1875   is] was Ed
1877   desert receyved] disceyt deserued Ed
1878   The woundid] This woundid T H Ed      vale] valley T H
          Ed
1879   herd] herd me T H Ed
1885   mounte] mounten T; mounteyne H; monition of Ed
          the] this T H
1886   Afforcid] Aforsid T; Afforsed H; Aforsayd Ed       hond
          and foot] fote & honde H
1887   to hym a non] anoon to hym T H; to hym thus Ed
1888   broken] broke Li T Ed
1890   *upon*] on La

Thi broken ioyntes and bonys to restore.

f. 147 r.      "First of all ren to hym and tak heed
               To be made hool of thyn infirmyte.
               Vnto the bodi ioyne ageyn his hed,
               An in al hast thou shalt recured be                    1895
               From al siknesse and al aduersite.
               And aftir that do thi besi cur
               To ordeyn for his sepultur.

               "And sith thou art a knyht of his doctrine,
               Lat se what he may the now availe.                     1900
               To make the hool bi craft of medicyne
               Telle to hym fast, and loke that thou nat faile,
               And thou shalt fynde an vncouth gret mervaile
               Yif thou nat cese vpon hym for to crye,
               Ageyn al sekenesse to fynde remedie."                  1905

               This maymed knyht gaff good *audience*
               To that ther iuge seide in derisioun;
               All set a-fyr with sodeyn hot fervence,
               Gan for t'abraide, of gret devocioun:
               "*I* trust," quod he" Of hool affeccioun,              1910
               Oonly bi meritis and vertu of Albon,
               God vnto helthe may me restore a-non.

               "Thoruh his power and his magnificence
               The eternal Lord may, be his gret myht,

---

1891   broken] broke Li T H Ed       ioyntes] bones Ed
       bonys] woundes T H Ed
1894   his] the T H Ed
1895   And Li T H Ed
1900   the now] now do the Ed
1902   Telle to] Call vnto T H Ed.   See *Glossary*.      that]
       om. H       thou] thou do H
1903   an] and T      gret] om. T H Ed
1905   Agaynst Ed       to] thou shalt T Ed
1906   *audience*] audienence La
1907   ther] the T H Ed
1908   a] on T H; in Ed
1909   for] om. Ed
1910   *I*] In La
1911   meritis and vertu] vertu & meritis Li T H Ed
1912   may me] me may Ed
1914   be] by H Ed

Bi the praier and merciful clemence                1915
Off hym that is his martir and his knyht,
In that I am lame, make me gon vp-riht."
Thes wordis seide, with gret love and drede,
So as he myht, he crept vnto the hede.

f. 147 v.    With gret devocioun he gan the hed enbrace; 1920
To the body he brouht *it* anon riht.
Al be-dewid with wepyng was his face,
Off wooful hert to seen that pitous syht,
That hooly prince, Cristis owen knyht,
Bi whoos merite whan he crept *on the* grounde,   1925
Al sodeynly he roos vp hool and sounde.

And whan he was restorid to his strengthe,
He gaff preisyng, laude, and reverence,
With humble cheer fil prostrat a-lengthe,
Thankid God of enteer dilligence,                  1930
And in the peeplis open audience
Cesid nat Seynt Albon for to preise
For love of whom Crist Iesu did hym reyse.

His force a-geyn Crist made hym to recur,
The peeple present myht seen and knowe.            1935
*Than* he devoutly made a sepultur,
Gadrid stonys lyggyng on a rowe,

---

1915   and] of H
1916   martir] mastre T H Ed       his] he his T H
1917   In that I] I that T H Ed       lame] lame to T H Ed
          gon] to (above) go T; to go H
1918   Thes] And thes T H Ed
1919   he crept] he crope T; he crepte H; crope Ed
1920   Inner Temple MS resumes from II, 1849.       enbrace]
          to embrace T In H
1921   body] heed Ed       *it*] om. La
1924   prince] prince Albon T In H Ed
1925   whan] as In       *on the*] to La
1927   restorid] restored ageyne T In H Ed
1929   a-lengthe] on lengthe H; in length Ed
1930   Thankid] Thankyng T In H Ed
1934   a-geyn] a geynst T In H Ed
1935   seen] se T In H Ed
1936   *Than*] the La       he] om. H       a] an H
1937   Gadrid] Gadryng T In H Ed       lyggyng] lying H; lyenge
          Ed

Leide the martir in the ground doun lowe,
And al a-loft,-- his labour was weel seene,--
He clowrid it with turvis fressh and greene.   1940

Wher-of paynymes had gret envie
Whan the beheeld whow that the same knyht
Restorid was and hool on eche partie,
So sodeynly, to his force and myht;
Wher-of a-stoned was euery maner wiht;        1945
Thouht in *hem* silf that was a-geyn nature,
A brosid man so sone to recur.

f. 148 r.    A-geyns this knyht thei took ther counsail,
Among hem silf gan his deth conspir,
Thouht it shuld be to hem gret availe         1950
To slee this man, the wer so set affir,
His sodeyn deth so greetly thei desir.
Som seide he had to his entent
Som wichecraft or som experyment.

Som othir seide, in ther iugement,            1955
Lik ther owen fals ymagynatiff,
This thyng was wrouht bi enchantement,
Or bi som magik had a preparatiff,
Not to be slayn with daggar, swerd, nor knyff.
But so wer, the story doth remembre           1960
That he wer hewe on pecis euery membre.

Among hem silf was gret contraversie,

---

1940  clowrid] coverd T In H; couered Ed. See *Glossary*.
1942  thei All other MSS    that] om. T In H Ed
1943  on] in T In H Ed
1945  maner wiht] man and wyght T In Ed
1946  *hem*] hym La Li    that] hit T; it In H Ed
1949  silf] om. Ed
1951  slee] hold T In H; slee Ed    thei] All other MSS
      affir] on fir H
1952  sodeyn] hasty Ed
1953  seide] seiden that T In H; sayd that Ed    to] in T H
      Ed; in to In
1957  thyng] om. T In H Ed
1958  had] he had Ed    preparatiff] preservatyff All other
      MSS. See *Glossary*.
1960  wer] where T In H
1961  That] But Li    wer] was H    on] in Ed

And eche of hem gan his verdite shewe,
Til it be-fill, of malice and envie,
Fals paynymes in noumbre nat a fewe                    1965
On pecis many have hym al to-hewe.
Of his recuryng havyng a maner dreede,
Al of assent thei smyten of his hede.

This blissid knyht, as the story seith,
Stood alwey oon in his perseueraunce,              1970
Of wil, of hert, steedefast in the feith,
List nat chaunge for torment nor penaunce,
To hooly Albon egall of constaunce.
*As* he was made felaw of his victorie,
So is he now made partable of his glorie.          1975

f. 148 v.    Aftir al this vengeable cruelte
And all this mortall furious violence,
For to turne hom ageyn to ther cite
To alle the peeple the iuge gaff licence.
At ther partyng, al of oo sentence,                1980
*And* with oo vois, homward as thei resorte,
*Ther* language was, the story doth reporte:

"Woo to that iuge that doth non equyte!
Woo be to hym that dooth no rihtwisnesse,
And woo to hym that can have no pite!               1985
Woo to that iuge gouerned with woodnesse,
And woo to hym that of fals hastynesse

1963   shewe] to shewe In
1966   On] In Ed       many] fewe Li; small T In H Ed
1967   a] no Ed        maner] maner of Ed
1968   assent] oon assent T In H Ed        smyten] smote T In H
         Ed
1970   oon] in oon T In H Ed
1973   To] Tho H       of] in Ed
1974   *As*] And La Li
1975   he] om. H       made] om. Ed
1977   all] om. H       this] his T In H
1978   turne] go T H Ed; our In
1980   partyng] departyng T In H Ed
1981   *And*] As La
1982   *Ther*] The La       the story] as the story T In H Ed
1983   to] om. Ed
1987   that of] of that T In H

Werkith of wil bi fals collusioun
Without title *of* trouthe or *of* resoun!"

This was the noise, the rumour, and the crye
Whan thei partid hom fro the mounteyn.
Trouthe wil out, maugre of fals enuye;
Rihtwysnesse may nat ben hid certeyn,
As for a tyme it may been ovir-leyn.
Bi exaumple, as, passid the daungeer                    1995
Of stormy wedris, Phebus is most cleer,

Our Lord Iesu, most gracious and benygne,
Which al gouernyth bi his eternal myht,
List to shewe many gracious signe,
Folwyng vpon the silve same nyht                        2000
Aftir the passioun of his blissid knyht,
Out of whoos tumbe was seyn a gracious strem,
Ascendyng vpward, briht as the sonne bem.

f. 149 r.    The same tyme whan folk to bedde went,
Ovir the cite this briht strem gan shyne,              2005
Last al that nyht,-- no man knew what it ment,--
Vpward, erect, riht as any lyne,
The peple saugh how that did enlumyne
The long nyht, as God did ordeyne
To alle four parties strecchyng of Breteyn.            2010

---

1988  Werkith] Werkes T In      of] vpon Ed      collusioun]
         collorysion H
1989  *of* trouthe or *of*] or trouthe of La; of trouthe or H
1991  partid] departid T In H Ed
1992  of] om. T In H Ed.  See *Glossary* s. v. "maugre."
1993  hid] hid it is T Ed; hid this H
1995  exaumple] ensaumple T In H Ed      passid] passid is
         ("is" above in T) T In H Ed
1998  his] om. T In H Ed
1999  many] many a T In H Ed
2002  tumbe] towne H      gracious] heuenly All other MSS
2003  Ascended vpward brighter then te sonne beme [sic] H
2004  folkes Ed
2006  that] the T In H Ed      it] he H
2007  erect] dyrecte H
2008  that] that it T H; that ("it" above) In; that Ed
2010  of] ouere H

With this, vncouth merveilous myracles
Wer seyn and herd duryng al that nyht.
Peeple gadrid to looke on tho spectacles
Tween ioie and drede, reioisshyng of that liht
As thei coude discerne and knowe of riht.          2015
This was the ditee which in that liht was songe,
As heer be-nethe is writen in Latyn tonge:

> "Albanus vir egregius
> martir extat gloriosus."

And ther wer seyn ascendyng vp and doun
In that celestial glorious briht skye
Heuenly angelis that made noise and soun          2020
With this refreite in ther armonye:
"Lat vs with song vpreise and magnyfye
The laude of Albon notable and glorious,
This day with martires maad victorious.

> "Albanus vir egregius
> martir &c."

This song was herd bi report thorugh the toun
And remembrid vpon eche partie
For a synguler comendacioun
Of hym that was prince of ther chyualrye,
Stiward of *Bretonys* to gouerne them and guye,
Whoos syngler laude and tryumphe glorious          2030
This day with martires is made victorious:

> "Albanus vir eg &c."

---

2011  mervayles T          myracle T In Ed
2012  Wer] Was T In H Ed          that] the T In H Ed
2013  on] vpon T In H Ed          tho] La reads "that" corrected
     to "tho"; that T In Ed; the H          spectacle T In H Ed
2014  Tween] Betwene T In Ed; By twene H          that] this In
2015  As] And as In
2017  As heer be-nethe] As be nethe T In H; As folowyng Ed
     exstat T In H Ed          MS Li contains the two cancelled
     stanzas given here as ll. 1801-14
2018  ther wer] ther was H; were there Ed
2019  that] the Ed
2021  ther] her H; this Ed
2026  vpon] by H
2028  ther] his T In H Ed
2029  Bretonynys La          them] hem T In; him H

f. 149 v.     This noble prynce of Brutis Albioun
          Hath soffrid deth and mortal tormentrie,
          Stable of hert, this Cristis chaumpioun,
          Hauyng despite of al ydolatrie;          2035
          This blissid martir crounyd a-bove the skye
          With angelis song, soote and melodious,
          This day with martires is made victorious:

                     "Albanus vir &c."

*Epilogue to Book II and Prologue to Book III*

*Oracio Translatoris*

          O prothomartir, ful famous of renoun,
          Among paynymes havyng the maistrye,          2040
          To be cause, grond, and destruccioun
          In Verolamye of al fals maumetrie,
          Thi liff for Crist put in iupartie,
          For which this day, with song melodious,
          Thou art with martirs made victorious:        2045

                     "Albanus vir &c."

          Be to that cite supportour and patroun.
          Keepe hem fro sore siknesse and maladie,
          Fro pestilence, and al infeccioun,
          And of ther enmyes represse the tyrannye,
          Which be franchised with the regalye        2050
          Of thi presence, O martir glorious,
          With all that longe to the and to thyn hous.

---

2036    the skye] so hygh Ed
2039    T (right margin) "verba translatoris"
2040    maistrye] victory H
2041    and] of H
2043    put] hast put T In; to put H; hath put Ed
2045    La and Li only repeat "Albanus vir &c." In : "Oracio
        Translatoris."
2046    to] vnto Ed
2047    sore] sorow T In H Ed
2048    and al] & from al H; and yll Ed
2049    And] om. H      the] all All other MSS
2052    longe] longeth T In H Ed

And blissid martir, most lowly I requeer,
Which abidist in the heuenly mansioun,
With laurer crowned, aboue the sterris cleer,      2055
Oonly of mercy to have compassioun.
Yiff ouht be seid in this translacioun
Thorugh ignoraunce, vnconnyng, or rudenesse,
Of gracious support rewe on my symplenesse.

f. 150 r.      In my labour though ther be founde offence, 2060
My wille was good, though smal was my cunnyng.
Medle mercy with thi magnyficence,
O gracious martir, of pite remembryng
The widwe offrid part of a ferthyng,--
The Lord above hir menyng vndirstood;         2065
Sauff oonly will she had non othir good.

Semblably, *thi* parfytnesse to qweeme
I am ful set, of humble affeccioun,
Hopyng eche man lyk myn entent shal deeme;
I wil procede, vndir correccioun,            2070
To wryte in ordre thi translacioun,
First set afforn, breeff and compendious,
The martirdam of Amphibalus.

With this, O martir, that from thi heuenly see
Thou list doun cast on me thyn heuenly look   2075
To ferther my penne, of mercy and pite,
In compilacioun of this thridde book
Bi the biddyng, as I first vndirtook,
Of hym which is this day bi Goddis grace
Fadir and abbot of that holy place,         2080

---

2053   I] I the T ("the" <u>above the line</u>) H Ed
2058   vnconnyng] unknowyng T H      or] of In
2059   rewe] and rewe T In H Ed        on] of H
2061   was] be Li T
2063   gracious] glorious T H
2066   oonly] of oonly T In H Ed
2067   Semblable H      *thi*] thei La; the H      to qweeme] "the
          queene" <u>struck through</u>, "to queme" <u>in margin of</u> T;
          the queene In H
2069   shal] wyll Ed
2071   thi] the Ed
2078   Ed <u>lacks</u> ll. 2078-84      Bi] Att T In H      first] <u>om.</u>
          T In H
2080   that] thy H

Off whom I have remembrid her-to-forn,
His name braidyng on a stede of whete,
Whoos moral garner hath many a greyn of corn
Compyled to-gidir of rethoriques sweete.
O blissid Albon, make the dew doun fleete          2085
To my penne, of merciful habundaunce,
This book t'accomplissh aftir thi plesaunce.

Explicit liber 2us

---

2082  on] of H
2085  Ed resumes at this line.      the] thi T In H Ed
2087  t'accomplissh] to A complessh T; to acomplessh In; to
      accomplissh H Ed      aftir] vnto Li T In Ed; to H

In the margin of Li, mutilated, "...t lib 2us"; H :
   Explicit passio sancti Albani"; Ed : "Here endeth the
   seconde boke of the glorious prothomartyr saynt
   Albon." There is no "explicit" in T or In.

Incipit Liber 3us

f. 150 v.     Myracles shewid and *mervayles* manyfold,
              This blissid martir for to magnyfie
              (As her-to-forn ye han herd me told),
              The nyht enlumyned with the golden skye,
              Song of angelis with heuenly armonye,                    5
              The peeple astoned, troublid in the derk,
              To seen how Crist list for his martir werk.

              "...Bete on your breste, remembryng on your tres-
                                                              pace;
              To the erthe fallith prostrat doun;
              Pray to the Lord for to don you grace              10

---

      T <u>and</u> In <u>have</u> <u>no</u> "incipit"; H : Incipit passio Sancti
      Amphibali sociorumque suorum cum translatione Sancti
      Albani.  Ed : Here begynneth the thyrde boke whiche
      telleth of the conuersion of many of the paynims vnto
      the fayth.  And also of the martyrdome of holy Amphi-
      balus which conuerted saynt Albon to the fayth of
      Christe whiche Amphibalus was the princes sonne of
      wales.  Li <u>corresponds</u> <u>exactly</u> <u>to</u> La.
   1  *mervayles* T In] merueilous La Li H; maruayles Ed
   3  han] haue T In H Ed
   4  illumyned Ed
   6  astonyd <u>All</u> <u>other</u> <u>MSS</u>        troublid] trembled T In;
      tremblyng Ed
   7  his] the T H Ed
   8-14  See *Explanatory Notes*.
   8  Bete] <u>But</u> T In H Ed      on] in In      remembryng on]
      remembr (remembrer?) on Li; remembre T In H Ed
   9  fallith] fall T In Ed; fell H
   10 Pray] Prayth T In; Prayeth Ed

Of your offence and transgressioun
Or that he take vengeance on your toun.
Trustith pleynly, wher ye be wroth or fayn,
Al this is wrouht for hym that ye haue slayn.

"This liht from hevene which that is descendid
For Albon shewid, and the golden skye.
Lat vs repent of that we have offendid,
For our trespace mercy to Iesu crye,
And for-sak all ydolatrye,
Takyng exaumple, al bi oon accorde,                    20
Of this martir that *whilom* was our lorde.

"In our opynyoun we have be foule blent,
Our goddis fals and verray disceyvable;
In hem no vertu, our dayes be mys-spent;
Our tyme is lost, our trust nat profitable;            25
Our hope is ydel and our feith vnstable,
Cast in errour of clowdy ygnoraunce,
That to come out we can no chevisshaunce.

f. 151 r.   "We may *considre* (a thyng a-geyn nature)
How the nyht with his blak dirknesse,                  30
Passyng resoun of any creatur,
Is bi myracle turned to brihtnesse,
Of angelis herd *melodious* swetnesse,--
And al this thyng, breeffly to comprehende,

---

12   on] of T In
13   wher] whether In H Ed      or] La reads "of" corrected
       above (other hand?) to "or."
14   haue slayn] ha slayn Li; did slayne T H
15   from] forme H      that] om. H
16   and] in In
18   For] Of T In H Ed
20   exaumple] ensaumple T In H Ed
21   *whilom*] om. La only
22-28  Stanza missing from Ed
23   Our] On T In H
24   no] is no T H
25   trust] tyme H
27   of] and H
29   cosidre La
31   any] euery T H
33   *melodious*] melodious of La Li; a melodious Ed
34   this] om. T In H Ed

For the meritis of Albon to comende.                    35

"Maugre maumetis which can nat but disseyue,
*Impotent* and verray feeble of myht,
Bi experience as ye may conceyve,
Brihter than day hath made the dirk nyht
To declar the meritis of his knyht,                    40
Pleynly to shewe liht of his parfitnesse,
Which may nat clipse be no foreyn dirknesse.

"Ageyn this Lord which is of most myht
We have errid in our opynyoun,
And doon to hym gret wrong and gret vnriht      45
To make our feith and our professioun
To fals ydolis, which in this roial toun
We have so long, in our paynym wise,
As ydolatrers doon froward sacrifise.

"Lat vs now dampne al sich old errour           50
And for-sake with enteer diligence
All fals godis, which may do no socour
To ther seruantis, present nor in absence.
Wher-fore lat vs, to clense our conscience,
Axe forgyffnes to that Lord Iesu                 55
Which hath in Albon shewyd so gret vertu.

f. 151 v.      "Lat vs nat tarie, but, in al hast we can,

---

36  nat] om. T H Ed
37  In potent La
40  his] his owne H
41  to] om. H      his] om. H
42  Which may not be clypsed by no foreyne derkenesse T H Ed
      Which may no clipse bi no voroyne derknesse In.  See
      *Glossary* s. v. "clipse."
43  of most] most of All other MSS.
45  doon to hym] do hym H; done vnto hym Ed      wrong and] om.
      In      gret vnriht] om. "gret" In Ed
47  this] the In
48  peynmes H
49  ydolatres Li Ed; ydolastres T In; ydolatries H      doon]
      do T In H Ed      froward] om. H
50  old] om. T In H Ed
54  to clense] now clere T H Ed; clere In
55  Axe] And aske T In H Ed      to] of Li T In H Ed
57  we] that we T In H (In has "that" above line)

Go seeke menys for our salvacioun,
In dyvers contres to fynde vp the man
Which bi his labour and predicacioun                    60
Conuertid Albon in this same toun
To Cristis feith, that martir most benygne,
This nyht declarid bi many vncouth sygne.

"From our rihtis and cerymonyes old,
And fals *errours*, enclipsid with dirknesse,           65
Don to mauhmetis, with whom we wer withold,
Of ygnorance, bi *conswet* rudnesse,
And to direct and clarifye our blyndnesse
From al errour of old ydolatrye,
The best wey that I can espye                           70

"Bi these myracles which Crist Iesu hath wrouht
For love of Albon this silve same nyht,
That his maistir in al hast may be souht.
For it is likly, accordyng weel with riht,
Sith God hath shewid siche myraclis for his knyht,
He that was cause of his convercioun
Myht best provide for our savacioun.

"I meene as thus, of verray equyte,
Sith God in Albon hath *shewid* sich vertu,
His maistir shold have gret auctorite,                  80

---

58  Go seeke] Go seche T In Ed; So suche H
59  fynden Li T In      the] that H
62  most] full T In; <u>om.</u> H
63  many] many an T In Ed; many a H
64  cerymonyes] sermons H
65  *errours*] errorus La; errors Li;      enclipsid] eclipsid
      Li T In; eclepsed H; enclypsed Ed
67  *conswet* Li] cosuetude La; conceyte H
68  blyndnesse] derknesse H
69  al] al olde T H      of old] and T H Ed; and all old In
70  wey] was H
72  this silve] the Ed
73  maistir in al hast may] mastre may in hast T In H Ed
74  with] to T (<u>above line</u>) H Ed
75  for his knyht] is inough H
77  Myht] May H
78  of] in T In H Ed
79  *shewid*] <u>om.</u> La Li

That was sent hym bi grace of Crist Iesu,
To put our doute at a pleyn issu,
Bi myraclis declaryng new and newe
His maistres techyng feithful was and trewe."

f. 152 r.    All that peeple, beyng in presence,              85
Off God enspired as bi on assent,
With o vois comendyng *his* sentence,
Gaff the favour in al ther best entent,
Took ther wey bi gret avisement
Toward Walis and souht on euery side,             90
Cerchyng the contre wher he shold abide,

Of whoos prechyng, notable was the fame,
Bothe of his lyvyng and parfit holynesse.
Ful glad thei wer whan thei herd his name,
And toward hym fast thei gan hem dresse,          95
As the story pleynly berith wittnesse,
Cam bi grace wher he did teche
The worde of God and to the peeple preche.

And ful devoutly vpon hym thei abod,
Havyng afforn hym riht gret audience,            100
And thei cam to hym *evene* ther he stood,
Salued hym with ful gret reverence,
Gretly reioisshyng of his devout presence,
Offrid on-to hym, or thei ferther gon,
The same cros which he gaff Seynt Albon,          105

The which cros was newly spreynt with blood

---

81    sent] sent to In
82    put] put oute In
85    that] the In
87    *his* ] om. La only
93    of] in T H Ed
94    thei] he H
95    towardes Ed       hem] him H; them Ed
98    to] om. H
101   thei] there H       *evene*] evenen La; evyn T H; even In Ed
          ther] as Ed
102   Salued] And salued T In; And saluted H; And hym saluted
          Ed       ful] om. Ed
104   on-to] vnto Li; to T In H Ed
105   seynt] to T In H; vnto Ed
106   newly] mekely H

Whan he for Crist sofred passioun,
Bi which tookne ful weele he vndirstood
That he was slayn.  Fil on his knees adoun,
Kyssyng the cros with gret devocioun.                    110
In his armes with teres al be-reyned
The holy relique ful streite he hath restreyned.

f. 152 v.    Thankid God with devout obseruaunce
Off that martires humble pacience.
This newe peeple, with devout attendaunce,               115
Which was come to yeve hym audience,
All at ones with ful gret reverence
And hert contryte, knelyng on ther knee,
For-soke ther ydolis and ther old vanyte.

Ther myspent tyme to them was a gret los,               120
To all vertu an odyous spectacle,
Til tyme thei wern markid with a cros,
In ther forehed bi grace and bi myracle
With that victorious tryumphal signacle,
An folwyng on, lik ther first entent,                    125
Receyued of baptem the hooly sacrament.

Withynne a while the fame went a-brood,
Ferr a-boute (the story as I rede)
Dyvers contrees, of this thyng how it stood,
Til atte last the noise gan to spreede,                   130

---

108   weele] yll H
109   adoun] downe T In H Ed
112   The] That T In H Ed        streite] streiht Li; streyth In;
      _om._ H; swetely Ed        hath] then H        restreyned]
      resceyved T In H; streyned Ed
113   Thankid] He thankid T In H Ed
114   Off] And T In H Ed
118   ther knee] her knees T H; his knees In; ther knees Ed
119   ther old] ther In; old Ed        vanytes T In Ed; vanyteis
      H
120   Ther] For H        a] _om._ T In H Ed
122   thei] thyne H        a] the T In H Ed
123   and bi] and T In Ed; of H
125   And _All other MSS_        ther] the In
126   of] the H
128   the] yn T In H Ed
130   to] _om._ T In H Ed

Off Verolamye how verraily in dede,
Citeseynes ther goddis have for-sake,
A ful gret noumbre, and ther iorney take

To folwe the tracis of Amphibalus,
A newe prechour, a straunger and foreyn.              135
Ther old rihtis, fals, supersticious,
Thei have renouncid, and hold al that but veyn.
Thei have also, of verray high disdeyn,
From them abiect (myn auctour list nat lie),
All ther ydolis and all fals mauhmetrie.             140

f. 153 r.    Whan this rumour was come to the cite,
Thei wer troublid, havyng gret mervaile
What it ment, or what it shold be.
At prime face lik a gret disavaile
To comoun profite, thei dempte in ther counsaile.
It was ful lik ther cite to encoumbre.
Enquerid first what failed of ther noumbre.

In ther rollis wer a thousand founde
And ther namys entitled euerychon,
A thyng likly ther cite to confonde               150
But remedie ordeyned wer anon,
That sich a noumbre bi assent wer gon.
Bi gret avis cast, as it was dewe,
A myhti power tho folk to pursewe

And *with* gret power cerchyn out the roote       155

---

132   goddis] goodes Ed
135   a straunger] straunge T In H Ed
136   fals] and fals (abbrev. "and" supplied between words by
      correcting hand) T H; fals and Ed        supersticiouns
      T; superstions H
137   but] ben T In Ed; be H
138   high] om. In
140   all] om. Ed
141   this] the H Ed        to] vnto Ed
144   disveyle H; dissauayle Ed
148   rollis] Rulis H
150   ther] the T In H Ed
158   as] om. T In H Ed
154   tho] the H
155   *with*] wit La        gret power] stronge honde T In H Ed
      cerchyn] sechen H; serched Ed

Of this mater, in hope it shold a-vaile.
The gadrid hem on horsbak and on foote;
Gan ordeyn a myhti strong bataile
Of sondri folk, armyd in plate and maile,
Geyn fugitivis gon from the cite                         160
And on Amphibalus avengid for to be.

Off whoos persone so notable was the fame
Thorugh al Walis and contrees enviroun
That the report of his good name
Gan so t'encrece thorugh al the regioun,--                165
Of his doctrine and predicacioun
Which thoruh Walis shon lik a lode sterre,
Them to directe which in our feith did erre.

f. 153 v.   Tho folk that wer come to hym of newe
Fro Verolamye his prechyng for to her,                   170
Lik a doctour in Cristis feith most trewe,
Receivid them with al his hert enteer,
Enformed hem, and tauth hem the maneer
Of Cristis lawe with besi dilligence,
And thei wer glad t'abide in his presence.               175

Litill and litill in he gan hem drawe
To catche savour and feith in his doctryne.
Of hool hert for-sook the paynym lawe

---

156   shold] shall H
157   Thei All other MSS
158   Gan] And gan H Ed
160   Geyn] Ageyne T In H; Agaynst Ed      from] oute of T In H
      Ed
161   And on] An one H      avengid] venged T In H
165   so] om. Ed
168   did] doth Ed
169   Tho] The H
170   for] om. H
173   hem] om H; them Ed
176   MS H, f. 31 r. continues from 62 v. (see note to II, 1.
      1157). The manuscript hand changes markedly at this
      point and so continues for sixteen leaves (31-47) and
      further to f. 63 r. Folio 63 v. and following are in
      a third hand which resembles the first more than the
      second.
177   savour and feith] fayth and sauour Ed
178   paynym] paynyms Ed

And with gret wil ther corage did enclyne
So to persever and so ther lyff to fyne              180
In Cristis lawe as folk that list nat tarie,
So for t'abide, and neuyr more to varye.

Othir ther wern which that gan pursewe
The saide peeple of malice and of hate,
This new doctrine of Crist to transmewe,             185
Which cam vpon, armyd in maile and plate,
Sent from that cite of purpos to debate
Ageyns him which, for Cristis sake,
Feith of paynymes vnwarly hath for-sake.

Folwed aftir, with rumour, noise, and soun,         190
To falle on hem of sodeyn aventur,
Cerchyng in Walis aboute, toun bi toun,
Of Amphibal the presence to recur,
Which, lik a clerk groundid in scriptur,
To that peeple, at reverence of the Lorde,          195
Stood a-mong hem and prechid Goddis worde.

f. 154 r.    And oon ther was, for angir almost wood,
That brak first out, shewyng his conceite
To Amphibalus, among hem ther he stood,
Wher-of that peeple was al the hool receite.         200
        "O thou," quod he, "ground of al deceite,

---

179-80  <u>Order</u> <u>reversed</u> <u>in</u> La; <u>corrected</u> <u>in</u> <u>margin</u> <u>with</u> "B"
        <u>and</u> "A."
180     to] <u>om.</u> H      persever] preserve H
185     to] <u>om.</u> T In H Ed
187     that] the H
188     which] which that Ed
189     hath] han Li T In; haue H; hath Ed
191     on] vpon T In H Ed      of] with In Ed
192     bi] and T H Ed; to In
193     Amphibalus T In H Ed
195     the] owre T In H Ed
197     oon ther] another H
198     first out] oute first H
199     hem] <u>om.</u> H; them Ed
200     the hool receite] and hole receyte T Ed; and hool of oo
        receite In; hool of receite H
201     T In H Ed <u>not</u> <u>indented</u>

Rote of fraude, falsnesse, and treacherye,
To all our goddis traitour and enmye,

    "What thou hast doon, thou maist nat it for-
                                          sake,--
Of froward contempt, maliciously practised,     205
Geyn our goddis a quarel for to take,
Ther lawis old presumptuously despised,
All this peeple contagiously disguysed,
To gret damage of vs and our cite,
Which, trust me wele, shal nat vnpunysshid be.  210

    "It is no doute, it shal nat a-bide longe!
Of ther iniurie and ther godly grevaunce,
As thei that been most myhti and most strong,
*Thei* sodeynly shal take on the *vengeaunce*.
But if thou wilt exchewe ther puyssaunce,      215
First do repent, to fynd hem more tretable,
And seek a mene to make hem merciable.

    "First of all, do thi besynesse
Of ther gret ire t'apese ther rigour;
Affor this peple shewe outward thi meeknesse  220
To lose the bondis which bi thi labour
Thou hast hem brouht in ful gret errour.
Be besy a-geyn, with feithful attendance,
Them to counsaile to falle to repentaunce.

---

202  of] and H       falsnesse] of falsnesse H     treacherye]
      In La the letters "eache" are over an erasure in
      different hand; trecherye Li Ed; treyterye T In;
      trayery H
204  nat it] hit nott T; it not Ed
205  practised] La has "contryvid" in text and "practised" in
      margin in another ink; practised All other MSS
208  All] As Ed
209  our] of our Ed
213  that been] be T In H Ed
214  *Thei*] The La      *vengeaunce*] vegeaunce La
215  exchewe] eschewe Li H Ed; esschew T; eschew In
216  to fynd] the to fynd T In H Ed     more] om. H
217  merciable] mercyfull Ed
219  ther rigour] the rigour T In H Ed
220  this] these Ed
223  Be] Be so T H Ed
224  to repentaunce] in repentaunce All other MSS

f. 154 v.      "Giff hem consail and make hem to assent        225
               With hert and bodi, no danger for to make,
               To axe mercy and sore to repent
               Or sodeyn vengeaunce vpon hem be take
               Eeke, that thei have our goddis for-sake;
               For this is no doute, but *it* be doon in deede,    230
               We shal ageyn hem vengeably proceede.

               "For yiff thei stonde in ther first errour,
               As thei began, froward and obstynate,
               Thei shal of mercy fynde no favour,
               With-out excepcioun, of hygh or lowe estate,        235
               But lik as peeple most infortunate,
               Deye on the swerde (take this for ful sentence
               As is concludid) bi marcial violence."

               Yet ther was oon supprised with feruence
               Of Cristis lawe, steedfast in the feith,            240
               Which had bothe connyng and eloquence,
               And for his maistir holy writte he leith.
               To thilk paynyme euen thus he seith:
               "Our Lord God, which is callid Iesu,
               Shal be this day our refuge and vertu                245

               "And our cheeff helpe in tribulacioun,
               Which shal, parcas, shewe som myracle,
               Bi his most myhti *domynacioun*,
               To-forn these folk as an vncouth spectacle,
               That ther a-geyn shal be noon obstacle               250
               Thorugh Goddis myht and mercyful goodnesse
               Som man to save of his sodeyn siknesse.

f. 155 r.      "Our maistir her, whom that ye repreve,

---

228   vpon hem be take] be vpon hem take Li T In H; be on them
        take Ed
229   Eeke] Of T In H Ed
230   is] _om._ Li Ed        *it*] in La; yf it H
235   or] and H
244   is callid] callid is T In H Ed
246   our] _om._ In H
248   domynacoun La; domination Ed
249   To-forn] To fore T In H; Therfore Ed        these] this T In
        H        as] _om._ T In H Ed        an] and H
252   save] sauf T In; same Ed
253   that ye] ye nowe H

In Cristis name to shewe an evidence,
From al myscheff som sike man shal releve,          255
Which lithe outraied bi mortal violence;
But to declar the magnyficence
Off Crist Iesu, anoon, without more,
To helthe a-geyn sich oon he shal restore,

"Nat in covert, but in your alder siht.            260
We have sich trust in his perfitnesse
Fro whoos doctryne, as we have behiht,
We shal nat chaunge for deth nor no distresse,
Without feynyng or any doublinesse,
Yow counseylyng in Cristis holy name,              265
Folwe his techyng and do ye the same.

"Ye threten fast to make vs a-ferde,
But God allone, he is our defence.
Iesu is strong ageyn sper and swerde,
Vndir whos pavis *of* perfite pacience             270
We shal a-bide, concludyng, in sentence,
We for-sake al fals ydolatrie,
For Cristis sake redy for to die.

"Favour of blood, nor non alliaunce,
Cherisshyng of tresour, nor promysse of kynrede,
Expert kynreede, *nor* non old acqueyntaunce,
Fayr be-hestis, manasse, nor haterede,
Al sett a-side, bothe love and drede,
The feith of Crist of hool hert we have take;
Al fals ydolis and mauhmetis we for-sake."         280

f. 155 v.     Of this answer paynymes, almost wood,

---

255  <u>sykman</u> T      shal] to T H Ed
256  outraied] outraged T In H Ed
260  alder] al their T In H; al ther Ed
263  nor no] or T H; or no In; nor Ed
265  Yow] Your T In H Ed
266  do ye] to do <u>All</u> <u>other</u> <u>MSS</u>
270  pavis] paveyce T; paveis In; pauise Ed      *of*] our La
      <u>only</u>
273  For] And for T H Ed
275  promyssyng H
276  *nor*] no La      old] <u>om</u>. T H Ed
277  manasse] manaces T In Ed; manacesse H      nor] and H
281  answer] awnsuere T; aduersite and answere H
      paynymes] the peyneyms T In H Ed

Lik tigris fel, vengeable as leouns,
Off innocentis to sheeden Cristen blood
With sharpe swerdis lik raveynous felouns
Thei kille and sleen of al condiciouns                285
As hungry wolvis in ther bestial rage,
Without excepcioun of old or yong of age.

The fadir ther, ageyn al skil and riht,
Of the sone took his dedly wounde;
Brothir of brothir was slayn in that fiht;            290
And with ther speris that wer squar and rounde,
Ther nygh cosynes *thei* wer glad to confounde.
Ther was no spare of blood nor of knyreede,
Without mercy eche othris blood to sheede.

Off agid folk ther was no reverence                   295
In that vnkyndly sodeyn cruel shour;
Mydil age nor age of innocence
Nor blood of blood fond ther no favour;
Nor no man ther list to knowe his neihbour.
Echon wer slayn, the story tellith vs,                300
That wer convertid bi Amphibalus.

Toward thes tirauntis that thes peeple sleeth,
Most merciles with swerd, pollex, and knyff,

---

282   vengeably H
283   sheeden] shede the T In H Ed
286   ther] her T H; om. In
287   or] and H
288   al] om. H
289   the] his T In H Ed
290   of] and Ed        fiht] sight T; flyght In; sight H
292   *thei*] the La only
293   no spare] none spared T In H Ed. See *Glossary*.        of
         kynreede] kynred Ed
294   othris] other In; others Ed
297   nor] no In
298   fond ther no favour] lyst knowe his neybour Ed
299   ther] the In        list] list not In        neyghborough T;
         neyghborowe In        Nor none to other lyst shewe his
         fauour Ed
301   That] And T In H Ed
302   Toward] Froward T H Ed        thes tirauntis] this
         tirauntis Li; tirauntes T In H Ed        thes peeple]
         this peple T In H Ed

Eche presid forn othir toward ther deth,
So charitable was that amorous striff,                305
Lik folk that wer glad to lese ther liff,
Off o corage and o pacience,
To deye for Crist so hool was ther feruence.

f. 156 r.    Among these hooly seyntis euerychon
*That* for-sooke ther toun and ther cite                310
Ther was a-liff left no mo but oon
Of al that cam Amphibalus to se,
Which bi the occasioun of his infirmyte
A-bood be-hynde, feble and impotent,
Which at ther deyng myht nat be present.                315

Whan Amphibalus sauh hem all dede,
Liggyng in the feeld, turnyd vp-so-doun,
With pitous cheer sauh the woundis bleede,
Of woful hert and compassioun
Devoutly made his comendacioun,                320
Prayng Iesu with vois, most pitously,
On all tho sowlis for to have mercy.

At Litchefeeld fil this aventur,
This gret slauhtir, as made is mencioun,--
Off which slauhtir, record of old scriptur,                325
Bi daies olde namyd was the toun.
This woorde, Licchefeeld, bi interpretacioun,

---

304  forn] inne aforn T In H Ed    ther] the T In H Ed
305  charitable] charitably T In H; amerous Ed    amorous]
      charytable Ed
307  and o] and of oo T In H; and of one Ed
310  *That*] That we La. "We" perhaps meant to be cancelled by
      a dot above "w" and illegible mark in right margin.
311  a-liff left no mo but oon] none alyve lefte but oone T
      H; none lyve lefte no mo but one In; none left alyue
      but one Ed
317  so] set Ed
318  the] ther Li; their T H; her In; theyr Ed
321  most] full T Ed; om. H
322  tho] the T In H    for] om. Ed
323  this] all this T H Ed
324  as made is mencioun] recorde of old scripture H; and
      made is mention Ed
325  record of old scriptur] as made is mencioun H

Is to seyn in that tonge, as I reede,
A feeld that lith ful of bodies dede.

Wher thes martires soffred passioun,                    330
Of oo corage and oo stabilnesse,
The paynymes, in ther opynyoun
Most obstynat, in ther cursidnesse
Made a vow and swore in ther woodnesse
Nevir to ete for non occasioun                          335
Til Amphibalus wer brouht in-to ther toun.

f. 156 v.    Lik woodmen thei aboute hym ride;
The hooly man (pleynly to declar)
With speris woundid, body, bak, and side,
Went afforn hem on his feet al bare.                    340
The more vngoodly thei did with hym far,
The more the martir with cheer and visage
Paciently soffrered ther outrage.

To hym thei had froward fel language,
The stony wey did hym gret duresse,                     345
And though he felt in his passage
Vndir his feete constreynt of gret sharpnesse,
Mitigacioun of al his hevynesse
Was whan that he the place did aproche
Wher Albon lay grave vndir a roche.                     350

The homycydes of whom to-forn I told
Had in this while a *maner* repentaunce,
Bakward among so as thei gan behold
The peeple slayn of ther alliaunce

---

329   lith] lyggith T In H; lyeth Ed
330   Wher] There T In H Ed
331   oo stabilnesse] of oo stablenesse T In H Ed
336   in-to] vnto Li; to T In H Ed
337   ride] rode T In
340   hem] hym H; them Ed      on] with Ed
343   soffrered] suffrid Li; suffyd T; suffred In H Ed
345   stony] stone Ed
346   though] though that T In H Ed
347   constraynt] constraynyd H
349   that] om. Ed
352   *maner*] maner of La
353   so] om. T In H Ed

Bi ther owyn furious governaunce;                    355
For thei hem silf, lik folk that wer wood,
The slauhtir made vpon ther owen blood.

Lookyng bi-hynde, first whan thei took heed,
Ther owyn cosyns, brethre, and kynreede
Bi ther handis lyn slayn in the feelde;              360
Thei gan wepe to se ther woundis bleede.
This same tyme, or thei took any heede,
Thei fond a man that lay languysshyng,
Vpon ther way, most pitously pleynyng.

f. 157 r.   This sik man with a ful dedly face       365
For gret constreynt of this maladie,
Saugh Amphibalus for-bi shuld pace,
With dedly vois gan vn-to hym crye:
"Seruaunt of God, do socour or I dye.
For Iesu sake lowly I requeer                         370
To helpe his seruaunt that lith in myscheeff her.

"For bi the callyng of his hooly name,
I have sich trust in Crist Iesu and the,
Though I lie her, impotent and lame,
Bi thi meritis that thou maist helpe me              375
To be made hool of this infirmyte."
Maugre paynymes that gan a-boute hym prese,
Of this clamour he wold nevir cese.

---

356   folkes T In H
358   took heed] took heed (struck out; other ink, in margin,
         "beheld") T; token hede In; toke hede and beheld Ed
359   cosyns, brethre] brethre cosyns Li; bretheren cosens T
         In H; brethern cosyns Ed
360   lyn] lyen T; leyn In; lying H; lay Ed
361   Thei gan] They gan to T In Ed; Began to H
364   Vpon ther way] Vpon the m... (illegible, crease; inserted
         above, "grounde") T; Vpon the In H; Upon the felde Ed
         pitously] pitous T In Ed; pitevous H        pleynyng]
         compleynyng Ed
366   this] his T In H Ed
367   Amphibalus] seynt Amphiball In      shuld] ther In
369   God] Crist In      do] do me T In H Ed
373   Iesu Crist T In H
375   that] om. T In H Ed
377   gan] can Ed
378   he wold nevir] wold nott he T H Ed; wold he nott In

In his praier he doth al-wey contune,
Sich feith he had in his opynyoun.                    380
Paynymys saugh how he was inportune
And so stable in his affeccioun,
Had in disdeyn and in derisioun
His gret noise, but maugre ther felnesse
He roos vp hool of al his old siknesse,              385

This sik man that lay bonde in peyn
Of old siknesse grevous and importable,
Bi Amphibalus, *lad* boundyn with a cheyn.
Was made al hool and of his lymes stable.
Thus can this Lord, *which* is most merciable,       390
Of sik folk her the compleyntis,
Werk myraclis for his holy seyntis.

f. 157 v.     This myracle, gracious and vncouth,
First, of this man relevid fro siknesse,
Deth of these martires gan spryng north and south,
Of ther wilful soferaunce with meeknesse.
Homward ageyn paynymes gan hem dresse,
But this myracle whan thei did aduerte,
Thei wer gretly astonyd in ther herte.

A-mong hem silf thei brak out opynly               400
Thouh thei to Crist wer contrarious;
Of *this myracle* wrouht so sodeynly
Thei sparid nat pleynly to sei thus:
"The God of Cristen is gret and merveilous;
Gret is his vertu, the deede berith witnesse,-- 405
To hele a man so sone of his siknesse."

---

379   contyune T In H; continue Ed
382   affeccioun] action Ed
383   Had] Hadden T In Ed; Hadden hym H
385   roos] aroos T In H Ed
386   in] in his H
388   *lad*] lay La Ed        with] in T In H Ed
390   this] the T In H Ed        *which*] which that La only
391   the] her T In; ther H; theyr Ed
392   Werk] And worche T In H Ed
394   fro] from his T In H; of his Ed
395   Deth] The deth T In H Ed        these] the Ed
400   out] om. Ed
402   *this myracle*] these myracles La Li        so] om. T In H Ed

As I told erst, paynymes atte last
(Wondir desirous toward ther contre,
Thei rood armyd) began to high hem fast,
And sped hem so that thei myht se                           410
The crestid wal of ther roial cite;
As thei thouhte that tyme for the best,
Aftir labour a while for to rest.

Thei wer oppressid with hungir and with thurst,
For that tyme list no ferther ryde,                        415
And eche of them, folwyng his owen lust,
Ches his ground a certeyn hour t'abyde.
Ther sheeld, ther sper, set hem doun be-side;
Them to refressh, leiser thei ha founde,
Whil Amphibalus lay in his fetris bounde.                  420

f. 158 r.     The tormentours, refresshid at the best,
As I have told, aftir ther werynesse,
The holy martyr myht have no pes nor rest.
Bounde in cheynes bi ful gret *duresse*,
In his most labour and grettest distresse,                 425
Maugre paynymes, whan he a leyser cauht,
To his most foon the woorde of God he tauht.

This mene while that al this thus was wrouht

---

407  I] thei T In H Ed        atte] at T In Ed; at þe H
408  desirous] desired T In H; desyrous Ed        toward] to
         go toward H        ther] her T In; your Ed; þeir H
409  began] and began T In H Ed
411  wal] walles T In H Ed        ther roial] her T In H;
         theyr Ed
412  thei] the H
414  thrust Li
415  ryde] for to ryde T H Ed
416  eche] eche one Ed        his] her T In H; theyr Ed
417  his] hir T H; a In        hour] there H; home Ed
418  sper] speres Ed        be-side] a syde Ed
420  Whyles Ed        fetris] fethers T; feteris H; feters Ed
421  the best] best T In H
422  ther] om. T In H; theyr Ed
424  Bounden T In H Ed        duresse] La only has "distresse"
         in text and "duresse" in margin in lighter ink but
         similar hand.
427  of God] þerof H
428  thus] thyng T In H Ed

As ye have herd, cam tydyng to the toun
How Amphibalus was to the cite brouht,                    430
Maistir to Albon, as made is mencioun.
At whoos entryng gret peeple ther cam doun,
Thouht in hem silf al ther hevynesse
Bi his comyng was turned to gladnesse.

Dempt a-mong hem bothe oon and all            435
The mater had stonden othir-wise,--
How Amphibalus was fro Cristis feith fall,
Off that lawe left al his old emprise,
Cam to ther goddis to do sacrifise;
All ther freendis with hym wer repeired,                  440
Of whom to-forn thei stood disespeired.

The bestial folk sopposid in certeyn
How all the peeple that went bi assent
With Amphibalus wer come hom a-geyn
Bi force of them that wer *for* hem sent,              445
But thei failed foule in ther entent,
For thorugh the toun the noise went a-non,
Lik as it was, how thei wer dede echon.

f. 158 v.       Geyn Cristis feith of malice set affyr,
Homycidis, tormentours that did this cruel dede,
Which fil vpon them in ther cruel ire,
Thei that made the martirs for to bleede
Off indignacioun and of gret hatereede,
The silff-same made relacioun

---

429   cam] come T In Ed        tydingis H
431   to] vnto T In Ed
434   to] vnto T; into Ed
436   mater] martyr In Ed        stonden] standyng Ed
437   was fro Cristis feith] fro Cristes feith was T In Ed;
        for Cristes feith wall H
441   stood] om. Ed
444   With] To T In H Ed
445   *for*] fore La
446   in] of H
448   echon] euerychone T In H Ed
449   Geyn] Ageyne T In H Ed        feith] om. Ed        affyr] on
        fyre T In H
451   ther] om. In
452   Thei] Tho Ed        martirs] martyr In
453   of] om. T In H

Of ther slauhtir thoruh Verolamye toun.    455

    The fadris wept with sorweful sighes grete
Whan thei herd ther sones wer so dede;
Pitous moodris ther sobbyng can nat lete,
Whoos wattry eyen with wepyng wer made rede;
Thorugh the cite, bothe in lengthe and brede,    460
Widwis, maidenes ran with ther her to-torn,
That so sodeynly have ther frendis lorn.

T, f. 51    *Suche pitous wepyng I trow nat ther was*
r.    *At brynnyng of the famous Illioun,*
    *In-to Troy whan the stede of brasse*    465
    *Was be sleyght compassid of Synoun,*
    *For thorough euery strete of Verolamye towne*
    *This noyse was herd, dedly and mortall,*
    *Like as men syng at festis funerall.*

La, f.    In ther most woful lamentacioun    470
158 v.    Thei seide among hem, of high and lowe estat,
(cont.)    "The tyme is come of our destructioun,
    Cite of citees, for-sake and desolat,
    *Most outeragious and most disconsolate,*
    To be notid of furious fel haterede,    475
    Blood a-geyn blood so felly to procede.

    "For our defence we have now non excuse,
    Folk infortunat bi divisioun;

---

455  toun] the toun T In
456  sorweful] sorowe H
457  so] om. T H Ed
459  wer] om. T In H Ed
462  *so*] om. La Li    have] they have T H
463-69  Stanza missing in La and Li; present in T In H and
    Ed. Stanza seems genuine; the text here given is from
    Trinity MS.
464  *At*] Atte H; At the Ed
465  *to*] om. Ed
468  *noyse*] vois H
471  *of*] with T In H Ed
473  citees] citezennes T In H Ed
474  Line missing, space left blank in La, Li. Line supplied
    from T. Line occurs also in In, H and Ed. The line is
    surely genuine, modelled on the same passage in Troilus
    as l. 475; see *Exp. Notes*.  *outeragious*] vngracious In

We shal hens-forth be callid the refuse,
As folk abiect, of euery nacioun.                        480
So importable is our confusioun
That we be nevir lik to fynde grace
Among no folk for to shewe our face.

f. 159 r.    "We can nor may our selven nat acquyte,
For our excuse a resoun for to make,                     485
But her-aftir that folk wil vs attwyte,
Our kyn, our blood, ther goddis had for-sake,
On whom vengeaunce so mortaly was take
In straunge contre, pleynly to descryve,
Among all that noon was left a-lyve.                     490

"Allas, allas! vnburied in the feeld,
Cast out to beestis that walkid in the pastur,
Kyn ageyn kyn in armys bar a sheeld
(An hateful werr, a werr a-geyn natur!),
Which lyn now dede, withouten sepultur,--               495
So late doon it may nat be socoured,--
Off foule and best a pray to be devoured.

"Allas our hope is turnyd to dispeir,
The staff brooke of our vnweldi age;
Our happe troublid, our Fortune is nat fair,            500
Froward to vs she turnyth hir visage.

---

479  hens-forth] fro hens forth T In H; from hensforth Ed
     be] om. H        refuse] refuge In Ed
482  nevir lik] lyke neuer T H Ed
483  for] om. H Ed
484  nat] om. T In H Ed
486  But] Bi La       folkes Ed        attwyte] adwite T; edwyte
     In H; awyte Ed
487  had] have T In H Ed
490  all] all so T In H; also Ed
492  to] of In; to the Ed       walkid] walk oute T In; walke
     Ed       the] om. Ed
493  a] on T In H Ed
494  An] And H        a werr] om. H
495  lyn] lyen T In; lieth H; lye Ed
496  be socoured] so be couered H
498  hope] ioy T (inserted above) H Ed        to] in to T In H
     Ed
500  happe] harpe T In Ed; harte H

Woo to that man that with his language
Causid Albon our goddis to for-sake
And maugre them the feith of Crist to take.

"Which hath, allas, perturbid our cite,                505
Brouht our welfar to desolacioun,
Grond and gynnyng of this mortalite
Of our allies and citeseynes of this toun
Whoos bodies lye turned vp-so-doun.
O myhty goddis of power immortall,                    510
Defende the peeple of your cite roiall!

f. 159 v.    "To our request your eeris doun enclyne;
Takith vengeaunce vpon your gret enmye
Which is cause of our mortal ruyne,
And of our myscheeff the rote, fynaly.                515
Revenge our wrong, ye that be most myhty,
On hym that causith that we sigh and grone.
Lat the vengeaunce rebounde on his persone."

Off ther pleyntis and ther so woful clamours
Thei cesid nat, lik folk most vengeable,               520
Til it fil so that the tormentours
Parceived weele that thei wer nat tretable,
Whow ther sorwe was in-tollerable;
Of compassioun list no lenger spair
Of all this thyng the trouthe to declare.              525

f. 159 v.    Al sodeynly thei began t'abraide,

---

502  that] om. H
505  our] the Ed
507  this] his T In; this Ed
508  this] the Ed
509  lye] lyggen T In H; lyen Ed        turned] om. T In H Ed
        vpsetdowne Ed
511  of your] of our T H Ed; and our In
513  Takith] Take Ed        your] our Ed        gret] om. T In H Ed
516  our] your T H Ed
517  On] Of H        sigh] sike T H; be seke Ed
519  and] and of T In H        so] om. T In H Ed
520  folkis H; folkes Ed
522  that] how Li T In H; om. Ed
523  Whow] How All other MSS; "also" above line in similar
        hand, In
526-637  Two leaves of Lincoln missing.

Ther dedly sorwis and pleyntis to refreyn;
To the most worthi of the toun thei saide:
"O Citeseyns, whi list ye so compleyn?
Leve your weepyng, your teris doth restreyn.          530
For bi report of vs that wer present,
Voide of deceyte or meenyng fraudulent,

"Ye have more cause of gladnesse than wepyng
And gretter mater of consolacioun
Than of distresse or of conpleynyng.          535
For yiff the ground be souht out, of resoun,
Touchyng your frendis slauhtir and passioun,
Ye have more ground (vs list nat for *to* feyn)
For to be glad than for ther deth to pleyn.

f. 160 r.     "Bi sondry toknys that wer contemplatiff,          540
Of signes shewid, the deede berith witnesse
Ther deth was entre to euyr-lastyng liff,
Ende of ther sorwe concludid on gladnesse;
Fro this dirk vale went up to brihtnesse,
Wher day is evir departid from the nyht,          545
And briht Phebus lesith neuyr his liht.

"It is accordyng ful weel vn-to nature,--
A man to wepe for frendis that be dede.
But ageynward, bi record of scriptur,
For Cristis sake who list his blood to shede          550
A thousand-fold shal receyve his meede,
And for this liff, which is but transitorie,
Eternaly a-bide and live in glorie,

---

527    refreyn] above line (later hand?) in T; the original
         word is scratched out and illegible.
529    list ye] lust T In; lust ye H     so] so to In; om. H
533    than] þat H
536    of] by Ed
538    to] om. La only
539    pleyn] prayne Ed
542    entre] entreed T In; entred H Ed     to] into Ed
543    ther] om. T In H Ed
544    Fro this dirk vale] For this that valey H
545    is evir departid] is partyd T In H; departed is Ed
546    neuyr] none of In
552    this] his T In H Ed
553    a-bide] to abide T In H Ed

"Wher is no partye of compleynt nor sorwe
But euyr-lastyng gladnesse in that place,            555
Bothe i-liche newe at eve and morwe.
Fro wo to ioie, fro sobbyng to solace,
Wher deth hath lost his power to manace.
Fi on dispeir, for deth to make striff,
Wher ioie folwith of euyr-lastyng liff!             560

"Deth in this world shuld nat be compleyned,
Off hem that passe from worldly vanyte,
Such as bi grace and mercy han atteyned
With Crist to regne in his eternal see
Wher ioie is evir and al felicite.                  565
And for sich folk, myddday, eve, or morwe,
It wer woodnesse for to make sorwe.

f. 160 v.        "Ye be bounde, pleynly to conclude,
To thank God for frendis that ye mysse,
Which hath chose so gret a multitude                570
Of this cite, and brouht hem vnto blisse
Of ioie perpetuel. Ye may nevir mysse,
Makyng a chaunge from this liff temporall
For thilk liff a-bove celestiall.

"Takith heed her-to, yeuyth good audience          575
Of thyng that we shal make rehersaile,
And it enprentith in your aduertence,
Touchyng your frendis slayn in bataile
Whom that we did so mortally assaile.
Al this considrid, to pleyn ye do wrong,            580
As ye shal knowe peraventur or long."

Afforn rehersid, the same tormentours
With a gret oth, present al the toun,

---

554  partye] part T In H; Where is no complaynt nor no parte
      of sorowe Ed
556  Bothe i-liche] i leche T In H; ilyche Ed      at] bothe
      at T H Ed; bothe on In      morwe] at morowe T H Ed
566  or] and T In H Ed
572  ye] they T H Ed; ther In
573  from] fro T; for In H      liff] om. T In H Ed
575  yeuyth] and yeueth T In H Ed
580  pleyn] complayne Ed      ye do] ye do no In; ye did H
581  or long] or ought long T In H Ed
583  present] present ther In H Ed

To them nat only but to ther successours
To be reportid, to al that regioun                                    585
Made ther-vpon a protestacion
Touchyng this matir (thei cast to expresse)
Shal have no touche nor spot of falsnesse.

Thei gan ther mater breffly to conclude,
Touchyng this story to seyn al ther entent       590
In Verolamye to al the multitude
Of gret and smale beyng ther present,
Rehersyng first whow that thei wer sent
With myhti hond to al contres enviroun
To seke ther freendis that wer fled from the toun.

f. 161 r.   Vndir these woordis spak for ther partie:
"Bi your biddyng we went, as ye wele knowe,
With force *and* armys to serche and espie,
To North Walis, in contres high and lowe,
Til it fil so, withynne a litil throwe                                600
And bi fortune, we founde hem euerychoun
With hym that whilom was maistir to Albon.

"Of this cite thei that wer fled and gon,
Some that wern ful nygh of your allye,
Vpon the maistir a-bidyng of Albon                                    605
We fonde eke gadrid a gret companye,
And of *Pictis* we did also espye,
With Walissh men of newe that wer drawe

---

585   to] thorough T In; thurgh H; through Ed        that] the In
586   ther-vpon] thir opyn T In H Ed        a] <u>om.</u> T In H Ed
588   spot] spice H
590   this] the T In H Ed
593   whow] how <u>All</u> <u>other</u> <u>MSS</u>
594   contres] the Contreys T In H
595   that] <u>om.</u> Ed
596   spak] spake T H Ed; spoken In
598   *and*] of La        to serched T; to serchen In; serchyng to
        Ed
600   throwe] thorough T H
601   And] Ladde T In H Ed
604   wern] were T (<u>above</u> <u>line</u>) In H Ed
606   gadrid] gadred T; gaddred In; gadered H; gethered Ed
607   And] <u>om.</u> H        *Pictis*] La <u>has</u> "p̃tĩs," <u>to</u> <u>be</u> <u>expanded</u> <u>to</u>
        "picticis"? Pictes T In H; Pectis Ed
608   Walshemen T In H; Walsemen Ed

And conuertid vnto Cristis lawe

"Bi thilk clerk that all these thyngis wrouht,
From whom thei wold departe in no manere.
Among all, our kynrede out we souht,
Took hem apart and with frendly cheer,
With fair speche and requestis and praier,
Meynt *with* manacis and sofftnesse of language          615
Fro that doctrine to reuoke ther corage.

"But evir thei stood in sich obstynacie,
On hym a-bydyng eche hour and moment.
Bi ther answer rather for to dye,
All of accord and echon of assent;                    620
List in no wise folwe our entent.
Whan we myht our purpos nat recur,
We left our tretee and *toke* on our armour,

"Of which thei wer nat a-stonyd nor afferd,
For Cristis sake eche redier than othir.               625
Who myht first renne vndir the swerd?
In ther metyng, brothir slayn of brothir,--
Ther was sich prees it myht be non othir,--
For Cristis sake echon thei wer fayn
Who myht first, for a prerogatiff, be slayn.           630

"Vpon the sone which was the fadris heir
The fadir shewid most cruel violence,
Which in nature is nothir good nor fair;
The sone also, void of benyvolence,

---

609  vnto Cristis] to the Cristen T In H; vnto christen Ed
610  thyngis] tydyngis H
612  all] all other H (T has "other" ruled through)
613  with] with full T In H Ed
614  and requestis] om. "and" T In H Ed
615  wit La
623  tretee] tretis T In H; tretes Ed      toke] tooken La; Li
      missing.      on] om. T In Ed
628  myht] wold In
629  thei] om. T H Ed
630  For A prerogatyf whoo myght furst be slayne T In H Ed
631  which] the which In
632  fadir shewid] Faders swerd H
633  is] was T In H Ed
634  of] of all T In H Ed

To his fadir did no reuerence.                              635
Ther was no mercy, but marcial outrage,
Without excepcioun of old or yong of age.

"Pacience was capteyn in the feeld
Of them that soffred *deth* for Cristis sake,
Ther sper was hope, meeknesse was ther sheeld;   640
Othir defence thei list nat for to make
In thilk quarel which thei had take;
List nat depart til spent was al ther blood,
Which on the pleyn ran lik a large flood.

"The Lord that sitt a-bove the sterris cleer 645
Saw and beheld the *grete* pacience
Of his knyhtis whos blood lik a river
Ran in *the* feeld bi mortal violence.
Whom to comfort, of his magnyficence,
The heven al opyn to shewe his gret vertu,     650
Saide on-to them that blissid Lord Iesu:

f. 162 r.       "'Comyth vp to me, my knyhtis most enteer,
Previd in bataile most victorious;
Ascendith vp a-bove the sterris cleer.
My *gate* is open, and redy is myn hous         655
A-geyn your comyng, most riche and glorious,
With the triumphe that neuyr shal dissevir,
And with a palme that shal lastyn evir.

"'Of paradis O chose citeseynys,
For your notable tryumphal prowesse             660

---

635  no] no maner of T H Ed; no maner In
638  MS Li <u>resumes</u> <u>at</u> <u>this</u> <u>line</u> <u>from</u> III, 525.     the] that
       In H
639  *deth*] <u>om</u>. La Li
643  al] <u>om</u>. T In H Ed
644  lik a large flood] large as a flode Ed
645  sitt] sittith T In H Ed
646  gret La
648  *the*] <u>om</u>. La <u>only</u>
650  opyn] opend In
653  most] riht <u>All</u> <u>other</u> <u>MSS</u>
655  *gate*] grace La Li
657  the] <u>om</u>. Ed
659  Of] O T In H Ed
660  tryumphaunte H

Makyng your *cleyme* as verray deynseynys,
Ther t'abide in your knyhtly noblesse;
To spende your blood was shewid no scarsnesse
For me to suffre deth bi gret outrage.
Dygne among martires, come tak your heritage!    665

"'*The* amerous fir of your fervent desirs
In your conquest of most sovereyn pris
Hath yow yove title to be possessioners,
Eternaly to cleyme, lik your avis,
A bidyng place in the heuenly paradis            670
To be regestrid, fre from al wordly striff,
With holy martirs in the book of lif.'

"Fro this world her we saugh hem flee to heuene
Bi many sygnes which that did appere,
Fro deth to liff, a-bove the sterris seuene.      675
We stood a-stoned be-holdyng the maneer
Whow Crist Iesu with a benygne cheer
List to receyve in-to his regioun
Thes holy martirs of Verolamye toun.

f. 162 v.    "In this noumbre of martirs ther wer founde    680
Ful nyne hundrid nynty rekned cleene,
Nyne addid to, slayn with many a wounde,
Of whoos blood, as it was weel seene,
All in-to red steyned was the grene,

---

661  *cleyme*] cheyne La Li
662  in] om. T In H Ed       noblenesse T; noblenes H; nobylnes
      Ed
665  Dygne] Syn H
666  *The*] Off La Li      fir] feyre T; fayre In H Ed
      desirs] desirous H
668  yow yove] yeve yow T In H; gyue you Ed
      possessioners] possessours T H
670  place] space T In H Ed
671  fre] all other MSS read "fre"; La has "fle" in line,
      corrected to "fre."
672  holy] the holy T In H Ed
673  her] om. Ed       hem] he In
677  Whow] How All other MSS
680  this] thes T; the In; these Ed      wer] be H
681  nynty] and nynty T In H Ed
682  Nyne addid to] And ·ix· therto T H Ed; And also nyne In
683  was weel] wele was H

The flood so gret of blood that cam doun lowe,     685
Oon from a-nothir that noman coude knowe.

"Thei lay oppressid vndir the hors feet;
No mann myht have verray knowlechyng.
The blody strem did ovir-flow and fleet
Ther dedly facis vpon the ground liggyng.          690
But sodeynly ther fil a wondir thyng:
Eche from othir, oonly bi Goddis grace,
Was thorugh the feeld knowen bi his face,

"Bi the prayer of Amphibalus
Off ded bodyes with ther woundis greene            695
(A gret myracle, the story tellith thus)
Ther woundis hol, that no carect was seene,
Ioyned to-gidre and sowdid eke so cleene.
A straunge siht, a siht of gret delite,
The blody strem as mylk ran doun *al* white.       700

"Thus bi the praier of oo rihtful man,
Of ther woundis, first ferful and terryble,
Ther was no carect, as we reherse can,
Bi apparence that outward was visible,
For vnto God no thyng is inpossible:               705
For thei that wer manglid and deformyd
Bi grace and praier wer sodeynly reformyd.

f. 163 r.     "The peeple, froward in ther opynyoun,
Seyng this myracle and wer ther-at present,
Bi a contrarious exposicioun                        710

---

686   Oon] And Li; That oon T In H Ed      that] om. T H Ed;
      "that" struck out, In.      coude] "kowde" struck
      through, "myght them (?)" inserted above the line, T;
      coude hem In
687   lay] lay so T In H Ed      appressid In
691   woundre T; wondre In; wonders Ed
693   his] the T H Ed
694   the] om. H
695   Off] Of the T In H Ed      ther] om. T In H Ed
697   carect was] carectes wer T In Ed; caracters were H
698   sowdid] sowed T In H      so] to H
700   doun] om. Ed      al] as La
701   Thus] This was In      the] om. Ed
707   sodeynly were Ed
709   ther-at] there T In H Ed

Saide ay the werst in *ther* fals iugement
And vengeably, echeon of assent,
Of fals malis did ther besy cur
To denye hem ther kyndly sepultur,

   "Cast hem to beestis, of malis and disdeyn,   715
To sich as wer disposid to ravyne,
Without reverence, lik an old careyn,
Thei a-geyn hem so felly gan maligne.
But Crist Iesu most gracious and benygne
To preserve his martirs bi myracle                 720
A-geyns paynymes hath shewid an obstacle:

   "A wolff cam doun with sturdy violence,
Terryble of look and furious of cheer,
Geyn bestis wilde to make resistence,
Toward the seyntis that the cam no neer.            725
An egle also, with persant eyn cleer,
Planyng a-loft, as all men bi-heeld,
From touche of fowlis kept al day the feeld.

   "Wher-of Pictis gretly gan mervaile,
Thei of Walis had a maner dreede;                   730
Thouht in hem silf, 'These tooknys may nat faile
To come of God and of no mannys deede.'
Of that resoun whan thei tokyn heede
First of the wolff and of the egle a-loft,
Stood a-stonyd and gan to wondryn oft."            735

f. 163 v.    It is approprid to wolvis of natur,
   As clerkis seyn, mannys flessh to attame;

---

711  *ther*] the La
715  Cast hem] But cast them T In H Ed
716  wern Li; weren T In Ed; weron H
721  hath] haue T In H Ed
724  Geyn] Ageyne T In H Ed
725  thei Li T In H Ed       no] noon H
726  persant] persyng Ed
727  Planyng] Hovyng T In H Ed
728  fowle T H Ed
730  had] hadden T In       dreede] of dreede T In H Ed
732  To come] Hit comyth T In H Ed       mans Ed
733  Of that] And of· T In H Ed       tokyn] toke T In H Ed
734  the egle] om. "the" In
736  to wolvis] vnto the wolfes T In; vnto the wolf H; to the
    wolfe Ed

Mong al careyns whan thei may it recur,
Thei most reioissh and ha ther-of game.
But he that makith wilde bestis tame,                    740
Dauntith serpentis which low on ground creepe,
Hath made a wolff his martirs for to keepe.

Free from all bestis disposid to raveyn
Bi his myracle and gracious werkyng.
And bi his power hevenly and divyne                      745
Of latter date he gaff *eek* the kepyng
Of blissid Edmunde, martir, maide, and kyng,
Vnto a wolff, the hed most vertuous
It to preserve fro bestis ravynous.

In this myracle, who can vndirstonde,                    750
To be notid is gret convenyence
Tween hym that was kyng of Est Ynglonde,
Slayn for the feith bi humble pacience,
And thilk martirs which made no resistence
To be slayn for Crist, as it is founde,                  755
At Litchefeeld, with many a blody wounde,

Folwyng the *exaumple*, these martirs euerychon,
For Cristis feith soffryng ful gret peyn,
Of ther prince that was callid Albon,

---

738   whan] wher T In H Ed        may it] it may In; is may H
      recur] recouer H
739   ha ther-of] haue ther of Li; therof haue T ("haue" inser-
      ted above), In Ed; <u>om.</u> "ha" H
740   whilde T
741   low on ground] on grounde low T H Ed
743   Free] <u>om.</u> Ed
746   gaff] hath In        *eek*] hym La; heke In
747   mayde martyr Ed
750   who] who that T In H
752   In <u>and</u> H <u>omit</u> <u>this</u> <u>line</u>; H <u>leaves</u> <u>a</u> <u>blank</u> <u>space.</u>  Li
      <u>corresponds</u> <u>to</u> La.  T <u>has</u> <u>the</u> <u>following</u> <u>in</u> <u>different</u>
      <u>ink</u> <u>and</u> <u>hand</u>:  "Of many a martyr that were by violent
      honde."  Ed <u>reads</u>, "Of martyrs which were with violent
      hande."  <u>The</u> <u>sense</u> <u>demands</u> <u>the</u> La <u>reading.</u>
755   To be] So were T Ed ("were" <u>a</u> <u>correction</u> <u>over</u> <u>erasure</u> T)
757   *exaumple*] exaumples La; ensaumple T H Ed; ensaumple of In
758   Cristis feith] Crist deth T In H Ed        ful] and ful T
      In H Ed
759   ther] this In        was callid] callid was <u>All</u> <u>other</u> <u>MSS</u>

In his tyme stiward of Breteyn.                    760
As I trist, thes noble princes tweyn,
Edmond and Albon, thes martirs ioyned too,
Shal save this lond in what we have to do.

f. 164 r.     This kynges baner, of azeur is the feeld,
Ther-in of gold betyn crownys thre;                765
The same chaumpe berith Albon in his sheeld,
Bete in the myddis of gold a fressh sawtre.
Ageyn our enmyes whan thei to-gedir be
In oon assemblid, shal make our party strong
Maugre al tho that wold doon vs wrong.             770

Of Estynglond kyng and chaumpioun,
Blissid Edmound shal his baner spreede;
The prince of knyhtis in Brutis Albioun
And prothomartir shal halpe vs in our neede;
The thousand martirs that list her blood to sheede,
For Cristis feith slayn at Litchefeeld,
Shal vs deffende with sper, swerd, and sheeld.

"These tokenes seyn, the paynymes gan to cese
Of ther pursute furious woodnesse,
And bi myracle thei sodeynly gan prese             780
To kisse the reliques, on knees gan them dresse
With many sygnes and toknes of meeknesse,
And wher-as thei afforn gan to malygne,
Thei shewid themsilf most goodly and benygne.

"Ther old malis and ther froward disdeyn,          785
Havyng the martirs first in derisioun

---

762  martirs] om. T In H Ed
763  what] that In Ed
765  betyn] ben T; been In H; be Ed
766  chaumpe] campe Ed
770  wold] woll H
774  shal helpe vs] shal vs helpe T In H Ed       in our] at Ed
775  The] Tho H; A Ed     list] om. T In H Ed      to] om. T H
     Ed
776  feith] sake T In H
778  seyn] shewen (?) H
779  furious] and furious T In H Ed
781  the] their T In H
783  as thei afforn] as they to forne H; afore as they Ed

Fro that conceit thei turned be ageyn,
Cauht in ther hert a newe opynyoun,
Them to worship with devocioun,
Gaff thank to God, and ther-of wer ful fayn          790
That sich a noumbre in that lond was slayn

f. 164 v.      "Of holy martirs, and halwid with ther blood.
Which thyng to put, in tokne of ther victorie,
Perpetuelly, thei thouht that it was good
Ther noumbre and namys to set in memorie,          795
Which from this liff, failyng and transitorie,
Be now translatid *wher* the may nat mysse
Eternally with Crist to regne in blisse."

Whan tormentours had ther tale told
Riht as it fil in ordre of euery thyng,            800
Of Verolamye the peeple, yong and old,
Present that tyme, herd al ther talkyng,
The more partye left ther wepyng,
For bi report only of ther language
Of ther sorwe the constreynt gan asswaage.          805

Thei gan the Lord to magnyfie and preise,
And to reioissh the glorie of ther kynreede,
Which bi grace he list so high vp reise,
Bi martirdam ther precious blood to bleede,
For his sake deye withouten dreede.                810

---

787  La has 1. 795 after 1. 787 as well as in correct place;
       here it is marked "va...cat."
788  Cauht] And caught T In H Ed
789  with] with grete T In H Ed
790  Gaff thank] Gaf thankyng T H; Yaf thankyng In; Gafe
       thankyng Ed
794  thei] the In H       that] om. H
796  failyng] fleynge Ed
797  *wher*] wher that La       the] thei T In H Ed
799  Whan] When the T In H Ed       tale] tales Ed
802  Present] Present there T In H Ed
804  reported In
805  constrayne H
806  Thei] Than T In H
809  martirdome T; marterdome In; martirdom H; mertyrdome Ed
       bleede] shede H
810  deye] dye T H Ed; dyed In       withouten] with oute eny
       T In H Ed

All atonys, with o vois in sentence,
This was ther noise, with ful devout reverence:

"Gret is that God, grettest and glorious,
Above all goddis of most magnyficence,
þat makith his seruantis so victorious          815
To gete the triumphe bi ther meeke pacience,
And bi his *myhty* imperial influence.
This Lord Iesu, most gracious and benygne,
Shewid in ther deth so many an vncouth signe.

f. 165 r.    "There grene woundis, terrible to behold,    820
With sharp swerdis severid fer a-sondir,
For lak of blood whan thei wer stark and cold,
Oo partie her, a-nothir partie younder,
The red blood (was nat this a wondir!)
Turnyd mylk whiht, as openly was seyn,          825
Ther woundis large hath sowdid newe a-geyn.

"He may be callid a leche verrayly
Which hath practised so high a medicyne,
Sich mortal hurtis to cur them sodeynly,
Whos roial bawme is *hevenly* and dyuyne.       830
Galliene cowde nat ymagyne,
Nor Ypocras, duryng al ther lives
Sich consowdis nor no sich sanatives."

The vertu shewid and power glorious

---

811  atonys] om. Ed      in] and T In H
812  ful] om. Ed
815  þat] It Li; La may read "þt" or "It"
816  the] so Ed      triumphe] grete triumphe T In H Ed
817  *myhty*] undeciphered contraction in La: all other MSS
     as above.
819  an] om. T In H
823  Oo] A H      partie her] parte there Ed      a-nothir] and
     a nother T In H Ed      partie younder] om. "partie"
     In
824  was nat this a wondir] this was a grete wondre T H Ed;
     this was wondree [sic] In
825  Turnyd] Turned to T In H Ed
826  sowdid] sowed In
830  bawme] beme H      *hevenly*] roial La Li
831  ymagyney In

Of Crist Iesu bi gret experience,                        835
And of his martir, blissid Amphibalus,
That day declarid bi notable evidence,
Bi whos praier, ther beyng in presence,
These myraclis, who so list take heede,
The same day accomplisshid wer in deede.                 840

Which thyng remembrid, the iuge wex ny wood,
Whos sodeyn ire no man cowde appese;
Gret pres a-boute, in place ther he stood,
Thei of this mater felt so gret disese.
But, for he cast hym fynally to plese                    845
To the paynymes, in his malencolie
Distrauht, of rankour thus he gan to crye:

"How long shal we endur or susteene
This gret iniurie, sclaundir, and clamour?
Lat vs serche out what it shuld meene,                    850
This hateful noise and furious rumour.
But, I wote weel, ground of this errour
Is thilk clerk which nat yore a-gon,
As we wele knowe, was maistir to Albon,

"Whos doctrine, if it wer vertuous                        855
Or come of God, as ye report and seie,
He shuld nat have be demenyd thus,--
So gret a noumbir soffrid for to deie
Of innocentis that did his lust obeie.
But it is lik, I do wele apperceyve,                      860
This clerk was besy the peeple to deceyve

"Bi som fals craft of incantacioun

---

838    ther] thei T H Ed
841    wex] wax T In; was H Ed        ny] nygh T In Ed; right H
843    place] the place T In H Ed        he] om. Ed
844    Thei of] Therof H        mater] martyr T (first "r" erased),
       In H; matyr Ed
846    To] om. T H Ed
847    to] om. T In H
853    Is thilk] Is thilke Li; That this T In H Ed        yore]
       thore H        nat] no In
854    we] ye Li T In H Ed        Albon] saynt Albon Ed
855    vertuous] tuous H
857    be demenyd] demenyd him T H Ed
858    soffrid] suffre T H Ed

Or bi som sotil strange experience,
Folk for to blynde bi som illusioun,
Bi a collusioun of fals apparence,
Lik as it wer soth in existence,                                865
With som coniuracioun or som charme made of newe,
A thyng that is nat, to shewe as it wer trewe.

    "For bi his compassid fals decepcioun
The worthiest born of this cite
Have be perisshid, as made is mencioun,                          870
And brouht to nouht bi gret adversite,--
Wher-vpon I make now a decre,
Peyn of deth, yeuyng this sentence:
To these bochers who that yevith credence,                       875

f. 166 r.    "That al othir may ther-bi ben a-ferde
Bi pleyn exaumple of ther punycioun,
Wher thei be founde shal go to the swerde
Withoute mercy or remyssioun."
Aftir this he sent for al the toun,                              880
High estatis and lowe did calle;
Whan thei cam, seide vnto them alle:

    "Lat vs procede and werkyn fynally,
And ther-vpon set an ordynaunce,
All of assent, vpon our most enmye;                              885
As we ar bounde, tak on hym vengeaunce."
Than euery man gan hym silf avaunce
With sich wepyn, pleynly, as the founde,

---

863   strange] and straunge T H Ed
865   Bi] Or by T In H      of] or H
867   coniuryson T In H Ed
873   now a] a new T H Ed; now In
875   these] thes Li; the T In H Ed
876   may ther bi ben] therby may be Ed
878   shal] om. Ed
879   or] of eny T H Ed; of In
880   Aftir] And aftre T In H Ed
881   did] did to T In H; did do Ed
882   Whan] And when Li T In H Ed      cam] came he T In; cam
        he H; come he Ed
884   ther-vpon] therunto Ed
885   All] And La Li In      most] om. T In H Ed
886   ar] arne T In      tak] to take H
888   With sich] With such Li; With which T In H; With suche
        Ed      thei All other MSS

Swerd, knyff, daggar, or what cam first to hounde.

So gret a peeple *out of* the wallis cam            890
In ther furious rage and cruelte
That ther was left vnethis any man
Which that a-bood withynne the cite;
Eche cryed on othir, "Go we hens, lat now see
Who that *can* sonest make hym silff stronge      895
To ben avengid vpon our gret wrong."

Ther goyng out was to the north party,
A medlid peeple, folkis wis and rude,
That no man coude remembre fynally
The gret noumbre nor the multitude;             900
All the cite, pleynly to conclude,
Was almost voide, myn auctour telle can,
Left allone of woman, chylde, and man.

f. 166 v.    Among the bocheers and tormentours strong
Oon was markid afforn in that passage          905
Which that thouht his felawis bod to long,
Ran forth fast to gete hym a vauntage,
And lik a wolffe in his cruel rage
Stynte nevir til he had founde
The place wher Amphibalus was bounde.          910

Lik a bocher percid his entrailes,
This homycide *that* ran afforn the route,

---

889  Sworde Ed       hounde La Li] honde T H; hond In; hande Ed
890  a] om. Ed        out of] on La        the] om. T H Ed
     wallis] Walys T In H; Wales Ed        cam] came T H; come
     than Ed
892  was left] left was ("was" inserted above in similar hand)
     In
894  lat now] now lett T In H; let Ed
895  can] cam La; canne T In        sonest make hym silff]
     sonnest make hym selfen T; make sonnest hym selfe In;
     fyrst make hym selfe Ed
898  peeple] peeple of T In H Ed        wis] nyse T Ed
904  the] thes In
906  bod] abode T In H Ed        to] om. T H Ed
909  he had] that he Ed
912  *that*] than La

Roff his novil, took al his bowailes
To a stake which that stood withoute,
Teied his roppis evyn round aboute.                      915
With a scorge the martir he gan make
In cercle-wise gon a-boute the stake.

Bi the grace of God in his suffryng
Felly assailed with many a gret torment,
Shewid no tokne of sorwe nor grucchyng,                  920
But al-wey oon, stable in his entent,
Til his roppis wer racid out and rent
Bi tormentours in ther cruel rage,
He chaungid nat cher, look, *nor* visage.

To *tormentours*, accursid al ther livis,               925
Amphibalus was set vp for a sygne;
Thei cast at hym swerd, daggar, spers, knyvis,
An ay the more ageyn hym thei maligne,
The more thei founde hym gracious and benygne,--
A pronostik *merveilous in* natur,                       930
Sauff goddis grace how he myht endur.

f. 167 r.      To wondir vpon, a merveilous myracle

---

913  Roff] Rooff Li; Raff T; Raf In H; Raffe Ed       novil]
        novill Li; Navill T; navill In; navle H; nauyle Ed
        took] and took T In H Ed       al] out Ed       bowelles
        T In H Ed
914  To] And at T In Ed; And atte H
915  his] lyke Ed
916  With] And with T H Ed
917  gon] to gon T In H Ed
919  a] <u>om</u>. In
922  roppis] ropis T H; bowels Ed       racid] rasid Li T In H;
        rased Ed
923  Bi] With Ed
924  chaungid] chaungeth T In H       nat] no T In H Ed
        look] of look T In H Ed       nor] no La; nor of T In H
925  To] Two H Ed       tomentours La       cursid T In H
926  was] þey T; <u>om</u>. Ed
927  Thei] And T (<u>different</u> <u>hand</u>), Ed       knyvis] and knyfes
        T In H Ed
928  An] And <u>All</u> <u>other</u> <u>MSS</u>       ay] euer Ed       thei] they did
        T In H Ed
930  *merveilous in*] a merveilous La
932  To] The H

Was seyn that day in the peeplis siht,
How this martir, vp set for a spectacle,
So long lived a-geyn naturs riht.                              935
His blood was spent, and *lost* was al his myht,
And his humydite callid radicall
In senewe and veynes wastid was at all.

His sowle, his spirite, his gostly remembraunce,
Stood in ther strengthe of spirituall swetnesse,
His heuenly fervence, his charite in substaunce
Appallid nat bi no foreyn duresse.
Force bar his baner geyn his mortall feblesse
To preve this texte, seide sith go ful longe,
How perfite love as any deth is strong.                       945

Of bodily force feeble to stond vp-riht
Aftir his flesshly disposicioun,
In gostly strengthe lik Hercules of myht.
For vertuous noblesse egal to Sampsoun
Previd that day in Brutis Albioun                             950
Was Amphibalus, with whom, ho list adverte,
Was nothyng left but only tong and herte.

T, f. 58      *In his hert, as long as ther was lyff,*
r.            *He cessed nott Goddis worde to preche;*
              *Grace was guyde and trought his preseruatyff.*   955
              *Feith bare vp all, cherite was his leche.*
              *His tonge enspired, the peple for to teche,*

---

936   *lost*] ilost La only
937   humydite] humylite Li; humedite Ed
938   In] His H      senewe] synewes T In H Ed      veynes]
          ioyntes T H Ed
941   in] on In
942   Appallid] Applied In
943   feblenesse T H; febulnesse In; feblenes Ed
945   perfite] persid T In H Ed
946   Of] O T In Ed
949   vertuous] vertues T In; vartues H      nobles T H
950   that] this T In H Ed
951   ho] who All other MSS      list] ilist H
953-59 These lines are missing from La and Li but occur in
          all other MSS; they are supplied here from Trinity. See
          *Explanatory Notes.*
954   gods Ed
955   *was*] is In      *and*] om. In      *his*] is his In

> *His body feble, his membris impotent,*
> *Yet tonge and hert were of oon assent.*

La, f.          His herte stable, strong as a diamaunt,          960
167 r.          Feith had of steele forgid his ymage.
cont.           His hope in God was so perseveraunt
                Dispeir in hym myht have non avauntage,
                For bi his gracious influent language,
                And bi myracles shewid in hym than,          965
                That day to Crist was turned many a man.

T, f.           *His doctryne fyx in her remembraunce,*
58 r.           *Most soueraignely they gan theryn delyte,*
                *Let her ydolles gon vnto a myschaunce,*
                *Which myght hem nother help nor profite.*          970
                *God with his grace list them to visite;*
                *Of oone assent gan hem redy to make,*
                *Aftre his counceill the feith of Crist to take.*

La, f.          Thei wer compunct, made ther praier,
167 v.          With repentaunce and vois most lamentable,          975
                To grant hem part of that he suffrid her,
                Touchyng his passioun grevous and importable;
                In thilk ioie which is perdurable
                Touchyng the sihtis that thei had seyn,
                Ther-of bi grace to putte hem in certeyn.          980

                Lik as ther trust and ther perfite beleve

---

960   stable strong] stronge stable Ed          diamaunt] diamonde
          T H; diamounde In; dyamant Ed
963   in hym myht] myght in hym In
964   bi] om. T H Ed
965   shewid in hym] in him shewid T In H Ed
967-73   These lines are missing from La and Li but are present
          in all other MSS; they are supplied from T.  See
          *Explanatory Notes*.
967   *His*] This H          *her*] his Ed.  H has "his" corrected to
          "her."
968   souerently Ed          *they*] than Ed
969   ydols Ed          a] om. In
971   to] om. In
974   compount T          made ther] and maden her T In H; and
          maden theyr Ed
976   her] there Ed
978   thilk] that T In H Ed; thilke Li

Was in Iesu, of hert, thouht, and deede,
With hool affeccioun, that it shal hem nat greve
For Cristis sake ther blood in hast to bleede,
Thei stood so hool, havyng of deth no dreede,        985
In ther opynyoun, our feith to magnyfie,
That thei despised al ydolatrye.

Ther prynce and iuge, which in presence stood,
Lik a man falle in frenesie,
Voide of resoun, lik a tiraunt wood,                 990
Comandid hath his tormentours to hye
Withoute excepcioun of high or low partie
To sleen all, and no mercy take,
That have ther goddis of despite forsake.

Thei presid in the martirs to encombre.              995
Lik gredy wolvis *or* tigris of assent,
Thei *slouh* that day a thousand ful in noumbre
For to obey his fel comaundement,
Amphibalus beyng ther present,
Which in spirite gan besily entende                  1000
To Crist Iesu ther sowlis to commende.

f. 168 r.   A cruel paynym, stout, indurat, and bold,
Spak to the martir of hateful cruelte:
"What hath this cite, othir new or old,
In any wise trespacid ageyns the,                    1005
Which hast causid this gret adversite,
*Her* innocent peeple in so short a while

---

988    which] while T In H; the whyle Ed
989    in] in to a T In H Ed.  See *Glossary*.
990    lik] as Li; and as T In H Ed        a] om. T In H
991    Commandeth T H       hath] all T In H Ed
992    of] for H       high or low] lowe or hygh Ed
993    sleen all] om. "all" T H; kyll and sleye Ed
995    presid] percid T In H; preased Ed        martirs] martyr
          Ed
996    *or*] of La       assent] one assent T In H
997    *slouh*] shouh La
1000   besily] om. Ed
1004   hath] of T In H Ed       this] the Ed       new or old] of
          new or of old T In; of new or old H
1005   wise] wise hath T ("hath" above), Ed
1006   this] the Li; her T In H; theyr Ed
1007   *Her*] Ther La Li; These Ed

With thi treynes and sleightis to be-guyle?

"Our statutis and lawis thou hast soiled
Bi th'occasioun of thi pereilous language,          1010
And our cite most cruelly dispoiled
Of ther peeple, old and yong of age,
Cause of ther losse and ther mortal damage.
And thou afforn hem, forwoundid to the deth,
Stondist in poynt to yelde vp the breth.          1015

"In sich disioynte thou maist nat recur,
Disentrailed, boundyn to a stake,
And our goddis thou hast abovyn mesur
Felly provokid, vengeaunce on the to take;
Yit yiff thou woldist repent and for-sake          1020
Thi Cristen secte and fro that feith withdrawe,
And of hool hert turne vn-to our lawe,

"Worship our goddis whom thou hast offendid,
And been in wil to do so no more,
Of all thyn hurtis thou myhtist been amendid,          1025
And axe grace as I have told be-fore,
To helthe ageyn thei myht the restore.
Thi grevous woundis which semen incurable
Make hem ful hool, the be so merciable,

---

1009    soiled] foiled T Ed
1010    th'occasioun] the occasioun T In H; occasyon Ed
        pereilous] perlous T In; persone and perlous H;
        parlous Ed
1011    dispoiled] despised T H; spoyled Ed
1013    ther mortal] her mortal T In H; mortal Ed
1014    forwoundid] for wounde H
1015    yelde] yeldeth T; yelden In          the] thy T H Ed
1017    to] vnto T In H
1020    yiff] if T In H; and Ed
1021    Cristen] cristes T In H; cristis Ed          that] thi T In
        Ed; the H
1023    goddis] god Ed
1025    all] And of all H; om. Ed
1027    the] om. T In; wele Ed
1028    grevous woundis] woundes grevous T H Ed
1029    the] thei All other MSS

T, f. 59     *"Vpon wrecches benignely to rewe*                1030
r.           *Suche as listen to fall in her grace,*
             *And woll repente lowly and be trewe.*
             *Aske mercy of their old trespace;*
             *Thei may nott feyle with a litell space*
             *To be acceptyd, wounded, halt, and lame.*         1035
             *Be my counceill do thi self the same,*

             *"Which stondist now set as a spectacle*
             *Afore the peple, which haue the in disdeigne*
             *Pray our goddis to shew som myracle,*
             *Bi their power that it may be seyn*                1040
             *That thou maist be restoryd new ageyne*
             *To that mercy, and aftyrward assured*
             *Of all thi woundes to be recured.*

La f. 168    "Yiff thou thus do thei wole be gracious
v.           To modifie ther vengeable violence."               1045
             "Lat be, thou paynym," quod Amphibalus;
             "Feeble is ther myht and mortal, in sentence.
             In thi language thou doost gret offence
             To yeve laude, worship, or preysyng
             To fals ydolis that have no feelyng.                1050

             "For thei be voide of grace and of vertu,
             Have nothir mynde nor ymagynatiff;
             Ther is no god but my Lord Iesu
             That dede bodies restorith ageyn to liff;
             He is myn helthe and myn restoratiff.               1055

---

1030-43  These lines are not in La and Li. Yet, because they
         occur in T, In, H, and Ed, and clearly continue 1. 1029
         in Lydgatean style, they are here included.
1031     *listen to*] lyst Ed
1033     *Aske*] And aske H
1034     *Thei*] om. In    *with*] within Ed
1035     accepte Ed
1037     *set*] om. Ed
1038     *the*] them Ed
1042     afterwardes Ed
1044     thus] this T In H
1046     No indentation, T In H Ed
1048     gret] om. T H
1050     feelyng] seing Ed
1051     and of] and al All other MSS
1052     mynde] tyme Ed

All your goddis of which ye now telle
Be but feendis that suffre peyn in helle.

"In ther preisyng and worship ye be blynde,
For deepe in hell is ther a-bydyng;
Ye do gret wrong them for to have in mynde          1060
Which evir endur in compleynt and wepyng,
And wer tirauntis her in ther livyng,
And of fals dreede took ther origynall,
To be deified, knowyng thei were mortall.

"In helle is now ther habitacioun,                  1065
Perpetuelly ordeyned to a-byde;
Of your fals goddis the commemoracioun
Is hold ther with al ther pompe and pride,
With fir be-set vpon every side,
Which nevir is queynt, of infernall fervence,       1070
Nor the worme ded of ther conscience.

f. 169 r.     "Al tho that serve them in ther live
Shal of ther peynes be with them partable,--
Out of charite folk that list to stryve,
Fals avoutrees, detractours detestable,             1075
And homycides most abhomynable
That wern or ben her of ther assent
Have and shal have parte of ther torment.

"Lik ther decertis thei must have ther meede.

---

1056  All] Of all ("all" <u>above</u> <u>the</u> <u>line</u>) H     ye now] now ye
      T In H Ed
1058  In ther preisyng] Them to prayse Ed     worship]
      worshiphyng T In H
1060  in] and Li
1062  wer] where H
1064  deified] defied Ed     were] be T In H Ed
1067  commemoracioun] <u>See</u> <u>Latin</u> <u>source,</u> <u>in</u> <u>Explanatory</u> <u>Notes,</u>
      III, 1046-1134.
1068  hold] holden T In H Ed
1070  nevir is] is neuer In H
1072  tho] they Ed     serve] serven T In H     them] hem T
      In H     ther] her T In H
1073  ther] her T In H     them] hem T In H
1075  avoutres T; avowtrers In; aveutrers H; aduoutrers Ed
1079  ther] her T In H

And thou, paynym, shalt have thi parte in peyn;
Of thi fals errour but thou repent in deede,
Shalt eek with hem, I telle the in certeyn,
Ben enbracid in the firy cheyn,
With Sathan stokkid amyd the smokis blake,
But yif thou wilt thi mawmetry forsake.                    1085

"Forsake thi rihtis of fals mawmetrye,
Thi secte, thyn errour of old vanyte!
Dispeir the nat, for gret is the mercye
Of Crist Iesu, which wil accepte the,
With al othir that her present be,                          1090
So that ye wil of feith and hooll entent
Receyve of baptem the holy sacrament.

"First of baptem the vertu to devise,
Lik as it is i-groundid in scriptur,
It wasshith away, who list advertise,                      1095
Off mannys synne al filthe and al ordur,
Causith a man al grace to recur,
Openeth heuen, and as seyn these clerkis,
Forsakith Sathan and all his mortall werkis.

f. 169 v.      "Thei that wer childre of perdicioun,       1100
Vndir the devil bi synne and wretchidnesse,
Bi grace of baptem, as made is mencioun,

---

1080   thi] above the line in T; om. H
1081   Of] For T In H Ed      in deede] sone T (struck out; "in
          dede" inserted in margin, other hand), sone In H
1082   hem] them Li In Ed
1083   the] a T In H Ed
1085   wilt] will T H
1086   thi] the Ed      mawmetrye] ydollatrye T In H Ed
1090   her] there H
1091   ye wil] wollen ("they" above) T; ye wollen In; they
          willen H; they wyll Ed
1092   baptisme Ed
1094   i-groundid] grounded H Ed
1095   who] who so Ed      list] lustith to In
1096   ordur] odure T Ed; odour H
1098   and] om. T H Ed; In has "and" above the line.
1099   all] om. H T (T has "all" added above, perhaps in other
          hand)
1100   childryn T; children In Ed; childern H
1101   devil] fende T In H Ed

Our feith receivid, stond in sikirnesse.
Fleeth to that grace and dooth your besynesse,
As I to-forn have to yow devisid;                    1105
Forsake your goddis and beth in hast baptisid.

"Watir of baptem doth synnes purifie,
Watir of comfort and consolacioun,
Clensith the filthe of al'ydolatrie,
Origynal welle of our salvacioun,                    1110
Conduyt and riveer of our redempcioun,
Callid in scriptur watir regeneratiff
Which restorith man to gostly liff.

"It is the hed-spryng and the gostly strem
Which conveith a man to paradis,                     1115
Rivail and port to-ward Ierusalem.
Of all riveers this river berith the pris
Vnto folkis that be prudent and wis.
Such as wasshe hem in this holsom riveer
Avoidith from hem al infernal daunger.               1120

"Scowrith away al venym serpentyne
And spottis blake callid originall,
Bi grace causid which that is dyvyne
Renewyng men to be celestiall.
An for conclusioun in this mater fynall,             1125
Forsake your goddis which may do yow no good,
And be my counsail be bathid in this flood.

---

1103   stond] stondith T In H; standeth Ed
1104   Fleeth to] Fleet to T; Flete of H; Flete to Ed
          that] the Ed
1109   Clensith] Causeth In H
1113   man] a man All other MSS      to] vnto T In H Ed
1114   and] of In
1116   Rivail] Ryuer Ed
1118   Vnto] As to T In H Ed
1119   hem] them Ed
1120   daunger] "damage" struck through; "daunger" in margin
          in same hand (?), T
1121   Scowrith] And scowrith T In H Ed
1123   causid] causeth T In H Ed
1125   And All other MSS      for] for a T In H Ed
1126   Forsake] To forsake T In H Ed
1127   In has this entire line inserted (by same hand?) in l.
          margin.      And be] be T; by In H Ed      be bathid]
          beth bathid T In

f. 170 r.      "The strem ther-of shal glade your cite,
               Race away the rust of all outrages,
               And with a flowe of al prosperite          1130
               Renewe bothe your hert and your corages,
               And yow preserve from infernal damages;
               Ye stond free, cheseth oon of the tweyn:
               Eternal liff or euyrlastyng peyn."

               Aftir *thes* noble exhortaciouns          1135
               Groundid on feith and perfit charite,
               The paynyms, lik tigris or leouns,
               In ther hasty furious cruelte
               Fil on the martir boundyn to a tre.
               On eche side assailed hym attonys          1140
               With rounde caliouns and with sharpe stonys.

               A gret myracle God list that day shewe,
               That this martir lik goddis chaumpioun,
               Besette a-boute with panyms *nat* a few,
               Stood ay vpriht no party bowyng doun,      1145
               Stable in praier and in his orisoun,
               Erect to God, nat turnyng north nor souht,
               The woord of God nevir out of his mouth.

               Sauff grace of God sempt an inpossible

---

1129  Race] Rase Li In; And rase T H; And race Ed       all]
        old All other MSS
1133  oon] om. T H; nowe Ed     the] om. T In H Ed
1134  Eternal] Euer lastyng In
1135  *thes*] this La Li; these H Ed     noble] notable T H Ed
1136  Groundid] Grounde T In H
1138  hastyff T In H
1139  Fil] Fillen T H Ed; Fellen In
1140  hym] om. T In H
1142  God list] transposed In     shewe] to shewe T In H Ed
1143  That] And T In H Ed
1144  a-boute] all aboute T In H Ed     with] of Li     nat]
        na La
1145  bowyng] om. Ed
1146  his] om. T H Ed
1147  souht] La only; all other MSS read "south."
1149  Sauff] Saue the T In H Ed     grace of God] word of god
        and his grace Ed     sempt an] exempt and T In H; was
        Ed

T'abide that bront.   Wher he had force and myht,--
In sowle and spirite stondyng *invinsible*,
The eyen vp lift *of* his inward siht
Toward heuen, Phebus was nat so briht
At mydsomer in his mydday speer
As he saugh Iesu in the heuen appeer                1155

f. 170 v.        On the riht side of his fadir der;
Fyne of his tryumphe, ende of his tormentrie,
Herd of angelis with sugrid notis cleer
Celestial song, *which* in ther melodie
Gan preise the Lord, and ther he did espie       1160
His blissid Albon, clad in purpil wede,
Tokne for Crist he list his blood *to* bleede.

To that martir a-mong martirs all
Of trust assurd whilom tweene hem tweyn
Amphibalus for helpe gan to call:               1165
"O blissid Albon, that suffredist gret peyn
For Cristis sake, of mercy nat disdeyn
To prey Iesu, that list for vs to deye,
To sende his angel my iourny to conveye,

"That cruel Sathan trouble nat my passage,       1170
Nor that his malis may cleyme in me no riht."
Bi the martir rehersid this language,
*Cam* too angelis from heuen with gret liht,
This vois eke herd in al the peeplis siht
Wher-as he stood boundyn to a stake            1175
Vpon the poynt to deye for Cristis sake:

---

1150   that] the H        and] or All other MSS
1151   invisible in all MSS, though "invincible" was no doubt
          intended.
1152   *of*] on La
1153   nat] not T H; nott In; neuer Ed
1157   ende] and T In H Ed
1159   *which*] om. La
1160   did] gan T In H Ed
1162   for] of T In H Ed        to] om. La
1164   tweene] betweene T In H Ed
1165   gan] can H; began Ed
1169   Angel] Angil Li; Aungelles T In; angels H Ed
1172   this] his Ed
1173   *Cam*] Can La; Came In; Come Ed
1175   Wher] Ther T In H Ed        boundyn] i-bounden T In H
1176   Cristis] goddis T In H Ed

"O Amphyball, aftir thi devis,
With thi disciple, the glorious prince Albon,
Thou shalt this day been in paradis.
Riht in erthe as ye wer bothyn oon                      1180
With your tryumphe ye shal to-gidir gon,
And with your palmes ye shal in glorie
With a title of euyr-lastyng memorie;

f. 171 r.      "Among martires receyve *ther* your meede,--
Lik your desert, for eternal guerdoun,--             1185
A crowne of gold and a purpil weede
Forgid for seyntis in the heuenly mansioun.
Lik to rubies most souereyn of renoun,
Albon and thou perpetuelly shal shyne,
Of Verolamye the cite t'enlumyne."                     1190

In this while to Angelis doun descende
To the holy martir for his gostly socour,
On his sowle benygnly for to attende,
Whitter than snowe or any lily flour,
His gost conveyng vp to the heuenly tour,--             1195
Paynyms, this tyme a-bidyng in the feeld,
Gretly abassht whan thei this thyng beheeld.

Harder of hert than flynt or any ston,
Aftre his spirit was born vp to heuen
Tormentours, in ther malis alloon,                     1200
Fervent in ire as flawme of *fyry* leven,

---

1177   O] <u>om</u>. H        Amphyballus T In H Ed
1180   bothyn] bothe T; both In H Ed
1182   shal] shal be T ("be" <u>added</u> <u>above</u>), H Ed      in] on In
1183   memorie] victorie T In H Ed
1184   *ther*] ye La; ther Li T In H; this Ed
1185   for] of Ed
1187   for] with T In H Ed
1188   souereyn] souereygnly In
1190   Of] In T H Ed
1193   for] <u>om</u>. T In H Ed
1195   vp to] unto Ed
1196   this] in this H
1197   whan] whan that Li
1199   to] vnto T In H
1200   alloon] al oon Li; ay oon T In H Ed
1201   Fervent in fyry ire as any beuen Ed      in] on In
          as] <u>om</u>. H      of] or T In H      *fyry*] fir in La

Lik as Iewis fil vpon Seynt Stephen,
So wer thei besi, of hateful cursidnesse,
The ded body with stones to oppresse.

Thei had the martir in so gret dissdeyn,        1205
*Afftir* his deth gan make a newe affray
That no memorie shuld of hym be seyn
Vpon the ground wher as he ded lay,--
Sauff ther was oon which that stale away
The ded cors and dede his besy cur        1210
Most secretely to make his sepultur.

f. 171 v.    He was Cristen, the man which did his peyn
The ded cors to close it in the grounde
In secre wise til Iesu list ordeyn
Provide a tyme that he may be founde        1215
Which for the feith suffrid many a wounde.
*And* this was doon bi grace, for the nonys,
Maugre all tho that cast vpon hym stonys.

Dukis, erlys, and lordis of the toun
Wer ovir-comen almost with fastyng;        1220
Among paynyms roos a discencioun,
That wold have had the body in kepyng,
Which had *avowid* in ther out-goyng
To bryng the *martir*, bi oth and surete,
Othir quyk or ded, hom to that cite.        1225

A-mong hem silf of vengeaunce thei gan stryve,

1202   fil] fyllen T In H; fell Ed
1206   *Afftir*] Affitir La
1207   of hym shuld be H
1208   as he ded] that he T In H Ed
1212   his] his busy H
1215   Provide] And provide T In H Ed
1216   a] om. T
1217   *And*] As La        this] thus In        was] om. T In H Ed
1218   upon] on T In H Ed
1221   roos] a-rosse T; aroos In H; rose Ed
1222   have] om. H
1223   *avowid*] avoidid La; a-wowed In; avowid Li T H; a uowed
          Ed
1224   *martir*] martis La
1225   that] ther Li T H Ed; her In
1226   thei gan] gan to Ed

With swerdis drawe fel at divisioun
Bi the promys outhir ded or live
To bryng the martir with hem to the toun,
Which wer vnworthi to have possessioun          1230
Of sich a tresour tyl God list shape a tyme
Of gracious chaunge to sende a new pryme.

A-geyn ther promys God made an obstacle
Whann thei of newe the martir gan manace.
The bodi was besilid bi myracle                 1235
And i-buried in a secre place
Ther to abide, tyl God list of his grace,
As I seide erst, this tresour of renoun
May be founde to glade with al ther toun.

f. 172 r.   Thus whan paynyms had shewed ther vttraunce,
Off the martir the doctryne hool for-sake,
God vpon hem did opynly vengeaunce,--
Al ther lymes and membris *gan to* shake;
With a palsie ther toungis wer eke take,
With which *membre* afforn in many wise         1245
The feith of Criste *thei* list falsly despise.

The handis, touchid, of the homycidis,
Impotent of power and of myht,
Ther podagre, vn-weeldi bak and sides,
Ther leggis faltrid for to stonde vpriht;       1250
Ther mouht stood wrong, a-goggl stood ther siht,

---

1227   at] a T In H
1228   the] ther All other MSS       live] a-live T In H Ed
1231   shape] to shape H
1234   the martir gan] began the martir to T H Ed; gan the
         martir to In
1236   i-buried] eke buried Ed
1238   of] to H
1239   ther] this T H; her In; the Ed
1240   whan] when the T In H Ed
1243   *gan to*] did La only
1245   mebre La
1246   *thei*] om. La    despise] to despise T H Ed
1247   touchid] cowchid (?) H      the] these Ed
1249   podagre] bodies T In H Ed      bak and] bak eke and T In
         H Ed
1250   Ther] Her T In H
1251   a-goggl] a-gogil Li; a-gogull T In H; a-gogle Ed

Eche membre and ioynt out of ordre stood,--
And the iuge sodeynly wex wood.

Handis to Godward whan thei be vengeable,
Feet that renne for custom to damage,                    1255
Cruel eyn which be nat merciable,
Mortal tongis that dampne men in ther rage,
Bi detraccioun, mouthis for fals language,--
Lik desertes, of old who list remembre,
God of his riht can punysshen euery membre.              1260

The eye for lokyng receyuyth his guerdoun;
The tonge for speche takith his salarie;
Blood wrongly shad requerith of resoun
Hasty *vengaunce* thouh it a while tarie,
Mordre, homycide, which ben to God contrarie;           1265
Deth of martires, slauhtre of innocentis,
Crieth vengeaunce to God in ther tormentis.

f. 172 v.     Speciali, al the tormentours
That wer assentid for to sleen Albon
Fadid a-wey as dew on somer flours                       1270
And cam to nouht, almost euerychon;
Mynde of the martir abood al-wey in oon,
And day bi day the gret laude and glorie
Gan more and more encrece of his victorie.

This seide vengeaunce no while was conceelid,--

---

1253  the] ther Li; her T In H; theyr Ed        iuge] iuge also
      T In H Ed
1255  for] of T In H Ed        to] for T In H Ed
1259  Lik] Lik her T H; Like theyr Ed
1260  ponyssh T In H Ed
1261  eye] eighe Ed        receyuyth] resceyue T In H Ed
      his] this In
1262  speche] speakyng Ed
1263  wrongly] wrongfully T In H Ed
1264  *vengaunce*] vengenace La
1266  slauhtres In
1267  in ther] with her H
1269  for] om. H        sleyne T; slayne In H; slee Ed
1270  as] a H
1272  Mynde] The mynde T In H Ed
1273  and] to H
1274  his] om. T H Ed
1275  counceiled In H

Nor the gret noise of the aduersite
Take on paynyms wolde nat be heelid.
Ther trouble and rumour was nat kept secre,
For dreede of which the cheef *of* ther cite,
Medlid with grace, as the story seith,          1280
Wer all attonys turned to Cristis feith.

With riht hool hert and ful devout humblesse
From ther old sect thei *gan* a-wey declyne,
Gan preise the Lord for his rihtwisnesse,
And some bi grace heuenly and divyne,          1285
Bi influence that did vpon hem shyne,
Left al the world, tresour and substaunce,
Went to Rome for to do penaunce.

And bi the grace of our Lord Iesu
Thei renouncid al ther old errour,             1290
Saugh in ther goddis was no vertu,
Helpe at neede, comfort, nor socour,
But all attonys, with diligent labour,
Of fals ydolls forsook the sacrifise,
Be-cam Cristen in most humble wise.            1295

f. 173 r.    Miracles shewid and vertuous doctrine
Off Amphibalus, with fructuous influence,
Grace annexid, which did vpon hem shyne,
Causid the cite of all ther old offence
To axe mercy, and with hool diligence          1300
Ther fals goddis of newe thei have despised,

---

1276   the] ther Li In Ed; her T H
1277   on] vpon T In H Ed
1279   *of*] om. La
1282   humblenesse H Ed
1283   *gan*] om. La
1286   hem] hym Ed
1288   Went to Rome] And to Rome went T In H Ed
1289   the] om. In Ed      Iesu] Christ Iesu Ed
1290   Thei] The In
1291   Saugh] And saugh T In H; And sawe Ed      was] ther was
         T In H Ed
1292   at neede] neede "at" above, T; om. "at" In; ne (omit
         "neede") H      nor] nor no H
1297   fructuous] vertous Ed
1298   vpon] on T In H Ed

And most meekly bi grace thei *wer* baptised.

> He that whilom was besy to compile
> This noble story, trewly of entent,
> In Latyn tonge to direct his style,                    1305
> Riht as he sawe, so was he diligent
> It to conveie bi-cause he was present.
> Yit list he nat, I suppose, of meekenesse,
> Telle wat he waas nor his name expresse.

> To hym silf he gaff non othir name,                    1310
> Aftir the story as I reherce can,
> Except, he wrot, of dreede and honest shame
> He wolde be callid, as he told than,
> Of all wretchis the symplest man;
> Off othir name, as bi *his* writyng,                   1315
> To vs he left non othir knowlachyng,

> Sauff he, of trust and of confidence
> Which that aboode, in his oppynyoun,
> Ther shoold come with gret reverence,
> Tyme comyng, folk of religioun                         1320
> Specialli to Verolamye toun,
> Which that shold do ther besy peyn

---

1302  thei] <u>om</u>. T In H Ed      *wer*] we La
1303  <u>In</u> <u>l</u>. <u>marg</u>. T <u>has</u> <u>an</u> <u>asterisk</u> <u>and</u> <u>in</u> <u>r</u>. <u>marg</u>. <u>a</u> <u>note</u>
      <u>in</u> <u>later</u> <u>hand</u> <u>apparently</u> <u>taking</u> <u>notice</u> <u>of</u> <u>the</u>
      <u>reworking</u> <u>of</u> <u>the</u> <u>remainder</u> <u>of</u> <u>the</u> <u>poem</u> <u>by</u> <u>editor</u>
      <u>of</u> Ed. <u>The</u> <u>hand</u> <u>is</u> <u>difficult</u>; <u>the</u> <u>present</u> <u>editor</u>
      <u>reads</u>, "A signo (?) in quaternio papiri nouiter
      scripto usque hunc versum 0 blessed Albon folio
      tertio sequenti et tunc prosequimur ad finem ut ibi."
      <u>Horstmann</u> <u>reads</u> "Quere in quaternio (omits "papiri")
      ...." <u>The</u> <u>1534</u> <u>edition</u> <u>contains</u> <u>ll</u>. <u>1303-51</u> <u>at</u> <u>a</u>
      <u>later</u> <u>point</u> (Horst. <u>ll</u>. <u>1521</u> <u>ff</u>.), <u>after</u> <u>161</u> <u>lines</u>
      <u>of</u> <u>new</u> <u>verse</u> <u>certainly</u> <u>not</u> <u>by</u> <u>Lydgate</u>, <u>and</u> <u>certain</u>
      <u>displaced</u> <u>stanzas</u> <u>from</u> <u>the</u> <u>original</u> <u>poem</u>. <u>See</u>
      *Appendix* <u>for</u> <u>full</u> <u>treatment</u> <u>of</u> <u>Edition</u>.
1304  story] history Ed
1312  Except] Except that In      and] and of Ed
1314  symplest] sympilleste Li; semplest T; symple H
1315  *his*] <u>om</u>. La <u>only</u>
1316  non othir] no maner T In Ed
1317  of confidence] confidence Li T In H; good confidence Ed
1319  with] a T In H; in Ed

The feith of Crist to preche in Breteyn.

f. 173 v.    Than shal the trouthe opynly be knowe,
          Whan the errour is losid and vnbounde          1325
          Off paynyms and Cristis worde be sowe
          Thorugh al that lond, fals ydolis to confounde.
          Than to ther hertis gladnesse shal rebounde,
          At vnset hour whan Iesu list bi grace
          Off his mercy a tyme to purchace.              1330

          This same man of ful trewe entent
          Which besi was his story to endite,
          Vn-to Rome with the book he went,
          Bi gret avis his purpos for t'aquyte,
          And fynally, lik as he doth write,             1335
          All fals goddis and ydolis to for-sake,
          Baptem receyve, and Cristis feith to take.

          As I have told, this book with hym he brouht
          To be seyn ovyr; with lowe subieccioun
          To all that court meekely he besouht;          1340
          Afftir the dew examynacioun,--
          Crist Iesu of hool entencioun
          Callid to record,--this story maade of newe,
          Lik as he wrot, that euery word was trewe;

---

1323  to] for to Ed
1324  opynly be] be openly T In H Ed
1326  be] to In      sowe] sawe Ed
1327  that] the T In H Ed
1329  At vnset hour] That vsith hour T ("faith" above, other
        hand), H; That vsith our In; That useth our fayth Ed
1330  mercy] infinite mercy Ed
1332  his] this T Ed
1333  Vn-to Rome] Vnto the see of Rome Ed
1334  avis] avice H; aduise Ed      for t'aquyte] to aquyte T
        In H Ed
1335  doth] doth playnly Ed
1336  ydolis] falce ydolles T H
1338  As] And as T H Ed
1339  lowe] meke and lowe Ed
1340  meekely] and humbly Ed (T has "and" added above)
1341-42  order of lines reversed in T In H Ed
1341  the] their Li T In H Ed      dew] dewe and full Ed
1342  Crist Iesu of hool] Oure lorde Christe Iesu with
        deuoute Ed

This book accomplisshid, notable and vertuous,
Of hym that was in Brutis Albioun
Callid prothomartir most victorious,
That first for Crist sofred passioun,
The yeer accountid of his invencioun
Fro Cristis birthe and his nativite                                    1350
Ful .vii. hundrid nynty yeer and thre.

f. 174 r.   Idus of August was his invencioun,
His bodi founde, as it was Goddis myht,
Aftir closid with gret devocioun
In a chest forgid of sylver briht,                                     1355
At which tyme in al the peeplis siht
To gret encrece of al Holy Chirche
God of his grace myraclis list to wirche.

As the story pleynly dooth vs teche,
Thei that wer blynd recurid han ther siht,                             1360
To dombe also restorid was the speche,
Folk lame and podagre went vpriht,
Lepres made clene, only thoruh Goddis myht,
Pallatik folk, the story doth remembre,

---

1345  vertuous] famous Ed (T <u>has</u> "vertuous" <u>struck out</u>, <u>and</u>
     "famous" <u>in margin</u> <u>in other hand</u>.)
1347  victorious] vertuous T In H Ed
1348  first] <u>om</u>. T In H Ed
1349  The] That T In H Ed     invencioun] translation Ed
1350  Fro] For H
1351  Ful] Fully T In H    yeer] <u>om</u>. H
1352-58  Stanza <u>entirely</u> <u>omitted</u> <u>from</u> Ed
1353  as it was] by grace of T In H
1355  sylver] gold and sylver T H
1358  to] <u>om</u>. T In H
1359-1414  Ed <u>places these lines after the 161 non-Lydgatean</u>
    <u>lines on St. Germain (beginning at Horstmann's III,</u>
    <u>1458)</u>.
1359  Not without myracles as the story doth us teache Ed
1360  han] haue T In Ed; hath H
1361  To dombe] The dombe Li T In H Ed    restorid was]
    restorid ("was" <u>above</u>, T) T In; was restored Ed
    the] to Li; to her T In H; to theyr Ed
1362  Folkes T In Ed; Folke H    went] went than Ed
1363  only thoruh Goddis myht by prayere of this knyght Ed
1364  Pallatik] so <u>all other MSS</u>. See <u>Glossary</u>.

Wer in that hour made hool, euery membre.          1365

    Be glad and mery, this title is riche and good,
Lond of Breteyn, callid Brutis Albioun,
Which art enbawmyd with the purpil blood
Off blissid Albon, prynce of that regioun,
And specialy, *O* noble roial toun                 1370
Off Verolamye, reioissh and be iocunde:
So riche a tresour is in thi boundis founde!

    Richer tresour, worthi to be comendid,
More than in Troie was ther Palladioun,
For on *thi* soile of newe ther is descendid        1375
Celestial dewe of grace and al foisoun,
And specially bi revelacioun
Which on thi theatre of newe doth rebounde,
Now blissid Albon is in thi boundis founde.

f. 174 v.    Hector whilom was Troies chaumpioun        1380
And Hanybal protector of Cartage,
Marchus Manlyus savid Rome toun,
The Capitolie savid from damage,
And in Briteyn in more latter age,
Of holy Albon whan the cors was founde,            1385

---

1365   And all other diseased were hole in euery membre Ed
      made] <u>om.</u> T In H      euery] in euery Li T In H Ed
1366   this] thi T In H Ed
1368   the] <u>om.</u> In H; T <u>has</u> "the" <u>above.</u>
1369   Albon] Albion H; <u>Saint Albon Ed</u>
1370   O] a La     roial] and ryall Ed
1372   boundis] londis H
1373   worthi] and worthier T H; and worthy In; more worthy Ed
1374   More than] Moche better than Ed    ther] her T In H;
      euer Ed (T <u>has</u> "her" <u>underpointed</u> <u>and</u> "euer"
      <u>above.</u>)
1375   on] in In    ther] <u>om.</u> T In H Ed
1376   Celestial] A celestiall Ed   al] of T In H
1377   bi] bi angelicall Ed (T <u>has</u> "angelykall" <u>above in late</u>
      <u>hand</u>)
1378   theatre] lande T H; londe Ed; In <u>leaves</u> <u>blank.</u>
1379   Now] This T H; That Ed
1380   Troies] Troianes T In H; Troyans Ed
1381   Cartago Ed
1382   Manlyus] Malvius T H Ed; Malwyus In
1383   savid] conseruyd <u>All</u> other <u>MSS</u>

Made in that regioun al ioie to habounde.

Whilom Kyng Offa had a visioun,
Which of Seynt Albonys was patron and foundour,
Bi myracle for his devocioun
The place shewid wher was hid this tresour.          1390
He with gret cost and diligent labour
Let calle to-gidre of dyvers regiouns
Sovereyn maistris of wryhtes and masouns.

Aftir the tyme, as made is mencioun,
To bilde that chirche whan he was diligent,          1395
He ordeyned for his translacioun,--
Of all his kyngdam bi comaundement
Grettest prelatis to be ther-at present;
Took auctorite, the story telle can,
Grauntid be bulle of Pope Adrian.                    1400

He went hym silf, this noble worthi kyng,
Of gret devocioun to Rome the Cite,
Sparid no cost til he in euery thyng
Had of his purpos graunt and auctorite,

---

1386  ioie to] to T ("for" above), H; thynges to Ed
1387  Kynge Offa as I sayd hauynge this vision Ed.  T cor-
        responds to La but "Whilom" is struck out, and above,
        a partly illegible phrase added, which Horstmann
        reads:  "Before as I have said."
1388  Albonys] Albon T In H Ed
1389  for his] shewed for his good Ed; T has "schewed" and
        "good" added above in other hand
1390  shewid] om. Ed; struck through, T    was hid] hid was
        H     this] om. T In H    tresour] ryche treasure
        Ed; T has "this riche" added above.
1391  gret] om. Ed
1392  calle] cast In
1393  Sovereyn] Most cunninge Ed
1394-1400  Entirely rewritten in Ed.  See Appendix for text,
        lines H. 1423-57
1396  He ordeyned] He let ordeigne T In; To let ordeigne H
1398  Grettest] The grettest T In H
1400  La reads in same hand, in margin, "Adriani pape"
1401  Ed resumes correspondence to La (Horst. III, 1500).
        He] After Ed
1402  Cite] ryall citie Ed

Privilegis, fredam, and liberte,                        1405
Bi the pope confermyd to that place
For love of Albon, with many special grace.


f. 175 r.    Bi auctorite, as ye have herd devised,
He had is axyng bi power spirituall,
And for his parte, to be more auctorised,               1410
He hath annexid in especiall
Libertees and fraunchises ful roiall,
Perpetually boundid on brede and lengthe,
Reuerence of Albon, to stondyn in his strengthe.


Tyme of this pope callid Adryan,                        1415
Reyngnyng this kyng notable and glorious,
A fals errour in Breteyn ther began
Which was sustenyd bi oon Pelagius,
To God and man froward and odious,
For which at Londoun, of prelatis young and old,
The same tyme a seene ther was hold.


All the bisshopis of that regioun
To-gidre assemblid bi gret ordynaunce
To stynte all errour of oon entencioun,
Germayn the bisshop cam doun out of Fraunce            1425

---

1405  fredam and liberte] fredoms and liberte T In H; fredomes
      and libertees Ed
1406  pope] pope then Ed
1407  Albon] saint Albon        special] a special T H; especial
      Ed
1408  devised] avised T In H
1410  to be] for to be T H
1412  Libertees] With all liberties Ed         and] om. T In H
1413  Perpetual H       boundid] bounde H       on] in In H; yt
      in Ed
1414  Reuerence] In reuerence T In H; In honour Ed        Albon]
      Saint Albon Ed
1415-91  Not in Ed.  Similar matter is contained in Ed III,
      1297-1457 (Horstmann's numbering).  T has vertical
      line in margin running to l. 1470 with note, "vacat ...
      hucusque."  See Appendix.
1415  "Adriani primi" in margin La, Li
1419  and man] a man T In H        odious] contrarius H
1421  ther was] was ther T In H
1425  Germanye Li

And with hym cam a clerk of gret substaunce,
A famous prelat, whos name to termyne,
I-callid was Lupus Tercasyne

 This holy Germayn, wis and of sad age,
Cam out of Fraunce, to be ther-at present,   1430
Bi a maner of devout pilgrymage
Vnto Seynt Albon, in al his best entent,
And at his toumbe he was diligent
Certeyn reliques with al his besi cure
Them for to offren at his sepulture.     1435

f. 175 v.  Of holy seyntis forn-tyme that he souht,
Off the apostlis and martirs manyoon,
Blissid Germayn, reliques that he brouht,
Offrid hem vp devoutly to Albon,
Richely shryned with many precious ston,   1440
The same reliques in especiall
Ther for to abide for a memoriall.

 And ageynward (his entent was good)
Took with hym, of notable diligence,
Part of the poudir rubified with blood    1445
Of this martir shad with gret violence

                1447

---

1426 cam] ther came T In
1427 prelat] clerk H
1428 trecasine T In H
1429 wis] om. T In H
1434 al] om. T In H
1435 for] om. T H
1436 forn-tyme] for tyme T In H
1438 reliques] the reliques T In H
1439 vp] om. In  to] vnto T In H
1440 many] many a T In H
1441 especiall therfort [sic] H
1444 of] with full T H; with a In
1446 this] the In
1447 Although the stanza demands a line here, it is absent
   in La, Li, and In. Trinity MS has added in another
   hand in the right margin: "Lyke as by for ye haue
   herd in sentence." H has, more appropriately, "Bare
   hit before him in the peplis presence" in text. Neither line gives any strong indication of genuineness.
   Ed lacks the entire passage. See textual note to
   III, 1415-70.

Kept for a relique in provyncis mo than oon,
Did it worship in mynde of Seynt Albon.

This holy Germayn of high devocioun          1450
Hath made a vough on *this* sepultur
Of blissid Albon, and in his orisoun
Requerid hym to doon his besy cur
To pray for hym that he may recur,
In Cristis cause to be victorious          1455
Ageyn the errour of Pelagious.

Bi the merite of Albon and vertu,
And bi his owen diligent labour,
And speciali bi grace of Crist Iesu,
Quenchid and anullid was the gret errour          1460
Off Pelagious which had no favour
Off Holy Writ but of fals heresye
*Geyn* Seynt Germayn to susteene his partye.

f. 176 r.    The holy martir list for to enspir,
Wher as he lay translatid in his shryne,          1465
Bisshop Germayn bi grace to set affir,
Mynde and memorie with cunnyng t'enlumyne,
Off heretikes staunche the doctryne,
Which in this sene, to his encrece of glorye,
Off Pelagious hath wonne the victorie.          1470

Whos translacioun compendiously devised,
Tyme remembrid of his inuencioun

---

1448  Kept] Kept it T H
1449  End of Lincoln MS. The torn fragment (very small)
        which follows in Li is from "Churl and Bird," a por-
        tion of which immediately follows on next entire leaf.
1451  Hath] Had T In H      *this*] his La Li In H Ed
1454  that] the H
1457  vertu] by vertu T In H
1458  his] om. In
1460  Quenchid] Queynte T In      adnullid H
1463  *Geyn*] Gey La; Ageyne T In H      Seynt] om. T In H
1464  for to] om. T In H
1466  Bisshop] The Bisshop T H
1467  to enlumyne T In H
1468  staunche] to staunche T In H
1471  devised] T adds "thus" above the line.
1472  inuencioun] T adds "furste" above the line.

Bi Kyng Offa, the feste solennyzed
To gret gladnesse of al this regioun,
Which in his tyme, b'exaumple of Salomon,          1475
Of gold and syluyr sparid non expense
To the holy martir for to do reverence.

Prelatis chosen of notable memorie
At this celestial gracious iubilee
The arke in brouht and the propiciatorie,          1480
With too prerogatyffs, surmountyng of degre,
In Moyses table hauyng the souereynte,
First love to God with hool hert and mynde,
Next, our neighbour, Crist bit bi lawe of kynde.

These tweyn loves accomplisshid in Albon,          1485
It was previd bi gret experience:
Froom the deth he leet his maistir gon;
For Cristis sake, of brennyng high fervence,
Suffrid passioun with humble pacience;
For his neihbour cause, he list nat feyne,          1490
He bad allone the brount for them tweyn.

f. 176 v.     O Verolamye, as I have told beforn,
O famous cite among all naciouns,
Which in thi bondis haddist sich a prince born,
Notable in knyhthod, with all condiciouns          1495
Of high prowesse, bi many-fold resouns
Worthi bi vertu and bi roial lyne

---

1475  his] this In      by example T In H
1478  chosen] "chosin" struck through and "prynces" above in
      later hand in T      of notable] notable of T In H
1483  to] of T In H
1484  Next] Next him T In H      Crist bit] in Crist T In H
1485  These tweyn] Thus thei (altered in other ink to "ther")
      T; These twey In; This they H
1486  It] Thus H
1489  Suffrid] And suffred T In H
1490  neihbour] neyghbours T In H
1491  bad allone] allone abode T In H      them] om. T In H
1492-98  These lines occur later in Ed (Horstmann, III, 1514
      ff.)  See Appendix.
1492  Verolamye] blot in La
1493  O famous] blot in La; a famous In      cite] olde citie
      Ed
1497  Worthi] Wordy Ed.  Dare one hope this is Lydgate's own
      spelling?

     To be registrid a-mong the worthi nyne.     1498

Here endith the livis and passiouns of Seynt Albon and Seynt
Amphibal translatid out of Frenssh and Latyn bi Dan Iohn
Lidgate at the request of Maistir Iohn Whetehamstede
Abbot of Saynt Albon the yeer of our Lord M CCCC XXXIX.

### Prayer to Saint Albon

T, f. 65    O Blessid Albon, O martir most benigne,
v.        Callid of Bretons steward most notable,     1500
       Prince of knyghthode, previd by many a sygne,
       In all thi werkes iust, prudent and tretable,
       And in thi domes rightfull and merciable,
       *Be* our paveyce, sheld of proteccioun,
       O prothomartyr of Brutis Albioun.     1505

T, f. 66    Let all thi seruauntes grace and mercy fynde,
r.        Which that call to the in myschef and distresse
       And haue thi passioun and martyrdome in mynde,
       A-geyne foreyn enemyes and all froward duresse.
       Of thi benigne mercifull goodnesse     1510
       Them to defende, be thou her champioun,
       O prothomartir of Brutis Albioun.

---

1498  registrid] in degre Ed     a-mong the worthi] aboue all
     the worthies Ed. This "aboue" supra in later hand.
     MS La ends here. The colophon occurs at this point in
     La only, but with small variations it appears at end
     of T, In, H, and Ed, which continue for fifteen more
     stanzas. Li is missing from III, 1449 onward.
1499-1603  These fifteen stanzas appear in T, In, H, and Ed,
     and in part also in the Talbot Book of Hours. Their
     character as a prayer and their appearance separately
     from the poem in Talbot, with title "Oracio ad pro-
     thomartirem Albanum," suggest that at least one other
     scribe (of Landsdowne or its original) assumed that
     they constituted a separate work; indeed he may have
     been right. The text here presented is that of T.
1500  Bretons] Bretayne Tal; Brytaynes In; Brutis H; Brytons
     Ed
1501  assigne Tal
1504  *Be*] Be thou Tal; Be in T In H     of] and Tal In
1507  that] om. Tal
1509  A-geyne] Enyue Tal     foreyn] frowarde Ed
1511  her] their Tal Ed

Sith thou art namyd gracious, benigne and goode,
The first all-so which that in Bretaigne
Suffredist peynems to shede thi gentyll blode, 1515
For Cristes feith to die and suffre peyne,
O glorious prince, of mercy nat disdeyne
To here the prayers and deuowte orisoun
Of all thi seruauntes in Brutis Albioun.

Thou were a myrrour of mercy and pitee;      1520
Haddist a custome, her in this worlde levyng,
To cherissh pilgremes, and heldest hospitalitee,
All pouere folk and straungers refresshing;
Graunte oure requestes for loue of this kyng
Callid Kyng Offa, which had a visioun         1525
Where thou were buryed in Brutis Albioun.

Like a prynce of right thou must entende
To forther all thoo that lyve in thi servise,
All her greves and myschefes to amende,
And by thi prayer a path for hem devise        1530
To leve in vertu and vice to despise,
Be thi most knyghtly mediacioun,
O prothomartir of Brutis Albioun.

For his sake haue in remembraunce
To all thi seruauntes for to do socour,        1535
Which, of deuocioun, the for to do plesaunce,
Was in thi chirche chef bylder and founder,
Of thi libertees roiall protectoure,

---

1513  gracious namyd In
1515  Suffred Ed        to] om. Tal
1519  O Prothomartyr of Brutis Albioun In
1520-33  These two stanzas transposed in Tal, which ends at
      l. 1526.
1521  a] in Tal
1522  and heldest] helde Tal
1524  this] þylke Tal; thilk In; thylke Ed
1527  moost In
1528  forther] Foster Tal
1529  greves] greuous Ed
1530  thi] their In
1531  leve] lyue H Ed        vicys Tal
1534  T has an additional "sake" underpointed after "For."
1535  To] om. H
1536  for to do] to do the Ed

There brought inne first men of relligioun,--
On the heldest abbey in Brutis Albioun.        1540

T, f. 66        Amonge all other, remembre that place,
v.              Hit to conserue in longe prosperite,
                Where thou art shryned, to grete encrece of grace,
                As their protectour ageyne all aduersitee.
                And euer haue mynde vpon her citee        1545
                Which is made famous be thi passioun,
                O prothomartir of Brutis Albioun.

                To the citee be patron, prince, and guyde.
                In thi service make hem diligent,
                With longe felicite on the todyr side.        1550
                Conserue thine abbott and thi devoute covent
                Sith thei arne bounde of hert and hole entent
                Euer the to serue by ther professioun,
                O prothomartyr of Brutis Albioun.

                Sith in thi lyvyng thou were so good a knyght
                And of vertu thou haddist grete sufficiaunce,
                Pray for the Sixt like as he hath right,
                Of Goddis grace, by influent pyussaunce,
                Be thi prayer, in Englond and in Fraunce
                Longe to contynue and haue possessioun,        1560
                O prothomartir of Brutys Albioun.

                As verely as thou in thi lyvyng
                Were like a prynce, notable and vertuous,
                Pray for the syxt Henry, of thes roealmes kyng,

---

1540   On the heldest] One the oldest In; One theldest Ed
       Abbeys Ed
1542   conserue] preserue Ed
1543   grete encrece of grace] In has "grete" struck through,
       "honowre" above, "and grace" in the line.
1550   todyr] other In Ed
1555-61   Omitted in Ed and replaced by two stanzas (Horst.
       III, 1752-65) which are given in *Appendix*.
1557   "Sixt" has been struck out in T and over it inserted
       "viii."
1558   grace] om. In
1564   T reads "viii" over "vi"

Afore remembrid, that he may be famous                  1565
In all his dedis and victorious,
Since he to the hath grete deuocioun,
O prothomartyr of Brutis Albioun.


    Pray for princes that this lond gouerne,
To rule the peple by prudent pollicie;                  1570
Pray for the Church that like a clere lanterne
Bi goode example her suggetes for to guye,
And pray all-so that the chivalrye
May hold vp trought a-geyne falce extorcioun,
O prothomartyr of Brutis Albioun.                       1575

T, f. 67       Pray for marchauntis and artificers
r.          To encrese by vertu in their businesse,
That ther be founde no fraude in their desires,
So that falce lucre haue noone entresse.
Bi thi prayer do all-so represse                        1580
All tyranny and all falce extorcioun,
O prothomartir of Brutis Albioun


    And with these, O martyr glorious,
Sith thi prayer may so moche avayle,
Pray to the Lord aboue, most gracious,                  1585
Ageyne indigence to send inough of vitayll,
And specially pray for the porayll,
Them to releue with plenty and foisoun,
O prothomartir of Brutis Albioun.


    Noble prynce, most soueragne and entier,   1590
Corne, fruyte and greyne to encrece and multiplie,

---

1565-66  Lines underscored in T and the following inserted
    in r. margin; cf. H. 1760-61 of Ed in *Appendix*:
    And his quene Anna notable and famous / That all their
    isseu may be victorious
1567  he] altered to "they" by cramped insertion of first
    and last letters
1571  lanterne clere H
1573  that] for that ("the" above in same hand) In
1574  vp trought] vpryght Ed
1579  entresse] enteresse In; encreasse Ed
1587  the] om. In
1588  Entire verse omitted in H
1590  most] of most H

Blessid Albone, pray for the labourer
To plough and cart her hondys to applye,
That grace may so gouerne hem and guye.
To grete increce gyue all this regioun,                1595
O prothomartir of Brutis Albioun.

All thes estates remembrid in substaunce,
Ioyned in vertu by perfith charite,
Like a prynce take hem in gouernaunce
And them preserue from all aduersitee.                1600
Sett pees a-monge hem and vertuous vnitee
Like an ymage voide of divisioun,
O prothomartir of Brutis Albioun.

Here endith the glorious liff and passioun of the blessid
martyr, Seynt Alboon, and Seynt Amphiball, which glorious
lyves were translatyd out off Frenssh and Latyn by Dan Iohn
Lydgate, monk of Bury, at request and prayer of Masteir Iohn
Whethamsted, the yere of our Lord MCCCCXXXIX and of the seyde
Master Iohn Whethamstede, of his abesye XIX.

---

1593   to] so to H Ed; T has "so" above the line.
1598   Ioyned] T has "d" struck through and "them" added in
          other hand above; Ioyne them Ed
1601   T has "kepe" in later hand in margin for "Sett."
1602   All where now reigneth pride and deuision Ed; T has
          entire line underscored and "All wher now reyneth
          pride & division" in later hand in margin.

See n. to III, 1498 La. colophon.        at request] at the
   request In H    XIX] XIX yere In
The Edition of 1534 reads as follows:  "Here endeth the
   gloriouse lyfe and passyon of seint Albon prothomartyr of Englande."
In, at foot of page, after colophon reads "Qd Panox" in
   small hand.

## THE EDITION OF 1534

The edition of Lydgate's <u>St</u>. <u>Albon</u> which was published (very probably) at St. Albans in 1534 exists today in a u-nique copy at the British Library, shelf mark C. 34. g. 17, S.T.C. no. 256. Although late, this edition has some author-ity, concerning which see the discussion of the manuscripts in the Introduction. Certain portions of the text estab-lished in the present edition are missing from that of 1534; further, in the 1534 edition there are 161 lines of rewritten matter and 140 lines of entirely new content. The tables be-low will facilitate comparison of the two. For the matter following 1. 1302 of Book III, which alone gives evidence of having been purposefully edited, the contents of the first ta-ble have been restated, from the point of view of the 1534 linear arrangement.


TABLE OF LINE DIFFERENCES BETWEEN THIS TEXT AND THE 1534 ED.

| Present Text | The 1534 Edition (line numbers from Horstmann's edition of 1534 text) |
|---|---|
| I: No differences | |
| II: 604-73 | omitted between H. lines 603-04 |
| 744-50 | " " " " 673-74 |
| III: 22-28 | omitted between H. lines 23-24 |
| 1303-05 | same as H. 1521-69 |
| 1352-58 | omitted between H. lines 1569-70 |
| 1359-1414 | same as H. 1458-1513 |
| 1415-91 | replaced by H. 1296-1457 |
| 1492-98 | same as H. 1514-20 |
| not in Lydgate | H. 1570-1695 |
| 1499-1554 | same as H. 1696-1751 |
| 1555-61 | replaced by H. 1752-65 |
| 1562-1603 (end) | same as H. 1766-1807 (end) |

TABLE OF DIFFERENCES BETWEEN 1534 EDITION & CURRENT TEXT
(beginning at book III, 1. H. 1296)

| | |
|---|---|
| H. 1296-1457 | replaces 1415-91 |
| H. 1458-1513 | same as 1359-1414 |
| H. 1514-20 | same as 1492-98 |
| H. 1521-69 | same as 1303-51 |
| H. 1570-1695 | new matter, not in Lydgate |
| H. 1696-1751 | same as 1499-1554 |
| H. 1752-65 | replaces 1555-61 |
| H. 1766-1807 (End) | same as 1562-1603 (End) |

The omissions of the 1534 editor in book II and the early part of book III give every appearance of having resulted from carelessness or from the use of defective manuscripts for copy. The latter part of book III, on the other hand, was substantially revised because the monks of St. Albans were then engaged in a controversy with their fellows of the Abbey of St. Pantaleon in Cologne concerning the question of the location of St. Alban's relics.

It would seem that the Empress Theophano, journeying from Rome to Cologne in the year 984, brought the relics of a certain Saint Albinus to the monastery as a gift for the German church and people.[1] Since nothing was known of Albinus, he came to be identified with the British saint, whether through confusion or through a desire to make the relics more interesting. It was in time believed in Germany that Saint Germanus had taken the relics from Britain to Ravenna, whence they were later transferred to Rome, to remain there until Theophano's journey.

Although Cologne's pretensions were of long standing, they were of no great concern to the monks of St. Albans until 1502, when a volume, De incliti et gloriosi protomartyris Anglie Albani, containing their version of the Alban legend, was issued by the German monks and dedicated to Henry VII of England. The enduring effect of this volume is attested to by Sir Thomas More's comic allusion to the controversy in his Dialogue concerning Tyndale.[2] There a beggar who has not been cured at St. Albans proposes to try Cologne instead.

---

1. For a full account of the whole matter, see E. P. Baker, "The Cult of St. Alban at Cologne," Archaeological Journal, XCIV (1937), 211 ff.
2. English Works, II, p. 51.

Unfortunately for the monks of St. Albans who had decided
to put Lydgate's poem into print, Lydgate, in telling of St.
Germanus' visit to Alban's shrine and of Offa's finding of
relics, had followed an account (not found by the present
editor) which erred in making the two events simultaneous.
The Cologne book is similarly mistaken.  It will be seen from
book III, 1570 ff. as reproduced below that the best argu-
ments to controvert the German claims were founded, first, on
the fact that Offa lived three hundred years after Germanus,
and, second, on the alleged fact that Offa found only the
martyr's bones, whereas the relics of Cologne, reputedly
brought over by Germanus, were incorrupt.

It was clear that if Lydgate's poem were to be published,
it must be purged of the very errors which reinforced the
German case; such a revision would provide an opportunity for
direct controversy with the Germans.  The editor, presumably
a monk of St. Albans, proceeded to remove that part of
Lydgate's third book which deals with Germanus and Offa, to
rewrite it in keeping with the facts as he had them, to add
a section reviewing and answering the assertions of the monks
of St. Pantaleon, and then to fit the remaining parts of
Lydgate to the new passages as well as he could.  The new or
revised passages are given below.  It is ironic that this
attempt to defend the glory of St. Albans should close with
a prayer for Henry VIII, Anne Boleyn, and the Princess
Elizabeth.  The abbey would soon face an unanswerable foe.

Obviously the author of these Tudor lines had no experience in versification beyond a grasp of rhyme-schemes.  Otherwise the prosy discursive nature of his mind--one dare not
say talent, is evident throughout.  It remains a matter for
astonishment that Carl Horstmann did not detect the difference in style and subject which set them apart from Lydgate's
genuine work.


REVISION OF GERMANUS AND OFFA PASSAGE IN 1534 EDITION
(from pp. 158-163, Horstmann lines 1297 ff.)


And so longe continued / tyll at the last
By a rurall person / disciple of pelagiane
His heticall doctrine / longe tyme begon & past
Newly renewed and fast toke rote agayne                H. 1300
Peruerted the people of this Brutis Britayne
And specially in this citie of olde Uerolamy
Moche increased this doctrine of infamy

Wherwith sore troubled was all the hole clergy

Not stronge inough / by lernyng and prudence
These olde errours to refourme & rectify
But glad to sende for helpe and defence
To the clergy of Fraunce / to be theyr assistence
Where assembled a counsell of clergy in generall
To prouide remedy for this myschefe in speciall          H. 1310

    Lastely concluded by the hole counsell
Sent vnto Uerolamy two auncient clerkes
In lernyng and vertue / ryght famous and excell
The one called **Germayne** a myrrour in good warkes
Confounder of heretykes / & all fyry sparkes
Of scismaticall doctrine / by gostly influence
He was consecrate byshop of Antisiodorence

    And Lupus the bysshop of Trecassinensis
In his holy iournay / with hym was associate
And came to this citie of Uerolaminensis          H. 1320
Where the people perverted were greuously insensate
And from the trewe fayth / crokedly abrogate
By thereticall doctrine of the erroneus person
Declared to the people with deuylysshe illusion

    Good people afore this tyme / of feruent deuocion
For recours of pylgryms / had builded an oratory
Ouer the tombe and corps / of holy saynt Albon
Wheder these bysshops of blessed memory
Came and made prayer to the martyr instantly
That he for them in theyr batayle and conflycte          H. 1330
Wolde be meane to god / the heretyke to conuicte

    Theyr prayer to god / by the martyr preferred
As preueth the sequele / was ryght acceptable
For than the heretikes / day ne tyme deterred
Was clerely conuicte of theyr errours detestable
And reduced by grace / by treuthe infallable
By Lupe and Germane in playne disputation
Renounsyng theyr errours / made abiuration

    Than for that grace / gyuen them in especiall
Of god by meane of the martyrs intercessyon          H. 1340
To his tombe they returned / with hert & mynd effectual
Redoublyng theyr prayer with humble deuocion
For the great tryumphe / and utter subiection
That thenmyes of god / had susteyned that day
Exhortyng the people / to laude god and praye

    And mekely on theyr knees / with all dew reuerence

Uncouered the tombe / where the corps lay
There founde the reliques in state and essence
All though he had layne ther many a longe daye
And of the same reliques they toke no parte away          H. 1350
But of therth all blody saint Germane toke a porcion
To bere about with hym of feruent deuotion

    And for the same in full recompence
A cophyn inclosed with relyques many one
Of all thaposteles / and martyrs with reuerence
Whiche he gathered in places where he had gone
There he them offered to blessed saynt Albon
For a perpetuall memory of that his acte and dede
And to all pylgryms to haue rewarde and mede

    Than departed Germayne and his felowe Lupus          H. 1360
In to  theyr owne countres there to remayne
Within foure yeres after / agayne it happened thus
Newly to sprynge / theresyes of pelagyane
Than the clergy sent of newe for saynt Germayne
Who hastely graunted to come and discusse
All doutes associate / with holy Seuerus

    Who breuely confounded and brought to vtterance
All theretykes to theyr shame and confusyon
That done they retourned agayne into Fraunce
The people delyuered from deuyllyshe illusion          H. 1370
Albeit shortely after / theyr former abusyon
Returned theyr myndes and brought in appostacy
Theyr god forgettyng to laude and magnifie

    And all that was done by the greuous occasyon
Of the furyous saxons / and theyr pagan ryte
For after that they had in this lande made inuasion
Churches and clergy they distroyed quite
To adnull Christis lawe was all theyr delyte
And compell the christen to theyr false ydolatry
In suche miserable lyfe was all theyr felicite          H. 1380

    Thus by them all this region in maner peruerted
From Christis fayth / and holy saynt Albon
The chapell and tombe decayed and subuerted
Token or knowlege there was lefte none
Deuotion and prayer forgotten and gone
Tyll god of his goodnes and mercyfull pitie
Wold reuele his sayntes to the laude of his deite

    Thus duryng this tyme thre hundred yere & mo

The hertes of the people all derke & obumbrate
From the fayth of Christ was clerely lost and go          H. 1390
Worshyppyng ydols of power adnychilate
Reason of knowledge by wyll was obnubilate
By longe continuance accustomed and used
That good and trew doctrine / they vtterly refused

Thylke holy saynt Albon / to the godhed directed
His deuoute prayer / his countrey to reconcile
To Christis owne fayth / al heretyks reiected
With errours and scismes / from them put in exile
The disceytes of the deuyll / hath the long begyle
To abate and suppresse / to the christen releue          H. 1400
And to all heretikes shame and repreue

His prayer well herde / god hath prouyde
A captayne / a ruler / a prince of gret pleasance
Ouer this contre / to reigne rule and gye
Discended of blode from royall aliance
That by goddes helpe shortly made purueyance
These fautes to redresse / by grace as he may
This noble deuoute prince called kynge Offa

It happed that this kyng than beinge at Bygging
Besydes wynslowe his owne maner place                    H. 1410
Callyng to memory all his former lyuyng
How by the blody swerd his peace he had purchace
Compuncte by contrition callyng for grace
Besought God on his knees / with feruent deuocion
Some knowlege to haue of his synnes remyssyon

Than sodenly in the chapel came a maruelous light
Inflamed the king with a swete fraragraunt [sic] odour
The kynge fyrst astonyed / to se it so bryght
Than after coforted [sic] gaue laude prayse & honour
To that only god / grounde of all socour                 H. 1420
And set fast in hym / his trust and confidence
Dayly to serue him / with all dewe reuerence

This kynge then lyinge in the citie of Bath
Halfe slepyng in a slombre appered an angell
Shewyng that of god suche fauour he hath
And also commaundement as he dyd than tell
All scismes and heresyes / from the contre texpell
He shulde perceyue with all diligence anone
To translate the reliques of holy saynt albon

The kyng or this tyme of the pope had purchased         H. 1430

That Lychefelde shulde be / tharchebysshops see
Wherby Canterbury was greatly defased
But for that tyme there was no remedy
All whiche I omyt and returne to our story
Howe and by whom was done this translation
Of archebysshop and bysshops with feruent deuocion

After that the angell at Bathe had thus appered
Of this prothomartyr Albon / made the kyng relacion
He called Humbertus / whome he had than arered
Archebysshop of Lychefeld / and made declaration                H. 1440
Of thangelles commandement / for the translation
Of this holy martyr / than the bysshop anon ryght
Obeyed and prepared therto with all his myght

Accompanyed with suffraganes / two he had than
Theyr names to recount / I let ouer passe
The kyng & they to Uerolamy / with many noble men
Accompaned / came reuerently to the same place
Where as a fyrye pyllour bryghtly shynynge was
Ouer the tombe & place / where as lay saynt Albon
By whiche token / they founde the cophyn anone                H. 1450

They toke vp the bones with all humble deuotion
And bare them to the churche with ympnes and songe
The kynge and his nobles folowed the processyon
Where many fayre myracle was done than amonge
The relyques enclosed in a shryne great and longe
Of syluer and golde set with great ryches
Thus with all solempnite / endeth this busynes                H. 1457

NEW PASSAGE ON COLOGNE CONTROVERSY IN THE 1534 EDITION
(from pp. 167-172, Horstmann lines 1570 ff.)

Nowe perfyte reders / that dyuers stories hath sene
Marke well the tymes / of this here expressed                H. 1571
Whan that saynt Albon by the paynyms kene
For Christis fayth / from this lyfe was suppressed
The comyng of saynt Germayn for errours to be
After all these / the tyme of his inuention
Done by kynge Offa / with his holy translation

CC.lxxxx.iii. yeres of our lorde Christ Iesu
The reigne of Dioclesyon the .xix. yere
Christis holy fayth to reuyue and renewe
Suffred saynt Albon / the story doth appere                H. 1580
Maximiane & Asclepiodot / both his iuges were

It was in the seconde yere / of the pope Gaius
That holy saynt Albon was martyred thus

Than one hundreth & one yere after his passion
Began fyrst theresies of false pelagyane
Which was .CCCC.iiii. yeres / by iust computation
After that Christ / had take our nature humayne
The .xiii. yere of the Brittisshe kynge Graciane
In the .iii. yere of the fyrst Anastacious
And the .xvi. yere of themperour Theodosius          H. 1590

Foure hundred and forty / of our lorde .ix. yeres mo
And in the fyrst yere of Vortigern the kynge
And the fyfte yere of the fyrst pope Leo
Theodose the seconde emperour than beinge
In his .xxi. yere after iust rekenynge
Saynt Germayn come fyrst / and lupus also
To distroye theresies / that were begon tho

C.xiiii. yeres by iuste computation
After his passion / thus come saynt Germayn
And forty and two yere without variation          H. 1600
After the fyrst tyme of the falce pelagian
Yet within fyue yeres saynt Germayn come agayn
As is shewed before / with holy Seuerus
All former heresies by grace to discus

CCC.xliii. yeres after saynt Germayne
Which was seuen hundreth / lxxx.&.xii. yere
Of our lorde Iesu / as stories doth determyne
That thangell at Bath / to kyng Offa dyd appere
To translate saynt Albon / with all heuenly chere
The fyrst Adrian pope / the .vi. Constantine themperour
Whan this translation was done with all honour          H. 1611

Perceyue nowe good reders / & gyue true iugement
Betwene the monkes of Colen / & of blessed Albon
The Coloners wryteth after theyr entent
To cause the pylgryms to withdrawe theyr deuotion
From Uerolamy / & to folowe theyr affection
Sayinge that they haue the very body
To theyr shame and rebuke / defendyng suche foly

And to proue theyr intent / playnely they say
That these heresyes of false pelagiane          H. 1620
Began in the reigne of noble kynke Offa [sic]
And also in the tyme of pope Adrian
Affyrmyng that than shuld come in Germayne

And with hym Lupus / a clerke of gret substance
And all theresyes were brought than to vttrance

And so by Germayn / were brought vnto Rauenus
The body of saynt Albon / and there themperour
Valentiniane / he was nobly receyued than
And also the body / with all godly honour
Where Germayn sore vexed with a mortall dolour        H. 1630
Departed this lyfe and vale of all misery
To theternall lyfe / in the celestiall glory

After whose deth themperours mother
Placida by name / as Coloners doth say
To Rome brought this body / she with many other
With all dewe reuerence / there abode many a day
Tyll Otto themperour / with his mother Theophana
Brought it to Colen / to tharchebysshop Brunon
In to the monastery of holy Panthaleon

Also at the tyme of this translation in dede        H. 1640
Adrian was pope / and that they confesse
And whan Ualentiniane / to thempyre dyd procede
Liberious was pope / in his .xii. yere doutlesse
As diuerse historiographers / playnly do expresse
So that of the sees spirituall nor temporall
Agreeth with theyr accomptes / after theyr memoriall

They say also the body is yet incorrupt
From the thyes vpwarde / they haue in possession
Which sayinge me semeth of trouthe be interrupte
Onles they wyll graunt any vnsemyng diuision        H. 1650
Of a corporall body to be cut in perticion
Yet I can not knowe what parte they shulde haue
For kynge Offa founde nothyng / but the bones in his graue

They say also that kyng Offa & saynt Germayne
Was bothe at one tyme / at this translation
Whan therisies was destroyde of false pelagian
In whose tymes is a gret alteration
Who lust accompt by iust computation
Shall fynde .CCC. yeres .xliiii. also
That kyng Offa came after sayde Germayn was go        H. 1660

They say also that themperour Ualentiniane
Sholde mete .s. Germain / whan he came to Rauene
Whiche can not be trewe / but all spoken in vayne
For CCC.lxvi. was the yeres of our lorde than
Whan Ualentiniane fyrste began to reigne

That was .lxxx.iii. yeres before that Germayne
Came to distroye theresies of pelagiane.

Therfore good bretherne of holy saynt Benet
Monkes of Colen leue this your bablyng
Ye be so ferre hense / in dede ye can not let          H. 1670
Ony deuoute persons / for to do theyr offryng
I wyll not denie / but your vntrewe surmysyng
May brynge some people / pucyll and innocent
For lacke of trewe knowlege / in a wrong iugement

But they that be lerned can rede as well as ye
Conferre histories / and also accompte the yeres
Can well perceyue howe craftely ye do flye
From trouthe / thistories so playnly apperes
And are not they accursed Yt false wytnesse beares
And specyally in writing / to the derogation          H. 1680
Of theyr bretherne in god of a nother nation

Remembre ye ware in Englande but late
With the .vii. Henry that myghty ryall kynge
Where couertly ye sought meanes with many a noble
To staye & aide you in this vntrewe lesing estate
But ye durst not abyde thende of the rekenyng
For feare of afterclappes that myght haue ensued
Ye where afrayde to drynke of suche as ye brewed

Wherfore reduce your selfe / false wrytyng reuoke
Knowlege your offence / of wyll more than dede        H. 1690
For if ye continue / ye shall haue but a mocke
Men knoweth howe ye can in ony wyse procede
But if that other ye loue god or drede
Folowe the trouthe / so shall ye do best
And in lytle medlynge / ye shall fynde moche rest.


REVISION OF PRAYER FOR THE KING IN THE 1534 EDITION
(from p. 174, Horstmann lines 1752 ff.)

And specially pray / for our most reall prince
Our redouted lord / and most gracious souerayne
Most victorious kinge / our sheld and our defence
Bothe kinge & Emperour / within all this Britane
Defender of the faith / of Irlonde lorde & captaine
Henry the .viii. surmountyng in renowne
O prothomartyr of Brutis Albion

Pray for his spouse / his louynge lady dere

His riall quene Anna / notable and famous          H. 1760
Indowed with grace / and vertu without pere
Pray four oure princes / that she may be prosperous
Elizabeth by name / both beautifull and gracious
Pray that theyr issue / have fortunate succession
O prothomartyr of Brutis Albion.

*EXPLANATORY NOTES*

It is convenient to mention here that several recurrent Latinisms in St. Albon tend to make interpretation difficult at first reading. The most idiosyncratic of these (for an English writer) is the quite frequent omission of the personal pronoun subject. In a number of cases cited below, it might be objected that the absence is an illusion induced by the modern introduction of punctuation, and that in fact Lydgate was using long, extremely loose sentence construction, with a number of verbs at some distance from one another. However, there are places where such an interpretation is impossible, and Lydgate is unfortunately omitting the subject pronoun, just as he would have in Latin, to the considerable loss of clarity, given the comparative simplicity of English fifteenth-century verb endings. For the phenomenon generally, see the following:

| | | | | | |
|---|---|---|---|---|---|
| I, 342 (he) | II, 686 (he) | II, 1692 (they) |
| I, 386 (they) | II, 708 (he) | II, 1696 (they) |
| I, 655 (he) | II, 723 (he) | II, 1719 (he) |
| I, 735 (he) | II, 831 (he) | II, 1726 (he) |
| I, 789 (he) | II, 857 (they) | II, 1741 (he) |
| I, 826 (he) | II, 931 (they) | II, 1770 (they) |
| I, 830 (he) | II, 956 (he) | II, 1786 (they) |
| I, 868 (he) | II, 1063 (thou) | II, 1815 (you) |
| I, 894 (he) | II, 1140 (he) | II, 1828 (you) |
| II, 19 (they) | II, 1155 (he) | II, 1909 (he) |
| II, 57 (it) | II, 1180 (he) | II, 1958 (he) |
| II, 87 (he) | II, 1262 (they) | III, 39 (he) |
| II, 96 (he) | II, 1270 (he) | III, 113 (he) |
| II, 106 (he) | II, 1367 (they) | III, 147 (they) |
| II, 169 (he) | II, 1406 (he) | III, 153 (they) |
| II, 171 (he) | II, 1431 (he) | III, 172 (he) |
| II, 180 (you) | II, 1478 (they) | III, 178 (they) |
| II, 243 (he) | II, 1504 (they) | III, 190 (they) |
| II, 249 (she) | II, 1506 (he) | III, 418 (they) |
| II, 452 (he) | II, 1527 (they) | III, 433 (they) |
| II, 592 (they) | II, 1665 (they) | III, 544 (they) |

| III, 735 (they) | III,  920 (he)  | III, 1140 (they) |
|-----------------|-----------------|------------------|
| III, 769 (they) | III,  972 (they)| III, 1206 (they) |
| III, 826 (he)   | III, 1121 (it)  | III, 1386 (it)   |
|                 |                 | III, 1464 (he)   |

Another characteristic stylistic trait is the extensive use of the absolute construction, sometimes quite long, on the model of the Latin ablative absolute. Among instances of this construction are:

| I,    8 ff.  | II, 1706        |
|--------------|-----------------|
| I,  176 ff.  | II, 1707        |
| I,  304 ff.  | III,  778       |
| I,  391      | III, 1353 ff.   |
| I,  619 ff.  | III, 1415 ff.   |
| I,  743 ff.  | III, 1422 ff.   |
| II, 235 ff.  | III, 1471-1477  |

Other Latinisms are the use of "tyme" and occasionally "hour" to begin a phrase or sentence, as though it were an ablative, i.e., "at the time when. . .," for instance, at I, 811, 813; II, 2004; III, 1415, 1472. There are some places where the editor feels Lydgate is consciously using the relative pronoun to begin the sentence, as in Latin, though again, one may often attribute this apparent Latinism to the modern punctuation. Examples are I, 890; III, 1037, 1471.

Other difficult uses are the omission of the "to" of the infinitive (e.g. I, 230, 392, 801; II, 148, 1742), omission of the relative pronoun (I, 466 "that," I, 474 "which," and omission of the preposition "on" (I, 230; III, 874).

*Book I*

1-4       Ralph of Dunstable (see Introduction) mentioned Clio in his opening line; but Lydgate had previously invoked or nearly invoked her in his St. Edmund and St. Fremund, ed., C. Horstman, Altenglische Legenden, Heilbronn, 1881, I, 90-94.

> I dar not calle to Clio for socour
> Nor to tho muses that been in noumbre nyne,
> But to this martir, his grace to enclyne

To forthre my penne of that I wolde write:
His glorious lif to translate and endite.

It is interesting that Lydgate here, like Gavin Douglas in
the prologues to his Aeneid, seems to have had scruples about
straightforward invocation of a pagan deity, yet manages to
give the appearance of following the classical convention.

7        Poetical use of this phrase may have been in inept
deference to the interests of Abbot John Whethamstede, who
commissioned the poem.  Lydgate alludes to Whethamstede's
Granarium at I, 894 (see notes to I, 883, 889-903).  Whethamstede was in fact one of the first to "debunk" the Brutus
legends which in Geoffrey of Monmouth passed for solid history.  He refers to the Brutus story as "poeticus ... potius
quam historicus."  See Laura Keeler, Geoffrey of Monmouth and
the Late Latin Chroniclers, Univ. of Calif. Publ. in English,
XVII (1946), no. 1, pp. 81-85.

8-15     The epilogue to Fall of Princes (Bergen, 11. 3401
ff.) contains a "humility" passage with many verbal parallels.
Curtius has shown the frequency of this sort of thing; compare the note to III, 1303-16, though in this instance the
humility is non-literary.  In both of Lydgate's passages the
direct source is no doubt Chaucer's "Franklin's Prologue,"
V, 716 ff (see n. to III, 363).  The apparent belief that
Virgil and Maro are two people shocks until we remember
Chaucer's Brutus Cassius.  Gramatically, this entire passage
is the first instance of the absolute construction mentioned
at the head of these Explanatory Notes.

12       As Dr. Quistorp reminds us in her "Studien zu Lydgates Heiligenlegenden" (p. 181, n.), this play on words
occurs in Chaucer's "Squire's Tale," V, 105-06.

14       Here too, Miss Quistorp suggests, Lydgate echoes
Chaucer ("Clerk's Prologue," IV, 31).

15       Certainly another Chaucer reminiscence (House of
Fame, III, 1567 ff., especially 1. 1678).  The allusion is
inept, since in the source fame has little to do with one's
merits.

16       Perhaps, "With wings as swift as those of Pegasus"?
In any case, a mixed figure.

18-46    The "Cronicle" in 1. 19 is the Tractatus de

Nobilitate mentioned in the Introduction, or more properly
the conflation of which it formed a part, also discussed in
the same place.   Compare with Lydgate's lines the following
from Tractatus (Bod. 585 f. 1 r.):   Regnante in hac terra
seuero missi [sunt] romam ad placendum imperatori diocliciano
una cum filio regis seueri nomine bassiano filii d[omi]norum
& nobilium tocius cornubie cambrie albanie & hibernie....
Inter quos filius principis cambrie missus est cum maximo
apparatu amphibalus appellatus, iuuenis in latina lingua gallica greca & ebraica satis instructus.   Missus est eciam inter
illos filius domini civitatis verolamie dictus Albanus nomine,
pro recipiendo ordine militari iuvenis elegans corpore &
opere circumspectus....   Et quidem filium principis Kambrie
secrete conversit [S. Zephyrinus] ... qui abiectis pompis
mundi ... pro christo assumpsit paupertatem.

     It is Severus who had Diocletian's role of persecuting
emperor in the first extant version of the legend, the Turin
Passion.   However his recurrence in a new capacity here must,
I think, be set down to mere chance and the historical association of the Emperor Severus with Britain.   See n. to I,
38 ff. below.

18          Verulamium, today Saint Albans, Herts., was a considerable city in Roman times, as the modern excavations
attest.

22          Obviously "whos" cannot refer to Diocletian; see
the remarks on Latinisms at beginning of these Explanatory
Notes.

25          "Pegaseus welle" is doubtless the fountain Hippo-
crene.

27-28       Dr. Quistorp (p. 181, n.) points out the mixed metaphor and for the quaking pen refers us to Troilus and Cri-
seyde, IV, 13-14.

38 ff.      Severus, here figuring as a British king, and his
son Bassianus doubtless derive from Geoffrey of Monmouth's
Historia Regum Britanniae (ed. Acton Griscom, London and
New York:  Longmans, 1929, pp. 330-334).   Geoffrey writes of a
senator of that name, sent to restore Roman rule after the
death of King Lucius.   Severus was finally slain by the Briton Sulgenius.   Buried at York, he left two sons, Geta and
Bassianus, the one by a Roman mother, the other by a British.
The Romans made Geta king but the Britons backed their

countryman, who slew Geta and ruled until killed by the naval
commander Carausius (see I, 710 n.).

The historical M. Aurelius Antoninus Bassianus, called
Caracalla, emperor of Rome from the year 211, son of Septimus
Severus who died in that year in Britain, murdered his brother
and co-emperor Geta in 212.

43          The origin of the name Amphibalus is discussed in
the Introduction, p. xxi.

44          Zephyrinus was pope from 198 to 217.  He was thus
a contemporary of Septimus Severus and of "Bassianus" but
died years before the birth of Diocletian.  See note to I,
18-46.

45          One would expect "he," but see observations on
Lydgate's Latinate style at the beginning of these *Explanatory
Notes*.

48          See note to I, 18-47 for light on "myn auctour."

58-60       See II, 2002 ff.; "stremys" seems to be the subject
of "directe."

64-65       Possibly from English "all" and Irish "baine,"
white, though in the unpublished De Inventione & Translatione
S. Albani in 8 Lectiones, in Trinity College Dublin MS E.1.40,
f. 52 r., Alban's name is derived from "almus" (bountiful?")
and "bonus"; then from "albedo"; last, from "regio albionen-
sis"  See Lydgate, Edmund and Fremund, I, 356 and I, 897 ff.
of the present work, as well as Chaucer's "Second Nun's Tale"
and lives in the Latin Legenda Aurea for other etymologies,
usually divorced from the probable true origins.

67-82       In Chaucer's "Second Nun's Tale," the angel presents Cecelia and Valerian with crowns of red roses and white
lilies (ll. 218 ff.).  See also note to III, 764 and Lydgate's
"Prayer to St. Edmund," in MacCracken's Minor Poems I, p. 126,
as well as St. Petronilla and St. Thomas of Canterbury on pp.
140 and 158 of the same edition.

84          From John 12:24-25:  Amen, amen, dico vobis nisi
granum frumenti cadens in terram mortuum fuerit, ipsum solum
manet:  si autem mortuum fuerit, multum fructum offert.

90          Lydgate also uses the term "laureat crownes" in
connection with martyrs in Edmund and Fremund, II, 769.

99-103    This paronomasia occurs also in <u>Fall</u> <u>of</u> <u>Princes</u>,
IX, 3397-3400:

> Off gold nor assewr I hadde no foyson
> Nor other colours this processe tenlumyne
> Sauff whyte and blak & they but dully shyne.

In <u>Edmund</u> <u>and</u> <u>Fremund</u> I, 88-89 we find

> In rhetorik thouh that I haue no flour
> Nor no coloures his story tenlumyne

In <u>Troy</u> <u>Book</u>, II, 196-97 and II, 184 we read

> So riche colours biggen I ne may;
> I mote procede with sable and with blake

> I toke non hede nouther of schort nor long

All seem modelled upon Chaucer's "Franklin's Prologue," V,
723-26:

> Colours ne knowe I none, withouten dreede,
> But swiche colours as growen in the meede,
> Or elles swiche as men dye or peynte.
> Colours of rethoryk been to me queynte;

106-82    With Lydgate's lines compare these from <u>Tractatus</u>,
f. 1 r.: Julius cesar primus Romanorum imparator [sic] postquam gallias subiugauit britannie que nunc apellatur anglia
arma intulit temporibus Cassivelani & post conflictus uarios
licet cum difficultate victor extitit. terram posuit sub
tributo, ediditque statuta que postea fuerunt longo tempore
in insula obseruata.  Interquas [?] statuit ut nullus in hac
terra susciperet ordinem militarem sed ille ordo a solis
romanis imperatoribus rome donaretur ne videlicet rurales vel
indigni passim accedentes ad dictum ordinem tantam dignitatem
ignavia deshonestarent.  Et ne umquam milites contra romanos
insurgerent q [sic] non de gestandis armis contra imperatores
sacramentum pupplicum [sic] edidissent.  Quod statutum non
solum ab huius terre regibus seruabatur sed a cunctis regibus
tunc existentibus in orbe Romano usque ad tempus seueri regis
Britonum qui fuit postea imperator.

Most of the additional matter Lydgate seems to have derived directly or indirectly from Geoffrey of Monmouth, IV,
i-ix (Griscom ed., pp. 306-18, Thorpe trans., pp. 107-18.
H. N. MacCracken in his edition of the <u>Serpent</u> <u>of</u> <u>Division</u>,

p. 16, points out the close resemblance of a passage in that
work to the one under discussion.  He did not know the Tractatus, and seems to have missed the origin of the reference
to Lucan (see n. to I, 120) in Geoffrey.  He comments, "Note
particularly the emphasis on the very word division,  an emphasis not suggested or needed in any way by the purpose of
the Life of St. Albon,  but wholly because Lydgate was writing from his memory of the Serpent."  In the Serpent, a passage derivative from Geoffrey and dealing with the invasion
of Caesar occurs on pp. 50-51.

106      The Latinate construction with "tyme" or "hour" is
discussed at the beginning of these notes in the remarks on
style.

110      The contracted "by" of "b'assent" (the apostrophe,
my editorial addition) is analogous to "b'experience" (II,
1535)  and "b'exaumple" (III, 1475) as well as to the Li
reading "bamaner" for "by a maner."  J. Norton-Smith is wide
of the mark in his comments on "b'assent" in his review of
Van der Westhuizen's edition, Medium Aevum, xliv (1975), 325.

116      For absence of the pronoun, see remarks on style
referred to in 106 and n. to 45 above.

120      Lucan's Pharsalia,  II,  572:  "Territa quaesitis
ostendit terga Britannis?"  This passage Lydgate took from
Geoffrey of Monmouth, who quotes it, IV, ix.

126 ff.   Eleanor Hammond in English Verse between Chaucer
and Surrey.  Durham, N.C.: Duke University, 1927, p. 94,
says of Lydgate:  "One thing of which he feels real personal
horror is dissension within the State:  to that subject he
returns again and again ...."  See also my n. to I, 106-82.

133 ff.   Historically, after his first excursion into Britain, Caesar invaded in force in July, 54 B.C., and fought a
campaign against Cassivellaunus, king of the region north of
the Thames and west of the Lea.  Mandubricius, heir to the
throne of the Trenovantes, deposed by Cassivellaunus, won his
people to Caesar's side.  Though nothing conclusive took
place, Caesar being called back by unrest in Gaul, Cassivel-
lanaus made a peace involving hostages, tribute, and immunity
for Mandubricius.  See Cambridge Ancient History, IV, Cambridge:  University Press, 1923, pp. 560-61, and Geoffrey of
Monmouth (Griscom, pp. 306-08; Thorpe trans., pp. 107-13).

133      Duke Androchee is probably to be identified

ultimately with the historical Mandubricius, but in Geoffrey Androgeus, Duke of Trinovantium, is a mighty vassal whose quarrel with his king springs from the accidental slaying of the king's nephew by the duke's, and a difference as to the proper venue for the trial. See Geoffrey, IV, viii (Griscom ed. pp. 314-16, Thorpe trans., pp. 113-15. Androgeus is not in any major source or contemporary analogue, even the Gilte Legende. Later, Caxton's Golden Legend might easily have derived it from Lydgate. However, Caxton's statement that Androgeus was duke of Kent may come from a misreading of a passage in Geoffrey, IV, iii.

136-39     Mark 3:24, "Et si regnum in se dividatur, non potest illud stare." Luke 11:17, "Omne regnum in seipsum divisum desolabitur, et domus supra domum cadet." Though it would at first appear that Lydgate believed Caesar's conquests to be mentioned in the New Testament, this interpretation is not necessary, for "scripture," in l. 135, may refer to writings other than the Bible.

143     On the absence of the subject pronoun, see note to I, 45 above and the remarks at beginning of these notes.

153     The change in number from "persones" above may perhaps be ascribed to copyist's error of "hym" for "hem" and a subsequent "improvement" to "he"; however Lydgate is as careless elsewhere.

183-96     Derived or inferred from Trac. f. 1 r. and v.: Statuit eciam ut in omni terra foret princeps militum & alius senescallus qui populum regerant & ei iusticiam exhiberent & a conspiracionibus contra romanum imperium cohiberent.

188     "They" is omitted; see note to I, 45 above.

197-217     Lydgate's own moralizing expansion of matter in the source. See note to I, 183-96.

197-203     From Ovid's Remedia Amoris 91:

> Principiis obsta; sero medicina paratur
> Cum mala per longas convaluere moras.

218-31     Cf. Trac., f. 1 v: Et sicut diadema siue corona est insigne regis ita voluit ut pilius ["pilion" (cap) in Harleian MS of Gilte Legende. See OED under "pileus" and "pilion"] foret insigne principis, & vestis aurifri[n]giata esset vestis senescalli.... uterque gradus foret ab

imperatore donandus; ut dum princeps milicie & senescallus
unum cum imperatore sentirent non esset in ullo regno qui
contra eum presumeret dissentire.  Neither the offices nor
the insignia seem to have historical authenticity.

230      This might be expanded to "for fear of the pain of
death to rebel" but see the remarks on style at the beginning
of these notes.

232-280    Cf. Trac., f. 1 v:  Regnante in hac terra seuero
missi romam ad placendum imperatori diocliciano una cum filio
regis seueri nomine bassiano filii dominorum & nobilium tocius
cornubie cambrie albanie & hibernie, usque ad numerum mille
quingentorum & quinquaginta.  Inter quos filius principis
cambrie missus est cum maximo apparatu amphibalus appellatus
iuvenis in latina lingua gallica greca & ebraica satis instructus.  Missus est inter illos filius domini civitatis
verolamie dictus Albanus nomine, pro recipiendo ordine militari iuvenis elegans corpore & opere circumspectus.  Omnes
pervenientes romam prospere ab imperatore cum honore maximo
sunt suscepti.  Compare I, 18-46 and n.

237      Whereas Lydgate has 1500 as the number, Tractatus
has 1550, and the Harleian English Gilte Legende has 1560.

239-245    This syntax is most difficult.  Might "prevaile" be
taken as an adjective meaning "most worthy" and preceded by
a comma, as well as followed by a semi-colon?  The meaning
would then be "most worthy, to the extent that Nature knew
her trade."

281-303    These lines are Lydgate's moralizing expansion of
lines 232-80.

286-87    Cf. Edmund and Fremund, I, 408-09, where the lines
apply to Saint Edmund:

          And yf he shal be shortly comprehendid
          In him was no thyng to be amendid

295-99    Miss Quistorp compares Edmund and Fremund, I, 347
ff.  See also I, 977 in the same poem.

304-46    Cf. Trac., f. 1 v:  Eo tempore sanctus zepherinus
papa rome sedit qui videns tantam iuvenum pulcritudinem,
quantum potuit laborauit convertere eos ad fidem christi.
Et quidem filium principis kambrie secrete convertit & fidem

docuit &...baptizavit. Qui abiectis pompis mundi voluntariam
pro christum assumpsit paupertatem & in omni perfectione con-
tinuauit vitam suam. Conversi sunt alii de praefata turba
multi sub eisdem diebus. Quod cum comperisset dioclicianus
iratus est vehementer iussitque ut per terras & per mare re-
quirentur & eius presencie sisterentur sed cum nullo sense
potuissent inueniri.

The pope's being struck by the appearance of the young
Britons and wishing to convert them is most reminiscent of
Bede's account (Eccl. Hist., II, i) of Pope Gregory and the
English slaves.

305        See note to I, 44 concerning Zephyrinus.

342        Pronoun subject absent.

346-585    This passage is vastly expanded by didactic discussion of duties of knights and the ceremonial of dubbing,
but essentially derives from Trac., f. 2 r: Dioclicianus
ommissa inquirendi diligencia, statuit diem in quo noui tirones susciperent arma militaria per manus suas. Quos omnes
manu sua cinxit informans eos de statu suscepti ordinis &
militaribus disciplinis iubens ut de cetero essent viri per-
fecti & corpora sua ab omni stultacia ["folie" in the Gilte
Legende] custodirent & delectacionibus incompositis & inor-
dinatis audaciam sumerent & vecordiam ["cowardise" in Leg.]
deuitarent pugnarent pro iusticia & si instaret necessitas
morti se offerrent hillariter pro eadem. De cetere non
gestare contra eum qui eos tali donasset honore & pro nulla
re mundi cuiquam iniuste facerent calumniam siue dampnum.
     Cf. Ramon Lull's Ordre of Chyualry (Caxton's trans.,
ed. A. Byles, E.E.T.S., O.S., clxviii, London: Oxford University Press, 1926 (for 1925), pp. 24-46.
     The ineptness of Diocletian's halting his persecution
only long enough to give a commencement address seems to
have escaped both the author of Tractatus and Lydgate.

353-59     Lydgate himself seems to have originated the tem-
ples of Mars and Bellona, with a glance at the "Knight's Tale."

370-78     The idea may derive from John of Salisbury: "What
is the function of orderly knighthood? To protect the Church,
to fight against treachery, to reverence the priesthood, to
fend off injustice from the poor, to make peace in your own
province, to shed your blood for your brethren, and, if needs
be, lay down your life." See G. G. Coulton's Medieval Pano-
rama, Cambridge: University Press, 1939, p. 242.

393          See note to I, 136-39.

411          "Common profit" is a key idea of the age, found in
Gower, Chaucer, and previously in Lydgate (e.g. Fall of Prin-
ces, IX 2335, 2531); see F. N. Robinson, Works of Geoffrey
Chaucer, 2nd ed., Cambridge: Houghton Mifflin, 1957, p. 711.

415          This line can best be interpreted as dependent on
the preceding, the whole to be paraphrased, "To become involved in no quarrel, the basis for one's stand in which is a
falsehood, especially one by which the poor are oppressed."

435-539  The elaborate ceremonial seems to have been derived
from historic medieval rites such as those described in G. G.
Coulton's article, "Knighthood," Encyclopaedia Britannica,
11th edition, xv, p. 855. Coulton mentions the shaving, bath,
white shirt and russet mantle. See Sir Nicolas Harris Nicolas, History of the Orders of Knighthood of the British Empire, London: J. Hunter, 1842, iii, pp. 1-28. It was apparently Lydgate who introduced this ceremonial into the Alban
legend. Gerard Legh in Accedens of Armory, ed. of 1576, gives
Alban's shield (the saltire) and comments (ff. 27 v. and 28
r.): "This shield I saye, was the Armes of that gentilman
sir Albone, knight of the Bath, and lord of Verolane nowe
callid sainct Albons...." Legh then gives a synopsis of Lydgate's poem, then continues, "Vigetius saith, there be two
maner of knighthoods one with the sworde and an other with the
Bath. He affirmeth that the bathe is worthiest...." Legh's
work had its first edition in 1562. The work he refers to as
"Vigetius" is not De Re Militari.

474          Interpolate "which"; see remarks on style, p. 210.

477
             "Tokne of chastite" is perhaps what Lydgate wrote or
intended, but all MSS. support the other reading, which per-
sonifies chastity.

484-87   This difficult elliptical sentence may perhaps be
paraphrased, "Books will show, if one wishes to consult them,
that if one wants to become full of virtue, the best road is
the choice of humility as a foundation-virtue. The mixed
figurative language of "weye," "spede," and "fundacion" is
unavoidable.

498-504  Dindimus of the "Bragmans" is treated in F. P. Magoun
Gests of King Alexander, Cambridge, Mass.: Harvard, 1929, pp.
44 and 176. See Walter Skeat, The Alliterative Romance of

<u>Alexander</u> <u>and</u> <u>Dindimus</u>, E.E.T.S., E.S. xxxi, 1. 249. For the
fourth century source, see George Cary's <u>The</u> <u>Medieval</u> <u>Alexan-</u>
<u>der</u>, Cambridge: University Press, 1957, pp. 13-14 and 91-94.


515        Syntax would seem to require "A knight must be..."
at the beginning of this line. This ellipsis may be an extreme example of one of the stylistic characteristics mentioned at the beginning of these notes or (as is more likely)
a mere lapse.


586-707    Cf. <u>Tractatus</u>, ff. 2 v. and 3 r.: Expletis que ad
sacramentum militarem pertinent, Bassianus regis seueri filius agens annum tricesimum rogauit imperatorem ut rome possent
primicias ordinis sui dedicare per hasti ludia & alia exer-
cicia militaria coram eo. Cui dioclicianus gratanter annuit
animositatem iuvenis approbans & collaudans. Per hanc inquit
ebdomada hastiludiabitis [all one word] & torneamenta facietis
cum militibus meis presentibus donec veniant alii a remotis
quos interim faciam euocari vt tuum desiderium compleatur.
Igitur per illam septimanam bassianus cum his britonibus sic
agebat in armis ut laudari ab imperatore & romanis omnibus
mereretur. Interea continuatum est torneamentum per bassianum & suos contra romanos siculos hispanos & sardimenses [sic]
milites elemannicos [sic] ciprios & certenses [sic] tirones
per multos dies & victoria britonibus cessit semper precipue
tum sancto albano cuius arma vt asseritur fuerunt de colore
azoreo cum sautur aureo que ex post inclitus rex offa fun-
dator monasterii eiusdem casualiter seu pocius miraculose por-
tavit sub quibus armis semper gloriose triumphavit eaque post
mortem suam sancto albano & eiusdem monasterio pocius reddidit quam legauit. Creuit igitur per Ytaliam fama britonum in
imnensum [sic] & apud imperatorem prevaluit laus eorum, &
his itaque gestis magnifice, bassianus ab imperatore petiit
licenciam repatriandi cum suis comilitonibus universis. Imperator vero pro elegancia corporali & strenuitate armorum
prae ceteris omnibus Albano dixit: Cum summo nostro fauore
redibitis, praeter albanum qui nostri corporis custos esse
debet. Itaque repatriantibus cum bassiano britonibus & qui
cum eis venerant. Albanus remansit in imperatoris obsequio
septem annis.


624        Ficuluees: <u>Trac</u>. has "siculos." See passage quoted
in previous note.


628-30     Ideas are telescoped here. What is meant is that
the Britons were outstanding, and that among these, Alban
was officially acclaimed as best.

638-39    It may be conjectured that these lines refer to some old representation of Alban, perhaps a miniature, with the shield borne contrary to fifteenth century practice.

642       If "Leicester" (see textual note) is correct, some manuscript or work of art at Leicester Abbey may be alluded to.   Leicester is within the boundaries of Offa's Mercia, and Unwona, bishop of Leicester, is one of the traditional signatories of the St. Albans charter.  MS Trin. Dublin E.I.40 disagrees by depicting a crowned lion on Offa's shield; of course Offa antedates formal heraldry.

645 ff.    Concerning Offa and St. Albans, see notes to III, 1345 and following lines.

659       "Aftir whos hond" seems to mean simply that the masons' hands went on working after the laying of the cornerstone.

664       By devotion to St. Alban's arms, or by adopting them as a token, people will be strengthened against those who do them wrong.

665       This line reminds us that the abbot's commission must have been at least in part motivated by the wish to stimulate the pilgrimage cult.

669       The confused syntax would be helped if we assumed "Bi" to be intrusive, but there is no textual reason for so doing.

687       Sense and meter both suggest "Non" as the first word of the line, but none of the manuscripts have this word.

690       This hero of the last books of the Vulgate Old Testament is one of the nine worthies alluded to in III, 1498.

691       Scipio:  cf. Fall of Princes, V, 1778-1782:

          ...the thridde worthi Scipioun
          Called Nasica,...
          Passyng all othir in wisdam & corage.

See also Albon, II, 1398.

705       This is a hard reading; it is offered faute de mieux.  See the Latin in n. to I, 586-707.

708-63    Cf. <u>Trac</u>., f. 3 r. and v:   Interea quidam miles
vocatus caraucius qui permissione senatus factus fuerat custos maris britannici bassianum qui regnum susciperat post
mortem seueri patris sui prodicione peremit & regnum britannie usurpauit & contra fidem prestitam tributum soluere renuit
quod romanis imperatoribus debebatur.   Ipse dedit pictis locum mansionis in albania que nunc scocia nominatur.  Allectus
igitur magnus senator missus est in britanniam contra carau-
cium cum tribus legionibus militum ad occidendum carausium
memoratum.   Quo perempto romani nimis populum britannie op-
preserunt.   Quamobrem dux cornubie asclepiodotus nomine elec-
tus est ad resistendum romanis.   Qui & Allectum peremit in
campo & gallum collegam suum fugauit & tandem occidit londo-
mis [sic] super torrentem qui de suo nomine walbrok hoc tempore nominatur.

    The source of <u>Trac</u>. here is Geoffrey of Monmouth, V, iv
and v (Griscom, pp. 333 ff., Thorpe, pp. 127-29).  The historical Carausius, admiral of the Channel fleet under Diocletian, rebelled, defeated Maximian in A. D. 290, and ruled in
Britain as emperor for three years.  See M. Cary's <u>History of
Rome</u>, 2nd ed., London: Macmillan, 1954.

731, 735  In both lines we find the characteristic omission of
the subject pronoun.  See the beginning of these notes.

736       Geoffrey of Monmouth:  "...dedit pictis locum mansionis in albania."  (Griscom, p. 334, Thorpe, p. 128).

740       The historical Allectus, Carausius' chief minister
(see <u>Camb</u>. <u>Anc</u>. <u>Hist</u>., XII, 327 ff.) killed Carausius in 293
A. D.  He in turn was killed by an expedition under the Cae-
sar Constantius and his praetorian prefect Asclepiodotus in
the year 296.

752       See note to I, 740.

756-63    According to Geoffrey of Monmouth, Gallus, Allectus' lieutenant,was besieged in London by Asclepiodotus
(Griscom, pp. 335-6; Thorpe, pp. 129-30).  Gallus surrendered
and was killed by the Britons at Walbrook.

764-812   Cf. <u>Trac</u>., ff. 3 v. and 4 r:  Britones ergo con-
corditer elegerunt asclepiodotus ducem cornubie in regem suum.
Qui licet eleccioni consentiret coronam regni gestare noluit
sine fauore imperatoris romani.  Cumque comperisset [?] dioclicianus augustus quod romani qui missi fuerant occisi

fuissent pro depopulacione britonum & aliis iniustis Maximianum commilitonem suum misit ad coronandum asclepiodotum.

Eodem tempore recordatus obsequii & fedelitatis albani
dioclicianus augustus creavit eum principem milicie totius
britanie & eiusdem insule senescallum & remisit ad natale
solum ut & coronacioni noui regis interesset & maximiano
fidelitatem cum iuramento faceret iuxta morem racione dignitatis sibi collate. Quem eciam dominus prius inuestiuit
creans eum dominum verolamie civitatis. Quibus expletis maximianus romam reuersus est cum tribus milibus librarum debitis
de tempore karausii tiranii & aliis exemius preciosis missis
ad placandum animum diocliciani.

The source of the first paragraph only is Geoffrey (Griscom, pp. 336 ff.; Thorpe, p. 130).

777          Maximian was Augustus of the West while Diocletian
ruled in the East. In Geoffrey, he is "Maximianus herculius,
princeps milicie predicti tyranni" (i.e., of Diocletian), who
conquered Britain, presumably overthrowing Asclepiodotus, and
began to persecute Christians at Diocletian's order. (Griscom, p. 337)
          The title bestowed on Maximian by Geoffrey may have been
the inspiration for the author of Tractatus when he made
Alban "princeps milicie." See notes to I, 183-96, I, 218-31,
and I, 764-812.

813-63          Cf. Trac., f. 4 r. and v: Per illud tempus sanctus
poncianus papatui presidebat qui per semetipsum & infinitos
alios non cessauit predicacionibus et miraculis romanos convertere ad fidem christi. In tantum in opere perfecit ut in
urbe romana quadraginta sex milia conuerteret ad rectam fidem.
Quod cum cognouisset imperator turbatus est non modice &
iussit convenire senatores & regni proceres ad audiendum quid
sentirent faciendum in tam arduo negocio quod tangebat omnes.
Qui conuenientes censuerunt papam fore [sic] vocandum ad
cetum [sic] publicum & ibidem dampnandum cum universo populo
christiano & non solum in urbe romana sed ubique terrarum
decreuerunt christianos inquirendos ac variis suppliciis pun-
iendos. Et insuper ordinauerunt ut omnes libri christianorum
flammis consumerentur et detentores iugularentur. Ecclesie
quoque subverterentur ubique & ecclesiastici necarentur.
Quod decretum mox ut vulgatum est christiani qui fuerunt rome
de diversis partibus oriundi suas patrias petierunt.

815          Pontianus was pope from 230 to 235. Maximian ruled

with Diocletian from 286 to 305. Pontianus was actually a
contemporary of Severus Alexander, grandson of Severus'
sister-in-law. The <u>Cambridge</u> <u>Ancient</u> <u>History</u> suggests that
"he may indeed have been a well-brought-up and charming
youth." (XII, 57 ff.)  This, added to the fact that he died
in Vicus Britannicus, today Bretzenheim, may be responsible
for the characterization of Caracalla in the <u>Tractatus</u>. See
notes to I, 38 and I, 44.

817       Pontianus' activities in Sicily and Lombardy are not
mentioned in the <u>Tractatus</u>, and may have been added from some
reference work or merely for the sake of the stanza and rime,
as representing the northern and southern extremes of Italy.

826, 829, 835  The characteristic omission of the third person
sing. subject pronoun.  See note on style at beginning of
these notes.

848-61    These details of the persecution of Diocletian
occur in Bede (I, vii), in Geoffrey (V, v) and in the <u>Trac-
tatus</u> (see note to I, 813-63).

851       An omission of the plural pronoun subject.  See the
remarks at the beginning of the *Explanatory Notes*.

853       The phrase is perhaps suggested by the reference to
Augustus' decree in Luke, 2:1.

861       The meaning can best be grasped if one substitutes
"thus" for "so" at the beginning of 1. 859.

864-75    Cf. <u>Trac</u>. f. 4 v:  Inter quos sanctus Amphibalus
qui iam multis annis rome & in locis sanctis manserat versus
natale solum dirigit iter suum & domino ducente pervenit
verolamium nobilem civitatem.

868       Another omission of the pronoun subject.

871       One would expect "faith" after "strong."

876-930   From internal evidence, these lines are clearly
original with Lydgate and have no parallel in the sources.

883       John Bostock, usually called Whethamstede, Abbot of
St. Albans, commissioned Lydgate's poem.  See R. Weiss,
<u>Humanism</u> <u>in</u> <u>England</u>, 2nd ed., Oxford:  B. Blackwell, 1957, pp.
30-36, and introduction to this edition.

889-903    One of Whethamstede's encyclopedic compilations
(unpublished) is called Granarium. Portions of it occur in
the Bodleian MS of the Tractatus.

894        Yet another omission of the pronoun subject.

897        This etymology, resembling that for Albon in I, 65
ff., differs from most medieval attempts in being probably
correct. The village of Wheathampstead is only a few miles
from St. Albans.

911        The word "bound" (see also "bounde" at 1. 924 and
"undirtook" at 1. 925) recalls Lydgate's financial arrange-
ments with the Abbot.


*Book II*


1-127      These lines are original with Lydgate, and depend
on sources only in that they refer to the story as told in the
sources (and in Lydgate). Lines 65-69 are drawn from the
Tractatus, though not closely. Compare Trac., f. 3 v: Eodem
tempore recordatus obsequii & fedelitatis albani dioclicianus
augustus creavit eum principem milicie totius britanie &
eiusdem insuli senescallum....

1-64       In these lines only does Lydgate turn from Rime
Royal; the eight-line stanza of this passage, like Chaucer's
"Monk's Tale," rimes ABABBCBC (ballad-stave). However, see
II, 2017 and n.

8          The sense can be gramatically explained only as a
case of extreme ellipsis.

24         Cornelius was the centurion miraculously converted
in Acts, 10. Eustace, like Cornelius, was virtuous even
before his miraculous conversion. According to the Legenda
Aurea he was a high military officer of Trajan's who, while
hunting a stag, saw a crucifix between its antlers. The
figure on the cross speaking to him, he and his family em-
braced Christianity. Both allusions are apt, since these
saints, like Albon were virtuous pagan Romans, military men
converted by miracle.

25-40      The Emperor Trajan's virtues were such that he was
traditionally said to have been released from hell by prayer

of Gregory the Great.  See The Golden Legend under "Gregory,"
Piers Plowman, C-text, passus 13, ll. 74-165 and 15, ll.
205-06, along with Skeat's notes, and Lydgate's own "St.
Austin at Compton," ll. 343-352, Minor Poems (MacCracken),  I,
pp. 203-204.

55        The comparison of Albon to the sun is probably
founded in part on his presumed Trojan, hence eastern, origin.

57        "Processe" seems to be the subject of "shal be."

73-127    This description of Albon is, in effect, Lydgate's
picture of a good ruler.

85        This subjunctive suggests some omitted phrase like
"he maad so that," but perhaps "indigence" is a plural
spelled for eye-rhyme, meaning indigent people, in which case
the punctuation at end of II, 84 ought to be a semi-colon.

94        Though none of the manuscripts add "the" before
"like," this word would clarify the line and improve its meter, the latter only if we prefer La's reading of "which" to
Li's of "which that."

101       Thomas Aquinas termed Prudence, Temperance, Courage
and Justice cardinal virtues.  The germ of the idea is in
Plato's Laws.  These virtues were thought of as natural, not
supernatural, and therefore to be achieved by pagans as well
as Christians.  See "Cardinal Virtues" in the Catholic Encyclopedia, 1st ed., New York: Encyclopedia Press, 1913-22.

106       Here again the third person subject pronoun is absent.

125-27    Cf. John 21:25.

128-64    Cf. Trac., ff. 4v. and 5 r:  Sanctus Amphibalus qui
jam multis annis rome & in locis sanctis manserat versus
natale solum dirigit iter suum & domino ducente peruenit verolamium nobilem civitatem ubi dum nullus eum hospicio vellet
suscipere circumit plateas urbis expectans consolacionem dei.
Tandem Albanus urbis dominus princeps militum & prouincie
senescallum fit illi obvius stipatus caterva familiarium ves-
titus vestibus auro textis.  Cui cuncti cives & extranei honorem maximum deferebant.  Quem ut vidit Amphibalus illico
recognouit.  Sed Albanus amphibalum non cognovit quamvis in
una societate mare transierant versus romam.  Tandem

Amphibalus ... hospitium pro deo petiit ab Albano.  Cui nimi-
rum Altanus qui semper cunctis peregrinis & pauperibus fuerat
hospitalis hospitium clerico libenter concessit....

163-69    In this stanza Lydgate drops the Tractatus as his
source and takes up the Interpretatio of William of St. Albans.  From this point on, the Tractatus gives a much con-
densed version of the legend.  The Gilte Legende also takes
up William at this point in the narrative.

163-83    Cf. William, p. 149 E (all numerical references to
the Interpretatio refer to the page number and marginal letters in Acta Sanctorum for June 22):  Hic sanctum virum hospitio benigne suscipiens, vitae necessaria ministravit.  Quem
tandem, remoto servorum strepitu, secretius allocutus; Quomodo, inquit, cum sis Christianus homo, per Gentilium fines
transitum habere & ad hanc urbem illaesus pervenire potuisti?

171       The missing pronoun subject again.  See p. 211.

177-82    The syntax seems impossible.  We may hazard the
intended meaning to be:  By many signs and tokens, various
examples of foreignness or stand-offishness, hard to overcome,
I know that you are a Christian; indeed you have foolishly
dared to assert this yourself, thus putting your life in
jeopardy among pagans.

184-90    Cf. William, p. 149 E :  Dicit ei Amphibalus:
Dominus meus Jesus Christus... iter meum jugiter prosecutus,
securum me inter discrimina custodivit.  Hic pro multorum
salute me misit ad istam provinciam, ut videlicet fidem quae
in Christo est Gentibus annuntians, ei populum acceptabilem
praeparem.

191-218    Cf. William, p. 149 E and F:  Quid est quod Deus
natus esse asseritur?  Nova sunt haec & mihi hactenus inau-
dita.  Nosse vellem, quid super hac re vos Christiani sentia-
tis.  Tum B. Amphibalus, euangelicam ingressus disputationem,
dixit ei:  Assertio nostrae fidei haec est, ut Deum Patrem &
Deum Filium esse dicamus; qui videlicet Filius, pro salute
hominum carnem dignatus assumere, hoc procuravit, ut qui carnem fecerat, caro fieret; et qui creator Virginis extiterat,
ipse mirabiliter ex Virgine crearetur.

219-28    A typical example of that particular kind of poetic
ornament advocated by the rhetoricians which finds its most
famous expression in the first lines of the Canterbury Tales.
Compare with II, 919-53 infra, which marks the beginning of

summer just as the Annunciation marks the early spring. See
also II, 1199-219 and Lydgate's Life of Our Lady, II, 429 ff.

226-32    The Annunciation is celebrated by the Western
Church on March 25. The sun enters Aries on March 21 according to the Gregorian calendar, but according to the Julian
calendar of Lydgate's day, about a week earlier. Still, the
religious and astronomical events were fairly close together.

227       The La reading, "wast" would be prosodically idiosyncratic, chiming with "past" immediately following and
making an interminable spondee.

232       See Isaiah 11:1. The "tree of Jesse" is one of the
most familiar of medieval symbols, a family tree tracing
Jesus' descent from David's father.

233-95    Cf. William, pp. 149 F to 150 A:  Ut igitur exhi-
bendae hujus novitatis tempus advenit, caelestis ad Virginem
nuntius destinatur:  qui ingressus ad eam dixit; Ave gratia
plena, Dominus tecum:  benedicta tu in mulieribus. Quae cum
audisset; turbata est in sermone ejus. Et ait Angelus ei:
Ne timeas Maria; ecce concipies & paries filium, & vocabis
nomen ejus Jesum. Dixit autem Maria ad angelum:  Quomodo
fiet istud quoniam virum non cognosco?  Et respondens angelus,
dixit ei:  Spiritus sanctus superveniet in te & virtus Altis-
simi obumbrabit tibi, ideoque & quod nascetur ex te Sanctum
vocabitur Filius Dei. Dixit autem Maria:  Ecce ancilla Domini, fiat mihi secundum verbum tuum. Hoc modo Virgo Deum,
ancilla Dominum, Patrem filia meruit generare. Virgo mater
facta est; sed virginitatis insignia non amisit. Hoc quoque
futurum fuisse non latuit Prophetas; sed multis illud oraculis
a seculo praedixerunt.

238       One would expect "knewe," but all manuscripts have
forms in "o."

296-358   (11. 335-358 are a free amplification)  Cf. William,
p. 150 A:  Si haec hospes ita esse credideris; cuncta quae ad
fidem Christi pertinet circa te digne poterunt adimpleri:
factus vero Christianus, debilibus, aegrotis, & cunctis male
habentibus, invocato Christi nomine, poteris subvenire:  tibi
nulla nocebit adversitas, mors non appropinquabit, priusquam
ipsius voluntas fuerit Creatoris:  tandem hanc vitam finies
per Martyrium, felicique beatus excessu, de seculo migrabis
ad Christum. Idcirco hanc urbem ingressus sum, ut in ea prae-
co tuae fierem passionis:  benignus enim dominus humanitatis

officia, quibus insistis, caelestis vitae praemio recompensat.

307-08    The first verbal element refers only to the first
substantive, the second only to the second.  This kind of
construction is not too unusual in the poem.  Whether it is
to be classed as idiosyncrasy or rhetorical figure is not
clear.

336-44    The serene corporal works of mercy; see J. M.
Perrin, "Mercy, works of" in New Catholic Encyclopedia, ed.
of 1967.  Lydgate omits two, giving drink to the thirsty
and clothing the naked.

345       The "and" is superfluous and makes the sentence
meaningless.  Otherwise, "all" becomes the subject of the
verb, "been regestryd."  In the MS, "and" usually appears as
an ampersand.

358       The first palm is the reward for a virtuous life,
as stated in 1. 349; the second is no doubt the reward for
a martyr's death.  New knights were sometimes given palms.

359-407   Cf. William, p. 150 A and B:  Dicit ei Albanus:
Quid reverentiae Christo, quid honoris impendam; si Christi
fidem forte suscepero?  Et ille:  Crede dominum Iesum, cum
Patre & Spiritu sancto, Deum unum esse:  & opus magnum in ejus
oculis peregisti.

       Lines 380-407 are primarily Lydgate's amplification of
the foregoing.

385       This line seems to be influenced by lines V, 1863-
64 at the end of Chaucer's Troilus.  Cf. note to 394-405 below.

393       A commonplace stemming from the "Celestial Hierarchy" of the pseudo-Dionysius (cf. Lydgate's "St. Denis,"
Minor Poems, I, p. 127, esp. 1. 63).  The nine ranks or
choirs of angels are grouped into three larger divisions.

399-405   These lines, especially 1. 405, recall Troilus, V,
1853-54.

408-35    Cf. William, p. 150 B, noting that Lydgate has
changed Alban's motivation.  Whereas his anger is feigned and
his disbelief far from positive here, in the source they are
genuine; this is perhaps Lydgate's most substantial change of

his source-material, as Dr. Quistorp suggests.  However, the
<u>Gilte</u> <u>Legende</u> (f. 99 r., col. 1) shows tendencies toward the
interpretation found in Lydgate, and may indicate some alteration in the hypothetical conflation.  The text of William
follows:

Tunc dicit ei Albanus : Quid est quod loqueris: insanis:
nescis quid dicis.  Assertionem tuam non capit intellectus,
ratio non admittit.  Si nossent viri hujus civitatis te talia
locutum fuisse de Christo, sine mora blasphemos sermones secundum publicas legum sanctiones capitis abscissione vindica-
rent.  Ego vero omnino pro te solicitus, ne quid tibi con-
tingat adversi, priusquam ex hoc recesseris habitaculo, vehementer pertimesco.  His dictos surrexit, & abiit ira commotus.
Nullatenus enim adhuc patienter audire quae dicebantur, nec
aurem placidam praebere voluit admonenti.

429-35    See note to II, 408-35.

429       "Fortune" as opposed to "Nature"; a personified
aspect of God's providence.

436-70    Cf. William, p. 150 B and C:  Solus in loco remansit Amphibalus; noctemque totam per vigil in oratione transe-
git.

Albano vero in solario quiescenti, miranda quaedam nocte
illa divinitus ostenduntur.  Cumque novo visu fuisset exter-
ritus, ac insolito perturbaretur aspectu; surgens continuo
ad inferiora descendit; & accedens ad hospitem, dixit:  Amice
si vera sunt quae de Christo praedicas; veram mihi solutionem
somni mei quaeso ne metuas indicare.  Aspiciebam, & ecce de
caelis homo veniebat; quem apprehendens innumera hominum multitudo, diversa expendit in eum genera tormentorum.

440       An allusion to the new knight's vigil over his
armor.  Cf. 1, 355.

471-540   The events of Christ's passion, resurrection and
ascension are very closely paralleled in William, 150 C and D.

527       These words, spoken by the British Albon, are rather
appropriate (though anachronistic), and were suggested by
Chaucer's "Franklin's Prologue," V, 709-13:

Thise olde gentil Britouns in hir dayes
Of diverse aventures maden layes,

Rymeyed in hir firste Briton tonge
Which layes with hir instrumentz they songe
Or elles redden him for hir plesaunce.

541-610    Cf. William, p. 150 D and E:    Haec & multa alia,
quae nec volo, nec licet ulli mortalium indicare; mihi nocte
per visionem sunt ostensa....

His auditis B. Amphibalus, sentiens cor ejus visitatum
a Domino; supra quam cuiquam credibile est in Domino est
gavisus; statimque Crucem Domini, quam secum habebat, proferens, ait:    Ecce in hoc signo potes manifeste dignoscere,
quid visio tua nocturna velit, quid portendat. Homo namque
veniens de supernis, Dominus meus est Iesus Christus:    qui
crucis supplicium subire non renuit, ut nos a reatu, quo per
praevaricationem primi parentis Adae tenebamur adstricti suo
sanguine liberaret.    Qui vero manus homini injecerunt; et
diversis poenarum generibus afficerunt, populum significat
Iudaeorum:    qui cum promissum haberent, quia Deus eis filium
suum de caelis mitteret, & tandem venisset quemdiu expectaver-
unt; non receperunt venientem, nec suae salutis auctorem
cognoverunt; sed in omnibus ei contradicentes, semper ei mala
pro bonis, odium pro dilectione rependerunt.

Lydgate has much expanded the reference to Adam and
Christ.

572-83    Miss Quistorp shows the parallel with Lydgate's
"Vexilla Regis," Minor Poems, I, p. 26, 11. 59-60.    There
Christ is "medycyne," "bawme," and "triacle."    These compari-
sons are not in the Latin hymn.

584        Samson:    The same comparison is made in "Virtues of
the Mass," Minor Poems, I, p. 103, 1. 373 (Quistorp).    See
Judges 14:5-6.    Samson and the lion are established proto-
types of Christ and Satan; see D. W. Robertson, Preface to
Chaucer, Princeton: University Press, 1963, p. 141.    The symbol is often associated with Hercules; see II, 142 and 636.

600-03    In the hymn "Pange Lingua" sung, like the "Vexilla
Regis," in the liturgy of Good Friday we find the likely
source for Lydgate's lines:

Crux fidelis, inter omnes
Arbor una nobilis:
Nulla silva talem profert,
Fronde, flore, germine.

De parentis protoplasti
Fraude factor condolens
Quando pomi noxialis
In necem morsu ruit
Ipse lignum tunc notavit
Damna ligni ut solveret.

611-52    Cf. William, p. 150 F, which Lydgate has much expanded by metaphor and rhetorical devices:  Sic begninus
Dominus pretio sanguinis sui nos redemit, sic mortis moriendo
victor extitit, & in cruce exaltatus ad se traxit universa,
sed ad claustra sponte descendens, suos qui illic tenebantur
absolvit, & aeternis nexibus diabolum alligans, ad infima
tenebrarum loca dejecit.

622       For the symbolic significance of "Edom," see Isaiah,
63:1 ff.

628-31    Doctor Quistorp notes that Christ  is compared to
Orpheus in Lydgate's "Testament," MacCracken, ed., Minor
Poems, I, p. 335, ll. 158-60.  D. W. Robertson in his Preface
to Chaucer, Princeton, 1963, pp. 106-08, has a footnote essay
on Orpheus symbolism in the Middle Ages, mostly derived from
Ovid.  The early Christian comparison of Orpheus and Jesus
survives as late as a twelfth-century Latin hymn.  Robertson
(p. 355) traces the Hercules-Christ comparison back to Patris-
tic times, though more usually in an Alcestis context than
among the Hesperides.  More recently J. B. Friedman, Orpheus
in the Middle Ages, Cambridge, Mass.: Harvard, 1970, treats
the Christ-Orpheus figure at length, pp. 125-28.

634       Prof. B. J. Whiting has called the editor's attention to John Metham's "Amoryus," Works, ed. Hardin Craig,
E.E.T.S., O.S. cxxxii (1906), p. 46, l. 1253.  Craig calls
attention to a similar passage in John of Trevisa's Bartholo-
maeus Anglicus.  See M. C. Seymour et al., On the Properties
of Things, Oxford: Clarendon Press, 1975, p. 1184.  Lydgate's
figure is based upon the legendary conflict waged by
the dragon and elephant, which the dragon usually wins.  But
in Trevisa the dying elephant falls on the dragon and kills
the "dragon that him sleeth."  (p. 1185)

635       For purity see the apocryphal Judith, 15:11 and 16:26.

636-38    See n. to 628-31 above and Robertson, pp. 141-42.

653-80    Cf. William, pp. 150 F and 151 A:  Tunc Albanus
super sermonibus illius vehementer admirans, in haec verba

prorupit, dicens:   Vera sunt, inquit, vera quae de Christo
memoras; nec possunt ullatenus argui falsitatis.   Ego enim
evidenter hac nocte cognovi, qualiter Christus diabolum
vicerit, alligaverit, & ad inferni profundiora detruserit.
Propriis oculis ipse conspexi, quia catenarum nexibus teter
ille jacet irretitus.   In hoc cognoscens quoniam omnia quae
locutus est vera sunt, amodo fidelissimum me tibi polliceor
auditorem.   Dic ergo obsecro (quia nosti universa) quid Pa-
tri, quid Spriitui sancto facturus sim, accedens ad Filii
servitutem.

681-715     Cf. William, p. 151 A:   Quibus ille auditis cum
ingenti exultatione dixit.   Gratias ago Domino meo Jesu
Christo, quod haec tria nomina per temetipsum proferre jam
nosti.   Tres igitur personas, quas aperte suis designasti
vocabulis.   Deus unum crede, firmiter & fideliter confitere.
Respondens autem Albanus; Credo, inquit & ex hoc fides mea
est, quod nullus Deus nisi Dominus meus Jesus Christus, qui
ob salutem hominum hominem dignatus assumere, crucis sustin-
uit passionem; ipse cum Patre & Spiritu Sancto Deus unus est,
et praeter eum non est alius.

686, 688     Two omissions of the pronoun subject.   See p. 211.

716-85     Cf. William, p. 151 A and B; the bracketed sentence
appears marginally and in another hand in Trinity Coll. Dublin MS:   His dictis saepe prosternitur ante crucem:   & quasi
pendentem in cruce Dominum Iesum cerneret, veniam sibi beatus
poenitens deprecatur.   Sic pedes, sic vulnerum loca assidua
exosculatione demulcet, acsi ad ipsius, quem crucifigi vider-
at, vestigia prorecumberet Redemptoris.   Sanguine mixtae per
ora volvuntur lacrymae, super illud venerabile lignum ubertim
decidentes.   Ego, inquit, diabolum abnego, omneque Christi
detestor inimicos; in illum solum credens, illi me committens,
qui (sicut asseris) a mortuis die tertia surrexit.   [Quod cum
constanter confiteretur Albanus; baptizavit eum Amphibalus in
nomine ejusdem sanctae Trinitatis, ex corde factum integrum
Christianum.]   Dicit ei Amphibalus:   Forti animo esto:   Dominus tecum est, & illius gratia tibi non deerit unquam.   Fidem,
quam ceteri mortalium homine tradente percipere consueverunt,
tu non ab homine, neque per hominem didicisti, sed per revel-
ationem Iesu Christi.   Quare jam securus omnino de te reddi-
tus, longius ire dispono, viam veritatis Gentibus ostensurus.

752-55     Lydgate's choice of words is influenced by the re-
nunciation of Satan and his works and pomps in the rite of
Baptism.   This portion of the rite, according to Gerald

Ellard (<u>Christian Life and Worship</u>,Milwaukee: Bruce, 1940, p. 252) is of the second century. The priest asks, "Abrenuntias Satanae? Et omnibus operibus ejus? Et omnibus pompis ejus? to which the one to be baptized thrice replies, "Abrenuntio."

777     An honorific, perhaps an adaptation of Latin "serenitas," as applied to the Roman emperors. See <u>OED</u> s. v. "serenity," 4.

785     Chaucer's <u>Troilus</u> has it, "alwey frendes may nat ben yfeere" (V, 343).

786-820   Cf. William, p. 151 B to D:  Nequaquam, inquit Albanus, sed una saltem septimana maneas apud me, ut interim dum mihi solicitudinem exhibueris Doctoris, cultum Christianae religionis plenius instructus agnoscam.  Amphibalus ergo, sentiens quod discessum suum graviter Albanus acciperet, trahitur ad consensum.  Igitur diebus singulis cum jam in vesperam hora declinaret, magister & discipulus hominum frequentiam devitantes, ad domum remotiorem, quae tugurium vulgo solet appellari, se proripiunt; noctem totam ibidem in Dei laudibus transigentes.  Et haec faciebant, ne secretum suum palam fieret infidelibus; qui cultores Christianae religionis, non in fide sequi, sed pro fide persequi contendebant.  Verum aliquanto tempore interjecto, Gentilis quidam ad judicem audaciter ingressus, quod factum fuerat indicavit.  Nihil omnino reliquit intactum, quo facilius vel obesset innocentibus, vel judicem impelleret ad furorem.  Quibus cognitis Iudex mox iracundiae furore succensus.

816     The mere judge, deriving from William, becomes at l. 1001 Asclepiodotus, king of Britain.  This alteration is also found in the English prose version; the Latin conflator felt forced to accommodate this court proceeding to the high rank of Alban as established in the <u>Tractatus</u>.  The conflator botched the job, so that in both English versions the sequence of events is puzzling and repetitious.

821-90   Cf. William, p. 151 D and E (ll. 835-63, a rhapsody on the friendship of the two saints, is original with Lydgate):  Albanum & Magistrum ejus ad suam praesentiam jussit evocari.... Sed hujusmodi decretum Albanum non latuit, qui Principis insidias modis omnibus cupiens praevenire, hortatur Amphibalum at urbe secedat; dans ei chlamydem auro textam, quo tutior ab hostibus redderetur : vestis...tantae dignitatis erat..., ut illa indutus cuneos hostium penetraret

illaesus. Ipse vero Magistri sui caracallam sibi retinuit,
certissime sciens, quod non aequis oculis eam saevientes as-
picerent inimici. Igitur Amphibalus, Albani precibus acquies-
cens, ante lucis exortum fugam arripuit, per viam tendens quae
de civitate vergit ad Aquilonem. Albanus vero eum deducebat,
quamdiu ambobus visum est expedire. Cumque discederent ab
invicem, & ultimum sibi valefacerent; quis eorum lacrymas sine
lacrymis ad memoriam possit revocare.

837-38    An apt allusion to I Samuel 18 to 20, especially
18:3-4: "And David and Jonathan made a covenant, for he
loved him as his own soul. And Jonathan stripped himself
of the coat with which he was clothed, and gave it to David,
and the rest of his garments...."

841    Antropos: i. e. Atropos, Milton's "blind fury with
the abhorred shears." Cf. Lydgate's Troy Book, II, 142 and
also Troilus, IV, 1546 and V, 7.

844    Cf. Chaucer's "Knight's Tale," I, 1191-2:

           A worthy duc that highte Perotheus,
           That felawe was unto duc Theseus....

845    For Orestes and Pylades see Euripides' Orestes.
Lydgate's source is not evident, but if one can judge from
the form of the names, must have been French.

847-51    Cf. Lydgate's Troy Book, III, passim.

878    "Garlement" is an interesting scribal form forecast-
ing the disappearance of the middle syllable in "garnement."

862    Quoted from Song of Solomon, 8:5.

891-97    A transitional paragraph of no originality in content, but not corresponding to any specific passage in William.

898-918    Derived from William (p. 151 D), but not in same
context:  ...ut cum ea qua dignum erat reverentia diis suis
victimas immolarent; nolentes autem, vi et violentia com-
prehendi, vinculis arctari & aris deorum loco victimae jug-
ulandos imponi. Sed hujusmodi decretum Albanum non latuit....

919-55    Cf. William, p. 151 F, which Lydgate has greatly
expanded by rhetoric. Cf. n. to II, 219-28. Lydgate omits

the fact that Alban was barefoot: Ubi dies exortus est, ex
improviso equites cum magna manu peditum, efferatis animis in
aedes Albani irruunt: scrutantur abscondita, strepitu & tum-
ultu universa pervenientes ad tugurium, illic illustrem virum
Albanum reperiunt in habitu peregrino, nudis pedibus ante
crucem Domini precibus incumbentem.

921-22    In other words, just as spring becomes summer.
Saints' feasts are traditionally celebrated on their death-
day, and St. Alban's feast is traditionally June 22.  Cf.
notes to II, 2]9-28 and II, 226-32.

938       Miss Quistorp (p. 203, n.) points out that Phlegon
is one of the four steeds of the sun in Ovid's Metamorphoses,
II, 154.  Lydgate mentions "Febus...his stede...Flegonte" in
Troy Book, III, 11; "drawith" may be a scribal error for
"drawn," or perhaps "drawid."

956-95    This passage does not derive from the major source.

971-96    This vast expansion of Ephesians 6:10-17, giving
symbolic value to each piece of contemporary armor, is anti-
cipated in a smaller way by St. Edmund, II, 710-16.  The development of the Pauline idea is not new with Lydgate: see
Felix's Life of St. Guthlac, B. Colgrave, ed., Cambridge;
University Press, 1956, p. 106, and Dorothy Whitelock's The
Audience of Beowulf, Oxford:  Clarendon, 1951.  Note also
Caxton, Order of Chivalry (see n. to II, 346)  Prof. D. Hart
writes me:  "The poet has started with one naked saint and
dressed him before us, though all that metal must have been
shivery with no jupon beneath.  Our saint is armed to the
teeth and all wrapped in metal; he will sorely need some "pacience" when he sallies forth to battle, because he's not
wearing a helmet...."  Prof. Hart agrees with the editor that
there is little aptness to the various equations of virtue to
pieces of armor.  These differ from those in the Order of
Chivalry.

995       Compare "Squire's Tale," V, 593, and the "Complaint
of Mars," 1. 9.  The expression means "with Saint John for a
surety," and seems to have been a catchphrase of the period.

996-1014 Cf. William, p. 151 F to 152 A:  Rapitur, trahitur,
dirisque constrigitur nexibus catenarum:  ab illiis vestibus, ab aliis trahitur & capillis.  Quem variis afficientes
injuriis, & satis inhumane tractantes, ad idola sua perdux-
erunt:  ubi tunc omnis civitas una cum Judice fuerat congre-
gata.  Albanus ut servum crucis palam se cunctis ostenderet,

signum Dominicum jugiter in manibus praeferebat.  Gentiles
signum novum & incognitum intuentes turbati sunt & exterriti.
Judex vero qui praeerat civitati, truci vultu, minacibus
oculis, beatum virum signumque salutis aspexit.  Cujus iracundiam in tantum dicitur, Albanus contempsisse, ut nec genus
suum, nec cujus esset familiae, dignatus sit ei confiteri:
sed de singulis interrogatus, nomen tantum indicavit; Chris-
tianumque se esse libera voce respondit.

    Lydgate, under the influence of the fame and civic im-
portance of Alban in the Tractatus, omits the judge's threat-
ening attitude and his questions as to Alban's origins.
These are still present in the English Legende, and therefore,
presumably, in the Latin conflation.

1001        Lydgate agrees with the Harleian MS of Gilte Legende
and therefore probably with the hypothetical Latin conflation,
in identifying William's judge with King Asclepiodotus of the
Tractatus.

1015-79    Cf. William, p. 152 A and B:  Quem Iudex hujusmodi
verbis aggreditur, dicens, Albane, Clericus ubi est, qui nuper
a Christo nescio quo huc directus, ut civibus nostris illud-
eret, hanc urbem latenter ingressus est?  Si reatus eum con-
scientia non remorderet, si de causae suae qualitate non dif-
fideret; sponte se nostris obtutibus ingessisset, ut pro se
suoque discipulo magister egregius allegaret.  Verum in ejus
doctrina quanta latuerit falsitas, quantaque fraudulentia,
suo tandem patefecit exemplo:  quandoquidem eum, quem in causa
tueri debuerat, inerti resolutus timore deseruit & aufugit.
Qua in re (nisi fallor) satis evidenter intelligis, quam
fatuo homini praebueris in errore consensum:  cujus instinctu
ad tantam devolutus es insaniam, ut omnia quae mundi sunt
repente desereres, & Deos magnos habere contemptui non tim-
eres.  Unde ne injuriam Deorum inultam praeterisse videamur,
eorum contemptum in nece contemptoris placuit vindicare.  Sed
quia  nemo est qui falli non posiit; eorum poteris indigna-
tionem poenitendo declinare:  quorum gratiam hoc modo tandem
promereberis, si haec secta nefandissima fuerit a te penitus
segregata.  Igitur saluberrimis acquiesce consiliis, & diis
magnis sacrificare ne differas; a quibus non modo peccatis
veniam, criminibus indulgentiam, verum etiam urbes & gentes,
exercitus, pecunias, provincias, potestates facile consequeris.

1080-1135 Cf. William, p. 152 B and C:  Albanus intrepidus
inter minas, integer inter munera, Judici respondit:  Verba
tua, o Judex, quibus diutius insudasti, quam vana sunt &

superflua, satis in promptu est.  Clericus enim, si bonum,
si utile videretur, si denique utrique nostrum cordi esset;
ad vestram utique audientiam occurrisset:  sed adventus ejus
mihi certe placere non potuit, qui sciebam populum hunc semper
ad mala fuisse proclivem:  nec ei Judices unquam placuerunt,
qui verum in judicio non discernunt.  Hujus doctrinam me
fateor suscepisse:  nec facti poenitet.  Quod enim non imper-
iti, non alicujus de plebe verbis fidem accommodaverim, ex
posterioribus forsitan cognoscetis.  Fidem hanc quam suscepi,
debiles et aegroti, sanitati pristinae restituti, veram esse
salutis suae testimonio comprobabunt.  Haec mihi fides carior
est cunctis opibus quas promittis, pretiosior cunctis honor-
ibus quas proponis.  Licet enim quis ditatus fuerit supra
modum, ad extremum tamen moritur vel invitus:  nec valet aurum
illud, tanta diligentia conservatum, suum custodem ex mortuis
revocare.  Sed quid in longum sermo producitur?  Diis...falsis
& fallacibus non sacrifico; qui omne genus meum spe vana
demulcentes, dum eis sedulo deserviret, miserabiliter deceper-
unt.

1085      "Atwene bothe" refers to the alternating threats
and blandishments of the judge.

1136-88    Cf. William, p. 152 C and D:  His dictis, sit subito
dolor in populo, hinc luctus, illinc clamor insultationis
exoritur:  sed martyr beatissimus nec Judicis comminationem,
nec circumstantis populi fremitum pertimescit.

     Statim conveniens turba Gentilium, sanctum virum colla-
tis viribus ad sacrificia daemonum coepit impellere, jubens
ut diis eorum quantocius immolaret.  Sed unius viri mentem
tanta nequit infringere hominem multitudo, ut nefandis riti-
bus in aliquo consentiret.  Tunc ex praecepto Judicis appre-
hensus, extenditur ad flagella.  Qui cum graviter caederetur,
ad Dominum conversus, hilari vultu dicebat:  Domine Jesu
Christe, custodi quaeso mentem meam, ne vacillet, ne a statu
decidat quem dedisti.  Tibi, Domine, animam meam in holocaus-
tum libenter offero, fusoque sanguine testis tuus fieri con-
cupisco.  Haec verba inter verbera resonabant.

     At this point, the Dublin MS bears in the margin the
note "Hoc de libro Johannis Mansel:  Erat namque dux et magister totius Britannie."  See Introduction, p. xxix.

1165-68    An allusion to Matthew 7:24-27.

1167-68    If La reading of II, 1167, is correct, "nat" of II,

1168, is a mistake, though metrically preferable; on the
other hand, if 1167 should read "ful often" (no manuscript
authority) then no change would be needed in 1168.

1168        This passage probably alludes to Colossians 2:6-10.

1180        An omitted pronoun subject.

1189-1219 Cf. William, p. 152 D and E:   ...facit eum sub cus-
todia Iudicis mensibus sex et eo amplius detineri.

His ita gestis, mox injuriam martyris elementa testantur.
A tempore namque comprehensionis illius, usque in diem quo...
vinculis erat absolvendus, terram ros aut pluvia non insudit,
venti non spirarunt; sed in dies singulos omnis regio sub
sole ardentissimo torrebatur:  nocturnis quoque horis aestus
erat nimius et intolerabilis:  non agri, non arbores quid-
quam fructum protulerunt, orbe terrarum pro justo contra imp-
ios dimicante.  Cives autem Verolamii plagam hujusmodi non
serentes, convenerunt in unum & dixerunt:  Praevalente male-
ficio artis magicae, deficit germen....

1191        Note that Ed agrees with La and Li; contrast II,
1132 and n.  The Latin source (see n. to II, 1189-219) has
"months" but Gilte Legende (Harl. f. 99 a v.) has "wokes."
Six weeks bring us into late June (Leo); cf. II, 1551.  This
coincides with the Feast of St. Alban (the traditional day of
his death, June 22.

1204        "Smyth" may be compared to II, 1747-48, "smothe
wind ... callid Zephirus."

1220-1366 Lines II, 1220-1345 contain matter probably taken
by the hypothetical conflator from Tractatus in order to harmonize the trial episode with the earlier matter from the
Tractatus, in which Alban is described as a high official.
Obviously, a man of such importance would not appropriately
have his case submitted to a mere judge, and therefore the
conflator identifies the judge with King Asclepiodotus (see
II, 1001) and associates the co-emperor Maximian with the
action as well.  The conflator has done his work carelessly,
and in following his crude insertion Lydgate has made Book
II much less coherent.  Lines 1346-66 are substantially a
repetition of Lydgate's own II, 1196-1219.  Lines 1220-1345
may be compared with the Gilte Legende, ff. 99a v. and 100 r;
in this prose version the insertion is similar, but after the
insertion much of William's prose (p. 152 E - F) is omitted,

though it occurs in Lydgate, II 1367-1415.

1220-82   Cf. _Tractatus_, f. 5 r. and v:  Timebat nempe asclepiodotus eum occidere ob familiaritatem quam habuerat cum
diocliciano... donec diocliciano de sua conversione plenius
significasset...Dioclicianus, visis asclipidoti litteris
direxit collegam suum maximianum herculeum, dans ei potesta-
tem per totam britanniam faciendi iusticias gencium ... des-
truendi fidem christianam ... praeter albano pro quo solli-
cite solicitabatur.  Albanum, inquit, pulcris promissionibus
allicias.... ...si nostris noluerit obtemperare precibus
monicionibus aut iussi omnibus [?] in hac parte ubicumque sibi
placuerit in toto mundo magnum eum faciam & honoratum.  Si
vero converti noluerit, ... decolletur per ictum alicuis
militis qui honorabilis fuerit in ordine militari.

1283-1303 Cf. _Trac._, f.6 r:...decreverunt ut amphibalus ubicumque posset inveniri caperetur & crudelissime flagellaretur
deinde nudaretur & ad palum fixum in terra firmissime sister-
etur.  Ubi aperto umbelico intestina extraherentur.  & in palo
necterentur & ipse ... circuire compelleretur donec omnia
viscera in palo predicto expenderentur extracta.  Quibus
peractis decretum est ut caput eius amputaretur.  Hec fuerunt
scriptis iudicia inlata contra albanum & amphibalum per maximianum & asclepiodotum.

1302      Not an infinitive; "both two."

1304-45   Cf. _Trac._, ff. 6 r. and v, 7 r:  Tunc summoniti
sunt burgenses Verolamii & Walyngcestrencium & londoniensium
seu trinouancium & omni villarum vicinarum ut convenirent die
Jovis proximo sequente ad audiendum iudicium et eius execu-
cionem per maximianum et asclepiodotum latum in albanum principem militum quondam urbis verolamie dominum & tocius britannie senescallum.  Convenerunt igitur ad diem praefixum innum-
erabiles populi ad videndum & audiendum tante rei nouitatem.
Die statuto albanus eductus de carcere amonetur libare Joui
et appollini diis precipuis civitatis.  Quo sacrificare no-
lente sed in super sic predicante ut multi converterentur ad
fidem Christi....

   Tempore imperatoris diocliciani Albanus dominus civitatis
verolamie princeps militum tocius britannie & senescallus ad
terminum vite despexerit iovem & appollinem & illis irrogavit
iniuriam quamobrem iuxta leges morti adiudicatus est per
manus alicuius militis quia miles esset.  Caput eius a corpore amputetur & ut corpus eius sepeliatur in eodem loco ubi

capite privatus est.  Cuius sepultura sit nobilis propter
honorem milicie cuius princeps fuit.  Crux quam adoravit cum
clamide quam gestavit cum eo mittatur in terram & sic in lo-
cello plumbeo corpus involutum in sarcophago recondatur.

1346-66  See note to II, 1220-1366.

1367-1412 At this point Lydgate once more takes up new matter
from William, p. 152 E and F:  Quibus tandem in unum congre-
gatis, beatissimus Albanus de squallore carceris ejectus,
nudis pedibus procedit in medium.  Quo viso, mox sapientes
ad invicem colloquuntur, consentiunt universi.  Albanus ab
omnibus innoxius judicatur:  injuriae condolent, vinculis in-
gemiscunt.  Sed & per parentes & genus ejus magnum & valde
praeclarum, quod erat in civitate, non minima perturbationis
rabies et dissensionis exoritur.  Injuriam namque tanti ac
talis viri aequanimiter ferre non poterant; ut videlicet homo
liber, acsi alicujus furti auctor extitisset, coram Iudice
ferro staret oneratus:  cum de moribus nec saltem sinistrae
suspicionis aliquando fama exorta sit; et certissimum apud
omnes haberetur, hujusmodi eum scelera summo semper studio
refugisse.  Cumque sedito gravis oriretur in populo, & tumultus incresceret; vir beatus omnium judicio nexibus exuitur
catenarum, quatenus liber a vinculis causam facti sui Iudici
redditurus adstaret.

The Gilte Legende (our only evidence for the hypothetical
conflation) for no clear reason omits most of this matter,
though it does refer to Alban's "kynne and his frendes" (Harleian 4775, 100 r), translating "parentes et genus ejus" in
the paragraph above.  Neither Lambeth MS 72 nor British Library Additional 35298, consulted to see if the omissions
were Harleian's only, vary from that manuscript.

1374      Van der Westhuizen may be right in retaining the La
reading; he points out that Tractatus reads, "Tunc nudatur
Albanus," (pp. 177, 282).

1388-94   These lines are clearly influenced, though not word
for word, by the Tractatus.  They are not paralleled in the
Harleian Gilte Legende.

1396      Ector: see Troy Book, II, 1129 for Hector's virtue.

1398      See note to I, 691.

1402-07  A reminiscence of II, 73-127; see note to those

lines.

1413-99    Cf. William, pp. 152 F to 153 B:  Hoc genus miser-
icordiae graviter Albanus accipiens, vehementer coepit formi-
dare, ne disseretur a martyrio, ad martyrium praeparatus.  Et
stans in medio multitudinis, cum gemitu suspexit in caelum:
et proferens Crucem Domini adoravit & dixit:  Domine Iesu
Christe, ne permittas in hac parte adeo diaboli praevalere
malitiam, ut per machinationes suas callidas, & istius populi
concordiam, meam impediat passionem.  Conatus ejus a te quaeso fiant irriti, reprimatur audacia, virtus dedicat in defec-
tum.  Dein ad populum se convertens ait:  Quid sustinetis?
Videtis certe quod tempus sub hac dilatione praetereat.  Si
non nostis ferre sententiam, legis vestras consulite, civitatis vestrae statuta requirite:  ipsa vobis insinuent, quid
agere debeatis.  Quid moras patimini?  Sciatis universi me
deorum vestrorum gravem existere inimicum.  Numquid honore
sunt digni qui nihil divinitatis in se dignoscuntur habere;
cum sint opera manuum hominum?  Vos estis eorum testes, quia
nihil vident, nihil audiunt, nihil intelligunt.  Optatne ali-
quis vestrum sic videre, sic audire, sicut dii quos adorat.
Nequaquam.  Quid ergo dicemus de talibus quorum similitudinem
habere cultores sui contumeliam credunt?  O multum detestanda
vanitas! ab his vitam sperare qui numquam vixerunt; his offere
preces qui numquam audiverunt; ab his salutem quaerere quibus
numquam bene fuit.  Unde absolute pronuntio; quia qui tales
colit, insanissimus est.  Rogo, quid infelicius homine, cui
sua figmenta dominantur! Vae ergo idolis, & vae cultoribus
idolorum.  Quid vobis videtur?

1417       In connection with Li reading, "bamaner" for "bi
a maner of" note significance as regards meter.  See note on
the "by" contraction at I, 110; cf. II, 1535 and III 1475 for
other "by" contractions.

1498       A clear case of the omission of the pronoun subject.  See remarks on p. 212.

1500-41   Cf. William, p. 153 C and D:  His auditis, Gentiles
mutuo colloquuntur, collatoque utrimque consilio, omnes un-
animi consensu in sanctum virum mortis tulere sententiam:
illudque mox in loco qui vulgi consuetudine Holmhurst vocab-
atur, fieri delegerunt, sed contentio inter eos ingens exorta
est, non invenientes quonam mortis genere suum perderent inimicum.  Quidam namque eum, tamquam discipulum Crucifixi,
crucifigendum; alii, quia deorum hostis extiterat, vivum
terrae infodiendum; non nulli, evulsis oculis post magistrum

suum dirigendum esse decreverunt:  denique Iudex populusque
civitatis universus, capitali eum sententiae addixerunt;
igitur ex judicio vinculis iterum constrictus Albanus ad supplicia trahebatur.  Tunc populus, in civitate Iudice derelicto, certatim proruit ad spectaculum:  qui sanctum virum con-
vitiis jugiter insectantes, Egredere, inquiunt, egredere hostis civitatis, deorum omnium inimice.  Vade quo tua te vocant
scelera; ut meritis tuis digna rependatur vicissitudo:  beatus
vero martyr non respondit eis verbum.

1506       Holmhurst is also mentioned in Tractatus, f. 7 r.

1523       An ellipsis, presumably omitting "that he be."

1535       See note to I, 110 on "by" contractions.

1542-76    Cf. William, p. 153 D:  Tanta congeries illuc con-
fluxerat populorum; ut loca prius ampla et spatiosa, nunc
prae hominum densitate angustissima viderentur:  vis quoque
tanta solis erat, ut nimiis ejus ardoribus terra sub itine-
rantium pedibus ureretur.  Cumque iter ageretur; tandem ad
flumen rapidissimum pervenerunt:  ad cujus ripam populo sub-
sistente, non minima transeundi facta est difficultas.  Dum
enim ruunt sine ordine, dum alter alterum praeire contendit;
nulli facilem transitum pontis angustia concedebat.  Tunc
quidam hanc dilationem non ferentes, sed vasto flumine se
credentes, in ulteriorem ripam natatu celeri transmearunt.
Alii, vero, opus simile praesumentes, ab aquis vehementibus
intercepti, vitam miserabiliter amiserunt.  Quo viso, factus
est dolor & luctus magnus in populo.

1551       The construction "as he is cours hath ronne" is
much like Chaucer's famous one in the General Prologue of the
Canterbury Tales, ll. 7-8.

1577-1622 Cf. William, p. 153 D and E:  Albanus quoque haec
videns ingemuit, & pereuntis populi damna deflevit:  & posi-
tis in terram genibus, misericordia motus super populum,
oculos ad caelum, mentem direxit ad Christum, Domine, inquit,
Jesu, de cujus sanctissimo latere sanguinem simul et aquam
manare conspexi; fac quaeso ut minorentur aquae, fluenta
recedant:  quatenus omnis hic populus, sanus & incolumis meae
valeat interesse passioni.  Mira res!  Cum genua curvaret
Albanus, alveus ille repente siccatus est.  Albani lacrymae
dum funduntur, aquas in flumine non relinquunt:  orationis
virtus flumen exhaurit, & inter undas viam populo patefecit.
Crebrescunt miracula, & virtutibus virtutes dum succedunt,

potentia Albani merita in populo clarius elucescunt.  Quos
paulo ante fluminis impetus secum rapuit, involvit, atque
perdidit; hi nunc inventi sunt, nihil habentes laesionis, nec
signum aliquid mortis in se praeferentes.

1623-1713 Cf. William, pp. 153 F to 154 A:  Tunc miles ille,
qui Albanum trahebat ad supplicia, tandem per Albanum pervenire meruit ad salutem.  Visis namque mirabilibus, quae
gloriose fiebant ab eo, poenitentia ductus ensem proiicit,
pedibus ejus advolvitur, fatetur errorem, veniam deprecatur;
obortisque lacrymis ait:  Albane serve Dei, vere Deus tuus
Deus verus est, & non est alius.  In illum me jam noveris
credere, illum mihi tecum pro Deo vendicare.  Fluvius iste,
quem precibus tuis in momento perduxisti ad nihilum, quodammodo loquitur & testatur, quod non sit similis, potens, &
faciens mirabilia super terram.  His auditis, scelerum min-
istris furor accrescit, invidiae stimulis agitantur, & homines
acerrimi fiunt acriores.  Qui efferatis animis ad eum rever-
tentes; Non est, inquiunt, per Albanum (sicut asseris) quod
flumen istud repente disparuit:  sed nos quibus deorum benig-
nitas scientiam contulit secretorum, res ista quare contigerit
novimus indicare:  nos deum solem colimus; & illi prae ceteris
reverentiam deferimus ampliorem.  Hic nostrae non immemor
devotionis, propter nos aquam fluminis vi caloris absumpsit;
ut sani & numero integri necem inimici nostri laetis oculis
cerneremus, tu vero, quia deorum beneficia ad alios sinistra
interpretatione torquere praesumis, dignam blasphemiae poenam
lues.  His dictis hominem arripiunt, dentes excutiunt:  &
illud os sacrum, quod testimonium perhibuerat veritati, graviter ab impiis laceratur.  Sed cum tot manibus non sufficeret
una pars corporis; ad reliqua membra transeuntes, omnia illius membra constringunt:  & cum nihil in corpore remaneret
illaesum; fides tamen qui servebat in pectore, laedi non
potuit.  Toto igitur corpore laniato, hominem in arena semi-
necem reliquerunt; ad scelus de scelere transitum facientes.

1662     Araclyus:  Though Miss Quistorp (p. 177, n. 382)
suggests that Lydgate may have taken this name from the
Sanctilogium (Nova Legenda Angliae I, p. 33) where it appears
as Heraclius, it seems more likely that in Lydgate's manuscript of William the same rubric occurred which is found in
the Trinity Dublin MS E.1.40:  "Credit Araclius miles visis
miraculis tantis."  The name also occurs in Tractatus as
Haraclius and Heraclius, and in the Auban, where it seems to
have originated, as Aracle.  The Gilte Legende does not mention the name in any form.  Maximian is Herculius in Geoffrey.

1665     The pronoun subject is again omitted.

1714-93    Lydgate continues to follow his source quite
closely; cf. William, p. 154 A to C:  Quis vero jam sine
lacrymis possit recordari, cum per dura lapidum loca, per
vepres et aspera quaeque, B. Albanum homines crudelissimi
ducerent ac reducerent:  spinae quoque & radices arborum etiam de pedibus avulsa secum frusta diriperent, & saxa pretio-
sus sanguis insiceret?  Tandem cacumen montis ascendunt; ubi
Dei athleta cursum sui certaminis erat impleturus.  Jacebat
illic hominum turba sine numero; qui sub ardenti sole siti
aestuantes; extremum spiritum jam trahebant.  Hi cum vidissent Albanum, fremebant in eum, dicentes:  Ecce malefico
praevalente, tantis urgemur incommodis, ut nulla nobis ulter-
ius remanserit spes vivendi; per artes magicas, quas Albanus
iste non desinit exercere, dies nostri defecerunt, & ipsi
defecimus.  Quorum miseriis Albanus intimo affectu condoluit,
caritatisque gratia fervens, pro suis persecutoribus preces
fundere non neglexit.  Deus, inquit, qui hominem de limo cre-
asti, ne sinas quaeso creaturam tuam mei causa qualemcumque
sentire jacturam.  Aeris adsit laeta temperies, aquarum copia
tribuatur; ventus incipiat spirare clementior; ut aestus, quo
populus laborat, tuo munere citius restinguatur.  Adhuc sermo
in ore loquentis volvebatur; & ecce subito fons ante pedes
ejus in medio vulgi circumstantis erupit.  Mira virtus Christ-
ti!  Terra nimiis ardoribus solis torrebatur; & tamen de
cacumine montis, de terrae pulvere, fons frigidus repente
scaturiens, venis exundantibus largiter profluebat.  Cumque
rapido impetu rivus ad inferiora descenderet; occurrit populus, ut aquis refocillatus cladem tantem qua vexabatur evad-
eret.  Quibus haustis, mox unius merito omnium sitis extincta
est:  sed adhuc tamen humanum sanguinem sitiebant.  Aestus
quidem corporum relevatus est, sed fervor furentium animorum
non est imminutus:  infirmi salutem adepti sunt, sed salutis
auctorem minime recognoscunt; Christum quippe blasphemantes;
Laus, inquiunt, Deo magno Soli, qui servis suis in arcto con-
stitutis tale dignatus est providere remedium, ut aquarum riv-
ulus subito de terra prosiliens, nobis ocurreret ad salutem.

1794-1849 In two manuscripts and the 1534 edition, there is
at 1. 1794 the rubric "Verba translatoris." Miss Quistorp
(p. 200 and n.) finds no device comparable to this apostrophe
to exist in the other legends of Lydgate.  She compares it to
Chaucer's "Man of Law's Tale," II, 288 ff., and "Knight's
Tale," I, 2831 ff.

1801-1814 Paraphrases and alternates of 11. 1794-1800, 1815-21.

1815       "creatouris" in La rises from scribe's taking a flourish for an "-is" sign.  See  II, 1817 and, for reverse, 532.

1828    The omitted pronoun subject is second person, rather than the more common third singular, thus is certainly stylistic, not phonetic.

1850-77    Cf. William, p. 154 C and D:  His dictis ad fundendum sanguinem populi furor accenditur:  cincinnique Martyris ad stipitem relegantur.  Ex omni populo carnifex unus eligitur, qui scelus pro omnibus perpetraret.  Qui mox expeditus, sublatum alte consurgit in ensem, eumque summis viribus librans in cervicem, uno ictu caput sancti Martyris amputavit.  Cadit in foveam cadaver exanime, praeparatam caedi:  pendet caput in stipite capillis irretitum.  Crux vero quam vir sanctus jugiter in manibus ferre consuaverat, felici jam cruore respersa, super herbam decidit:  eamque occulte quidam Christianus, Paganis omnibus rapuit & abscondit.  Carnifex autem, cum adhuc staret juxta corpus, luminibus ejus in terram cadentibus totus efficetur tenebrosus:  nec potuit miser objectu manuum oculis labentibus obsistere, nec lapsos in locum pristinum revocare.  Quo viso plurimi Gentilium mutuo colloquentes vindictam hanc plenam justitia profitentur.

1876    Note the latinate construction; see the remarks at the beginning of these *Explanatory Notes*.

1878-1975 Cf. William, p. 154, D, E, and F:  Cumque haec ita geruntur, ecce ex improviso miles illi, quem paulo ante semivivum in inferioribus Pagani reliquerant, annisu quo potuit montem manibus reptando conscendit.  Tunc Iudex, quem illuc miraculorum, quae per Beatum fiebant Albanum, rumor attraxerat; insultans viri vulneribus:  Eja, inquit, debilis obsecramus Albanum, ut ossa tua dignetur in statum pristinum reformare.  Curre, festina, reliquo corpori caput appone; statimque plenam ab eo mereberis consequi sospitatem.  Quid moraris?  Sepeli mortuum, refer obsequium; nec dubium quin servi sui manibus celerem conserat medicinam.  At ille, fidei calore succensus:  Ego, inquit, firmissime credo, quod B. Albanus suis meritis integram mihi reddere sanitatem, & ad clementiam possit perducere Salvatoris.  Facile enim hoc, quod vos irridendo nunc dicitis, per eum circa me poterit adimpleri.  His dictis, beati Martyris caput amplectens, sanctam caesariem reverenter exsolvit.  Tunc pium onus fragilis vector assumens, illudque corpori manibus devotius apponens; mirum in modum mox convalescere, ac desperatum coepit robur corporis recuperare.  Qui sanitati pristinae dicto citius in integrum restitutis, Christi potentiam, & Albani meritum, omni populo audiente, non destitit praedicare.  Et jam fortior ad laborem, propriis manibus debitum Sancto reddidit

obsequium.  Ipse humo corpus operit; tumulum desuper ipse
componit.

Videntes autem Pagani quae fiebant, repleti sunt zelo:
& conserentes ad invicem, dicebant, Quid faciemus?  Homo iste
ferro non potest interire.  Corpus ejus omne contrivimus; et
ecce jam versa vice vires pristinas, primamque speciem caro
recepit.  Et quid amplius faciemus.  Inite consilium quid
agere debeamus.  Tunc unus ex eis in medium prosiliens; Homo,
inquit, iste gladio non poterit occidi, nisi membratim prius
distrahatur.  Magus enim est, et per artes magicas ferro ne
sibi noceat novit obviare:  omnem ferri aciem hebetat nec
audet gladius hominis malefici corpus attingere.  Quibus auditis miles jubetur apprehendi, & vinculis arctari:  & nimis
horrendo supplicii genere, sanctum illud corpusculum discer-
pentes, ad ultimum gladio caput amputarunt.  Sic beatus miles,
usque ad mortem in fide Christi perseverans, una cum sanctissimo Albano corona martyrii solus ea die meruit sublimari:  &
qui factus est consors passionis, gloriae quoque consortia
non amisit.

1976-96    Cf. William, p. 154 F:  Per acta tandem Martyrum
caede, Judex soluto concilio populo dat licentiam abeundi.
Discedentes autem, saevitiam Judicis detestantur, & dicunt:
Vae Judici, apud quem locum non habet aequitas, partes suas
contra rationem exercet.  Vae Judici, in cujus judicio dom-
inatur furor, non justitia; sententiam dictat non ratio sed
voluntas.

1997-2045 Cf. William, p. 155 A (Lydgate has greatly expanded
the episode of the angelic song):  Nocte igitur insecuta,
Dominus Jesus Christus famuli sui Albani merita signis evi-
dentibus declaravit.  Nam cum tempus quietis advenisset; ecce
columna lucis e tumulo beati martyris in caelum usque extend-
ebatur:  per quem descendentes Angeli & ascendentes, noctem
totam in hymnis & laudibus deducebant.  Inter cetera vero
quae canebant, vox ista frequentius est audita:  Albanus vir
egregius, martyr extat gloriosus.  Cumque ad hoc spectaculum
subito fieret concursus hominum, magis ac magis intuentium
numerus augebatur.  Qui stantes eminus lumine turbantur insolito, novitasque rei vertitur in miraculum.

The column of light issuing from the tomb is paralleled,
and perhaps eventually derived, from Bede's Ecclesiastical
History, I, 33 and III, 11, where similar events are recorded
of the Abbot Peter's tomb and the relics of St. Oswald.  See
also the note to III, 1387-89.

2008        "that did" with force of "it did" seems to be an
East Anglian regionalism.

2017        This Latin phrase quoted directly from the source
and reappearing at the end of each of the next five stanzas
is the only variation from strict Rime Royal found in St.
Albon except for the eight-line stanzas of the Prologue to
Book II.

2046-87    These lines, marked "Oracio translatoris" in MS In,
and from internal evidence obviously by Lydgate, have no parallel in the sources.

2051        "Thyn hous" is the church and abbey of St. Albans.

2064        The widow's mite, Mark 12:42.

2080-84    Abbot Whethamstede; see notes to I, 883 and 889-
903.

## Book III

1-7        These lines are a recapitulation of the matter of
Book II.  It is to be noted that Book III has no prologue
as such, though the epilogue to Book II is really a transi-
tion, looking both forward and back.

8 ff.      It seems certain, as Horstmann points out in his
note, that one of the citizens of Verulam is speaking.  We
must therefore conclude that a substantial portion of the
text introducing this speaker has been lost, unless this is
an instance of Lydgate's carelessness.  As evidence of the
latter possibility, note the similarity between Lydgate's ll.
6 and 7 and the first words of William quoted below.

8-84       William, p. 155 C and D: Tunc unus ex eis, cum
prae timore omnes stare videret attonitos, ait:  Haec miranda
quae videmus, Christum Dei filium liquido constat operari.
Dii quos hucusque coluimus, potius probantur esse portenta
quam numina; quippe quibus virtus nulla, nulla divinitas in-
esse facile deprehenditur.  Opera nostra, opera inutilia;
diesque nostri inaniter defluxerunt.  Ecce noctis tenebrae
caeli cedunt splendoribus; superni cives eunt & redeunt; &
ab his Albani sanctitas assidue commendatur.  Tenebrarum
caligine mundus involvitur, sed Albani claritas tenebras non

admittit; Albani merita nequeunt obscurari. Nos, quia nihil utilitatis habet religio illa, quam hucusque tenuimus, veterem tandem damnemus errorem; de falsis ad vera, ad fidem de perfidia convertamur. Eamus & inquiramus Dei virum, qui (sicut nostis) Albanum, praedicando convertit ad Christum. Quam sint autem vera quae de Christo loquitur; ex his quae per Albanum fiunt mirabilibus liquido potestis advertere. Opera quae fiunt per discipulum, magistri procul dubio sermonibus attestantur.

39        "Hath made" lacks a subject.  Presumably either "God" or "He" is intended (cf. 1. 43).  If the latter, we have yet another example of the omitted pronoun subject.

85-161    Cf. William, p. 155 D and E:  Dum hac & alia vir ille prosequeretur, laudabilem ejus sententiam omnium favor excepit:  mox errorem pristinum detestantur, Christi fides ab omnibus praedicatur, iter in Walliam sub festinatione dirigitur, ubi Dei servus Amphibalus manere putabatur.  Nec eos sua fefellit opinio; nam procul adhuc positi, quod ibidem consisteret, famae celebritate cognoscunt.  Ad quem cum pervenissent, repererunt eum verbum vitae regionis illius hominibus praedicantem.  Cui adventus sui causam exponentes, Crucem, quam suo Albano quondam commendaverat, obtulerunt; quae beati Martyris recenti cruore perfusa, signa sui martyrii satis evidentia praeferebat.  Vir autem Domini gratias agens in omnibus Creatori, inclinat se & adorat, signumque salutare devotione debita veneratur.  Qui dum novis auditoribus faceret de religione sermonem, mox omnes ei in fide consenserunt; abjectaque superstitione vanitatis, signaculum quod in Christo est ab ejus sacris manibus alacriter susceperunt.  Cumque dies plurimi praeterissent, fama facti per omnem diffunditur regionem:  quae processu temporis per loca singula convalescens, tandem Verolamium vario sermone replevit, asserens quosdam de civitate toto corde hominem sequi transmarinum, ejusque suasu deorum culturas & leges patrias abjecisse.  Quo audito concutitur civitas, turbantur universi, requiritur qui abierint & compertum est mille viros non adesse:  eorumque nomina mox jubentur annotari.  Adversum quos nimio furore commoti, totis viribus se praeparant ad insequendum:  instructique armis bellicis cum ingenti strepitu iter ineunt, acsi essent ad praelia processuri.

111       The detail of Amphibalus' tears seems to come from the Anglo-Norman Auban; see Introduction, p. xxvi.

113       The subject pronoun is omitted.

122-24     Lydgate seems to interpret as a miraculous event a
statement in William which would seem to mean simply that
they were marked with the sign of the cross by Amphibalus.

148        For an interesting account of how it happened that
a thousand were thought to have been martyred with Alban, see
the Rev. Hippolyte Délehaye's "In Britannia dans le Martyrologe Hieronymien," Proceedings of British Academy, xvii (1931),
300.

153        "Cast" ordinarily would require a pronoun subject.

162-68; 183-238  Cf. William, p. 155 F: Audientes autem cel-
ebre nomen Amphibali, ad eum post aliquot dies fama ducente
perveniunt, & in circuitu ejus, quos quaerebant, intendentes
verbis illius, inveniunt.  Quibus visis, mox unus ex eis
Sanctum Dei cum nimia severitate verbis aggreditur hujusmodi:
Seductor pessime (inquit) cur istos imprudentes, & qui cavere
tuas nescirent insidias, verborum fallacis circumvenire vol-
uisti?  Quid egisti?  Impulsu tuo leges calcare, deos contem-
nere praesumpserunt.  Cur deos magnos irritare non metuis,
quod tibi non cedet in prosperum?  Si suam in te coeperint
injuriam vindicare, nulli dubium quin cito de terra dispereas:
sed si vis, una cum his quos in erroris tui vincula conjec-
isti, coram diis & hominibus inculpabilis apparere; praecipe
ut resipiscentes ab errore, simul nobiscum ad propria rever-
tantur.  Quod si tanta eis fuerit in errore pertinacia, ut
nullatenus redire consenserint; non remanebit ne unus quidem,
qui non occidatur.  Stat sententia.

    It is easy to misunderstand Lydgate and to assume that
the pursuers were also converted, and that a third group came
out against them.  Lydgate probably misunderstood the first
sentence quoted above ("Audientes..."), thinking it referred
to the converts, but having caught his mistake, did not see
fit to undo what he had written.

169-82     These lines are a repetition and expansion of ideas
in the passage from William quoted in note to III, 85-161.
See also note to III, 162-68.

172-178    "Receivid" would ordinarily require a subject pronoun, as would "for-sook" a few lines later.

183-238    See note to III, 162-68

187        "Hem" is apparently object of both "cam vpon" and

"debate ageyns."

190          The omitted subject pronoun again.

228-29     For better comprehension read aloud.  The heaviest
stresses should fall on "hem" in l. 228 and "thei" in l. 229.

239-80     Cf. William, pp. 155 F to 156 A:  Tunc unus ex
Christianis, fidei calore succensus, pro Clerico respondit,
dicens; Hunc virum quem cernitis, cultorem esse veri Dei,
forsitan hodie comprobabitis.  Considimus enim quod in con-
spectu vestro, more solito, per eum infirmo alicui salus
pristina in Christi nomine sit reddenda.  Ad illius profecti
sumus sanctitatem, ut cunctis, quae ad fidem Christianam pertinent, circa nos rite peractis, aeternae vitae nos faceret
esse participes.  Absit a nobis hoc scelus; ut hujus sancti
viri vestigia relinquamus, & vanis iterum vobiscum supersti-
tionibus involvamur.  Vos potius a lite cessantes, nostro
saltem provocati exemplo, fidem Christi suscipite:  ut una
nobiscum ad ejus possitis gaudia pervenire.  Mortem minamini:
sed quam pro Christo libenter amplectimur.  Deus autem &
Dominus noster Iesus Christus de servis suis faciat quod vol-
uerit.  Quid nos a proposito bono & utili revocare conamini?
Quid inaniter & superflue laboratis?  Quae semel pro Christo
dimisimus, ad ea nullatenus denuo revertemur.  Stat sententia.

253-60     A similar miraculous cure is recorded of Augustine
of Canterbury by Bede, II, 2.  To prove the validity of his
authority, Augustine cures a blind man after the dissident
British bishops have failed to help him.  Such contests go
back to Elijah in I Kings 18:20 ff.

270          See II, 971-95 and n.

281-315    Cf. William, p. 156 B:  His auditis Paganorum furor
magis accenditur:  ad arma prosiliunt, extractisque gladiis
sanguis funditor innocentium.  Proh dolor! Ministri scelerum in sua (ut ita dicam) membra desaeviunt, dum filius a
patre, pater a filio trucidatur; dum fratres a fratribus,
cives a civibus occiduntur.  Non reverentia senum, non parentum miseratio dura carnificum corda mollivit.  Sancti vero
Martyres certatim cervices suas gladiis objiciunt:  & dum
prior trucidatur, moras arguit secuturus.  Ex hoc sacro colle-
gio unus omnino superfuit, qui in via corporis infirmitate
detentus adesse non potuit.

305          The oxymoron, "amorous striff" is reminiscent of the

Petrarchan phraseology of <u>Troilus</u>, I, 400 ff.  It bears a certain kinship to Marvell's "To His Coy Mistress," ll. 43-44.
Perhaps both reflect some classical original, possibly Marvell
was directly influenced by Lydgate.

316-22; 330-64  Cf. William, p. 156 B and C:  S. Amphibalus
vallatus undique corporibus occisorum, beatas animas laetus
domino commendabat.  In quem carnifices cruenti omnem iracundiam suam refundentes, juraverunt, qui nihil cibi sumerent
donec inimicum deorum suorum seu vivum seu mortuum ad suam
perducerent civitatem.  Cujus brachia loris durissimis as-
tringentes, ante equos suos eum ire impulerunt:  illi quippe
sublimes in equis ferebantur, solus Amphibalus nudis pedibus
iter peragebat.  Sed quo magis suo Albano appropinquat, eo
amplius asperitas viarum & laboris iniuria mitigatur.  Carnifices vero semper ad locum caedis respicientes, seria jam
poenitentia ducti, super cognatos amicos suos, quos in furore
suo trucidaverunt, amarissime flere incipiunt.

316-20    Dr. Quistorp (p. 186) may be right in maintaining
that the tears of Amphibalus were added on Lydgate's own in-
itiative, but the French <u>Auban</u> has the same detail at ll. 1201
ff.

323-29    Although the name Lichfield does not appear in
William's text, it was included, not, as Miss Quistorp suggests (p. 187) because of an old tradition, but more likely
because Lydgate's MS. of William bore the same rubric which
appears in Trin. Dub. E.1.40, f. 25 v. of the <u>Interpretatio</u>.
This note is partially lost through trimming:  "...apud
lichefeld ... evenit inde Lichfeld dictum quasi campus cada-
verum."  The <u>Tractatus</u> also mentions (f. 8r.) but does not
etymologize Lichfield.  The Harleian prose version contains
no reference to the city.

    Lydgate's ineptness in not realizing that the tongue in
question is English deserves notice.

330-64    See note to III, 316-322.

363    The man referred to here should by all the conven-
tions of storytelling be the only one left alive among the
thousand converts previously martyred (III, 311).  But Lydgate does not seem to make the connection.

365-427  Cf. William, p. 156 C and D:  Dumque iter agitur,
intuentur hominem languidum secus viam jacere:  qui

cognoscens quod S. Amphibalus praeteriret, coepit clamare &
dicere:  Serve Dei excelsi, adjuva me; ut qui propria jaceo
depressus infirmitate, tua merear relevari intercessione:
credo enim quod invocato super me Christi nomine, celerem
mihi possis reddere sospitatem.  Carnifices autem, importuni-
tatem clamoris illius non ferentes, hominem incipiunt irri-
dere.  Nec mora sub oculis irridentium, qui jacebat exurgit;
& per hominem vinctum, vinculis diutini morbi, quibus tene-
batur, absolvitur.  His ita gestis, coepto itinere perrex-
erunt.  Res gesta diu celari non potuit:  sed mox per univer-
sum regionem facti fama difunditur.  Mirantur & ipsi carnifices; in tantum ut quidam ex ipsis Deum glorificarent, dicentes:  Quam magnus Christianorum Deus, et quam magna virtus
ejus!  Denique cum ad natale solum pervenissent, & suae jam
possent moenia cernere civitatis; paululum in loco deserto
fame & labore confecti requiescentes, defigunt telluri hastas
& scuta reclinant.  Ceteris autem quiescentibus, solus Amphibalus inter vincula constitutus, requiem non habebat.  Et
licet gravibus vinculis esset coarctatus:  suis tamen persecutoribus verbum vitae non destitit praedicare; Verbum quippe
Dei non potuit alligari.

365-85    This passage may have been originally suggested by
the healing of the son of Timeus in Mark 10:46.

428-518    Cf. William, p. 156 D, E, and F:  Interea nuntiatur
in civitate, quod cives in patriam remeassent; & magistrum
Albani, magnum & diis suis acceptabile sacrificium adduxis-
sent.  Quod cum percrebuisset, ingenti gaudio vitas reple-
batur.  Aestimabant enim, quod eos, pro quibus ierant, in-
columes ad propria revocassent.  Sed dum inter eos mira
fieret exultatio, quidam ex carnificibus adsunt improvisi,
dicentes; omnes, pro quibus tam laboriosum iter assumpserant,
in externis finibus pariter in gladio cecidisse.  Quo cognito
protinus omnis illorum hilaritas & gaudium in luctum & trist-
itiam convertuntur.  Patres a pignoribus, cives a civibus se
queruntur destitutos:  hic fratrem, ille propinquam se deflet
amisisse:  matres quoque, cognita filiorum nece, sparsis crin-
ibus, veste conscissa, subito moestam incendunt clamoribus
urbem:  ubique luctus, ubique gemitus:  nec erat quem ad
lamenta doloris non cogeret magnitudo.  Et dicebant:  Heu;
cur venerunt super nos haec mala? vae nobis!  Quid adhuc
vitam trahimus infelicem?  Ad mortem nos praecesserunt, quos
habere decrevimus successores.  Heu filii! quid egistis?
Propter vos cunctis in circuitu nationis facti sumus in op-
probrium:  nec jam prae confusione faciem hominum possumus
intueri.  Frequenter enim ante oculos nostros revocabitur,

quod filii nostri deos suos deseruerunt; & idcirco in externa
patria procul ab amicis miserabiliter fuerint interempti.
Totis dispersi agris jacetis exanimes, jacetis insepulti,
volatilibus in escam, bestiis in devorationem. Proh dolor!
Ad hoc reservati sumus? ad hoc superstites vobis existimus?
ut quod filii commiserunt, parentibus imputetur. O miseria!
Periit spes nostra: requies senectutis nostrae sublata est.
Vae homini sacrilego & fraudulento, qui dudum ab Albano recep-
tus hospitio, illud Christi nomen execrabile nostrae civitati
primus invexit. Ille perturbavit omnia: ille causa necis
omnium esse convincitur. Dii immortales, si vobis unquam
servivimus, nefandum hominem disperdite, & talem terris aver-
tite pestem. Cum damnis nostris, & vestras injurias in eo
vindicate: & mala, quae in nos commisit, in caput proprium
retorquete.

438-41    Both these clauses refer to "Dempt" above and ex-
press conditions contrary to fact.

463-66    The language is imitative of Chaucer in "Nun's
Priest's Tale," VII, 3355-57 and "Squire's Tale," V, 209-10
and 3355. Knowing Guido delle Colonne, Chaucer may have believed the Trojan horse to be of brass (See H. Bergen on Guido
in Troy Book, IV, E.E.T.S., E.S., cxxvi, 1920, p. 183: (equum
ereum). Chaucer might seem to refer to brass, but never quite
says so. Lydgate, nowever, does, using Guido, in Troy Book,
IV, 11. 6010 ff. The "brazen horse of Troy" is also in Lydgate's "Misericordias Domini," 1. 59 (MacCracken, Minor
Poems, I, 73).

The comparative frequency of echoes of the Franklin's and
Squire's Tales causes one to wonder whether Lydgate did not
have by him a MS of Fragment V (Skeat F) of the Canterbury
Tales. See notes to I, 8-15, 12, 99-103; II, 527, 995.

472-74    Cf. Troilus V 541-42,

          ... O paleys desolat
          O hous of houses whilom best ihight,
          O paleys empty and disconsolat.

478       See note on "division" at I, 106-82 and I, 126 ff.

519-81    Cf. William, pp. 156 F to 157 A: Cumque carnifices
vidissent, quod populus intolerabili dolore conficeretur;
prosilientes in medium, Nolite inquiunt, cives, nolite flere,
nolite supra modum contristari. Reprimite lacrymas,

consolationem admittite:  ne videamini filiorum gaudis invi-
dere.  Non necesse est super mortuos magnopere contristari,
quorum mortem vita, quorum dolores gaudia prosequuntur.  Nihil esse crudelius, quam parentes a filiis morte interveni-
ente separari, nec nos quidem abnuimus:  sed illic ubi mor-
ientes multam de se materiam gaudendi posteris derelinquunt.
Istis nequaquam condolendum est, imo magis congaudendum,
quos semper beate victuros constat in caelo regnare cum
Christo.  Non ergo dolere, sed gratias agere Christo debemus;
qui tantam ex hac urbe multitudinem dignatus est assumere,
& secum in caelestibus collocare.  Non sunt quasi mortui
plangendi in terris, qui feliciter cum Christo vivunt in
caelis.  Damna deflere, humanum quidem est; sed dolori nolle
modum ponere, insaniae proximum est.  Audite quae circa de-
functos gesta sunt; & quia incassum plangitis, forsitan cognoscetis.

528        "They" seems to mean the slaughterers of the nine
hundred and ninety-nine converts.  This preposterous speech
is in William (see note to 519-81 above).  Lydgate can only
be blamed for retaining it.  It adds to the somewhat chaotic
quality of the narrative of Book III.

544        The pronoun subject is again omitted.

545        "Procurage," though not listed in OED, is doubtless
founded on OED procure (66) and hence would mean much the
same as "brocage" (see textual note).  "Surmytted" (see Glossary) makes good sense but utterly destroys the meter.

581-679    Cf. William, p. 157 A, B, and C:  Tunc jurantes,
quia narrationi suae nihil falsitatis admiscerent, ad omnem
multitudinem locuti sunt, dicentes:  Egressi (sicut scitis)
ut parentes & amicos quaereremus; tandem in Walliam fama
ducente pervenimus:  ibique Clericum, ad fidem Christi Wallenses, Pictos, civesque invenimus exhortantem.  Tunc sine
strepitu parentes nostros a ceteris segregare, & sic nobiscum
reducere cupientes; nunc monitis, nunc minis eos coepimus
convenire.  Sed tanta inerat omnibus pertinacia, ut nulla
possent verborum industria vel ad horam ab illius viri con-
sortio separari.  Nos ergo in iram versi, ad arma prosilimus;
& iniuriam nostri contemptus, in caede civium vindicamus.
Ipsi vero certatim cervices suas gladiis objectantes, mortem
pro Christo libenter excipiunt.  Et erat spectaculum misera-
bile; cum filii in patres, patres in filios insurgerent,
prosternerent, interficerent.  Nulla ibi miseratio, nec reverentia senectutis.  Proh dolor!  quod dicturi sumus, sine

gravi gemitu loqui non possumus. Dum patris vulnera filius
alligaret, fratris manum, frater superveniens amputavit.
Itaque funduntur parentes, carissimi trucidantur: inundant
campi sanguine, cadaveribus obteguntur. Dum haec agerentur,
ecce Iesus ipse, pro quo ponebant animas, de caelo prospici-
ens, dixit clara voce: Transite ad me milites mei: ecce vobis aperta...janua paradisi...praeparata beatitudo quae non
minuitur.... Quibus auditis, nos, qui caedem exercuimus, in-
credibili memoratu est quanto gaudio repleremur; intelligen-
tes, quod amici de mundo ad caelum, de morte migrarent ad
Christum. Felices nobis esse videbamur, qui tales habuimus
parentes; quorum jam concives Angeli, quibus ipse Christus oc-
currere dignaretur. Verum ex insolito divinae vocis auditu
conturbati sumus & perterriti.

598     The latinate "force and arms" of the other manuscripts is quite possibly what Lydgate intended.

615     "And" is probably a scribal addition (ampersand in
the MSS), since both sense and meter profit by its absence.

621     The pronoun subject, "they" is omitted. See p. 210.

638-42     See n. to II, 971-95 as well as the text which it
glosses, for a fuller version of the Pauline metaphor.

655-58     A reminiscence of John 14:1-3?

680-735     Cf. William, p. 157 C and D: Volentes autem scire,
quot in illa caede corruissent, recensere coepimus interfec-
tos: & inventi sunt nongenti nonaginta novem, omnes pro
Christi nomine trucidati. Iacebant singuli equorum ungulis
calcati, nec poterant propter vulnera & sanguinis copiam qui
prefluxerat recognosci. Sed dum vir sanctus hujus rei Deo suo
preces effunderet; subito praeter spem redintegrantur omnium
vulnera mortuorum. Sanguis in speciem lactis convertitur,
cutis ad formam pristinam revocatur; adeo ut nec vestigium
vulneris in eis potuerit deprehendi. Factumque est ut agni-
tionem humanam, quam nostra crudelitas prius abstulerat, oratio Justi denuo repareret. Tunc populus terrae, beneficia
Christi sinistra interpretatione pervertens, divinis per omnia
virtutibus contradicit; & ne in suis finibus mandentur sepul-
turae, qui fidem Christi susceperunt, vehementer obsistit.
Supremum naturae debitum defunctis negatur, & devorandi bestis
ac volatilibus exponuntur. Sed aderat Dei gratia, quae servos
suos post mortem quoque glorificans, dura furentium corda mollivit, & hostes circa mortuos reddidit mitiores. Ut enim

liquido daretur intelligi, divinam Christi cultoribus non deesse custodiam; ecce lupus & aquila, ex improviso venientes, ad Sanctorum cadavera substiterunt.  Lupus feras, aquila volucres abigebat:  ut eos ad illorum missos esse praesidium facile sensus humanus intelligeret.

681          See note to III, 148.

722-28     The association of the eagle and the wolf (along with the raven) with descriptions of gory battlefields is very frequent in Old English verse, e.g. Beowulf, 3024-27, Wanderer, 81-83, Brunanburh, 61-63.  See Magoun, "The Theme of the Beasts of Battle in Anglo-Saxon Poetry," Neuphilologische Mitteilungen, lvi, 81-90.  A. Renoir suggests continuity between the versions, Neophilologus, lxx (1976), 455-59.

736-77     These lines are on matter original with Lydgate and are not paralleled in the sources.  As a "verbum auctoris" this device resembles II 1794 ff.

746-49     This legend is treated in detail in Lydgate's Edmund and Fremund, II, 841-68.

763          "What we have to do":  It is likely that Lydgate has here in mind the retrieving of England's fortunes in France. Charles VII had reentered Paris two years earlier.

764-65     The symbolism of Edmund's coat of arms, the three crowns, is explained in Edmund and Fremund, I, 49-56.  They symbolize earthly kingship, virginity, and martyrdom.

769          "Thei" in the preceding line is presumably the subject of "shal make."

778 ff.    Lydgate, led astray by his aside on St. Edmund and the current political situation, has forgotten that the speaker is a member of the group who killed their fellow citizens. The "they" and other third-person pronouns should more correctly be of the first plural.

778-840    Cf. William, p. 157 D and E:  Quibus perspectis, mirantur Picti, Wallenses contremiscunt:  humana rabies mitigatur, impugnare jam desinens, quos divina dextera defendebat. Undique visendi studio vicinia tota circumfusa ruit:  Reliquias Martyrum piis amplexatur affectibus, & dignis obsequiis veneratur:  & quos paulo ante habuerunt in derisum, nec pati poterant ut eos terra susciperet; nunc versa vice miris

laudibus extollunt, & habere desiderant; gratias agentes
omnium Creatori, qui suam regionem tot taliumque virorum dignatus sit sanguine consecrare.   Ad perpetuandam quoque memoriam occisorum, ab ipsis incolis eorum numerus & nomina des-
cribuntur.   Haec omnis multitudo quae convenerat, priusquam
ad propria remearet, vidit, audivit, & in his omnibus nobiscum testis extitit.   Cum haec & alia carnifices prosequuntur;
sedantur lacrymae populi, dolor mitigatur.   Multi quoque qui
audierunt, potentiam Christi collaudant; de parentum gloria
laetantur, & dicunt:   Magnus Deus Christianorum, qui servos
suos ita reddit gloriosos.   Non posset homo peccator mortuorum vulnera in integrum reformare.   Vere bonus medicus, qui
tam subito servorum vulnera ad pristinam revocat sanitatem.
Ex hoc manifeste colligitur, Clericus ille quanti sit apud
Deum meriti, quamque amplectenda sit illius praedicatio; qui
solis precibus cuncta quae audivimus potuit obtinere.

804-05    The first "thei" refers to "tormentours," the second
to the rest of the citizens.

827-33    Cf. II, 572-83 and n.

841-903   Cf. William, p. 158, A and B:   Judex autem cum
audisset hos sermones; volens placere Paganis, in haec verba
furibundus erupit:  Usquequo patiemur hoc scandalum?   non est
hic homo a Deo, qui sermone suo perimit innocentes.   Clericus
ille quibusdam verborum praestigiis novit decipere oculos
intuentium; ut ea quae falsa sunt, vera faciat aestimari.
Per illius verba deceptoria urbis nostrae cives optimi peri-
erunt.   Praecipimus ergo, ut omnes qui sequuntur hunc hominem,
aut carnificum verba magnificant & mirantur, ubicumque fuerint
reperti, gladio puniantur.   Post haec mandavit omni populo,
dicens:   Egrediamur universi, & inimico nostro quantocius
occurramus:  ut qui omnes cognoscitur offendisse, ab omnibus
sibi vindictam sentiat irrogari.   Dicant omnes quod voluerint:
sed nos nostrae civitatis injuriam negligere vel inultam re-
linquere non debemus.   Hoc mandatum postquam in civitate di-
vulgatum est; Gentiles hinc inde concurrunt, & quidquid teli
furentibus venit in manus arripitur.   Alter alterum ut velo-
cius est hortatur, & in suum sese invicem excitant inimicum.
Tendentes ergo per viam, quae de civitate vergit in Aquilonem,
urbem vacuam reliquerunt.   Erat autem populi numerus infini-
tus, nec poterant plateae multitudinem capere confluentem:
& quia stipatis agminibus incedebant prae densitate sua lento
gradu iter agere cogebantur.

904-63    Cf. William, p. 158 B and C, which Lydgate has

greatly expanded.  Both the English prose legend and Lydgate,
as opposed to William, have a single pagan rushing ahead;
see Introduction, p. xxxiii.

     Interea quidam ex eis hujuscemodi moras non ferentes,
animorum levitate ducti, a reliquo populo diverterunt:  &
ingressi semitam, cujus compendio stratae publicae obliqui-
tatem declinarent; citius ad virum Dei in vinculis constitutum, & a fociis suis longius remotum pervenerunt.  Quem mox
arripientes, & tractantes atrocius expoliaverunt, visceraque
ejus ferro patefacta, palo in terram defixo circumligantes,
& flagellis nimiis Sanctum Dei concidentes, in circuitu ejusdem pali ambulare fecerunt.  Cumque beatus Martyr, Dei munere,
inter tot angustias constitutus, nulla daret doloris indicia;
illi acriores effecti eum quasi ad signum statuunt, & cultel-
lis lanceolique quod reliquum erat corporis confodiunt.  Vir
autem Domini, tamquam nihil mali pateretur vultu hilari stabat
constantior; & signa sui martyrii toto jam corpore praeferebat:  prodigiosum cunctis de se praebens spectaculum, quod
post tanta supplicia, post tot mortis genera, adhuc vivere
potuisset.

935     The expression "naturs riht" may mean the human
right to die, but more likely refers to "natural law."

937     "humydite callid radicall":  OED s.v. "humidity"
cites Thomas Stanley, History of Philosophy VI (1701), pp.
260-61:  "Death...cometh...when through the want of Refriger-
ation the Radical Humidity is consumed and dried up."

944-45   Canticum Canticorum (Song of Songs) 8:6.

953-59   This stanza, missing in the best MSS, is not needed
for the continuous sense of the poem, nor does it correspond
exactly to the source, but its style is a strong argument
for authenticity.  Cf. III, 967 and n. below.  Its resemblance
to preceding stanza suggests that it was suppressed to make
room for 946 ff., with its rich allusions.

964-1001  Cf. William, p. 158 D, much expanded and amplified
by Lydgate:  Eadem hora plurimi, quorum corda Deus tetigerat,
compuncti sunt corde; renuntiantesque idolis, Christianae se
fidei subdiderunt, orantes Martyrem, ut ipsius intercessione
beatitudinis aeternae, quam illi Deus praeparaverat, & quam
se jam videre perhibebant, participes fieri mererentur; pro
quo etiam omnes, animas ponere minime formidabant.  Quo cognito, Princeps vocatis mox speculatoribus, omnes qui deorum

suorum culturam abjecerant, & doctrinam Clerici sequebantur,
jubet interfici. At illi ferale complentes edictum, mox
mille viros morti tradiderunt; beato Amphibalo intuente,
eorumque animas Domino commendante.

967-73    The authenticity of these lines is indicated by
their closeness to the corresponding passage in William
(158D).

1001-45   Cf. William, p. 158, D and E:  Tunc unus qui ceteris audacior videbatur, sic eum prior alloquitur:  Crudelissime hominum, cur imprudentes illos persuasionis tuae fraude
decepisti; & perversis ac feralibus tuis monitis irretitos a
cultura deorum submovisti?  Quid in te civitas nostra pecca-
vit, ut eam suis civibus spoliares?  Diligenter attende, vir
bone, quid feceris.  Tuorum subtilitate verborum parentes &
amici nostri in perditionem abierunt.  Tu causa necis omnium:
tu eos ad mortis laqueum impulisti.  Hinc justis odiis te
persequimur:  maxime cum ipse quoque justitia justitiae adver-
sariis jubeat adversari.  Ubi te jam miser esse conspicis?
Hostium undique vallaris agminibus, nec est locus evadendi.
Sed quamvis deos & homines ad iracundiam supra modum provo-
caveris, eorum tamen gratiam poenitendo poteris promereri.
Perfectae vero poenitentiae hoc erit indicium, si sectam illam
quam hucusque tenuisti, deserueris; & deos invictos, quos ig-
norans forsitan offendisti, coeperis adorare:  nec dolebis de
facto; quia mox rerum omnium affluentiam consequeris; insuper
omnes quos neci nuper tradidisti, per suae divinitatis potentiam dii nostri a mortuis revocabunt.

1020 ff.   Compare the temptation of Alban in II, 1075 ff.

1046-1134 Cf. William, p. 158 E and F (Lydgate has expanded
the praise of baptism to forty-two lines):  Dicit ei Amphibalus:  Dum deos tuos, o Pagane, nimiis laudibus conaris
extollere; in verbo tuo te noveris offendisse.  Solus enim
Dominus Jesus Christus suscitat mortuos & vivificat.  Illos
vero quos quasi deos & potentes aestimatis in caelo, poten-
ter tormenta patiuntur in inferno.  Illic deorum vestrorum
commoratio & mansio sempiterna:  ibi fletus & stridor den-
tium, ibi vermis qui non moritur & ignis inextinguibilis.
Horum participes & locii fient in tormento injusti, adulteri,
maledicti, ceterisque, qui dum hic viverent, similes se demon-
ibus per actus reprobos reddiderunt; ut quorum voluntatem
secuti sunt per convenientiam vitiorum, eorum quoque consor-
tio non careant in perpessione tormentorum:  talium quippe
cultores numinum talis decet retributio meritorum.  Tu quoque

o Pagane, tu cum ceteris cultoribus idolorum, nisi citius
relicto gentilitatis errore ad fidem Christi convertaris,
eisdem doloribus habes subjacere. Sed dum vacat, abjiciatur
vanitas, error condemnatur: misericordia Dei nostri magna
est, nolite desperare. A viis vestris pravis resipiscite, &
ad baptismi gratiam convolate. Quid vero baptismus conferat
diligenter advertite. In baptismo peccata donantur, caelum
homini referatur; & vetustate deposita, nova quodammodo effi-
citur creatura. Qui enim prius erant per culpam filii diaboli, fiunt postmodum per gratiam filii Dei. Ad hanc ergo
gratiam confugium facite; ut poenas possitis evadere sempi-
ternas.

1062 ff.  This euhemeristic theory probably stems directly or
indirectly from Cicero.  See De Natura Deorum, III, xxi, and
De Republica, VI, xxiv.

1067     Miss Quistorp points out (n. 406) that Lydgate has
"Commemoracioun" for William's "commoratio" (n. to III, 1046-
1134).  The Harleian MS of the Gilte Legende has "mynde,"
i. e. commemoration, an instance of the correspondence of the
two English versions, suggesting a common Latin source not
found.

1098     "As seyn these clerkis":  Common in Chaucer, e.g.
"Merchant's Tale" (IV, 1972, 1362); the next line is paraphrased from the rite of baptism.  "Forsakith" may be an im-
perative parallel to "causeth" and "openeth" rather than an
indicative.

1122     Original sin is commonly portrayed as spots or
stains on man's pristine state escaped by Mary the mother of
Jesus, who is therefore styled "immaculate."  The phraseology
seems to derive ultimately from Song of Songs, 4:7.

1135-97  Cf. William, p. 158 F to 159 A:  His auditis, hinc
inde concurrunt:  crudeles dexterae lapidibus onerantur.
Fervent impii in nece innocentis:  & ut beatum spiritum eji-
ciant, totis viribus elaborabant.  Sed licet Dei Martyr saxo-
rum grandine graviter undique caederetur:  immobilis tamen in
oratione persistens, loco suo motus non est, nec in partem
alteram vel ad horam declinavit.  Denique cum invictum spiritum esset caelo rediturus; elevatis oculis Jesum stantem ad
Patris dexteram intuetur:  Angelorum quoque concentum in
caelis audivit:  & inter eos Albanum suum recognovit.  Quem
sibi in auxilium advocans, Sancto, inquit, Albane communem
Dominum quaeso depreceris, ut mihi Angelum bonum obviam

mittat, ne mihi praedo truculentus obsistere, ne iter meum
pars iniqua valeat impedire. Vix verba compleverat: & ecce
duo Angeli caelesti fulgore radiantes ad eum de supernis ven-
iebant. Vox etiam caelitus hujusmodi ad eum facta est: Amen
dico tibi, quia hodie cum discipulo eris in paradiso. Pagani
autem caelestem sonum audientes, stabant stupefacti. Igitur
Angeli beati viri animam, niveo candore fulgentem, secum as-
sumentes in caelum, cum hymnis & laudibus detulerunt.

1179      Suggested by the episode of the good thief, Luke
23:43.

1198-1239 Cf. William, 159 B. Lydgate has placed the detail
of the Christian's hiding Amphibalus' body in a different order:   Sed viri animo concitati, corpus exanime & in vinculis
constitutum lapidibus adhuc obruere non cessabant. Nec poterant opem ferre morienti nec de manibus eruere saevientium,
duces ejus & comites, jejuniis & fatigatione confecti. Tunc
grave inter Paganos certamen exoritur; & usque ad conflictum
gladiorum, contentio nefanda procedit. Agmine denso pars
utraque cucurrit, & supra membra beatissima gravis pugna com-
mititur. Sed noluit nec permisit Deus omnipotens ut fierent
veridici, veritatis inimici; qui dudum juraverunt, quia sanctum virum seu vivum ad suam perducerent civitatem. Dum enim
tumultus incresceret, & inter se Pagani turbarentur; quidam
fidelis in Christo clam beati Martyris corpus auferens, sub
terram occuluit diligenter, quandoque (ut considimus) divino
munere in lucem proferendum.

1202      Cf. Acts of the Apostles 7:54-58.

1212-15, 1230-39 A reference to the finding in 1178 of the
supposed relics of Amphibalus, after a dream-vision of one
Robert Mercer, citizen of St. Albans, an account of which is
in Matthew Paris' Chronica Majora, v. II, pp. 301-308. ˙ See
Introduction to present volume, p. xxii.

1240-60   Cf. William, p. 159 B and C: Interim caelestis in
populum vindicta desaevit, distorquentur labia, varia defor-
mitas vultus apprehendit, obrigescunt digiti; nervi officiis
non funguntur: ardent linguae, quibus beato Martyri fuerant
illata convitia. Quid multa! Brachia, manus & omnium omnino
membrorum flexibilitas ita repente diriguerat, ut ne lapidem
quidem de terra levare jam possent. Variis ergo poenis affla-
ti, sic demum a praelio quieverunt. Judex autem, amisso
rationis intellectu, amens effectus est. Nec erat qui posset,
se Domino Jesu & servo ejus Amphibalo contumelias irrogasse,

& tamen periculum evasisse, jactando gloriari:  quotquot enim
manum erexerant contra Dominum dignam pro meritis a justo
judice senserant ultionem.

1261-67    Lines expanding and moralizing upon III, 1240-60
and not found in sources.

1268-74    Cf. William, p. 159 D (not in same context as in
Lydgate):  Decessit omnis ille coetus infidelium, qui in B.
Albanum mortis quondam tulere sententiam, nec jam de eis multum tractant homines aut loquuntur:  Albani memoria non dele-
bitur, sed ejus laudabile meritum, si quid mea carmina possunt, longe lateque per orbem diffundetur.

1275-1302 Cf. William, p. 159 C:  Res autem gesta diu celari
non potuit.  Exciti rumore vicini accurrunt; quod auditu per-
ceperant, oculis comprobantes.  Mox fidem Christi civitas tota
suscepit, deumque justum in suis judiciis collaudavit.  Multi
divini amoris instinctu sua relinquentes, Romam adeunt:  de-
flent commissa, fatentur errores, undamque lavacri expetunt
salutaris.  Igitur a die illa & deinceps, omnis populus civitatis, deos quos coluerat vanos esse cognoscens, Christum Dei
filium omni tempore colere studuit & timere.

1296-99    "Myracles" and "doctryne" seem to be the subjects,
"causid" the verb of this difficult passage.

1303-16    Cf. William, p. 159 D:  Haec & alia multa quae divina pietas noluit hominibus occultare, diligenter litteris
commendavi.  ... Sed ne posteri super meo nomine reddantur
nimium soliciti:  sciant quia si voluerint verum mihi ponere
nomen, me miserum, me peccatorem ultimum nominabunt.

1314      The similarity of the passage, here and in William
above, to the "wretch" pseudonym of the translator of Gilte
Legende is noted by Richard Hamer (Three Lives from the Gilte
Legende, Heidelberg:  Winter, 1978) pp. 17-18.

1317-30    Cf. William, p. 159 D:  Tempus erit, ut confidimus,
quo viri religiosi, viri Christiani, ad praedicandum Gentibus
venient in Britanniam.  Isti cum venerint, Dei magnalia hoc
modo libris adferta reperient, legent, & ad notitiam deferent
plurimorum.  Tunc veritate cognita laetabitur insula:  tunc
Gentiles errorum vinculis absoluti multiplici gaudio reple-
buntur.  Verum tempus praedicatae visitationis & gratiae quando venturum sit, quia certum non habeo; istic jugus laetitiae
magnitudinem non expecto.

1331-44    Cf. William, p. 159 E:  Romam autem profisciscar, ut illic gentilitatis errore deposito, & lavacro regenerationis adepto, veniam merear assequi delictorum:  libellum quoque istum, qui habetur in manibus, asseram examini Romanorum; ut si quid in eo secus quam debuit forte prolatum fuerit, hoc per eos dignetur in melius commutare Dominus Jesus Christus, qui vivit & regnat Deus per omnia secula seculorum. Amen.  (End of Interpretatio Guillelmi)

1340       "that court" is of course the Roman Curia.

1345-53    This and the following passages concerning Offa have no direct known source.  The matter is fairly closely paralleled in Vitae Duorum Offarum of Matthew Paris, pp. 17 ff.  See also my Introduction, p. xxxiv.  The following is from p. 18 of the Vitae:

Acta autem sunt haec a passione saepedicti Martyris anno quingentesimo septimo, ab adventu Anglorum in Britanniam trecentesimo quadragesimo quarto.  Indictione prima, Kalendis Augusti.  Compare M. Paris, Chronica for A.D. 793 (I, 358).

Note Kalends rather than Ides; the year would seem to be A. D. 793.

1354-55    Cf. Vitae Duorum Offarum, p. 18:  Martyris igitur corpus ... in theca lignea (in qua prius a Christi fidelibus, propter barbarorum saevitiam fuerat tempore discriminis occultatum) reperiunt....  Quem utique thesaurum ... transtulerunt in quamdam ecclesiolam, olim extra urbem Verolamium.... Rex igitur Offa christianissimus, locellum memoratum, laminis aureis & argenteis gemmisque pretiosis ... decenter adornari....  Cf. Chronica Majora, I, 357-58 for this and next note.

1356-65    Cf. Vitae Duorum Offarum, p. 18:  Nam mortui ad vitam revocantur, semineces ad sospitatem restaurantur, leprosi mundantur, paralytici solidantur, febricitantes curantur, contracti eriguntur; muti, surdi, caeci, & arreptitii, imo omnes languidi & se male habentes malorum remedia recipiunt.

1366-86    These lines are apparently original with Lydgate.

1370-72    See note to III, 1354-55.

1373-74    For the palladium see Troilus, I, 153 and Lydgate's Troy Book IV, 5586 ff.  Note especially l. 5611, "this relik."

1382     Marcus Manlius is discussed at length in Fall of
Princes, IV, 211 ff.

1387-89   Cf. Vitae Duorum Offarum, p. 17:  Rex Offa ... divino est admonitus oraculo, ut Sanctum Dei Anglorum sive
Britonum Protomartyrem Albanum de terra levaret, & reliquias
ejus in scrinio dignius collocaret.  ...Rex vero, dum illuc
iter expediret, lucis radium, in modum ingentis faculae caelitus omissum, super locum sepulcri quasi fulminare conspexit.

1390-93   Cf. Vitae Duorum Offarum, p. 19:  Rex ecclesiam
coepit aedificare, ponens primum lapidem in fundamento....
In Matthew Paris, the construction of the church comes after
the translation and journey to Rome.

1394-98   Cf. Vitae Duorum Offarum, p. 18:  Thesaurum, super
aurum & topazion pretiosum, diu sub cespite absconditum, &
jam divinitus inventum, archiepiscopus Humbertus, cum suis
coepiscopis et Clericis, astante Rege reverenter levantes de
sepulcro ... transtulerunt in ecclesiolam.  See note to 1390-
93 above.  For this and two prev. passages, Chronica I, 356-7.

1399-1414 Cf. Vitae Duorum Offarum, p. 18:  Eodem quoque mense
Rex ibidem provinciale statuit concilium:  ... Cumque trac-
tarent diligenter ... de conventu monachorum in illo loco
congregando....  Et haec omnia ut digniorem ... fortiantur
affectum, consilium virorum sanctorum suscepit ... ut per
Legatos solemnes a latere Regis destinatos, aut potius in
propria persona Rex ipse, super his cum Curia tractet Romana.
Offa igitur Rex piissimus ... transalpinum iter arripit....
Romam tandem perveniens ... Adriano summo Pontifici sui causam
adventus explicans, & de loco simul & B. Albano canonizando &
magnificando, coenobioque constituendo, devote preces porri-
gens, petitioni suae Romanam de facili curiam inclinavit....
Rex... B. Albano amplas contulit terras & possessiones innum-
eras.  Cf. Chronica Majora I, p. 359.

1399     The pronoun subject is omitted again.

1415-70   This matter is found substantially (except for con-
temporaneity with Offa and Pope Hadrian) in Bede, I, xviii.
Lydgate might well have got it second-hand from a variety of
sources.

1415-18   The error of assigning Offa and Germanus (for whom
see Introduction, p.xix ) to the same period is also to be
found in the Cologne volume of 1502, discussed in the Appendix

on the edition of 1534. See 1. H. 1619 in Appendix, p. 427.
Some unknown source of the shared error is indicated, for it
is unlikely that the German monks would have derived their
mistake from Lydgate.

1417-70  Pelagius was born in the British Isles in the later
fourth century. His teachings were condemned as heretical in
416. He denied the significance of original sin and stressed
the power of man to achieve his own salvation, in contrast to
those who taught that man had fallen and salvation could come
only from the merits of the death of Christ.

Germanus, bishop of Auxerre in Gaul was sent to  Britain
by Pope Celestine in 428. He returned there in 445. Part
of his mission was to combat Pelagian doctrines. He is said
to have visited the burial place of Albanus.

For further data on Pelagius and Pelagianism see Karl
Baus et al., The Imperial Church from Constantine to the
Early Middle Ages, trans. Anselm Biggs, v. II in History
of the Church, eds. Hubert Jedin and John Dolan, New York:
Seabury Press, 1980, pp. 161-71 and (for Germanus) pp. 211
and 518. See also B. B. Warfield, Studies in Tertullian and
Augustine, 1930, reprint, Westport, Conn.: Greenwood Press,
1970, pp. 289-307.

1471-84  See note to III, 1354-55.

1475-80  For Solomon, the ark, etc. see II Chronicles, 5:1.

1484     Loving one's neighbor next to God and putting him
before oneself is not a natural attribute (lawe of kynde)
but rather, according to medieval theologians, a supernatural
virtue deriving from Deuteronomy and the gospels; thus
Lydgate is inadvertently heretical in this passage.

1498     The identical line occurs in Edmund and Fremund, I,
1. 150. For a list of the worthies and the sources of the
list see the detailed modern treatment, Der Topos der Nine
Worthies in Literatur und bildener Kunst by Horst Schroeder,
Göttingen: Vandenhoeck, 1971; also The Parlement of the Thre
Ages, ed. M. Offord, E.E.T.S., O.S., ccxlvi (1959), 11. 297-
583 and notes.

1525     See n. to III, 1387-89 for Offa's vision at Bath.

1557-64  Henry VIII, Anne and Elizabeth replace Henry VI in
the 1534 print. Schirmer (John Lydgate, pp. 169-70, takes

the lines of the 1534 editor (H. 1760 ff. in the <u>Appendix</u> to
the present volume) to be part of Lydgate's own work, referring the "Anne" to Anne of Armagnac.

1602      The term "ymage" is used in <u>Edmund</u> <u>and</u> <u>Fremund</u>, I,
935-83, to refer to the commonwealth as a moral body, with
the various classes representing various parts of the anatomy.

1602      For the terms "frenssh and Latyn" in the colophon,
see <u>Introduction</u>, p. xxix and xxxi.

*GLOSSARY*

This *Glossary* records the more uncommon or difficult words and forms of the foregoing text. In general, modern words having recognizable forms and words well-known to readers of Chaucer have been passed over; these constitute about two-thirds of the words used; since these common words occur more frequently, the glossed words constitute far less than a third of the bulk of the text.

In a few cases readings of the Lansdowne Manuscript rejected by the editor have been included in the *Glossary*. So have readings accepted from other MSS. So too have the substantial passages not in Lansdowne but inserted from MSS. Lincoln and Trinity College, Oxford.

When a word occurs quite often with the same meaning, only a few occurrences are cited. Such omissions are indicated by "etc." Otherwise, all occurrences of the word with a difficult meaning are noted; thus "but" meaning "without" is included, whereas "but" in its ordinary modern meanings (89 occurrences) is omitted.

Initial "i" equalling "j" alphabetically follows "i" equalling "i"; initial "y" having a vowel force is entered under "i"; consonantal initial "y" is entered separately at the end of the alphabet. Initial "u" equalling modern vowel "u" precedes "u" equalling modern consonantal "v." These last are intermixed with initial "v" words equalling modern consonantal "v." "V" words equalling modern vocalic "u" are placed with "u."

Number references are commonly given to subdivisions under the given word in the Oxford English Dictionary (OED). In some difficult cases, references are also made to A Middle English Dictionary (MED).

A

A prep. of (MED "a" prep.) II 1367.

ABIECT pa. p. cast out, rejected (OED 1) II 1065, 1518;
III 139, 480.

ABRAIDE, A-BRAIDE v., pa. t. broke out abruptly into speech
(OED "abraid" 3b) I 588; II 242, 1155, 1431, 1909; III
525 etc.; awakened (OED 2) II, 450.

ACCOMPLYSSHID pa. p. perfected, fulfilled (OED 1?) III
1485.

ACCOUNTID pa. p. reckoned, of a number (OED 2) III 1349.

ACQUYTE v. pay a claim, debt (OED 1, with a glance at OED
II) I 930; to clear of a crime etc. (OED 11) III 484;
discharge a duty (OED 13) II 40.

A-DAW v. awake (OED "adaw¹" 1) II 860.

ADIORNE v. adjure, charge solemnly (OED "adjure," 2) II
1264. This spelling affected by the -en inf. form, not
in OED.

ADUERTE v. take note of (OED 2) II 924, 1663; III 398, 951;
turn one's attention to (OED 4) I 876.

ADUERTENCE n. attention (OED); The meaning "memory" seems
more likely, though neither in OED nor MED. III 577.

ADUERTISE v. take note of, heed (OED 1) II 361, 681; III
1095.

AFFORCID v., pa. t. forced, constrained (OED "afforce" 2)
II 1886.

AFFRAY n. attack, disturbance (OED 1) III 1206.

AF(F)ORN prep. and adv. before (OED "afore" B3) I 551, 832;
beforehand (OED "afore" A2) II 83, 294.

AGEYN, A-GEYN(E) prep. against (OED "again" B1) I 581, 664,
751; in response to, in welcome of (OED B3b) II 223,
1140.

AGEYNWARD  adv.  on the other hand (OED 5)  II 215; III 549;
in return (OED 2)  III 1443.

A-GOGGL  adv.  squinting? protruberant? (cf. OED "goggle,"
adj. and modern "agoggled," pa. p.)  III 1251.

AGON  compound v.  have gone, have apostasized (see OED "a" v.
and MED "agon" 3b)  II 1036.

AGON  adv.  "ful yore agon" a long time ago (OED "ago, agone"
adv. B)  I 4; II 153.

AGRYSE  v.  shudder, feel terror (OED "agrise" 1)  II 498.

A-LIFF  adj.  ("a-lyff" form in OED "alive," adv.)  III 311.

ALLEGEAUNCE  n.  act of a vassal (OED "allegiance" 2) or re-
lief, help (OED "allegeance[1]")  II 1417, 1748.

ALLIAUNCE  n.  people united by kinship or friendship (OED 4);
perhaps more exactly, those related by marriage  I 159;
II 1382; III 274, 354.

ALOON  adj.  unique, without competition (OED 2a)  III 1200.

AMONG  adv.  at same time  (OED B 1)  II 809, 1264; at inter-
vals, repeatedly (OED B 2)  I 201; III 353.

AMPTE  n.  emmet, ant (OED records form for 15th c.)  I 888.

ANCILL(E)  n.  handmaid, female servant (OED "ancille")  II
277, 291.

ANULLID  pa. p.  annihilated (OED 1)  III 1460.

APPARAILE  n.  clothing and arms (OED "apparel" 5a)  I 254.

APPELLE  v.  revoke, call away (from Fr.) (not in OED or MED
but see MED 4, "to call")  II 1759.

APPERCEYVE  v.  perceive, notice (OED "apperceive")  II 1068;
III 860.

APPLIE  v.  submit, comply (OED 18, 19)  II 1182; devote, put
to special use (OED 5)  I 460; II 58, 723; put in practical contact (OED I,2)  III 1593.

APPLIED  pa. p.  "were applied," busied themselves, undertook

to (decide) (see OED, "applied, pa. p." for modern analogue; neither OED nor MED seems to notice this passive
construction.)   II 1508.

APPROPRID   pa. p.   attributed as proper (OED "appropre 2)   I
513; III 736.

AR   conj.   ere, before (OED "aar" recorded as variant of
"ere")   II 460, 1514.

ARIVE   v.   "arive up," to land (OED "arrive" 2)   I 119.

ARKE   n.   a reliquary (see OED 1 citation of 1845) or figura-
tively the ark of the covenant III 1480.

ARME   n.   armada, armed expedition (OED "army 1)   I 119.

ARRABLE   adj.   capable of being plowed (earliest OED citation,
1577) II 1209.

ARRYVAIL   n.   disembarkation (OED "arrival" 1)   I 121.

ARTICLE   n.   matter, item (OED 10, 11)   I 582.

ASELID   pp.   sealed up (OED "asseal" 2)   II 512.

ASIDE, A-SIDE   adv.   in a hidden place (OED 3)   II 1025.

ASPECTIS   n., pl.   influence (OED "aspect" 4 is further developed here)   I 269.

ASSUR   v.   dare, be so bold (OED 8d)   II 180.

AT   prep.   in phrase "at reverence," out of reverence, in reverence (OED 23 may be compared, but no precise equival-
ent)   III 195.

AT ALL   adv. phrase   in every way (affirmatively) (OED "all"
9b)   II, 1764; III 938.

ATTAME   v.   cut into, penetrate (OED 1)   III 737.

ATTEMPERANCE   n.   temperance, moderation (OED 1) I 449; II 102.

ATTWYTE   v.   reproach, taunt, twit (OED "atwite" v.[1])   I 511;
III 486.

AUCTORISED   pa. p.   duly sanctioned or approved (OED var. of "authorized" 3)   I 219; III 1410.

AUDIENCE   n.   judicial hearing (OED 3)   II 113; II 1100, 1308;
     hearing, attention (OED 2)   II 668, 1456, 1478, 1930;
     III 100, 116, 575.

AVENTURE   n.   that which happens by chance (var. of OED "ad-
     venture" 2)   I 137; II 918; III 191, 323.

AVIS   n.   deliberation, conclusion of deliberation (OED "ad-
     vice" 4)   II 66, 151, 1242; III 153, 1334; resolve,
     opinion (OED 1 or 6)   II 562, 1853; inheritance, portion?
     (OED s.v.  "advice" cites OFr. "avis" with meaning, "por-
     tion des biens qu'un père assigne à ses puinés")   III
     669.

AVISEE   adj. or pa. p.   well-advised (OED "advisy")   I 691.

AVISEMENT   n.   deliberation, reflection; "bi avisement," deli-
     berately (OED "advisement" 1b) I 219, 696; II 913; III 89.

AVISIOUN   n.   dream or monition in a dream (OED 1 and 2)   II
     463, 521, 561, 589, 773, 1589.

AVOIDE   v.   clear away things material or immaterial (OED 1,
     4c)   I 361, 438, 522, 531; II 375, 985, 1670; to expel
     (OED 5)   II 173, 864.

AVOUCHE   v.   ask for confirmation from authority (OED 1) I 493.

AVOUTRE, AVOUTRY   n.   adultery (cf. OED "avouter" and by-
     forms of "adultery")   I 455, 475.

AVOUTREES   n. pl.   adulterers (cf. OED "adulter")   III 1075.


                              B


BAD¹   v., pa. t.   commanded (OED "bid" 10)   I 835; II 494,
     653, 1862.

BAD², BOD   v. pa. t.   faced, encountered, withstood (OED
     "bide" 7)   III 906, 1491.

BARONAGE   n.   the bad angels as peers of Satan (cf. OED 1b)
     II 753.

BAREYN adj. unprovided with, having an insufficient amount of skill, etc. (OED 6, 8) I 22, 97.

B'ASSENT contracted prep. phr. by assent; see expl. n. I 110.

BATAILE, BATAILL n. assembly of, body of, warriors (OED "battle" 8) III 158; otherwise used as meaning "fight or struggle" (OED 1, 7) e.g. I 765; III 578.

BAWME n. odor, perfume (OED 4) II, 940; aromatic medicinal ointment (OED 5 and 6) II 572, 579; III 830.

BEDILL n. one who makes a proclamation or delivers a message for another (OED 1a, 2) II 326.

BEHIHT, BE-HIHT pa. p. promised (OED "behight" 1) II 128; III 262.

BEKNOWYNG pr. p. acknowledging (OED 2) II 1632.

BENEFISE n. benefit, protection (OED "benefice" 2) II 1198. Compare "benefit," II 1348.

BE-REYNED pa. p. wet, as with rain, rained upon (OED "be-rain" 2) III 111.

BERN OFF v. repel a stroke (OED "bear" 34) II 982.

BESILED, BESILID pa. p. Made away with, spirited away (OED "bezzle" 1) II 1025; III 1235.

BESYNESSE, BUSINESSE n. "do thy besynesse," bestir thyself (OED 8) III 218, 1104.

BE-SPRE(Y)NT pa. p. sprinkled (OED "besprent" a) II 727, 1865.

BETE, BETYN pa. p. embroidered (OED "beaten" 5c) III 765, 767; compare "bete," v., strike II 1178; III 8.

BI prep. apparently meaning "after the manner of antiquity, in accord with its custom" (not in OED) I 639.

BLASPHE(E)ME n. blasphemy II 417; blasphemer (OED blaspheme s.[1] B) II 1057, 1345, 1537, 1694, 1785, 1815.

BLENT pa. p. blind, blinded (OED "blenk") II 1495, 1843;

III 22.

BLYVE   adv.   quickly, eagerly   (OED "belive" adv. 1)   II 476.

BOCHE(E)R   n.   executioner, torturer (OED "butcher sb. 2)   III
    875, 904, 911.

BOD   pa. p.   see BAD[1].

BOISTOUS   adj.   rough, crude   (OED 1)   II 469, 1083, 1476.

BOISTOUSNESSE   n.   rudeness, crudeness (OED 1 or 2)   I 151.

BOLLYNG   vbl. sb.   swelling, puffing up (OED "boll" v.[2])   II
    578.

BOND(E)   v., pa. t.   bound, I 41, 170; II 613 etc.

BORWE, TO   prep. phr.   as a pledge or protector (OED "borrow"
    2c)   II 995.

BOUNDIS   n. pl.   bonds, fetters (OED "bond" sb.[1])   II 623.

BRAIDYNG ON   pr. p. and prep.   resembling (OED "braid" v.[1] 10)
    II 2082.

BRAK OUT   v. pa. t.   burst forth into words or emotion   (OED
    "break" v. 54 e)   III 198.

BREDE   n.   breadth, II 479; III 460, 1413.

BRYHTNESS   n.   an honorific form of address (cf. "serenitas"
    in L.)   II 777.

BROOKE   pa. p.   broken (OED 1, but suggesting OED 14,
    "taming")   II 1185; III 499.

BROSID   pa. p.   crushed or mangled by heavy blows, bruised
    (OED "bruise" 1)   II 1947.

BURDOUN   n.   cudgel rather than merely staff (OED "bourdon" 2)
    II 972.

BUT   conj. or prep.   without (OED A 2) or (if "very" is ellip-
    tically omitted) "unless" (OED C 10)   I 774; III 1081.

BUT   adv.   only (OED B 2)   II 1409.

C

CALIOUNS n., pl. flint, pebble (OED "calion") III 1141.

CALLID pa. p. applied abusive names to (OED "call" 12) II 1693.

CARECT n. wound, scar, mark of nails on crucifix (perhaps OED "caract," "mark") II 736; III 697, 703.

CAREYN n. dead body (OED a 1) III 717, 738.

CAS n. chance (OED 1) I 137; case, situation (OED 4 or 5) I 330, etc.

CAST adj. chaste (OED cites St. Albon s.v.) I 485.

CAST v. decide, resolve (reflexive OED) I 234, 909; II 1129; III 153, 587, 845, etc.; "castyng" planning, foreseeing I 163; "cast a providence,"decide by the help of providence II 1367.

CATCHE v., CAUHT pa. t. be inspired with an idea, conceive an opinion (OED 32) I 783; III 788; obtain by one's own action (OED 6) I 158; "cauht a leyser" found the time III 426; "catche savour and feith" begin to grasp, feel pleasure III 177.

CAUSE conj. because (OED, but earlier than citations) II 1330; III 1490.

CERIOUSLY adv. seriously (OED by-form) I 23, 56; II 197.

CERTEYN n. certainty "in certeyn" (OED B1) I 482, 705; II 1105, 1621; III 442, 980, 1082.

CERTEYN adv. certainly (OED C1) I 810; II 1634, 1993.

CESSIOUNS n. periodical sitting of a court of justice (OED "session" 3) I 542.

CHAAR n. meaning uncertain, perhaps "hearse, burial car"; perhaps "lane, alley"; a Northern word found in Midlands at later date by Dialect Dictionary (OED "chare", sb[1], sb[2]) II 1046.

CHASE v. pa. t. chose I 334. See "ches(e)."

CHAUMPE   n.   field (in heraldry) (OED champ sb.$^1$2)   III 766.

CHA(U)NCE   n.   lot, fortune (OED 3)   II 811, 1536.

CHERISSH   v.   treat with benevolent care (OED 2)   I 212, 389;
II 1201, 1349; III 1522; hold dear (OED 1)   I 37; CHERIS-
SHYNG   v. sb.   fostering or cultivating a plant (OED
"cherish" 2b, cited for 16th c.)   II 224; III 275.

CHES(E)   v. CHOSE, pa. t. s. & pl., CHASE pa. t. sing., CHESYN
pa. t. pl., CHOSE pa. p., vb. sb. to choose (all forms
attested, OED)   I 80, 281, 334, 408, 753, 768; II 69
etc.; cf. "chase."

CHEVISSHAUNCE   n.   shift, means of helping oneself (OED "chev-
isance$^1$ 3)   III 28.

CHOSE   pa. p.   picked, chosen   I 85.   See "ches(e)" above.

CLAD   pa. t., pa. p.   clothed, covered as with clothing (cf.
"clothid" I 479)   I 523; II 519 etc.   For pa. t. see II
222; the pr. and inf. do not occur.

CLARIFYE   v.   to light up, enlighten (OED 1, 3d)   III 18.

CLEENE   adv.   with nothing left out (OED "clean" 4, 5)   III
681.

CLEER   adj.   shining, sparkling (OED A 1a)   II 403, 617; per-
spicuous (OED A 3 or 7)   II 1591; unambiguous (OED A 8)
II 660, 747; audible (OED A 13)   II 2055.

CLEER   adv.   brightly (OED B 1)   II 437.

CLENNESSE   n.   sexual purity (OED 2)   I 67, 79, 362, 448,
456, etc.

CLERKLY   adv.   to a scholar? learnedly (OED 1)   I 899.

CLYENT   n.   one under another's protection (OED 2)   I 550.

CLIPSE   v.   aphetic form of "eclipse" (cf. OED by-forms)   II
1817; III 42.

CLOISTRES   n. pl.   enclosed space, conventual enclosure (fig.
from OED 2)   II 37.

CLOWRID   v., pa. t.   covered with turf?   (v. not in OED or

MED; see "clowre" n. in OED)   II 1940.

COLLATERALL   adj.   attendant, subordinate (OED 2, 3)   I 779.

COLLUSIOUN   n.   deceit, trickery (OED 1)   II 1428, 1648; III
864.   I 830 and II 1988 may mean simply "evil action."
No OED definitions seem applicable, but cf. MED 2).

COLOUR   n.   appearance, pretext (OED 12)   I 549; "colours,"
I 99 is an intentional ambiguity, alluding both to pig-
ments and rhetorical figures.

COMBEROUS   adj.   troublesome, unwieldy (OED "cumbrous" 3)   II
1567.

COME   v., pa. t.   came II 1359.

COMMEMORACIOUN   n.   religious service (cf. OED 2b)   III 1067.

COMOUNTE   n.   community, commonwealth (OED "commonty" 2)   I
508; the plural form, "comountees" is not easily accoun-
ted for; perhaps "common people" I 206.

COMPARISOUNS   n. pl.   cumulative noting of differences or similarities (between Lydgate and the chronicles) (OED "comparison" 4) II 1392.

COMPASSID, COMPASSED   pa. p.   contrived, devised (OED 1b)   II
115; III 466, 869.

COMPELLE   v.   attempt to force, without success (not in OED)
II 1145; drive forcibly (OED 3)   II 1290.

COMPLISSH   v. intr.   finish, complete (aphetic form of "accomplish" (OED "accomplish" 2)   II 1435.

COMPUNCT   adj.   feeling sorrow for wrongdoing   III 974.

CONCEIT(E), CONSEYT   n.   personal opinion or thought (OED 4)
I 588; III 787   whim (OED 7)   I 783; II 426, 693; mental
capacity (OED 2b)   II 1844; II 693 suggests "query" or
"problem."

CONCEYVE   v.   perceive, understand (OED 9)   II 165; III 38.

CONCERNID   pa. p.   discerned, separated? (OED 1)   II 21.

CONCLUDID   pa. p.   decided, determined (of a judicial process)

(OED "conclude" 5) II 1299.

CONCLUSIOUN n. "for short conclusioun" to make a long story short I 580; II 208.

CONDESCENDE v. agree (OED 5) I 845; deign (OED 6) I 596, 607.

CONDICIOUN n. rank, state in life (OED 10) I 268; CONDI-CIOUNS n. pl. manners, morals (OED "condition" 11b) I 34, 291; II 1402; III 1495.

CONDUTIS n., pl. natural channels, media of conveyance (OED "conduit" 3, 4) II 574.

CONIURACIOUN n. compelling of demons to do one's bidding (OED 3) III 867.

CONSEYT n. see "conceyt(e)" above.

CONSERVE v. keep alive or flourishing (OED 2) III 1542, 1551.

CONSISTORIE n. court of God; company about his throne (OED 4) II 346.

CONSOWDIS n., pl. healing herbs (OED "consoude") III 833.

CONSTREYNT n. coercion (OED 1) II 480; distress, pain (OED 3) II 1425; III 347, 366, 805.

CONSTREYNED pa. p. forced (OED 1) I 866; II 82; afflicted, distressed (OED 6) II 1731.

CONSWET adj. accustomed, wonted (OED "consuete") III 67.

CONTAGIOUSLY adv. in a manner morally injurious (OED "contagious, adj. 7; adv. not in OED before 1615 or with this meaning) III 208.

COMTEMPLATIFF adj. worthy of being contemplated? tending to contemplation (cf. OED "contemplative" A 2) III 540.

CONTRARIOUS adj. hostile, perverse (OED 3 or 4) I 463; II 1301, 1544, 1867; III 401, 710.

CONTUNE, CONTYUNE (or CONTYNUE) continue (OED "contune") I 397; II 1355; III 379, 1560.

CONVEIE  v.  conduct, accompany, escort (OED 1 & 2)   I 104,
    869; II 533, 829; III 1115, 1169, 1195; transmit to pos-
    terity (OED 9b)   II 1393; III 1307.

CONVENYENCE  n.  congruity of quality or nature (OED 1)   III
    751.

CONVIVED  pa. p.  probably from "convivo," live with, have a
    common life.   (not in OED before 17th c. with meanings
    related to "convivial"; here the meaning is probably
    "dwelling in common with."   II 790.

CONVOCACIOUN  n.  meeting (OED 2)   II 1363.

CORAIOUS  adj.  full of virile force, lusty (OED "courageous"
    3)  I 465; having courage (OED 1)   II 1011.

COST$^1$  n.  side of the body or perhaps side or coast of the
    earth (OED "coast" 1 or 4)   II 508.

COST$^2$  n.  expense  (OED "cost," sb.$^2$)   expense I 660; III
    1391, 1403.

COTE ARMEWR  n.  garment painted or embroidered with heraldic
    arms (OED "coat-armour" 1)   II 988.

CROKID  adj.  bent (with age?)  (OED "crooked" 2)   I 12.

CUR  n.  "do one's cure" work diligently, painstakingly (OED
    "cure," sb.$^1$)  I 766; II 1897; III 713, 1210, 1434,
    1453.

CUR  v.  cure (OED v.$^1$ 4)   III 829.

CURAS  n.  "a peyr curas," piece of body armor consisting of
    breastplate and backpiece   II 979.

CUSSHEWIS  n., pl.  armor for protecting front part of thigh
    (OED "cuisse")   II 978.


                              D


DALIAUNCE  n.  talk, confabulation (OED "dalliance" 1)   II
    808, 1689.

DAMAGE  n.  injury, harm, pain, woe (cf. OED 1 & 2)   II 293,

827, 1497, 1705; III 209, 1013, 1132, 1255, 1383.

DA(U)NGE(E)R   n.   hesitation, reluctance, resistance (OED 2)
II 178; III 226; peril (OED 4)   II 186, 1573, 1995;
power as of a master (OED 1)   II 645; III 1120.

DA(U)NT   v.   subdue, tame   (OED 2 & 3)   I 118; III 741.

DAY-STERR   n.   sun? (fig.) (first OED cit. for "sun" 1598)   I
637; morning-star, Venus (OED 1)   II 1826.

DEBONAIRE   adj.   gentle, gracious (OED A)   I 412.

DECLYNE   v.   deviate from rectitude, fall away from religious
belief (OED 1, 3, 9)   I 539; II 87, 1101.

DEDIE   v.   dedicate (OED)   I 600.

DED(E)LY   adj.   deathlike (OED 7c)   II 1711; causing, likely
to cause death (OED 4)   II 1723; III 289; suggesting
death (OED 7b)   III 368, 468; being a sign of death III
690.

DEYNSEYN   n.   denizen (form in OED)   III 661.

DELUGE   n.   flood, fig. any great danger (cf. OED 3)   II 959,
1562.

DEMENYD   v., p. t.   managed (OED 3)   II 99.

DEPART(E)   v.   separate (OED 3)   II 1656; III 545; leave,
depart I, 683 etc.

DEPARTYNG   vb. sb.   departure (OED 3)   I 704; II 832.

DESPITE   n.   contempt, hostility, disobedience (OED 1, 5)   II
1062, 1233.

DEVIDID   pa. p.   perhaps akin to "devide words" (MED 5b), thus
"has been so discriminating in choice"; possibly a variant of "devisid" II 74.

DEVIS   n.   intent, desire (OED "device" 3b)   III 1177.

DEVISE   v.   formulate, as a phrase (OED 5b)   II 749.

DIFFAME   n.   slander, calumny (OED "defame" 3)   II 115.

DIFFER   v.   defer (var. sp. noted, OED)   II 1443.

DIFFERENCE   n.   mark distinguishing one thing from others
    (OED 4, not before Caxton)   I 224.

DILIGENCE   n.   favor, affection? (not in OED but see "dili-
    gent" 3 and etym.)   I 676; II 15, 1930; assiduity in
    service (OED 1b)   II 360.

DISAVAILE   n.   harm, disadvantage (OED)   III 144.

DISCEYVABLE   adj.   deceitful, treacherous (OED "deceivable")
    II 1122; III 23.

DISCIPLYNE   n.   instruction (OED 1)   I 47.

DISCRECIOUN   n.   discernment, judgment, faculty of discern-
    ment (OED 3)   I 190, 793; II 121, 1495, 1804, 1843.

DISCRE(E)T(E)   adj.   judicious, prudent (OED A 1)   I 692; II
    675.

DISENTRAILED   pa. p.   disemboweled (OED first cit. 1596; MED
    cites 1534 Albon)   III 1017.

DISESE   n.   absence of ease, discomfort (OED 1)   II 1778; III
    844.

DISESPEIRED   pa. p.   hopeless, dispairing (OED "desespeire"
    and "despaired," pa. p.)   II 1465; III 441.   See also
    "dispeir" below.

DISGUYSED   v., pa. t.   transformed (OED "disguise," v. 3)
    III 208.

DISHONESTE   n.   immodesty, sexual immorality (OED "dishones-
    ty" 2; by-form ending in single "-e" not noticed by OED)
    I 439.

DISIOYNTE   n.   strait, plight (OED "disjoint")   III 1016.

DISPEIR   v.   despair (cf. "disespeired" above)   III 1088.

DISPENCE   n.   act of spending or dispensing (often liberally)
    (OED "dispense" sb.[1] 1 or 2)   I 392, 466.

DISPITOUS   adj.   pitiless (OED "despitous" 1 or 2)   II 1664.

DISPOSICIOUN  n.  plan or dispensation (of God) (OED 3)  I
    250; natural tendency (OED 6)  I 32; frame of mind (OED
    7b)  II 99; physical constitution (OED 8)  III 947.

DISPOSID  v., pa. t.  planned, purposed (OED 7)  I 675.

DISSEVIR  v.  part, part company (OED 3b)  II 673; depart?
    (OED 3b)  III 657.

DISSEYUE  v.  deceive (OED notes by-form "dysseyue")  III 36.

DISSIMYLED  pa. p.  feigned, pretended (OED "dissimuled" and
    "dissimule" for form)  II 1432.

DISSOLUCIOUN  n.  enfeeblement (OED 4)  I 395.

DITEE  n.  any literary composition (OED 1)  I 10; song?  fine
    rhetorical passage?  (OED 2?)  II 2016.

DIVISIOUN  n.  dissension, discord, strife (OED 1)  I 126,
    132, 136, 393; III 478, 1227; "void of divisioun," uni-
    fied, integral, but with overtones of first meaning
    (OED 1)  III 1602.

DOUBLENESSE, DOUBILNESSE, DOWBILNESSE  n.  duplicity, ambi-
    guity (OED 2 or 1b)  I 361; II 853, 1490; III 264.

DRAW(E), DRAWEN  v.  attract by moral or invisible force (OED
    26)  I 328; II 9; III 176, 608; pulled like draught-
    animal  I 428; II 938 (the form "drawith" for pa. p. may
    represent "drawid" or be a scribal error); extract
    sword (OED 33)  I 557 etc.; pulled (pa. p. "drawen")  II
    479; tear apart (OED 5)  II 481; pull judicially behind
    horse (OED 4)  II 997.

DRESSE  v.  hold forth, offer (OED 14b)  II 551; make ready,
    prepare (OED 5)  II 688, 700;          turn in some di-
    rection (OED 15)  III 95, 397; move to a position (OED 3)
    III 781.

DUODEYN  n.  a kind of tax, a tax of one-twelfth (not in OED
    see Ducange, "duodena" and "duodenaria.")  I 809.

DURESSE  n.  severity, cruelty (OED 2)  III 424, 942, 1509;
    injury (OED 2)  III 345.

E

EGAL(E), EGALL   adj.  affecting all in the same manner (OED
    "equal" 4)   I 538; II 32; equal (OED "egall")   I 687; II
    1973 etc.

EMPRISE   n.  esteem, value set upon (OED 3b)   III 438.

ENBAWMYD   pa. p.  anointed (OED "embalm," 4a or b) or perhaps
    perfumed (OED "embalmed" 1526)   III 1368.

ENCHACE   v.  drive away (OED "enchase" v.$^1$)   I 54.

ENCLIPSID   pa. p.  cast a shadow on, obscured (OED 2b)   I 399;
    III 65.

ENCLOIED   pa. p.  rendered lame (fig.) (OED "encloy")   I 149.

ENCOMBRAUNCE   n.  molestation (OED 1b, earliest cit. c. 1450)
    II 810.

ENCOMBRE   v.  press hard, harass, give trouble to (OED "en-
    cumber," 3c)   I 757; III 146, 995.

ENLUMYNE   v.  increase the depth or truth of a composition,
    to brighten the style (fig. from OED 1)   I 28, 96; III
    1467; to illuminate I 627; III 1190 (though the real
    sense may be "adorn with brightness"; increase distinc-
    tion or prestige) I 9891.

ENTAILE, ENTAILL   n.  shape, pattern of garment or armor (OED
    sb.$^1$ 2)   I 242, 257 (I 242 may rather signify human
    physical build, bodily shape).

ENTEER, ENTIER   adj.  devoted, characterized by integrity,
    perfect (OED 2, 3c, 9)   I 284; II 15, 360, 646, 867; III
    172, 652, 1590; complete, total (OED 2)   I 676; II 616,
    1930; III 51.

ENTENDE   v.  apply oneself (OED "intend" 9)   I 195, 370, 606;
    III 1000; devote oneself (OED 8b)   III 1527.

ENTENT, OF   prep. phr.  on purpose (cf. OED "intent sb. 1)
    I 792; II 1002.

ENTENTE, TO HIS   prep. phr.  in mind, as his intention (OED "intent" 4)   II 1953.

ENTITLED   pa. p.   written of by (proper) title (OED "entitle"
2)   III 149.

ENTRECHAUNGING   vb. sb.   exchange (OED "interchange" 1)   II
857.

ENTREMEDLE   adj.   (from Fr. pa. p.)   intermixed (OED "inter-
meddle" 1; adj. form without "d" not noted)   I 535.

ENTRESSE   n.   interest on capital (OED "interess" sb. 4, cit.
of 1529)   III 1579.

ENTRETE   v.   treat, handle physically (OED 1,2)   II 1721; concern oneself with, treat of (OED 3, cit. 1513)   II 1836.

ENVIROUN   adv.   round about (OED A); from all about (MED 5)
II 1304; III 163, 594.

ERECT   adj.   upright (OED 1)   II 2207.

ERECT   pa. p.   (OED "erect" v. 1; the latinate participial
form noted)   II 721; III 1147.

ESCHAUFFYNG   vb. sb.   condition of being overheated (cf. OED
"eschaufe" v.)   II 1555.

ESEIL   n.   vinegar (OED "eisell")   II 486.

ESPECIAL(L), IN   prep. phr.   particularly (OED "especial" adj.
4)   I 226, 324, 782; II 34 etc.

EXCHEWE   v.   escape (text. n. and OED "eschew" 1)   III 215.

EX(C)ECUCIOUN   n.   carrying of a law into effect (OED 1c)   II
1241, 1447, 1684; DO EXECUCIOUN put to death (OED 8c)
II 1282, 1331.

EXPERIENCE   n.   sense data, that which happens or is under-
gone (OED 4)   I 398, 548; II 662 etc.; proof, confirmation (OED 2) experiment (magic?) (OED 1b)   III 863.

EXPERYMENT   n.   apparently, a magic procedure (not in OED)   II
1954.

EXPERT(E)   adj.   experienced (OED 1)   I 198; II 676; III 276;

in last case perhaps related to adv. meaning "clearly" (MED).

EXPLEITID   pa. p.   completed, filled (OED "explete")   I 485.

EXPOUNNED   pa. p.   expounded ("expoune, exponned" in OED)   II 1774.


F


FAVOUR, FAUOUR   n.   friendly regard, disposition (OED 1)   I 35, 244; III 274 (this last seems to mean "disposition to act to advantage of one's relatives"); aid, support (OED 5)   I 98; friendly action (OED 2)   I 146; partiality (OED 4)   I 537; look, appearance (OED 9)   II 171; indulgence (OED 3c)   II 418; regard, sanction (OED 1b) III 1461.

FEER, IN   prep. phr.   together (OED "fere" sb.$^2$ 2)   II 532, 785, 1112.

FEERIS   n. pl.   fires   II 901.

FELAW   n.   equal in rank, "collegam" (OED "fellow 1)   I 756; II 1247; companion (OED "fellow" 2)   II 1974; III 906.

FELNESSE   n.   ferocity, cruelty (OED "fellness" 1)   III 384.

FEMYNYTE   n.   assemblage of qualities pertaining to female sex (OED "feminity" and "femininity" 1)   II 248.

FETT   v., p. t.   fetched (OED "fet" 1)   II 630.

FYLE   v.   see "i-fyled."

FYNDE VP   v.   discover by search (OED "find" 21)   III 59.

FYNE   n.   end (OED "fine" sb.$^1$ 1)   III 1157.

FYNE   v.   bring to an end (OED "fine" v$^1$ 2)   III 180.

FIRST FRUTES   n. pl.   "primicias," earliest products or issues of anything (OED "first-fruit" 2)   I 599.

FITCHID   pa. p.   fixed (OED "ficche")   II 1108.

FLEET(E)   v.   drift through air (OED v. 9b)   II 940, 2085;
     overrun (OED 8b)   III 689.

FOISOUN   n.   abundance (of food and drink) (OED 1)   II 341,
     509, 1766; III 1376, 1588.

FOLTISH   adj.   foolish, besotted, silly (OED)   II 1804.

FOR   conj.   because (OED B1)   I 26; II 648, 1320.

FORBI   adv.   nearby (OED "forby" B2)   III 367.

FORBODE   pa. p., adj.   forbidden (OED notes form under "for-
     bid")   II 601.

FORCE   n.   moral strength, virtue of fortitude (OED 6)   I 669;
     III 943.

FORGE   v.   invent a tale, lie (OED "forge" v$^1$ 4)   II 110.

FORGED, -ID   adj.   made of metal (OED 2)   I 257; II 403; III
     961 etc.; constructed, made, fabricated (OED 1)   II 976,
     1453; III 1187; false (OED 4)   II 1480.

FORLORN   pa. p.   irrevocably lost (cf. OED 1)   II 981.

FORMOST   adj.   first, foremost   I 700.

FORN-TYME   adv.   beforehand (cf. OED "foretime," adv. of 1590
     and OED "aforetime" of 1535)   III 1436.

FORSAKITH   v. pr. 3rd s.   causes one to forsake (not in OED)
     III 1099.

FORTH   adv.   with vb, expresses continuity or progressiveness
     of an action (OED 3b)   I 572; away or out from a place
     of origin (OED 6)   I 254; II 57 etc.

FORWOUNDID   pa. p.   grievously wounded (OED "forwound")   III
     1014.

FRANCHISE   n.   immunity, privilege (OED 1)   I 569; III 1412.

FRANCHISED   pa. p.   invested with a privilege (OED "franchise"
     v.)   I 14.

FREDAM   n.   liberty to act (OED "freedom" 4)   I 608;

liberality (OED 3)  II 333; exemption from control (OED 2)  III 1405.

FREEL  adj.  weak, frail (OED "frail" 1)  II 1161.

FRENESIE  n.  madness, delirium (OED "frenzy" 1)  III 989.

FRE(E)NGID  pa. p.  fringed (OED lacks form "freengid"; earliest cit. 1480)  I 223; II 145.

FRUCTUOUS  adj.  advantageous, profitable (OED 3)  III 1297.

FRUMENT  n.  grain, corn.  (This is the first OED citation)  I 83.

G

GARLEMENT  n.  variant of "garnement" (OED cit. 1485)  II 878.

GARNEMENT  n.  garment (OED "garment")  I 222; II 145.

GARNE(E)R  n.  granary (fig.)  I 889; II 2083.

GAWRYNG  pr. p.  staring, gaping (OED "gaure" 1)  II 1139.

GLADE  adj.  bright, beautiful (OED "glad" adj. 1)  I 73.

GLADE  v.  to make glad (OED "glad" v. 2)  III 1128, 1239.

GLIDE  v.  motion of a weapon, prob. with notion of swift, unresisted movement (OED 4b)  II 1586.

GODWARD  adv.  (quasi-sb.) up (OED A and A2)  III 1254.

GOODLY  adj.  handsome (OED 1)  I 29, 246; kindly, gracious (OED 4)  I 677; III 784.

GOODLY  adv.  kindly (OED 2)  I 598; II 163, 169, 688, 778; well, virtuously (OED 3)  II 685.

GOSPEL  n.  the Holy Scriptures generally (OED 2c)  II 257.

GOVERNAUNCE  n.  authority, rule (OED 2)  I 156, 186.

GRACIOUS  adj.  yielding grace (not in OED)  II 2002.

GREE   n.   supremacy (OED "gree" sb. [1] 5)   I 622.

GRE(E)NE   adj.   recent (OED 10b); unripe, inexperienced (OED
     8c)   I 604; young (OED 8)   I 824; fresh, unhealed (of a
     wound) (OED 10a)   II 509; III 695, 820.

GREVAUNCE   n.   infliction of a harm or hardship (OED "griev-
     ance" 1)   II 295.

GREVIS   n. pl.   armor for leg below the knee (OED "greave[2]")
     II 976.

GRO(U)ND(E)   n.   solid base for an edifice (OED 4)   I 489;
     II 975, 1275 etc.; one's place to make a stand (OED 13b;
     first cit. 1616)   II 1081; III 417; earth (OED 8)   I 858;
     II 1201; III 690 etc.

GRUCCHYNG   vb. sb.   complaint (OED "grutching")   III 920.

GRUTCHE   v.   murmur, complain (OED "grutch" v. 1)   II 1159.

GUYE   v. refl.   act, direct oneself (OED "guy" v. 1 3b)   II
     60.


                              H


HA   v. (inf. and pl. pr.)   have (OED notices by-form for both)
     II 791, 1459, 1471; III 419, 739.   For other forms of
     "have" see "hath" and "have" below.

HABIRIOUN   n.   habergeon, sleeveless coat of mail (second "i"
     certainly with force of "j"; OED has by-form "habirjoun)
     II 971.

HABOUNDE   v.   abound (OED has by-form)   III 1386.

HABUNDAUNCE   n.   abundance (OED notes forms in "h")   II 1767,
     2086.

HALPE   v. pa. t.   helped (OED "help" A 1)   II 1784.

HANGYNG   pr. p.   in abeyance, payable? due? (OED closest in
     "hanging" pr. p. 3)   I 733.

HARNEYS   n.   armor (OED "harness" 2)   I 256.

HATH v. 3rd p. pl. pr. (by-form noted in OED "have") III 570.

HAVE A-DO v. phr. had business with, fought ("agebat in armis") I 616, 617; have dealings with (OED "ado" sb. 3) II 1129.

HED-SPRYNG n. fountainhead (fig.) (OED "headspring") III 1114.

HELDEST adj. superl. eldest (by-form in OED) III 1540.

HERBERGAGE n. lodging, place of lodging (OED "harbergage" 1, 2) II 136, 148, 157.

HERBERWE n. lodging (OED "harbour" 1) II 340.

HERTLY adj. genuine, earnest, sincere (OED "heartly" 1) II 297, 894, 1420, 1423.

HOLD pa. p. held (OED form noted) III 1068.

HOLDYNG pr. p. in phr. "holdyng his passage" seems to be "taking his passage." II 237.

HOME-COME n. homecoming (OED "home-come") I 716.

HOOL(E) adj. whole (OED cites form) I 361; II 235; III 376 etc.

HOUNDE n. hand (form not in OED, probably influenced by rhyme with "founde") III 889.

HOUR n. for prep. phr. at the hour; see "time" below; II 869.

HOUS n. religious house, abbey (OED 4a) II 2052.

HUMYDITE n. the fluid matter that makes a body humid; "radical humidity," the bodily fluid necessary to life (OED "radical" A 1) III 937.

I (vowel, incl. Y, vowel)

IDUS n. ides (OED cites Latin form, 1330) III 1352.

IERARCHIE n. each of three divisions of angels in the system of Dionysius the Areopagite (OED "hierarchy" 1; see OED "cherub")   II 393.

I-FYLED   pa. p.   filed, sharpened (fig. of a tongue) (OED v.[1] 1)   I 252.

YMAGE   n.   representation of an abstract concept?   perhaps in terms of the human body and its parts (cf. OED "image" 3b and 4)   I 386; III 961, 1602; see exp. note to III 1602; idol, statue (OED 1a)   II 1480, 1800; semblance, likeness (OED 3)   II 1494.

YMAGYNATIFF   n.   imaginative faculty (OED "imaginative" B) II 1956; III 1052.

YMAGYNYNG   pr. p.   pondering, forming designs concerning (OED 3, 4)   II 591.

IMPORTABLE   adj.   unbearable, intolerable (OED a.[1])   II 499, 1574; III 387 etc.

IN   prep.   into (OED "in" 30)   III 989.

INDEFFERENT   adj.   impartial (OED "indifferent" 1)   I 538.

INDE STOONE   n.   either any precious stone from India (OED "ind" sb. 4) or stone of indigo color (perhaps sapphires) (OED "inde" b)   I 283.

INDURAT   adj.   morally hardened, obstinate (OED "indurate" 2) II 1798; III 1002.

INFLUENCE   n.   God's invisible power, viewed as resembling the light and force of the planets in astrology; a pagan god's supposed power (OED 3)   I 27, 53, 326, 653; II 10, 321, 1669, 1820; III 817, 1286, 1297.

INFLUENT   adj.   exercising celestial influence (OED 2)   III 964, 1558.

INPORTABLE   see "importable."

INPORTUNE   adj.   persistent in solicitation; irksome through persistency of request (OED "importune" 4); earliest OED cit. 1447)   II 431; III 381.

INSOLENCE   n.   excess, want of moderation; cf. Latin

"insolentia" (not in OED)   I 464.

INTERESSE   n.   share, part (OED "interess" 1b)   I 462.

INTO   prep.   in (OED "into" 21)   II 923.

INTRUSIOUN   n.   act of thrusting oneself into a vacant estate
    or benefice to which one has no legal claim (OED 2)   I
    730

INUENCIOUN   n.   invention, the finding of a saint's remains or
    relics (OED "invention" 1, first two citations, also 1b)
    III 1352, 1359.

IS   pro.   his (by-form noted, OED "his")   III 1409.

ISSU   n.   decision, conclusion (OED "issue" 10c), "playn
    issu," full, complete conclusion   III 82.


                    I   (consonant)


IUBILEE   n.   joyful celebration (OED first citation, 1592)
    III 1479.

IUPARTE   v.   put in jeopardy (OED by-forms of "jeopard"
    include "iouperd, ieoparte")   put in jeopardy   II 182.

IUPARTIE   n.   jeopardy (OED cites by-form)   I 859; II 855,
    970, 2043.

IUSTIS   n. pl.   jousts, tournament (OED "just, joust" sb. a
    or b)   I 601, 673.


                    K


KALENDIS   n.   beginning, first days (OED "calends" 4)   II 4,
    225.

KYNDE   n.   Nature (see Glossary of Proper Names)   I 243: na-
    ture in the more abstract sense (OED "kind" 4)   I 249;
    II 1198; the last may also be the proper name.

KYNDLY   adj.   natural (OED 1)   III 714.

KNYHTLY  adv.  in a knightly, chivalrous way (OED "knightly")
    I 600; II 992.

KNOLACHYNG, KNOLECHYNG, KNOWLACHYNG  n.  action or condition
    of knowing, recognizing (OED "knowledging 3)  I 340,
    920; II 674, 766; III 688, 1316.

KOWDE  v., pa. t.  used idiom. in "kowde hem gret thank," was
    conscious of owing thanks, acknowledged thanks (OED "can"
    v.[1] 10)  I 611.


                                L


LAK  n.  blame (OED "lack" sb.[1] 2b)  I 101.

LAME  adj.  impaired in any way (OED 1)  II 118.

LANGAGES  n. pl.  individual utterances (cf. OED "language"
    4b)  II 1483.

LAUREAT  adj.  consisting of laurel (OED "laureate" a. 1)  I
    90; worthy of the laurel wreath (OED 3, cit. of 1535)  I
    14, 903.

LAURER  n.  laurel as a symbol of victory (by-form of OED
    "laurel" 1; see head and 2)  II 2055.

LAYES  n. pl.  short lyric or narrative poems; see exp. note
    to II 527; (OED "lay" sb.[4] 1)  II 527.

LEDNE  n.  the song or "language" of birds; bird latin (OED
    "leden" 2c)  II 950.

LEYSER  n.  opportunity (OED "leisure" 1b)  II 172; III 426.

LEITH  v. pr. t. 3rd sing.  presents, puts forth (OED "lay"
    v. 2 is perhaps correct)  III 242.

LEST  n.  desire, "atte lest," at the good pleasure of (OED
    "list" sb.[4] 3)  I 614.

LEVEN  n.  levin, lightning (OED levin)  III 1201.

LICENCE  n.  permission (OED "license" sb. 1) I 677, 712, 1979.

LIE, LYE  v. i.  to lie, recline III 374; LYTH  3rd s. pr.

II 652; LYE, LYN pl. pr. III 360, 495, 509; LAY
pa. t. II 342, 344, 445 etc.; LYGGYNG pr. p. II 1937;
III 317, 690 etc.

LIFT pa. p. lifted (form noted, OED) II 1155; III 1152.

LIK adv. (quasi-prep.) in manner of, as, acting as, with
identity implied (e.g. Amphibalus acts "lik" the clerk
he in fact is. OED "like" B1 covers meaning, though not
with precision.) I 216, 632; II 109, 440, 1194, 1375;
III 194; in accordance with (also covered by OED "like"
B 1) I 211, 367, 455, 800; II 79, 84; III 1259 etc.

LYMES n. pl. limbs (OED lists by-form) III 389, 1243.

LISSE v. alleviate (OED "lisse" v. 2) II 728.

LIST v. wish, desire (OED "list" vb.$^1$ 2) I 19, 484; II 107;
III 415 etc.; "listen," pl. pr., are willing III 1031.

LIVE n. life (by-form in OED) III 1072.

LONGITH v. pr. 3rd sing. is fitting, befits (OED "long" vb.$^2$
1) I 456, 512.

LOOK v. consult, see (OED 2) II 1448.


                                        M


MAGNYFICENCE n. title of honor (OED "magnificence" 6) I
590; bounty, munificence (OED 2) II 1641, 1913; III 257,
649; glory, grandeur (OED 3 and 5) II 384, 678, 2062;
III 814.

MAIDE n. man who has abstained from intercourse (OED 2c)
III 747.

MALENCOLIE n. ill-temper, anger (cf. OED "melancholy" 1)
II 1732.

MALIGNE v. inveigh (OED 3) I 161; II 1006; III 783?, 928;
contrive (OED 1) I 200; III 718.

MAMETIS, MAU(H)METIS, MAWMET(T)IS n. pl. idols, false gods
(OED "maumet" 1) II 396, 1471, 1499, 1845; III 36, etc.

280.

MANHEEDE   n.   humane quality, perhaps manly dignity (OED 2b or 4)   II 333.

MANHOOD   n.   manliness, courage, valor (OED "manhood" 3)   I 564; II 104.

MANYO(O)N   pro.   many a one (OED "many" A 1c)   II 1575; III 1437.

MANSIOUN   n.   heavenly abode (OED "mansion" 2d)   II 465.

MARKID   pa. p.   fore-ordained, destined (OED "mark" vb. 6) or "observed" (OED 13)   III 905.

MARTIS   n. poss.   See "Proper Names."

MASSAGE   n.   conveyer of a message (OED "message" sb.$^1$ 3)   II 230, 234.

MAUGRE OF   comp. prep.   in spite of (OED "maugre" sb. and prep.   3)   II 1992.

MAU(H)METIS, MAWMETTIS   see MAMETIS

MAUMETRIE, MAWMETRY(E)   n.   idolatry (OED "maumetry" 1)   II 2042; III 140, 1085, 1086; perhaps "idols taken all together" (OED 2)   II 1123.

MEDLE   v.   mix (OED "meddle" 1)   II 733, 983, 2062; "medled with grace," once associated with grace (OED 3)   III 1280.

MEDLID   pa. p. adj.   mixed (OED "meddle" 3 and after 8d)   II 983; III 898.

MEDWIS   n. pl.   meadows, pieces of land permanently covered with grass (OED "meadow" for by form)   II 940.

MEEUYD   pa. p. adj.   stirred up, excited (OED "meeve" and "move"   v. 7)

MEYNT   pa. p.   mingled, mixed (OED "meng")   I 68; II 486; III 615.

MENE   n.   instrument, means (OED "mean" sb.$^2$ 10)   I 58, 922.

III 217; what is in the middle (OED "mean" sb.$^2$ 1)   II
1750.

MEN OF RELIGIOUN   comp. n.   monks, members of a religious
house (OED "religion" 1b)   III 1539.

MENSTRE   n.   monastery (OED "minster" 1)   I 645.

MERCIABLE   adj.   merciful, compassionate (OED "merciable")
III 217, 390, 1503.

MEVEERS   n. pl.   movers, causers of an (illegal) action, in-
citers (OED "mover" by-forms and 3 (cit. of 1497)   I 209.

MEVID, MEEUYD   pa. p.   moved (OED "move" does not note precise
forms)   I 206; II 779, 826.

MEVYNG   vb. sb.   motivation?   (OED "moving" 3)   II 985, 1405.

MEWET   adj.   mute (form "mwet" listed in OED)   II 1464.

MYCH   adv.   much (form noted by OED)   I 547.

MYNDE   n.   memory, that which is remembered (OED "mind" 4)
III 1272, 1449; "have in mynde," commemorate, worship
III 1060.

MYSCHEEF   n.   evil arising from certain conditions (OED "mis-
chief" sb. 2b)   I 476; II 311.

MORID   v. pa. t. and pa. p.   increased, augmented (OED "more"
v.$^2$)   II 1075, 1617.

MORTAL   adj.   pursued to the death (OED 3c)   I 849; "mortal
myht," weak? (not in OED)   III 1047.

MORTIFIED   pa. p.   transformed in earth, as though dead (cf.
OED "mortify" 1)   I 85.

MOTLES   n. pl.   the material of the flowery "mantle" of earth,
prob. fig. from many-colored cloth (OED "motley" B 1b)
II 221.

MOUHT   n.   mouth (by-form noted, OED)   III 1251.

N

NA   adv.   not (OED "na" adv. 1)   I 556.

NEWE   prep. phr.   "of newe," lately, recently (OED "new" adv.
1)   I 174   as a second, later choice (OED "new" adv. 2?)
I 753.

NOBLES   n. sing.   noble birth, nobility (OED "noblesse" 1)
II 1397.

NO(U)THIR   conj.   neither (OED "nother" adv. and conj.)   I
193; II 1055, 1165, 1181, etc.

NOUTHIR   adj.   neither one nor the other (OED "neither" B 1)
II 876.

NOVIL   n.   navel (OED, by-form noted)   III 913 (cf. II 1289).


O


OBEDIENCE   n.   a subordinate relationship like a monk's, as a
result of the third religious vow (OED 2)   II 671.

OBEISAUNCE   n.   obedience (OED "obeisance" 1)   I 114; II 667.

OBSTACLE   n.   objection, opposition (OED 2)   I 820; II 217,
1785 etc.

ODIBLE   adj.   hateful, odious (OED "odible")   I 421.

ON   pron.   one, in const. "on the heldest," the oldest (OED
"one" 26)   III 1540.

OPPRESSE   v.   lie with, perhaps ravish (OED "oppress" 7)   I
471; burden, oppress (OED 2)   I 415; II 77, 438; III 414;
crush, subject to pressure (OED 1)   II 1572; III 687,
1204.

ORDEYN   v.   prepare, arrange (OED "ordain" 1)   I 118; II 1057;
III 158; command, order (OED 14, 15)   I 143, 188, 300,
565, 615; II 66, 945, etc.; appoint (OED 10)   I 214, 789.

ORDYNAUNCE   n.   order, decree, law, command (OED 5b, 6, 7)   I

922; II 910, 1023; III 884, 1423.

ORDRE  n.  society of knights (OED 7b)  I 21; rank or dignity
of knighthood I 259, 350, 408, 435; perhaps, mere member-
ship in the church (cf. OED 4?)  II 738; proper sequence,
arrangement (OED 15)  I 50, 145, 168 etc.

ORIGYNALL  n.  origin (OED "original" B 1)  III 1063.

O(U)THIR  conj.  or, either (by-form in "u" not noted, OED)
II 844, 845, 1025, 1039, 1353, 1356, 1807; III 1004, etc.

OUER-MAYSTRED  pa. p.  conquered (OED "overmaster" 1)  I 134.

OUER-RIDEN  pa. p.  crossed by riding (OED "override" 1)  I
112.

OVIR-LEYN  pa. p.  covered up (cf. OED "overlay" 1 and "over-
lie" for form)  II 1994.

OUTRAGE  n.  public, scandalous sins (OED 3)  I 196, 441;
III 1129; violence (OED 2)  II 227; III 636.

OUTERAGIOUS  adj.  excessive in cruelty (OED "outrageous" 3)
III 474.

OUTRAY(E), OUTRAIED  v.  overcome, vanquish (OED "outray" 3)
I 887; II 612, 633; III 256.


P


PALESTRE  n.  school for wrestling, here, apparently, a place
of knightly exercise (OED does not have extended meaning,
though the citations for "palaestra" seem to imply this
development.)  I 606.

PALLATIK  adj.  paralytic (OED offers by-form "parlytyk")
III 1364.

PARAGE  n.  lineage, descent, rank (OED 1)  I 293.

PARCAS  adv.  perhaps (OED "percase" 3)  III 247.

PARCEL  n.  a portion, some (OED A 1)  II 1383.

PARCELL  adv.  in part (OED B 1)  I 787.

PARTABLE  adj.  participating, due a share in (OED 2)   II
     1975; III 1073.

PARTY, PARTIE  n.   part (OED 1)   I 228; III 554, 803; oppon-
     ent (OED 5)   I 529, 537; side of a debated question (OED
     5)  II 435; direction, point of compass (OED 26)   I 816;
     II 1017; III 897; region (OED 2a)   I 726; II 2010;
     social division (OED 5 is closest)  III 992; part of the
     body (OED 1)  II 1599; III 1145.

PASSAGE  n.  travel from one place to another (OED 1)   II 237;
     III 905.

PASSYNGLY  adv.  surpassingly (OED "passingly" b)   I 280.

PAVEYCE, PAVIS  n.  a large convex shield covering the whole
     body (OED "pavis, pavise" 1)   II 984; III 270, 1504.

PEYN(E)  n.  suffering for a crime, penalty, punishment (OED
     "pain" sb.[1] 1)   I 230; II 328, 611, 1158, 1696; III 386,
     1057, 1073, etc.; trouble taken to accomplish something
     (OED 5, "do one's pain")   I 234; II 69, 1410; III 1212,
     1322; pain, suffering (OED 3)  II 479, 488, 499, 511,
     1058, etc.

PEYN  v. refl.  take trouble (OED "pain" v. 4)   II 1882.

PEISED  pa. p.  weighed in the mind (OED "peise" v. 2)   I 404;
     II 1053.

PERAVENTURE  adv.  by chance (OED "peradventure" adv. 2)   I
     148; (OED 3)   III 581.

PERLIOUS  adj.  perilous (by-form not in OED)   II 1045; see
     textual note.

PERISSHID  pa. p.  dead ("perished" in OED); perhaps one might
     read "be-perished" (an unrecorded form)   III 871.

PERSANT  adj.  keen, piercing (OED "perceant")   III 726.

PIKID  adj.  furnished with pikes?  (OED "piked" 1)   perhaps
     "out-pikid," perhaps "departed" (OED "pike" v.[3] 2)   I
     281.

PILLIOUN  n.  a hat or cap (OED "pillion"[2])   I 225.

PLENTEVOUS  adj.  abundant (by-form of "plenteous" noted in

OED)   II 945, 1762.

PLEYN[1]   adj.   level, flat (OED "plane" adj.)   I 858.

PLEYN[2]   adj.   full (OED "plain" adj.[2])   II 882.

PODAGRE   adj.   suffering from gout (OED "podagre" A)   III
1249, 1362.

POLEYNYS   n. pl.   armor covering the knees (OED "polayn")   II
977.

POLLEX   n.   pole-ax, battle ax (OED "pole ax" 1)   III 303.

POLLICIE   n.   political sagacity (OED "policy" 3)   I 181, 597;
II 63, 72 etc.

PORAILL, PORAILE   n.   the poor as a class (OED "porail" 1)   I
415; II 80; III 1587.

POSSESSIONERS   n. pl.   those in possession, occupiers (OED
"possessioner" a)   III 668.

POVERT(E)   n.   poverty (see OED "povert" and as by-form in
"poverty")   I 46, 334, 865; II 31, 882, 892.

POUSTE   n.   power (OED "pouste, poustie")   II 645.

PREPARATIFF   n.   perhaps "preparation" in the medical sense;
perhaps "something administered before medicine (or, fig-
uratively, torture) to prepare the system for something
(death?) to follow (cf. OED "preparative" sb. 1b)   II
1958.

PREROGATIFF   n.   peculiar right or privilege of a person or
body (OED 1b)   I 245; II 272, 287; III 630; sign of rank
or privilege (not in OED)   II 226; that which has preemi-
nence (OED 1a)   III 1481.

PRESENCE   n.   the place where a ruler or judge exercises his
office (OED 1c)   II 823, 1031; III 988.

PRESERUATYFF   n.   that which preserves from injury (OED B 1b)
III 955.

PREVE, PRE(E)VID   v. and pa. p.   prove, proved (OED by-form)
II 371, 1638 etc; II 1452; III 653, 950 etc.   (cf.

"provid" I 411; II 1124, etc.).

PRICE  n.  prize, value, excellence (OED "price" 8; OED
    "prize" for by-form)  I 629.

PRYME  n.  early morning; by extension, the beginning of any-
    thing (OED "prime" sb.$^1$ 6)  III 1232.

PRYME FACE  adj. and n.  at first sight (OED "prime" adj. 9c)
    I 196; III 144.

PRINCIPLIS  n. pl.  beginnings, commencements (cf. OED "prin-
    cipium"; a literal rendition of Ovid's "principiis
    obsta.")  I 199.

PROCESSE  n.  course of events (OED 2)  I 50, 519, 879; course
    of action (OED 1)  II 57; argument (OED 3)  I 930; II
    199, 1092.

PROCURAGE  probably formed from "procure" (OED 6) and meaning
    "a bribe"  I 545.

PROFESSIOUN  n.  solemn vow (like that of a religious order)
    (OED "profession" 1 a & b)  I 458, 530, 541; III 1553;
    declaration of belief (OED 5)  II 741, 797; III 46.

PRONOSTIK  n.  possibly "forecast" (OED "prognostic" sb.$^1$ 2)
    but possibly (from context) close to "phenomenon."  III
    930.

PROPICIATORIE  n.  the mercy seat or rich covering of the Ark
    of the Covenant, hence the feretory containing Alban's
    relics (cf. OED "propitiatory" A 1)  III 1480.

PROPORCIOUN  n.  metrical rhythm (earliest cit., OED 10, 1447)
    I 102.

PROTHOMARTIR  n.  earliest martyr of a particular nation (OED
    "protomartyr")  I 7, 272, 671; III 1347, etc.

PROVIDE  v.  get ready to act (OED 4)  perhaps merely "act"
    II 1448.

PROVIDENCE  n.  arrangement, provision (OED 1)  I 393, 656;
    foresight (OED 2)  I 451, 697; II 13; "cast a provi-
    dence" II 1367, see "cast"; divine providence (OED 3)
    II 310, 383.

PROWESSE  n.  profit, excellence (not in OED); perhaps "valor" if "prowesse" modifies "mantil."  I 522.

PUNYCION  n.  punishment (OED "punition")  III 877.

PURCHACE  v.  acquire (OED "purchase" 4)  I 887; bring about, effect (OED 3)  III 1330.

PURPURAT  adj.  purple, red, blood-colored (OED "purpurate" 1) I 76.

PURVEYAUNCE  n.  arrangement, preparation (OED "purveyance" 2) I 158.

Q

QUYNT ESSENCE  n.  substance of which heavenly bodies are composed, latent in all things (OED "quintessence" 1)  II 580.

QUYT(E)  v.  acquit, bear oneself (OED 1b, 3b)  I 632; repay, requite (OED 10)  II 356, 691.

QUYTE  adj.  free of blame (OED 1)  II 1379.

QWEEME  v.  please, gratify (OED "queme" 1)  II 2067.

R

RACE  v.  erase (OED "race" v.$^3$)  III 1129.

RACID  pa. p.  plucked, torn out (OED "race" v.$^4$ 1)  III 922.

RADICALL  adj.  fundamental (see "humidyte")  III 937.

RASCAIL(E)  n.  rabble (OED "rascal" 1)  II 405, 1126.

RAVEYN, RAVYNE  v.  prowl ravenously (OED "raven" v. 4)  III 716, 743.

RAV(E)YNOUS  adj.  voracious, rapacious (OED "ravenous" 1, 3) II 931; III 284, 749.

RAUHT   v. pa. t.   reached, thrust (form noticed, OED "reach";
    see OED 1 c)   II 485.

REBOUNDE   v.   redound (OED "rebound" 1c)   III 1378.

RECEITE   adj.   in state of having heard  or received?  (not as
    such in OED; see "recet" and textual note)   III 200.

RECHELIS   n. pl.   grains of incense (OED "rekels")   II 1132.

RECOMPENCE   v.   make up for, requite (OED "recompense" v. 2c)
    I 524.

RECORD   v.   go over in the mind, recall (OED 4)   I 136; II 24,
    202, 1316; III 325.

RECORD   pa. p.   borne witness to, perhaps set down in writing
    (OED 10 or 9 of verb; the participle without ending is
    not noticed)   II 294.

RECUR   n.   recovery (OED "recure" sb.)   II 1875.

RECUR(E)   v.   to redress?  (OED "recure" v. 2b)   II 178; to
    win or obtain (a place, a victory, an object)  (OED 4b)
    II 872, 974; III 622, 738 etc; to regain, recover (OED 4)
    II 1107; III 193 etc; to heal, cure, recover health (OED
    2 or 3)   II 178, 309, 1895; III 1016 etc.

RECURYNG   verbal sb.   recovery (of health)  (not in OED except
    under "recure" v. 1)   II 1967.

RED   n.   used adjectivally  reed (see text. n. and Mark 15:36)
    (by-form recorded, OED)   II 485.

REDRESSE   v.   amend, improve (OED "redress" v.7)   I 1.

REFO(U)RME   v.   restore (OED "reform" v.2)   I 208; II 603,
    1409; III 707; make a change for the better (OED 5)   II
    108.

REFREYN   v.   place a check on, restrain (OED "refrain" 1)
    III 527.

REFREIT(E)   n.   refrain, burden of a song, etc.  (OED "re-
    freit")   II 538, 2021.

REFUSE   n.   a worthless or outcast portion of a group (OED B

1b)   III 479.

REGALIE   n.   kingly power (OED "regaly")   I 727; II 2050.

REKLES   adj.   characterized by heedless rashness (OED "reckless" 3)   I 499; II 70.

RELLIGIOUN   n.   a religious order, hence "men of ..." members of an order (OED 2c)   III 1539.

REMEMBRAUNCE   n.   "in remembraunce" on record (OED 5a)   I 915; II 1309; memory, (OED 1)   I 919; II 152, 836 etc.

REMEMBRID   pa. p.   recorded, mentioned, perhaps reminded (cf. OED "remembered" 1 and 2)   I 84, 106, 135, 583; II 241; III 841 etc.

REMEVE   v.   to persuade from a purpose or resolve (OED "remove" 8)   II 1170, 1501.

REN(NE)   v.   to run II 1590, 1892; III 626, 1255; RAN   pa. t. II 484, 1587 etc.; RONNE   pa. p.   II 1551.

REPREVE   v.   reject, censure (OED "reprove" v., 1 or 3; by-form noted)   III 253.

REQUEER   v.   ask, petition (OED "require" 2; by-form cited) II 157, 2053; III 370, 1453.

RERBRAS   n.   armor for the upper arm, originally for back of arm only (OED "rere-brace")   II 981.

RESOUN   n.   debate?  translates "disputationem" in source (cf. OED "reason sb.$^1$ 1)   II 198; OF RESOUN   correctly (OED 13c)   II 1377; account or excuse (OED 3; cf. OED 5)   III 485.

RETCHE   v.   reck, heed (by-form not in OED under "recche") II 1834.

RETHORIQUE   n.   elegant expression, flourish (OED sb.$^1$ 2c)   I 901; II 2084.

REUOKE, REVOKE   v.   summon to apostatize (OED 5)   II 1187; REUOKE CORAGE   change from earlier determined stance (OED 7)   III 616.

REWM   n.   realm (OED "rewm(e) noted as by-form)   II 664.

RIGOUR n. strict enforcement of a law (OED 2) II 1238.

RIGHTFULL adj. just (OED "rightful" 1) II 1403; III 701, 1503.

RIHT n.[1] rite (OED "right" sb.[2]) I 567; III 64 etc.

RIHT n.[2] in phrase "of riht," as is proper, aright (OED "right" sb.[1] 5) I 437.

RIHT adj. straight, direct (OED "right" adj. 1) II 238, 2007.

RIHT, RITH adv. directly, straight (OED 1) II 210 with intensive force in "rith so" (by-form in OED "right" adv.).

RIVAIL n. landing place (OED "rival" sb.[1]) III 1116.

ROCHE n. cliff, rocky height (OED "roche" sb.[1]) III 350.

ROFF pa. t. of "rive" tore away (OED "rive" v.[1] Inflex. 2 and Sign. 2) III 913.

ROPPIS n. pl. entrails, intestines (OED "rope" sb.[2]) II 1292; III 915, 922.

ROUHT n. ruth, pity (by-form "rought" under "ruth") I 316.

ROUTE, ROWTE n. large disorderly crowd (OED "rout" sb.[1] 5) II 396, 1290, 1544; III 912.

RUBIFIED pa. p. reddened (OED "rubify") III 1445.

RUDENESS n. lack of gentle manners and upbringing (OED 2) I 149 etc.


S


SABATOUN n. broad-toed armed foot-covering worn by those in armor (OED "sabaton") II 975.

SACRAMENT n. act or oath resembling the sacraments of Christianity in placing a sacred seal upon some part of a man's life (OED 3) I 154.

SANATIVES n. pl. remedies (OED "sanative" B) III 833.

SAUFF  adj.  safe, whole (OED "safe" adj. 1)   II 189.

SAUF(F)  prep.  save, except, save for, save that (OED "save"
    quasi-prep. 1)   I 550, 682, 865, 929; II 2066; III 931,
    1149, 1209, 1317.

SAUTE  n.  probably "a-saute" is to be taken as one word (the
    hyphen is editorial); "saute" may be an aphetic form of
    "assault" (see all by-forms in OED under "assault" sb.)
    II 1733.

SAWTRE  n.  heraldic device like a St. Andrew's cross, saltire
    (OED "saltire")   I 641, 667; III 767.

SCARSNESSE  n.  niggardliness, stinginess (OED "scarceness"
    1)   III 663.

SCHYES  n. pl.  see SKYE.

SCLAVEYN  n.  slavin, pilgrim's mantle ("sclavyn" and "sla-
    veyn" both noted as by-forms of OED "slavin")   II 877,
    1339.

SCRIPTUR  n.  any writing or composition (OED "scripture" 4)
    I 135, III 325.

SE(E)  n.  throne, perhaps city from which rule is exercised
    (OED 1b, c)   I 803; God's throne (OED 1c) II 705, 2074.

SEENE  n.  synod, meeting of clergy (OED "sene"[3])   III 1421.

SENTENCE  n.  thought or meaning, as opposed to wording (OED
    7b)   I 169.

SERPENTYNE  adj.  deriving from the serpent in Genesis, Satan-
    ic (OED "serpentine" adj. 2)   II 605; III 1121.

SHEWYNG  verbal. sb.  appearance (OED "showing" 7)   I 279.

SHYRES  n. pl.  shire-courts (OED "shire" 3c)   I 542.

SHOUR  n.  battle, conflict (OED "shower" sb.[1])   III 296.

SIGNACLE  n.  a mark, sign (OED "signacle" 1)   III 124.

SIGNE  n.  a dummy, set up for a target, from source, "signum
    statuere" (not as such in OED but cf. "sign" 4)   III 926.

SIMYLITUDE  n.  simile, symbol (OED 3a and b)   II 639.

SYNGLER  adj.  personal, not common or general. preferring
    oneself (OED "singular" 8)   I 401; II 92.

SITH GO  adv.  ago (OED "sith" 4 for "sith ago")   II 784; III
    944.

SKYE, SCHYE  n.  cloud (OED 1, by-forms cited)   II 934, 1208,
    1602, also perhaps II 2019; III 4, 16.

SKIL  n.  a sense of what is fitting ((ED "skill" 1c)   II
    1052; III 288.

SLAW  adj.  slow (OED lists by-form "slawe" under sb.)   II 70.

SLOUTHE  n.  sluggishness? (OED "sloth" 1) no clear meaning;
    the author has lost the thread of his metaphor.   II 977.

SMET, SMYTE(N)  v. inf.  smite, strike off II 1280, 1296,
    1698, 1755, 1863, 1968; SMOT  pa. t.  II 1872; SMET  pa.
    p.  II 420, 1328, 1523 (by-forms in "e" cited in OED as
    northern).

SMYTH  adj.  smooth (OED cites "smith" as by-form of "smeeth")
    II 1204.

SOF(F)(E)RAUNCE, SUFFRAUNCE  n.  patient endurance (OED "suf-
    ferance" 1)   I 517, 914; II 323, 644; III 396 etc.

SOFRE  v.  wait patiently (OED "suffer" v. 6)   II 1438.

SOFFRERE  v.  suffer, not in OED but close to OF "soffrir"
    III 343.  Cf. "soffre" I 375; II 81, etc.

SOGET  adj.  subject (OED "subject" adj., by-form cited)   I
    115, 177, 182.

SOLLENYZED  pa. p.  commemorated by special observances (OED
    "solemnize" 1) III 1473.

SOLUCIOUN  n.  answer (OED "solution" 1b)   II 602.

SONDE  n.  dispensation or ordinance of God (OED "sand" sb.[1]
    1)  II 918.

SOTHFAST  adj.  genuine, veritable (OED "soothfast" 3)   II

1808.

SOWDID   pa. p.   caused wounds to heal (OED "sold" v.$^2$ 2b)   III
   698, 826.

SPARE   n.   leaving someone or something unharmed (OED "spare"
   sb.$^1$ 1)   III 293.

SPARID   v. pa. t.   stopped, withheld action (cf. OED "spare"
   v.$^1$ 6)   I 76.

SPECIFYE   v.   tell in detail (OED 1)   I 62; exhibit a quality
   in a special manner (OED 3b)   I 457.

SPEER   n.   sphere; unless "midday speer" refers to the sun in
   its sphere at midday the exact meaning is unknown (cf.
   OED "sphere" 2 or 3)   III 1154.

SPLAIED   v. pa. t.   bloomed, unfolded (of a flower), unfurled
   (of a flag)   (OED "splay" v.$^1$ 1 and 2)   I 75; II 994.

SPREDE   v.   unfold, expand (of flower-petals, leaves)   (OED
   "spread" v., 7, cit. of 1400)   I 74; unfurl II 625; III
   772.

SPREYNT   pa. p.   sprinkled (OED "sprenge" 1)   III 106.

SQUAR   adj.   pertaining to a spear's head, presumably shaped
   like a long four-sided pyramid, as opposed to "round" or
   cone-shaped spears (cf. OED "square"3)   II 1720; III 291.

STAGE   n.   position, as of heaven, with reference to relative
   height (OED 2); however cf. "theatre" below   I 95.

STALE   v., pa. t.   stole (noted, OED under "steal")   III 1209.

STARK   adj.   stiff in death (OED 4b)   III 822.

STEDE   n.   place, particular part of earth's surface (OED
   "stead" 2)   I 898; II 2082.

STILE, STYLE   n.   writing implement, pen, stylus (OED "style"
   1)   I 52, 880; III 1305.

STOKKID   pa. p.   subjected to rigorous imprisonment (OED
   "stock" v.$^1$ 1)   III 1084.

STRAUNGE   adj.   foreign to, different, uncommon, singular, out

of the way (OED "strange" 8)   I 541; II 178; unfriendly
(OED 11a) II 160; of a foreign place (OED 2)   III 489.

STRE(E)M(YS) eye beam   (OED "stream" 4e)   I 59; beam of light
(OED 7)   II 664, 935, 1550, etc.; water course as such or
as metaphor for baptism, flow of blood (OED 1, 4)   II
1656, 1757, 1762, 1769; III 689, 700, 1114, 1128.   See
"welle-streemys."

STRONG   adj.   evil (OED 113)   III 904.

STUBBIS   n., pl.   tree stumps (OED "stub" 1)   II 1714.

STURDINESSE   n.   fierceness, rebelliousness (OED 2 or 3)   I
417.

STURDY   adj.   fierce, cruel (OED A 1 and 2)   II 821, 1559; III
722.

SUFF(E)RAUNCE   n.   see "soffraunce."

SUFFICIAUNCE, SUFFISAUNCE   n.   satisfaction (OED "suffisance"
3 or 5)   II 85, 1091, 1770; III 1556.

SUPERFLUITE   n.   immoral excess (OED "superfluity" 4)   I 438.

SUPPORT   n.   assistance, used in formulas of supplication and
submission: "with support," "of support," "under support," (OED 1b for "under")   I 57, 589, 609; II 1258.

SUPPORTACIOUN   n.   assistance, countenance; "with supportacioun" used in formulas of supplication (OED 1)   I 103;
II 776.

SUPPRISED   pa. p.   of a feeling, come suddenly and unexpectedly (OED "surprise" 1)   III 239.

SURAUNCE   n.   pledge, guarantee (OED "surance" 1)   I 789.

SURFET   n.   action that exceeds the limits of law or right
(OED "surfeit" 2)   I 514; excess in sensual things (OED
3)   I 189, 450.

SURMYTTID   pa. p.   imputed, falsely alleged (OED "surmit"1)
I 545, text. n.

SURQUEDOUS   adj.   proud, arrogant (OED "surquidous")   I 500.

T

TABLE  n.  tablet inscribed with commandments, hence, the Law
    of Moses (OED 2)   III 1482.

TAKE  v.  assume or receive (a rank)   (OED 16)   I 153.

TARAGE  n.  quality (OED "tarage" sb.[1])  I 299.

TELLE  v.  pray, beg (OED "tell" v. 6)  II 1902.

TEMPRE  adj.  temperate (OED "tempre")  II 1772.

TERMYNE  v.  declare, name (OED "termine" 2)   III 1427.

TERRITORY  n.  the land surrounding a city (or building?)
    (OED 12)  I 358.

THAT  pers. pron.  it (so used in modern times in Norfolk--
    Wright's Engl. Dial. Dict. s. v.)  II 331, 2008.

THAT  conj.  lest, so that, while, when  I 462; II 1556, 1946.

THEATRE  n.  perhaps "church" (fig. from OED 1); in glossing
    Troy Book, II 943, Bergen suggests "a place suggesting
    an amphitheatre...." most likely signification from con-
    text (not in OED) "the whole of England as a place of
    action." III 1378.

THER-AGEYN  adv.  contrariwise, on the other side (OED "there-
    again" and "thereagainst" 2)  II 607.

THILK  dem. adj.  that (OED A)  I 138 etc.

THIS  contraction?  this is?  in "this our bileeve"  II 204.

THROWE  n.  space of time (OED sb.[1] 2)  III 600.

TIME, TYME  n.  standing for prep. phrase  at the time, in the
    time, reflecting introductory Latin ablative "tempore"
    (see "hour" above)  I 106, 811, 813; III 1320, 1415,
    1472.

TITIL, TITLE  legal possession, right (OED "title" 7)  I 123,
    142, 727; III 668; name, denomination (OED 4)  II 67;
    III 1183 (?) 1366; that which justifies a claim? (OED 6?)

II 1989.

TO  prep.  at (OED 4)  II 531.

TODYR  pron.  other, the other (OED "tother")  III 1550.

TO-FORE  prep.  before (OED "tofore" A)  I 174.

TO-FORN  adv.  before (OED "tofore" B)  I 163.

TOKYN, TOOKEN  v. pa. t. pl.  took (OED forms noted (forms,
    OED "take" A4)  III 623, 733.

TOKNED  pa. p.  marked with a sign (OED "token" v.1)  I 477.

TOOK KEEP  v. and obj.  heeded (OED "keep" sb. 1)  II 443.

TORMENTRIE, TURMENTRIE  n.  pain, torture (OED "tormentry" 2)
    II 500, 1181, 1217, 2033; III 1157.

T'OUTRAY  I 887; see "outraie."

TRANSLACIOUN  n.  transference of the remains of a saint from
    one place of interment to another (OED "translation" 1)
    II 2071; III 1396, 1471.

TRANSLATID  pa. p.  moved to another place (of a saint's re-
    mains) (OED "translate" 1)  III 797, 1465.

TRANSMEWE  v.  transmute, transform, in sense of causing con-
    verts to change their beliefs (OED "transmew" 1)  III 185.

TRAYTOURLY, TRETOURLY  adv.  traitorously (OED "traitorly"
    adj.; first cit. Sir Philip Sidney)  I 723, 744.

TREYNES  n. pl.  treachery, tricks, deceits (OED "train" sb.[2]
    1)  III 1008.

TRETABLE  adj.  tractable, affable, easily dealt with (OED
    "treatable" 1)  III 216, 522, 1502.

TRETOURLY  adv.  see "traytourly."

TREWE  adj.  functioning exactly, accurately made (OED "true"
    4d)  II 985.

TRIACLE  n.  medicinal compound, antidote to poison, snake

bites, remedy (OED "treacle" 1a and b)    II 572.

TRIED   pa. p.   separated (OED "try" v. 1)    I 81.

TROUBLY   adj.   opaque, hard to see through (OED "troubly" and "trouble" adj. 1)    I 54.

TUGURRYE   n.   outbuilding, from context perhaps summer-house (cf. OED "tugury")    II 883.

TURMENT   n.   tournament (form not in OED, possibly scribal error)    I 673.


V (vocalic)


VMBRAS   n.   defensive armor for forearm, vambrace (OED "vambrace" but by-form not cited)    II 980.

VNCOUTH   adj.   unaccustomed, strange (OED A2)    II 459, 535, 541; III 63, 249, etc; of a strange, unpleasant character (OED 4)    II 1696.

VNDIR   prep.   in (OED 16e)    II 1309; III 596; "undir support," with support (of a superior)(OED 9b)?    I 57.

VNGOODLY   adv.   roughly, rudely (OED 2)    III 341.

VNHABILED   pa. p.   disabled, deprived of (mental?) power (cf. OED "unable" adj., for form and v.$^2$ for meaning)    II 1063.

VNSET   adj.   uncertain (OED 1b)    III 1329.

VNWAR   adj.   sudden (OED 3)    II 1360.

VNWARLY   adv.   unexpectedly (OED 1)    I 394; III 189?; incautiously (OED 2)    III 189?.

VNWELDI   adj.   feeble, impotent (OED "unwieldy" 1)    III 499.

VPREISE   v.   lift up (as a voice) (OED "upraise" 1b; first fig. cit. with voice is modern)    II 2022.

VP-SO-DOUN   compound adv.   upside down (OED notes by-form under "upside down")    III 317, 509.

VPRIST  n.  rising of the sun (OED "uprist" 2)  I 357.

VTAS  n.  octave, eight-day period after a festival, the eighth day (OED "utas")  I 619.


## V  (consonant)


VAUNTAGE  n.  head start (OED "vantage" 3, cit. 1523) III 907.

VENGEABLE, WENGEABLE  adj.  cruel, dreadful (OED 2)  I 432; II 1976; III 520, 1045; vengeful (OED 1)  II 1143.

VENGEABLY  adv.  dreadfully, pitilessly (OED 1)  III 231, 712.

VOIDE  v.  remove, clear away (OED "void" 1)  I 450; II 120.


## W


WAN  adv.  when (OED, "when" notes by-form)  II 1866; there are many occurrences of "whan" passim.

WAT  pron.  what (OED, "what" notes by-form)  III 1309.

WELLE-STREMYS  n. pl.  streams flowing from springs (OED "well-stream")  II 508.

WELTHE  n.  well-being of a nation, city, etc.  (OED "wealth" 1c)  I 839.

WENGEABLE  adj.  see "vengeable."

WERDLY  adj.  worldly, of this world (cf. OED "werdliche")  II 1824.

WERE  v.  wear upon the body (OED "wear" $v^1$; by-form noted)  I 560.

WERKYNG  v. sb.  influential operation (as of God) (OED "working" 6)  II 1646; III 744.

WHAT  adv.  why (OED III 19)  II 1117.

WHOW  adv.  how (OED "how" for by-form)  II 1942; III 523,

593, 677; otherwise "how" (46 examples passim).

WIL(L)FUL(L)  adj.  intentional (OED 5)  I 189, 417; volun-
tary (OED 4)  I 46, 865; III 396.

WITHDRAWE  v.  restrain (OED 4c)  I 217; withhold (OED 4b)
I 810; II 461.

WITHHOLD  v.  retain, keep (not necessarily "keep back")
(OED 2)  I 698; III 66.

WITHSTOND  v.  oppose, resist (OED "withstand" 2d; see exp.
note)  I 199, 740.

WOMANHEED  n.  womanliness, womanhood (OED "womanhead")  II
252.

WONDIR  adj.  strange, wonderful (OED "wonder" adj.)  II 1763;
III 691 adv. II 448; III 408.

WOODMEN  n. pl.  madmen (OED "woodman" sb.2)  II 1139; III
337.

WORD  n.  world (by-form in OED)  I 45, 335.

WORDLY  adj.  of this world (by-forms as for "world" above)
II 853, 1113, 1116, etc.; III 671.  See "werdly."

WROOKE  pa. p.  revenged (by-form cited by OED for next cent.)
I 729.


Y (see "I" for vocalic "Y")


YALD  v. pa. t.  yielded (OED cites "yalde" for succeeding
century)  I 77.

YE(E)VE, YIFF, YEUYTH, YAFF, YOVE, YOVEN  v.  give, giveth,
gave, given  I 360; II 112, 303; II 376; II 506; I 630;
II 1278; III 668 etc.

YOOR AGON  adv. phrase  long ago (OED "yore" 4)  I 4; II 153.

YOUNDER  adv.  yonder (OED gives forms in "ou" for succeeding
centuries)  III 823; cf. "yondir" II 788.

*Index of Proper Names*

ACHILLES    II, 847, 851.

ADAM    II, 565, 569, 604, 622.

ADRIAN, Pope Hadrian    III, 1400, 1415.

ALBANYE    I, 735.

ALBIOUN, usually "BRUTIS ALBIOUN, i.e., "The Albioun of Brutus."    I, 5, 7, 29, 30, 134, 679, 775; III, 773 etc.

ALBON, ALBONE, ALBOUN, ALBANUS, St Alban    I, 48, 64, 73, 83, 265, 267, etc.; II, 191, 445-2017.

ALISANDRE    I, 501.

ALLECTUS    I, 740, 745, 755.

ALMAYN, Germany    I, 626.

ALPIES    I, 109.

AMPHIBALUS, AMPHIBAL, AMPHIBALL    I, 43, 248, 327, 330, 864, etc.

ANDREW, Apostle    I, 667.

ANDROCHEE, see *Explanatory Notes*    I, 133.

ANTROPOS, The Fate, Atropos    II, 841.

APPOLLO    II, 399, 1324.

ARACLYUS, converted executioner    II, 1662, 1879.

ARGUS    I, 191.

ASCLEPEODOT(E), ASCLIPIODOT, ASCOPLEODOTE, see *Explanatory*
     *Notes*     I, 752, 569, 796; II, 1001, 1220, 1301.

ATHLAS     II, 585.

AURORA     II, 1, 936.


BASSIAN, BASSIANUS, son of King Severus, see *Explanatory*
     *Notes*     I, 40, 236, 277, 586, 621, 675, 715, 720,
     723, 729, 744.

BEDLEEM     II, 256.

BELLONA     I, 359.

BRAGMANNYS pl., Brahmans; see *Explanatory Notes*     I, 502.

BRITEYN(E), BRETEYN, BRETAIGNE     I, 119, 140, 301; III, 760,
     1514 etc.

BRITEYN, adj., British     I, 268; II, 54.

BRITO(U)N, adj.     II, 525.

BRITOUN, BRETON, n., BRETONYS, pl.     I, 128, 288, 586, 678,
     748, 765; II, 2029; III, 1500.

BRITTYSH, adj.

BRUTIS, poss. noun with "Albioun," Pertaining to Brutus, Brut
     I, 7, 30, 134, 679, 775; II, 2032; III 773 etc.

BURY, Bury St. Edmunds     III, 1603 (colophon of Trinity MS).


CAPITOLIE, temple of Jupiter on the Capitoline     III, 1383.

CARAUSYUS, CARYUSYUS, CARAUCYUS, see *Explanatory Notes*     I,
     710, 722, 725, 741, 743, 811.

CARTAGE     III, 1381.

CASSIBALAN, CASSIBALLAN, see *Explanatory Notes*     I, 122, 133.

CECILE, Sicily     I, 817.

ENGLOND    III, 1559; see also "EST YNGLONDE."

EOLUS    II, 1204.

ERIDICE, Eurydice    II, 1204.

EST YNGLOND(E), East Anglia    III, 752, 771.

EWSTAS, St. Eustace    II, 24.


FICULUEES, Sicilians? See "CECILE"    I, 624.

FLEGONTE, Phlegon, one of the steeds of Phoebus    II, 938.

FLORA    II, 221, 1203.

FRANCEIS PETRAK    I, 14.

FRAUNCE    I, 117; III, 1425, 1430, 1559.


GABRIEL, Archangel    II, 234, 242.

GALIAN, GALLIENE, Galen, the physician    II, 583; III, 831.

GALLUS, see *Explanatory Notes*    I, 756.

GARNARIE, GARNER, Whethamstede's Granarium    I, 889, 894;
    II, 2083.

GERMANYE    I, 116.

GERMAYN, St. Germanus of Auxerre    III, 1425, 1429, 1438,
    1450, 1463, 1466.

GREGORIE, Pope Gregory    I, II, 35.

GREEKIS, n. pl.,    I, 473, 476.


HANYBAL    III, 1381.

HECTOR, see ECTOR.

HENRY, Henry VI of England; see also "SIXT"    III, 1564.

HERCULES    II, 636; III, 948.

HERCULYUS, Maximianus Herculeus, Emperor    II, 1250.

HOLMERST(E), Holmhurst, near St. Albans    II, 1506, 1523.

HORESTES, Orestes    II, 845.


ILLIOUN    III, 464.

INDE, YNDE    I, 283; II, 1110.

YNGLONDE, see "ENGLOND," "EST-YNGLONDE."

YPOCRAS, Hippocrates    II, 583; III, 832.

ISRAEL    II, 1606.

ITAILE    I, 112, 637.


IERUSALEM    III, 1116.

IESSE, father of David    II, 232.

IESU, IESUS    I, 273, 322; II, 184, 260, 1654; III, 18, 71,
        etc.

IEWIS, n. pl.    II, 17, 489, 591; III, 1202.

IEWRY, the Jews, collectively; Palestine?    II, 491.

IOHN, St. John, Evangelist    I, 84; undetermined, II, 995.

IONATHAS, Jonathan, son of Saul    II, 837.

IUBITER    II, 399, 1324, 1822, 1838.

IUDAS MACHABE    I, 690.

IUDITTIS, n. poss., Judith's    II, 635.

IULIUS, CESAR IULIUS    I, 107, 135.

IUNO    II, 400.


KYNDE, Nature personified    I, 243; II, 10.


LATYN, n.    II, 2015; III, 1305.

LEON, LEOUN, the constellation    II, 922, 1551.

LICCHEFEELD, LITCHEFEELD    III, 323, 327, 756, 776.

LONDON, LONDOUN    I, 759; II, 1306; III, 1420.

LUCAN    I, 9, 120.

LUCAS, St. Luke    II, 240.

LUCIFER, the morning star    II, 3, 935.

LUCYNA    II, 437.

LUMBARDIE    I, 817.

LUPUS TERCASYNE, St. Lupus or Lowe of Troyes    II, 1428.

LYDGATE, DAN IOHN    Colophons to Lansdowne and Trinity MSS.


MACHABE, Judas Maccabaeus    I, 690.

MARCHUS MANLYUS    III, 1382.

MARIA, Mary the mother of Jesus    II, 275.

MARO, Vergil    I, 8.

MARS, the deity    I, 458, 600, 694; II, 399, 1823; poss.
    MARTIS    I, 354, 525; MARTIS, poss., the planet    I,
    627.

MARY, the mother of Jesus; see also "MARIA"    II, 230, 234,
    274.

MAXIMYAN, the emperor; see also "HERCULYUS"    I, 777, 794,

SPAYN    I, 625.

STEPHEN, SEYNT    III, 1202.


TERCASYNE    See LUPUS.

THESEUS    II, 844.

TITAN    II, 55, 937.

TRAIAN    II, 25, 35.

TROIAN, adj.    II, 849.

TROIANS, TROIANYS, n. pl.    I, 476; II, 1349.

TROYE, TROY, TROIE    I, 473; II, 351; III, 465, 1374, gen.
    TROIES 1380.

TULLIUS CHITHERO    I, 10.


VENUS    I, 462, 469; II, 462, 1324, 1826.

VER, Spring    II, 223.

VEROLAMYE, St. Albans, Herts.    I, 18, 264, 924; II, 923,
    1362; III, 455, 467.

VIRGILE    I, 9.


WALBROK, Walbrook, London    I, 763.

WALIS    I, 240, 247; III, 90, 163, 167, 192, 730.    See
    "NORTH WALIS."

WALISSH, adj.    III, 608.

WHETHAMSTEDE, MAISTER IOHN    Colophons to La. and Trin. MSS;
    alluded to and etymoligized, I, 898.